Bob Shebib

Douglas College

Choices

INTERVIEWING AND COUNSELLING
SKILLS FOR CANADIANS

THIRD EDITION

PEARSON

Prentice
Hall

Toronto

National Library of Canada Cataloguing in Publication

Shebib, Bob
    Choices : interviewing and counselling skills for Canadians / Bob Shebib.—3rd ed.

Includes bibliographical references and index.
ISBN 0-13-197602-8

       1. Counseling—Textbooks. 2. Interviewing—Textbooks. I. Title.

BF637.C6S52 2006   158'.3   C2005-907813-8

ISBN 0-13-197602-8

Vice President, Editorial Director: Michael J. Young
Acquisitions Editor: Patty Riediger
Sponsoring Editor: Carolin Sweig
Executive Marketing Manager: Judith Allen
Developmental Editor: Jon Maxfield
Production Editor: Richard di Santo
Copy Editor: Nancy Mucklow
Proofreader: Nancy Carroll
Production Coordinator: Janis Raisen
Permissions Manager: Susan Wallace-Cox
Composition: Laserwords Private Limited
Art Director: Mary Opper
Cover and Interior Design: Jennifer Stimson
Cover Image: © Brand X Pictures / Alamy

5 6 7 8   10 09 08 07

Printed and bound in the United States of America.

Contents

Preface

*It is not for him to pride himself who loveth his own country, but rather for him who loveth
the whole world. The earth is but one country, and mankind its citizens.*
—Bahá'u'lláh

When I first became a counsellor in the late 1960s, I had an undergraduate arts degree with
courses in psychology, but no training in counselling skills or methods. I was well-meaning
but misguided in my belief that counselling involved giving advice to people with problems.
I thought that I could listen patiently to people's problems, make an assessment, and then
offer some prescription for change. In fact, that seemed to be what many of my clients also
expected and wanted. But after a while, I made a number of important discoveries. First, I
wasn't smart enough to have the answers for all of the complex issues that came my way.
Second, even when I did have answers, for the most part, my good advice didn't seem to be
very helpful to my clients. Finally—and this was clearly the most important discovery of
all—my clients were not as incapable as my need to give them "good advice" implied.

I began a learning process that still continues. I learned that my expertise would come not
from knowing what was best for people, but from being willing to become deeply involved in
a relationship with clients that would demand that I change my own ways of thinking, feeling and behaving. I had to struggle to control my own biases and to separate my experiences and feelings from those of my clients. I also learned to appreciate the inherent
strength, capacity and resilience of my clients, which enabled me to give up the need fix
and rescue them. Moreover, I learned that empathic listening is the cornerstone of helping, and often I found that empathetic listening was all many people needed to help them
organize their thinking and mobilize their energies for change. For others, systematic
exploration of problems, goal setting, and action planning was the cornerstone of change.
Overall, I learned that counselling should empower clients and strengthen their self-esteem,
not mine. Now I cringe when I see "quick fix" television counsellors who "solve" complex problems in minutes. I remind my students that the applause they hear is for the
counsellor, not the client, and to remember that what they are seeing is at best entertain-
ment, not counselling.

PURPOSE

*Choices: Interviewing and Counselling Skills for Canadian*s is an introductory text that
meets long unmet needs of Canadian counselling students and professionals. My goal has
been to provide a practical guide to assist professionals in the helping disciplines develop
knowledge, skills, and attitudes for effective interviewing and counselling. Although the
book is intended primarily as a textbook for Canadian introductory counselling and interviewing courses, it is also designed as a reference text for more advanced practitioners. The
book is targeted at students of counselling and professionals in disciplines, such as social
work and youth counselling. But it may also be of interest to practitioners in allied disciplines such as psychology, criminology, teaching, and nursing, who wish to develop their
interviewing and counselling skills.

This book aims to contribute to the development of professional competence in four ways:

1. It introduces basic concepts and models to help learners understand the theory and reasoning behind the use of counselling and interviewing skills.

2. It provides realistic examples to illustrate concepts in action.

3. It contains challenging exercises that promote skill development, conceptual understanding, and self-awareness.

4. It emphasizes the notion of a range of skill choices for interviewing, rather than rules and recipes.

Choices is a Canadian textbook. Throughout the book, the case examples, statistics and ethical references all reflect Canadian realities. In addition, Chapter 2 explores the codes of ethics of the Canadian Counselling Association and the Canadian Association of Social Workers. Finally, Chapter 10 deals with multicultural counselling in Canada.

This third edition draws on feedback from reviewers, readers, and students. All chapters have been rewritten to improve clarity and include current research, with updated references and web links. The third edition continues my commitment to producing a readable and practical text. In fact, one of my original goals was to write a textbook that I could share with clients. So as much as possible, I have avoided the use of unnecessary jargon, and I have tried to be transparent and explicit regarding my assumptions.

CENTRAL VALUES AND ASSUMPTIONS

I believe in the importance of intelligent choice in the use of skills and strategies. Making wise choices requires that counsellors develop a wide range of practice skills based on the unique needs of clients and situations, as well as supported theory (science) and proven practice. This book emphasizes cultural competence by encouraging counsellors to consider culture as a major component of rational choice. Clearly, cultural context is important when working with clients who are culturally different; but since everyone is unique, with their own mix of values and beliefs, culture is a variable for work with all clients.

But when working with clients from visible minorities and those who are marginalized by poverty or discrimination, counsellors must examine the socio-political realities that frame their circumstances. They also need to develop sufficient self-awareness to escape or manage any tendency to be culture-bound—the assumption that all clients share their values, perspectives, and ambitions, or, worse still, that client differences represent deficiencies. By sustaining a multicultural perspective that recognizes and prizes diversity, counsellors can avoid the pitfalls of ethnocentrism (the belief that one's one views and culture are superior). Culturally competent counsellors view cultural differences as opportunities to widen their horizons and deepen their versatility. They remember to be humble enough to learn from their clients.

Choices and Respect for Diversity

Diversity includes differences in such major variables as race, religion, age, sex, sexual orientation, physical and mental ability, economic capacity, language, culture, values, beliefs, preferences, and ways of thinking and behaving. This diversity of today's counselling caseloads requires that counsellors develop a range of interviewing and counselling skills. Competent counsellors are able to vary their style depending on the unique needs of different clients and situations. In simplest terms, the more choices counsellors have, the greater their ability to match their work to the needs and wants of their clients and the less their need to repeatedly use the same skill. Effective counsellors can use particular skills, but they are wise enough to know when not to use them. Similarly, the goal of counselling is to help clients achieve versatility in their capacity to solve problems and achieve goals.

Self-Awareness

Knowledge of self, including consciousness of one's values and beliefs and the impact of one's behaviour on others, is a prerequisite for effective counselling. Counsellors who lack self-awareness may confuse their clients' feelings with their own, or they may assume that clients will feel as they do. Moreover, when counsellors are unaware of their own needs, including those that are unmet, they risk unconsciously using their counselling relationships to meet personal goals instead of client goals. In addition, without self-awareness, counsellors will be ignorant of those areas of practice in which they are competent and those in which it will be difficult for them to work with objectivity.

Competent professionals know themselves, and they ensure that their values and beliefs do not become a burden to their clients. They accept that exploring and reflecting on one's competence and the limits of one's role and expertise are fundamental to professional practice. For counsellors, this process of self-examination continues throughout their careers.

Self-Determination

Best-practice counselling draws on the expertise of clients to participate in decisions related to the goals and process of counselling. For this reason, counsellors should demystify their work through open discussion of their methodologies, assumptions and intentions. Moreover, commitment to client self-determination restrains counsellors from unhelpful behaviours, such as advice giving and abuse of power or control. By promoting client self-determination, counsellors use a strengths approach that empowers clients by assuming their capacity to cope and change. In practice, this means

> ... believing that people are capable of making their own choices and decisions. It means not only that human beings possess the strengths and potential to resolve their own difficult life situations, but also that they increase their strength and contribute to society by doing so. The role of the social worker in clinical practice is to nourish, encourage, assist, enable, support, stimulate, and unleash the strengths within people; to illuminate the strengths available to people in their own environments; and to promote equity and justice at all levels of society. To do that, the social worker helps clients articulate the nature of their situations, identify what they want, explore alternatives for achieving those wants, and achieve them. (Cowger, 1994:264)

Although the topic is beyond the scope of this book, counsellors should also consider their responsibility to extend beyond their role as counsellors to social and political action. As advocates for social justice, they should strive to reduce gender, cultural, and other forms of discrimination. They should also promote changes in social policy as well as modification in the functioning of formal organizations and institutions to better meet the needs of clients.

The Nature of Counselling and Interviewing

Interviewing is an information-gathering process that is free from any conscious attempt to influence the subject. Interviewing is the foundation of counselling, a process that goes beyond interviewing to enable clients to cope with the problems of daily living. Counsellors negotiate a working relationship with clients in order to accomplish some agreed-upon purpose, such as assisting clients to make decisions, deal with painful feelings, solve problems, or learn new skills.

Counselling is a complex blend of skill, attitude, and art. Although core skills can be learned and practised, they are not recipes. The ideas in this book are presented as a starting point with the hope that they will be customized and adapted to fit individual counsellor–client interactions. Skill and technique can be impressive, sometimes even appearing to be magical, but alone they are insufficient. Counsellors need to be genuine, maintain warm and caring regard for their clients, and recognize the inherent worth of people. To some extent, professional training can shape these beliefs and values; but to a greater extent, they must come from the hearts and souls of counsellors. Kadushin discusses the important mix of skill and feeling:

> Many might say that if they had to choose between feeling and technique they would choose feeling as the more important prerequisite. Perhaps so, but if one has to make a choice between these qualifications, an injustice has already been done to the client. It should be possible to offer the client an interviewer who is both attitudinally correct and technically proficient. (1990:xii)

The counselling model featured in this book rests on the assumption that counselling and interviewing are most effective under these conditions:

- Interviews and counselling relationships have a clear contract and purpose.
- Working relationships with a clear understanding of roles have been established.
- A climate of trust and safety in taking risks has been established.
- Counsellor responses are genuine, based on real feelings and attitudes.
- Counsellors respect their clients' independence and their right to self-determination.

THE FOUR PHASES OF COUNSELLING

This book divides the counselling relationship into four phases: preliminary, beginning, action, and ending. Each phase involves common as well as unique tasks and skills. For example, the beginning phase focuses on relationship development and problem exploration. Predictably, skills for developing relationships, such as active listening, are most useful in the beginning phase, whereas skills such as confrontation are not recommended. But the subsequent action phase focuses on helping clients develop new perspectives, set goals, and implement change strategies; thus, skills such as reframing and confronting are used extensively in this phase. Thus, each phase has its own tasks and relevant skill sets.

The four phases are developmental, with success at one phase dependent in part on success at previous phases. For example, clients are more willing to accept confrontation in the action phase if a solid relationship or trust was already established in the beginning phase. In general, reference to the four-phase model allows counsellors to make some predictions about the climate of the interview and determine skills and tasks will be needed.

However, practitioners must be cautious in applying the model too rigorously to every counselling interview, because there are always circumstances for which the sequence of events may need to differ sharply from the model.

STRUCTURE OF THE BOOK

The book is divided into ten chapters.

Chapter 1 explores the basic nature of counselling skills and strategies. In this chapter, four major skill clusters are introduced: relationship building, exploring/probing, empowering, and challenging. The four-phase model of counselling (preliminary, beginning, action, and ending) is proposed as a model for understanding the evolution of the counselling relationship.

Chapter 2 introduces readers to the basic concepts of ethics, values, and self-awareness. New content has been added on the topics of self-determination, as well as a revised model for understanding and resolving ethical dilemmas.

Chapter 3 examines the helping relationship and considers the core conditions necessary for counselling to be effective. New and updated material on sessional and relationship contracting is featured in this chapter.

Chapters 4, **5**, and **6** explore the active listening skills of attending, silence, paraphrasing, and summarizing (Chapter 4), questioning (Chapter 5), and empathy (Chapter 6).

Chapter 7 is concerned with action-phase skills that motivate clients to think differently and make changes in their lives. The third edition includes the Stages of Change model, which has strategies for working with clients at each stage of their change process. As well, new principles of confrontation are featured.

Chapter 8 presents information for working in difficult situations, such as when clients are resistant or potentially violent.

Chapter 9 looks at concepts for working with various populations, including those who are seeking work, dealing with mental disorders, contemplating suicide, or coping with an HIV-positive diagnosis or AIDS. Updated material on mental health in Canada and suicide are new to the third edition.

Chapter 10 explores important concepts and issues related to counselling clients from different cultures. This chapter includes a discussion of spirituality and counselling, reflecting a growing interest in and acceptance of spiritual issues in counselling. All data has been updated to the 2001 census.

Appendix A reproduces the Canadian Counselling Association's Code of Ethics.

Appendix B reproduces the Canadian Association of Social Worker's Code of Ethics. These are followed by a **Glossary** of key terms and concepts, and a list of **References**.

FEATURES

People learn in different ways, so this book includes a range of features designed to assist learners to understand at cognitive, emotional, and behavioural levels. Each chapter contains the following elements:

- **Chapter preview:** key concepts that will be addressed in the chapter.
- **Summary:** a short review at the end of each chapter that summarizes important ideas.

- **Conversations:** a unique addition—teacher–student dialogues that offer reflections on frequently asked questions.
- **Sample interviews:** annotated interview excerpts that illustrate and explain chapter concepts.
- **Exercises:** end-of-chapter reflective questions to give readers practice developing skills, self-awareness, and creative thinking.
- **Weblinks:** links to websites related to the chapter's material.

TO THE STUDENT

If you are studying this book as part of a course on counselling skills, you will probably have the opportunity to develop skill competence in a number of different ways:

- Watching instructor demonstrations.
- Conducting practice interviews using role-played or (preferably) real-life scenarios.
- Completing the chapter exercises.
- Receiving feedback and evaluation from instructors and student colleagues who observe your work.
- Using audio and video recordings to understand and assess your verbal and nonverbal responses.
- Working with clients.

In most counselling skills courses, learning groups are used to practise skills. Usually, these learning groups use classroom simulations and practice interviews, in which you assume the roles of client, counsellor, and observer. Each of these roles offers unique challenges and opportunities for learning.

Role-Playing the Client's Perspective

The client's role offers a powerful opportunity for you to understand client feelings and expectations. You may find that your reactions are similar to those that clients experience:

- Ambivalence about sharing feelings or details about personal issues.
- Feelings of vulnerability, and fear of being judged, embarrassed, or ridiculed.

As a client, it will be up to you to control how much you wish to disclose; however, by taking reasonable risks, you can enhance your learning opportunities and insights.

Role-Playing the Counsellor's Perspective

When you are asked to practise your newly learned skills as a counsellor, you may feel clumsy and insecure as you take risks to change established communication patterns or experiment with new skills and strategies. As a student with limited training, you may be reluctant to ask questions that seem to invade the privacy of your colleagues. Moreover, when dealing with sensitive issues, you may fear that your lack of experience may damage your clients. You may also fear that your colleagues will judge you as inept. As well, when you are being observed by others, the intense focus on your work can be unsettling and anxiety-provoking. But all these reactions are common, and you will probably find that your colleagues feel the same way. Most professional counsellors take many years of practice and study to become competent and comfortable using a full range of skills. What is important is that you persist and avoid the natural temptation to stick with familiar patterns of communicating. Skills that are awkward in the beginning will, with practice, become part of your natural and preferred style. As Minuchin & Fishman (1981) note:

> Unfortunately, the teaching of new skills often disorganizes the beginning student. As in any learning or relearning process, the student finds himself concentrating so much on the trees that he misses the forest... As in the training of the samurai, the student needs a number of years to achieve expertise and many more to achieve spontaneity. (Minuchin & Fishman, 1981:10)

Acting as an Observer

Student observers are responsible for watching the interview and providing feedback to student colleagues who are practising their counselling skills. At first, you may be reluctant to offer feedback, perhaps worrying that your remarks will generate anger or hurt feelings. But keep in mind that the observer's role gives you an excellent opportunity to develop and practise giving feedback.

Helpful feedback is energizing and does not detract from another person's self-esteem. As people learn and practice interviewing and counselling skills, they may feel vulnerable and awkward. Hence, it is important to remain sensitive to their emotional and psychological needs while balancing their needs for information and correction.

Observer feedback may be of two types: supportive or corrective. Supportive feedback reinforces or acknowledges achievements—"catch them doing something right." Consider how you respond differently when your strengths are acknowledged rather than when your weaknesses are targeted. Yet despite how obvious this idea seems, many students and professional counsellors are very problem-oriented and fail to acknowledge client or colleague strengths. Moreover, to be effective, this supportive feedback must be genuine (true) and delivered without rescuing or patronizing. If you lie to others in order to avoid hurting them, your credibility as a source of feedback will diminish.

In contrast to supportive feedback, corrective feedback challenges others to examine or change behaviour. But before giving corrective feedback, consider your relationship with the other person. If your relationship is based on trust and caring, corrective feedback has the potential to be effective. However, if your relationship is stressed (for example, in situations where there is unresolved conflict), corrective feedback is more likely to be perceived as an attack. If people think your feedback is harsh, demanding or controlling, there is a higher probability of them resisting.

Don't use corrective feedback as a means to control, impress, or to punish. Pay attention to your tone of voice and other nonverbal behaviour. Make sure that you avoid lecturing and pointing fingers. Timing and pacing are also important. Supportive feedback is more useful when self-esteem is low. In addition, feedback is most effective when given as soon as possible, but ensure that you protect personal privacy. Also, avoid overwhelming student counsellors by remembering that you do not have to accomplish everything at once. As a general rule, ask people to self-evaluate before offering your opinions. You may be surprised to find that they already have insight into the problem areas. Then, the number of areas where you have to provide direct feedback is reduced.

Feedback has the most potential for success if it is invited and/or targeted to perceived areas of need. Contract with others to receive feedback. Ask questions such as: "Would you like me to offer my ideas on what happened?" or, "Are there specific issues that you are concerned about?" In addition, when you work with others (clients or colleagues), don't forget individual differences. Some people prefer feedback to be direct and to the point. Others may prefer it "sandwiched" between positives. Some others need time to reflect before responding or they may profit from visual and written illustrations.

Note that some people may have an immediate reaction to your feedback that differs from their reaction once they have time to ponder what you have said. Thus, a person who responds defensively or even with anger may on reflection come to accept your input. The opposite can also be true—people who react favourably may later develop other feelings, such as resentment or confusion. Checking back during future encounters is one strategy for keeping abreast of others' reactions.

Finally, remember that giving helpful and caring feedback is one way of developing and strengthening relationships. If you are honest and supportive with others, you greatly increase the probability they will be honest and supportive with you when you ask for their helpful feedback.

Developing an Effective Learning Group

When you work with student colleagues in each of the three roles, it is helpful to candidly discuss your fears as well as your expectations of one another. You will need to work to develop a contract or agreement on how you will work together. Practice interviews will be more powerful learning opportunities if they are based on real rather than role-played feelings and issues. Consequently, it will be important to establish a climate of safety, where confidentiality will be respected. Some important principles to remember:

- Colleagues who are in the client's role are disclosing personal issues and feelings, so it is essential to respect their dignity and right to privacy.

- Everyone has different capacities for intimacy. Don't expect that all members of a learning group will disclose at the same level. Accept individual differences.

- Learning the skills of counselling requires a certain willingness to give up familiar patterns of communication and attempt new approaches. Expand your limits by taking appropriate risks to try new skills, and be tolerant of colleagues who are engaged in similar risk taking.

- Expect that the process of learning and experimenting with new skills will result in a period of awkwardness and self-consciousness. For a time, it may seem as though your capacity to counsel others is regressing.

- Feedback from others is an important part of learning. Therefore, try to make it easy for others to give you feedback by consistently responding in a nondefensive manner. Help others give specific feedback by asking targeted questions.

Keeping a Personal Journal

A personal "for your eyes only" journal can be a significant adjunct to your learning. The journal is a tool for introspection that provides a private means for documenting and exploring your thoughts and feelings related to the development of your counselling skills. There are no rules for journal writing other than the need to make entries on a regular basis and to try to avoid self-censorship.

Using This Book

If you are using this book as part of a course on counselling, your teacher will propose a suggested reading schedule that structures your reading over the semester, and he or she will assign or adapt the chapter exercises to fit your learning needs. Another way to use the book is on an "as you need it" basis, using the index or chapter headings to locate specific content. As well, you are encouraged to use other books, journals, and tools, such as Internet research, to supplement your learning. However, you should read this book (or any book) critically and seek to understand and explore the ideas and try them out. But don't forget that there is room for other perspectives.

Counselling Skills as a Way of Life

You may be surprised to discover that the skills of counselling are also the skills of effective everyday communication and that the process of developing your counselling competence may begin to influence your personal relationships. As counselling skills become part of your style, you may find yourself becoming a little more inquisitive and more sensitive to the feelings of others. However, you may find that others in your life do not welcome the changes in your manner and style. When you change, others around you have to accommodate your changes. If you become more probing in your questions, they must be forthcoming with their answers. When you become more empathic, their feelings become more transparent. These changes move the relationship to a deeper level of intimacy, which may be frightening for some, particularly if the pace is too fast for their comfort level.

ACKNOWLEDGMENTS

The editorial staff at Pearson Education Canada has been instrumental in helping bring the manuscript to publication. In particular, I wish to thank Jon Maxfield, Developmental Editor, and Nancy Mucklow, Copy Editor, who provided great help in preparing the third edition for publication. I also want to thank the following members of the Pearson team: Michael Young, Heather McWhinney, Jessica Mosher, Judith Allen and Richard di Santo, for their invaluable support.

The three editions of this book have been enriched by the helpful comments of my colleagues: Bob Martel, John Fox, Sharon Smith, John Fleming, Ray Chapman, Garry Tennant, Julie Roper, Elizabeth Robinson, Doug Estergaard, Ellen Edwards, Roberta Neault, Maxine Davis, Jackie Yurick, and the late Dave Burgess. I also wish to thank the faculty at Vancouver Community College—Joanne Rykers, Lee McLeod, Susan Runytu, and Sara Menzel—who have given me many helpful suggestions that have been incorporated in this book.

The students of the Community Social Service Worker program at Douglas College offered candid and helpful recommendations to me when I field-tested the ideas in this book.

I have been aided by many reviewers who critically evaluated prepublication drafts, including Lourdes A.D. de la Cruz, Sheridan College; Brian Ouellette, St. Thomas University; Colleen Kamps, Centennial College; Maria Schnurr, Algonquin Collge; Sheri M. McConnell, Memorial University; Susan Kalles, Mohawk College; Frances Grunberg, Langara College. I want them to know that their input was extremely useful and much appreciated. Special thanks to Neil Madu from Simon Fraser University who offered extensive comments and suggestions on the prepublication draft.

This book is dedicated to Joyce Shebib, to whom I owe an enormous debt of gratitude. Her constant support, encouragement, and painstaking review of every chapter through many rewrites made the final product much better than it would have been otherwise.

Bob Shebib
Douglas College

chapter one

An Introduction to the Skills and Process of Counselling

PREVIEW

After reading this chapter you should be able to:

- Define the range of counselling activities.
- List the people who provide counselling services.
- Explain why it is important for counsellors to be versatile.
- Describe the necessary range of skill versatility.
- Classify the four skill clusters of counselling.
- Summarize the developmental objectives of the four phases of counselling.
- Describe counselling pitfalls.

AN OVERVIEW OF COUNSELLING

Counselling Careers

Many professionals, such as social workers, child and youth care workers, psychologists, psychiatrists, nurses, and psychiatric nurses, do counselling work. Most are members of professional associations like the Canadian Association of Social Workers (CASW) and the Canadian Counselling Association. As members, they are subject to codes of ethics governing acceptable professional behaviour. Membership in these associations usually requires a university degree and, in some cases, a master's degree or a PhD.

Social workers generally have university training with a bachelor's degree in social work (BSW) or a master's degree in social work (MSW) In addition, they may have specialized training in specialty areas, such as family therapy or group work. Social workers might work in private practice or be employed in hospitals, prisons, schools, or community social service agencies. Many social workers also work for government agencies investigating incidents of child abuse and neglect.

Counselling psychologists are usually qualified at the PhD level, but some jurisdictions allow registration for those with a master's degree. They may work as counsellors or may specialize in other areas, such as in administering and interpreting psychological tests. Psychologists are often employed in private practice, but they also may work in settings such as prisons, hospitals, schools, and private industry.

In contrast, psychiatrists are medical doctors with advanced training in psychiatry. They are specialists in the treatment of people with mental disorders. Psychiatrists are the only counselling professionals licensed to prescribe medication. Psychiatric nurses generally have two to four years of training. Historically, they worked in psychiatric hospitals and wards, but increasingly, they are working in community-based mental health settings.

Community college graduates with one to two years of college training also provide counselling services in settings such as transition homes, addiction centres, employment counselling agencies and community mental health. The non-profit social service sector also uses volunteers to deliver services in settings such as crisis phone lines, where people in distress call for assistance or referral. In addition, the professional counselling community is often supported or replaced by an array of self-help support groups, such as Alcoholics Anonymous (AA) or Narcotics Anonymous (NA).

What Is Counselling?

Counselling is a time-limited relationship in which counsellors help clients increase their ability to deal with the demands of life. Typically, people seek or are referred to counsellors because of an unmanageable crisis, such as the loss of a job, relationship problems, or feelings of distress. The immediate goal of counselling is to provide assistance so that people seeking help (clients) can gain some control over their problems. The long-term goal of counselling is to restore or develop a client's ability to cope with the changing demands of their lives (empowerment).

Counselling is defined by three variables: the needs and wants of the client, the mandate of the counselling setting, and the expertise or competence of the counsellor. Professional counsellors are aware of the limits of their competence and know when to refer their clients to other appropriate service. They are also aware of their own needs and unresolved

TABLE 1.1	Counselling Skills: Beginning to Advanced
Beginning Level Counsellors	**Advanced Level Counsellors**
Basic use of core listening and responding skills.	Exemplary use of broad range of listening and counselling skills and strategies. Capacity to be creative to meet unique needs of individual clients.
Sensitivity to overt nonverbal cues.	Responsive to subtle nonverbal cues and themes.
Basic content knowledge of field of practice.	In-depth knowledge of current science and practice in the field. Ability to analyze and adapt published material.
Rudimentary understanding of self.	Sophisticated knowledge of self, one's impact on others, and one's ability to selectively use aspects of self to influence others.
Struggle to manage biases, personal reactions.	"Second nature" capacity to stay appropriately detached and in control of self.
Tendency to "mimic" mentors and textbook responses.	Capacity to customize approach, development of individual styles.
Self-consciousness.	Focus on clients.
Tendency to want to fix, rescue or solve client problems.	Acceptance of the client as "expert." Focus on client empowerment.

issues, and they refer clients to other professionals when they cannot work with reasonable **objectivity**. In addition, they accept that no one counsellor is qualified to work with all clients. Table 1.1 summarizes how counselling knowledge and skills evolve from beginning to advanced levels.

The work of counselling may entail a broad range of activities, including the following:

- helping clients cope with painful feelings
- teaching clients new skills
- helping clients develop problem-solving skills
- mediating relationship communication difficulties
- aiding clients in identifying and accessing resources
- helping clients make decisions and implement action plans
- supporting or motivating clients

Interviewing skills are indispensable to effective counselling. The goal of **interviewing** is to acquire and organize relevant information through timely listening and responding skills. But when the interview is used as an information-gathering process, interviewers do not try to promote change. However, clients may feel relief from sharing, and organizing their thoughts in response to a systematic interview may help them to grow.

Moreover, good interviewers are comfortable with silence and know when to listen without interrupting. Counsellors who listen to their clients give them a chance to air their feelings, and this step can be therapeutic in itself. Patient listening shows clients that counsellors are willing to accept them without judgment and without burdening them with quick-fix solutions to complex problems and feelings.

At the beginning of counselling sessions or interviews, silent listening may also give counsellors valuable clues about the potential focus of the interview. Listening also helps counsellors learn about their clients' priorities. It reveals which methods clients may have used and not used to try to solve their problems.

Good listeners also know when and how to respond. Paraphrasing, summarizing, questioning, and showing empathy are the foundations of effective listening. These skills enable counsellors to focus and deepen the interview. Good listeners use questions to clarify meaning and seek details and examples, whereas they paraphrase and summarize responses to confirm understanding and highlight important information. A good interview involves methodical questioning and exploration of issues, a process that can help clients clarify and organize their thoughts. Finally, counsellors use empathy skills to confirm their understanding of the client's feelings.

Social Work and Counselling

One special feature that distinguishes social work counselling from that performed by other professionals is its dual focus on working with individuals as well as their social environment. Social workers assume that an individual can only be understood in the context of his or her environment; thus, they pay particular attention to the interaction of the person and the environment. Like other professionals in the helping professions, social workers counsel clients to help them develop insight, solve problems, deal with emotional pain, and enhance relationships. They may also support clients by providing information, social skills training, or resources.

But unique to social work is the important professional responsibility to promote social justice or "fairness and moral rightness in how social institutions such as government, corporations, and powerful groups recognize and support the basic human rights of all people" (Sheafor & Horejsi, 2006:6). Social justice commitment involves advocacy to promote human rights and more equitable income redistribution; political action to change oppressive legislation or policy; public education to shape public opinion; and efforts to build community. Social workers recognize that social problems arise, at least in part, from ineffective social systems.

While counselling is important for helping individuals cope, it is insufficient for dealing completely with these great challenges. Thus, because this book explores only the counselling component of social work practice, practitioners are cautioned to approach this task with the broader mission of social work in mind. Value 2 of The Code of Ethics of the Canadian Association of Social Workers (2005) outlines the obligations of social workers to advocate for social change:

Value 2: Pursuit of Social Justice

As a result, social workers believe in the obligation of people, individually and collectively, to provide resources, services and opportunities for the overall benefit of humanity and to afford them protection from harm. Social workers promote social fairness and the equitable distribution of resources, and take action to reduce barriers and expand choice for all persons, with special regard for those who are marginalized, disadvantaged, vulnerable, and/or have exceptional needs. Social workers oppose prejudice and discrimination against any person or group of persons on any grounds, and specifically challenge views and actions that stereotype particular persons or groups.

Principles:

- Social workers uphold the right of people to have access to resources to meet basic human needs.
- Social workers advocate for fair and equitable access to public services and benefits.
- Social workers advocate for equal treatment and protection under the law and challenge injustices, especially injustices that affect the vulnerable and disadvantaged.
- Social workers promote social development and environmental management in the interests of all people (p. 5).

CONVERSATION 1.1

COUNSELLING AND PSYCHOTHERAPY

STUDENT: What's the difference between counselling and psychotherapy?

TEACHER: The terms **psychotherapy** and counselling are often confused. Both counselling and psychotherapy are used to help clients learn skills, deal with feelings, and manage problems. In counselling and psychotherapy, appropriate relationships with clients are the crucial success medium that establishes a foundation of safety and security for clients to undertake the change process.

Although there is no clear dividing line between the two terms, the major difference between counselling and psychotherapy is that psychotherapy tends to be more long-term than counselling, with an emphasis on severe emotional and behavioural difficulties or disorders. On the other hand, counselling is targeted at assisting clients in managing situational problems.

CHOICES: THE NEED FOR VERSATILITY

The typical counselling caseload is characterized by its **diversity**. Culture, gender, age, religion, sexual orientation, language, education, economic ability, and intellectual capacity, as well as beliefs, values, preferences and personal style, make every client different. Therefore, there is no "one size fits all" model of counselling. Respect for client diversity requires counsellors to be versatile in adapting their methods to fit the needs of each client or context. Counsellors who persist in using the same strategy for all clients, without regard to individual differences, will never become effective.

Expert counsellors draw on research theory and experience as guides in determining which skills and procedures will best meet their clients' needs. They work from a model or process for exploring problems and helping clients build solutions, but they adapt that model to each client situation. Every client and problem circumstance will favour different skills, and each situation requires counsellors to know how to use skills, as well as when to use them and when to refrain from using them. Most counsellors now accept that no one counselling approach is best, and they are willing to draw ideas from different theoretical schools. In the process, they learn to use an assortment of counselling tools, including drama, role play, toys, music, art, films, visual charts such as genealogical diagrams, personality tests, and audio or visual recordings. However, as Lazarus and Beutler (1993) caution, counsellors must act based on "a logical decisional process that takes into account the client, setting, problem, and the nature of the counselor's skills" (1993:384).

Moreover, Brill and Levine (2005) stress the importance of considering the counsellor's personal influence in the counselling process. Counsellors "must consider their weaknesses as well as their capacities and strengths in selecting methods, techniques, and procedures. Because each individual is different, all workers must develop their own styles and their own ways of handling the tools of the trade. This is the element of artistry that is a vital part of such work" (p. 175). Successful counsellors model high congruence between who they are and how they act. They are sincere and real in the way they relate to clients.

Skill versatility also means that counsellors have choices that give them the freedom to adapt to individual differences. When one strategy fails, counsellors can use others.

Finally, skill versatility enables counsellors to customize their approach. For example, although most clients respond favourably to empathy, some clients see empathy as intrusive and respond with defensiveness, preferring to keep their feelings private, at least for a while. Effective counsellors are alert to such reactions and have the ability to use skills other than empathy with such clients.

But knowing how to use a skill is not the same as knowing when to use it. Although counsellors can make some generalizations about when a particular skill is appropriate, they need to apply these generalizations with caution and consideration for individual differences. For example, at the beginning of a counselling relationship, the counsellor usually wants to use skills that promote the development of the working alliance and avoids more demanding strategies such as confrontation. But once they have established a firm working relationship, counsellors will want to use skills that help clients gain new perspectives, so confrontation may be warranted. As another example, empathy often encourages clients to share deeper feelings. Therefore, counsellors who use empathy should be willing to invest the time that this sharing requires. But if the interview is near an end, the counsellor might decide to avoid empathic responses that stimulate emotions that cannot be dealt with in the time available.

Matching the Language of Clients

Careful listening helps counsellors learn their clients' communicative language and metaphors. In turn, this knowledge helps guide counsellors to modify their language to fit that of their clients. Counsellors need to pay attention to such variables as voice tone, volume, and tempo and then respond appropriately. To a depressed client, a high-energy, fast-talking counsellor might be annoying. Similarly, the counsellor who responds in a monotone to a client who is ecstatic about finding a job might come across as cold and indifferent.

Grinder and Bandler (1976) suggest that everyone has a different way of using language to describe their experiences. According to their theory, people process ideas in one of three major modalities: in the visual mode through pictures and images; in the auditory mode with sounds; and in the kinesthetic or feeling mode. A person who thinks visually will be more likely to say, "I see what you mean"; whereas a person who processes in the auditory mode might say, "I hear you." Someone else might say, "I have a handle on my problem" or "I feel in touch with that idea." These responses each suggest that person's processing mode. Counsellors may find it easier to establish rapport and build trust when they match their clients' words with similar language (see Table 1.2).

TABLE 1.2	Matching Clients' Language Styles	
Style	**Client Statement**	**Sample Counsellor Response**
Visual	My view of the problem is . . .	If I get the picture correctly, the way you see it is . . .
Auditory	When I listen to myself I know what I have to do.	Tell me more about what you are saying to yourself.
Kinesthetic	I can't seem to get a handle on my problem.	What prevents you from grasping the solution?

Other Versatility Variables

Versatility also means being flexible regarding other variables, such as the location of the interview, the duration, the pace, the fees, and the people involved. Although some counsellors work in office settings with scheduled 45-minute or hour-long interviews, many work in settings where counselling interviews are less structured. Process versatility gives counsellors choices regarding the sequence and pace of counselling activities. With most clients, the beginning phase is concerned with exploring problems and feelings; but with other clients, counsellors may move immediately to action and problem solving. With some clients, counsellors spend a great deal of time helping them explore their feelings; but with others, counsellors spend little or no time in this activity.

Versatility also extends to other factors, such as the amount of expected or desired eye contact, the seating arrangements, and the physical distance. Some clients are comfortable in an office setting, but others prefer to work in their own home or to meet in a neutral setting. Adolescent boys, for example, might prove more approachable if counselling interventions are combined with some activity. Some clients favour an open seating arrangement with no desk or obstacle between them and their counsellors. Others prefer to work over the corner of a desk (Kadushin, 1990).

VALUES AND ETHICS

Ethics are principles of acceptable conduct. Professional associations like the Canadian Association of Social Workers and the Canadian Counselling Association have formal statements that define ethics and standards of practice for their members. Similarly, **values** are ideas and principles that individuals and groups consider important or worthwhile. The behaviour of counsellors in their interviews is influenced to a great extent by their values, including their philosophical view of people and the way they are motivated. Counsellors who see people as basically good and goal-directed will behave very differently than those who believe people are selfish and lazy, needing to be controlled. In counselling, certain core values are of particular importance:

1. belief in the dignity and worth of people
2. respect for the client's right to self-determination (i.e., for freedom of choice and the right to control their own lives)
3. commitment to work for social justice

These professional values are at the root of the counselling model described in this book. By respecting the dignity of people, counsellors try to be nonjudgmental in their work and treat all clients with respect and caring. The second core value, the self-determination principle, values the right of clients to be involved in decision making and to control decisions that affect their lives. And the social justice principle requires counsellors to work to alleviate unfair social or system conditions. Chapter 2 considers these concepts in greater depth.

SKILL CLUSTERS

Today, there is no standardized method for classifying counselling skills. Nevertheless, it is useful to think about skills in terms of their function or intended purpose. In this book, four major **skill clusters** are discussed: (1) relationship building skills; (2) exploring or probing skills; (3) empowering skills; and (4) challenging skills. Each major skill is further categorized into subclusters of related skills (see Table 1.3).

Significantly, some skills achieve multiple purposes. Sensitive active listening, for example, contributes to the development of the relationship because it communicates acceptance and the sincere desire to understand. At the same time, active listening is also essential for getting information, so this skill can also be classified as a exploring/probing skill. Practitioners need to be versatile, building competence based on knowledge of (1) particular skills, including their intended purpose; (2) best methods and situations for using each skill; and (3) personal strengths and limitations with each skill.

Relationship-Building Skills

Relationship-building skills are the basic tools for engaging clients, developing trust, and defining the purpose of the counselling. They are of central importance during the beginning phase of helping; but effective counselling requires that the relationship be sustained and deepened through all phases of helping. Relationship-building skills can be organized into three clusters: those promoting core conditions, those involving active listening, and those defining the relationship.

Core Conditions

Rogers (1951, 1961, 1980) and others have written extensively about the core conditions necessary for forming a helping relationship—namely, congruence or genuineness, empathy, and positive regard. Rogers believed that people were essentially good, self-deterministic (able to make their own decisions), and goal-directed. Thus, he believed that these core conditions were necessary for establishing the rapport and therapeutic alliance needed in a purposeful counselling relationship.

Congruence, or **genuineness**, is the capacity to be real and consistent with clients. Congruent counsellors are open with their reactions and feelings and demonstrate consistency in what they believe, say, and do. Congruency also requires counsellors to be "transparent"—without hidden agendas or false demeanours. Rogers believed that the more counsellors were aware of their feelings and the more they genuinely expressed

TABLE 1.3	Skill Clusters		
Relationship Building	**Exploring or Probing**	**Empowering**	**Challenging**
Promoting core conditions • Congruence • Empathy • Positive Regard Active listening • Attending • Silence • Paraphrasing • Summarizing • Questioning • Empathy Defining and sustaining the relationship • Relationship contracting • Sessional contracting • Immediacy	Active listening • Attending • Silence • Paraphrasing • Summarizing • Questioning • Empathy Other interviewing skills • Directives • Simple encouragers • Counsellor self-disclosure • Humour • Open ended statements • Responding to nonverbal cues • Managing transitions	Searching for strengths • Defining client capacities and rights • Defining problems as opportunities • Identifying resources Teaching • Skills training • Modelling • Role playing Information giving • Advice and information • Referring • Answering questions Supporting • Reassuring • Fostering optimism • Reinforcing • Advocating • Providing direct aid • Praising	Confronting • Providing critical feedback • Promoting strengths • Encouraging • Correcting distortions • Reframing • Asking clients to take responsibility Action planning • Defining clear and measurable targets for change • Helping clients identify and evaluate alternatives for reaching goals • Helping clients choose, develop, and carry out change strategies Use of Power and Authority • Limit setting • Enforcement

these feelings in the counselling relationship, the more effective the counselling would become.

Empathy as a core condition means being able to see the world through the eyes of the clients. Essential to empathic understanding is the ability to understand feelings without imposing one's own feelings or reactions. "Empathy becomes judgmental when the counsellor not only reflects the client's feeling state but also applies his or her own emotional yardstick in measuring its appropriateness for the client" (Gilliland & James, 1998:117–18).

Positive regard, or respect for clients, is the ability of counsellors to recognize the inherent worth of people, regardless of their behaviour. As Gilliland and James conclude, "At any given time, the counselor needs to be willing to accept the confusion, fear, anger, resentment, courage, sorrow, and multiplicity of other feelings the client may have. Such caring is total and nonpossessive and lacks prior conditions of rightness or appropriateness of the client's feelings" (1998:117).

Active Listening

Active listening is crucial for building relationships. When clients feel heard, they respond with further disclosure. Moreover, unless counsellors listen, there is no way for them to understand the complexities and uniqueness of their clients' situations. Active listening involves six separate skills: attending, using silence, paraphrasing, summarizing, questioning, and showing empathy. **Attending** is the manner in which counsellors communicate that they are physically and psychologically interested in what their clients are saying or doing. Appropriate **silence** gives clients time to think and respond. Effective counsellors understand the multiple meanings of silence. Is the client confused? Have we reached the end of the topic? Is the client thinking? Skilled counsellors know when to interrupt a silence and when to allow it to continue. **Paraphrasing** involves restating (usually in shortened form) the client's thoughts to clarify the essence of what he or she has said. **Summarizing** means condensing the essential content and identifying essential themes and ideas. **Questioning** involves probing for information to confirm understanding and seek clarification, such as by saying, "Do you mean that . . . ?" **Empathy** is "the process of accurately understanding the emotional perspective of another person and the communication of this understanding" (Shebib, 1997:177).

Active listening skills also provide psychological incentive for clients to open up. When clients sense deeply that they have been heard, they are motivated to open up. In addition, when their ideas are not judged or rejected and when their feelings are validated, they learn to trust the listener. This trust results in a climate of safety, and clients begin to reveal more. Furthermore, active listening skills provide a structure for exploring thoughts and feelings. Paraphrasing and summarizing, for example, help clients organize ideas, identify key points, and recognize priorities. Questions also provide a systematic way of exploring ideas for detail, definition, and example. Finally, empathy opens opportunities for understanding and accepting feelings.

Active listening says to the client, "I have heard you," "I am willing to understand your problems and feelings without judgment," and "I accept you." Consequently, active listening is a powerful tool for establishing rapport and understanding, which are the bases for a strong working relationship. The skills of active listening will be discussed in depth in Chapters 4, 5, and 6.

Defining and Sustaining the Relationship

Rogers emphasizes the importance of avoiding moral judgment of clients in order to develop an effective helping relationship. He vividly captures the significance of nonjudgmental exploration to the development of the relationship: "It is only as I understand the feelings and thoughts which seem so horrible to you, or so weak, or so sentimental, or so bizarre—it is only as I see them as you see them, and accept them and you, that you feel really free to explore all the hidden nooks and frightening crannies of your inner and often buried experience" (1961:34).

Three major skills are associated with defining and sustaining the relationship: relationship contracting, sessional contracting, and immediacy. These counselling contracts may change, sometimes frequently, as the work proceeds. **Relationship contracting** involves negotiating the intended purpose of the counselling relationship, including agreeing on the expected roles of both counsellor and client. **Sessional contracting** is concerned with setting the purpose of an individual session. Sessional contracting defines a work plan that is individualized to meet the needs of the client. Consider, for example, three women who seek counselling for the same problem—a relationship breakdown. As a result of contracting, client one may conclude that she needs help in managing her stress and pain. The second client may want to focus on developing her assertive communication skills for dealing with an abusive spouse. The third client might want help with decision making in choosing between leaving the relationship or remaining in hopes of solving the relationship problems. (See Chapter 3 for a detailed discussion of relationship and sessional contracts.)

Immediacy (Egan, 1998) is a tool for examining and deepening the counselling relationship. It involves a process of evaluation that addresses the quality of the relationship in terms of its contracted objectives. The skill of immediacy can be used to troubleshoot relationship problems. It promotes candid discussion regarding ways the relationship might be changed in order to better fulfill its objectives. With immediacy, relationship problems and feelings are addressed before they have a chance to have a lasting destructive impact. (See Chapter 3 for an extensive discussion of this skill.)

Exploring/Probing Skills

Exploring/probing skills are basic tools of interviewing that counsellors use to gather information, clarify definitions, seek examples, and obtain necessary detail. These skills enable counsellors to avoid making **assumptions**. Active listening skills are the primary tools of exploration and probing. Because they communicate counsellor willingness to listen nonjudgmentally, they motivate and encourage clients to tell their stories.

Other Interviewing Skills

Directives such as "Tell me more" or "Please expand on your feelings" control the direction and pace of the interview. Directives can also be used to focus the client on relevant priorities. Directives are the "road signs" of the interview.

Simple encouragers are short verbal and nonverbal cues that motivate clients to continue. Verbal statements such as "Uh huh" or "Yes" and short directives such as "Please continue," along with nonverbal signals such as head nods and an attentive posture, make up this skill set. **Counsellor self-disclosure**, used sparingly, can be a useful tool that models appropriate sharing of feelings. Counsellor self-disclosure may reduce the clients' sense that their experiences or feelings are strange or abnormal. Subsequently, when experiences are "normalized," clients are more apt to open up and share. In this way, counsellor self-disclosure acts as an exploring/probing skill. **Humour**, if timely, can be used to reduce tension or encourage clients to take a lighter view of their situation. But humour must be used cautiously so that it does not offend clients or trivialize their problems.

Open-ended or incomplete statements give clients an opportunity to "fill in the blanks." One technique is to ask the client to complete a statement:

Counsellor: How might your finish this statement? The one thing I need most from my husband is . . .

Alternatively, the counsellor can simply present the incomplete sentence with a pause for the client to complete it.

Counsellor: It seems like the thing you need most from him is ...

By **responding to nonverbal cues**, counsellors pay attention to such things as voice tone, posture, eye contact and facial expressions. Sometimes the content expressed by a client's words is sufficient for understanding; but not infrequently, the major meaning or intent of a client's message comes through the nonverbal channel. Counsellors should never ignore the nonverbal channel, which enhances, contradicts or embellishes verbal messages.

Managing transitions involves paying attention to or suggesting shifts between phases or topics. This skill can be used to organize the flow of the interview or to link themes and ideas. (See Chapter 6 for an extensive discussion.)

Empowering Skills

Empowering skills help clients develop confidence, self-esteem, and control over their lives. But Cowger (1994) offers this important reminder that the role of social workers is not to "give" people power:

> To assume a social worker can empower someone else is naive and condescending and has little basis in reality. Power is not something that social workers possess for distribution at will. Clients, not social workers, own the power that brings significant change in clinical practice. A clinical social worker is merely a resource person with professional training on the use of resources who is committed to people empowerment and willing to share his or her knowledge in a manner that helps people realize their own power, take control of their own lives, and solve their own problems. (p. 264)

Five skill subclusters are the essence of empowering: searching for strengths, teaching, supporting, giving information, and managing anxiety.

Searching for strengths moves counselling from a process of identifying deficits and problems to one in which clients' strengths, capacities, and resources are recognized. Strengths are the resources that enable clients to overcome problems. In this sense, client assessment moves beyond identifying obstacles and problems to discussion of personal and environmental resources.

Helping clients realize their strengths empowers them with the belief that they are capable of change. For example, helping clients reframe how they think about problems can enable them to see their problems as opportunities. Saleeby (2002), a major proponent of the strengths approach, summarizes the goal of this philosophy: "Mobilize clients' strengths (talents, knowledge, capacities, resources) in the service of achieving their goals and visions, and the clients will have a better quality of life on their terms" (p. 1–2). Such an approach reduces some of the power differential that comes when client vulnerabilities and deficits are given priority over their strengths. Glicken (2004) offers this reminder that deserves attention by both clients and counsellors: "There is usually more about clients that is positive and functional than is negative or dysfunctional" (p. 4). With the strengths perspective, the client is the expert and the primary author of the change process. "Thus, the worker's role is to listen, help the client process, and facilitate by focusing on positive behaviors that might be useful to clients for coping with their current life situations" (Glicken, 2004:6).

Teaching may be used in counselling as a way to assist clients in developing strengths. Skills training, role playing, and other tools can be used to help clients develop their capacities.

Information giving empowers clients with knowledge of alternative courses of action, including resources that might assist them deal with their problems. Counsellors may also offer suggestions and advice regarding problem management.

Finally, supporting is used to bolster clients' energy and optimism. To some extent, all counselling skills are supportive. Supporting reduces clients' feelings of isolation and provides them with incentives to address their problems, express their feelings, and begin a process of change. Supporting can also be used to tell clients that they are on the right track and that their feelings and reactions are normal. As well, supporting helps clients manage anxiety and stress, thus increasing their energy, self-confidence, and capacity for problem solving.

Challenging Skills

Challenging skills are used to encourage clients to critically evaluate their behaviour and ideas. They push clients toward change and growth and in this way fulfill the fundamental reason for the counselling relationship. But excessive or premature reliance on challenging skills may strain the counselling relationship. As Young puts it, "when challenging skills are used, the aura of safety and support, so carefully constructed by the helper, is at risk. There is a fundamental shift from relationship building to a focus on the goals set by the client and helper, conveying to the client that the helping relationship is not a friendship but a business partnership" (1998:100).

Three subclusters are contained within this skill set: confronting, action planning, and using power and authority. **Confrontation** prods clients to critically examine their actions and/or consider other viewpoints. Counsellors may need to provide critical or corrective feedback, identify overlooked strengths, correct distortions, suggest other viewpoints (re-framing), or request that clients assume responsibility. Confrontation skills are most effective when there is a strong relationship of trust and when clients understand and accept the value of their use. Brill and Levine (2005) offer this perspective on the challenging skill of confrontation:

> Misuse of confrontation can be devastating, destroying all previous efforts. Workers must assess the amount and quality of confrontation the client is willing or able to use, and they must be able to give support if the reality is overwhelming. Workers must not use confrontation to express their own anger and frustration, although these are certainly a part of the reality with which both workers and clients must deal. (p. 186)

Ideally, confrontation skills increase clients' motivation for change. Counsellors develop the credibility necessary for successful confronting when they have listened to clients and persuaded them that they are accepted and understood. With this base, clients may be appropriately confronted when they:

- are working from false assumptions or incomplete information:
- misread the actions of others
- lack **self-awareness** regarding the impact of their actions (for example, when they blame others for their problems rather than examining their own responsibility)
- demonstrate contradictions in their behaviour, thoughts, and feelings
- deny or do not recognize their personal strengths, capacities, or resources.

Action planning is a way of helping clients bring about changes in their lives. These changes may include finding new ways of managing feelings, forming strategies for modifying ways of thinking, or developing new skills or behaviours. Action planning helps clients define clear and measurable targets for change (goals), identify and evaluate alternative strategies, and select and develop plans for reaching these goals.

Use of Power and Authority

Counsellors derive or are given power by virtue of their position. Such power comes from many sources: competence, knowledge, education, control of resources, position in the agency/status in the community, or simply the fact that the client is the one who is in the position of needing or seeking help. But counsellors are also representatives of agencies that wield power. For example, child protection social workers frequently make decisions and judgments that impact clients' lives. However gentle and caring counsellors are, from the perspective of clients, they are perceived as persons with power and influence, and often as people to be feared. As such, counsellors should heed Compton and Galaway's (1999) caution to accept and use their power wisely.

> Questions of power and authority are particularly relevant when we are required to enter a situation by court order or agency decision. Prior experiences of the misuse of professional authority may underlie the family's negative expectations, lack of trust and fear of commitment. When we intervene in people's lives at the request of others, we must be prepared to explain very clearly— many times, if necessary—what authority and power we carry, what the limits of our authority and power are, and how we will use it. This is often difficult because of our own feelings about authority. (1999:181.)

THE PHASES OF COUNSELLING

Counselling interventions usually move through a planned change process involving sequential steps or phases, each characterized by unique as well as common objectives and skills. For our purposes, four **phases of counselling** will be discussed: (1) preliminary; (2) beginning; (3) action; and (4) ending. This model builds on similar models presented by others such as Egan (1998), Shulman (1999), and Young (1998).

Each phase is distinguished by its focus on different activities. The preliminary phase is essentially for planning. Proper planning increases the likelihood that clients will perceive that their needs can be met through counselling. The beginning phase is a time of engagement, when both the client and the counsellor make decisions about whether they will work together and, if so, under what structure. The beginning phase is also a time for exploring problems and feelings. Although clients may begin to change their behaviour or manage their feelings more effectively during the beginning phase, the action phase is more concerned with initiating change. During the ending phase, the working relationship is brought to a close, perhaps with a referral to another resource or counsellor.

One common objective of each phase is forming and sustaining a working relationship. This counselling relationship is the vehicle for change and provides a base of safety and security for clients to explore and understand their emotions and difficulties. The counselling contract, an agreement on the goals and roles of the participants, is the reference point for the relationship. It is continually reviewed and revised as the work progresses.

A second common objective of all phases is to establish open, honest, and productive communication. Effective communication enables counsellors to learn about their clients' needs and feelings. As well, it empowers clients to learn new ways of handling old problems.

The third common objective of all phases is evaluation. Ongoing evaluation can review the essential elements of the counselling plan (goals and methods), the working relationship, or the overall satisfaction of all participants with the pace of the work and its results. By using a problem-solving approach, counsellors and clients can explore ways to ensure that the work is relevant and efficient.

Skill clusters help organize skills based on function. Since each phase of counselling supports different activities, each phase also favours different skills. For example, during the beginning phase of counselling, relationship-building skills are the priority, and challenging skills are usually avoided, at least until a foundation of trust and safety is established. Exploration/probing skills are also vital during the beginning phase. They enable counsellors to acquire information for understanding, thus helping them avoid assumptions. But challenging and directing/teaching skills tend to be more effective in the action phase, when a strong relationship and a solid base of understanding have been established. Table 1.4 summarizes the principal activities and priority skills of each phase.

Counselling tends to move through the phases sequentially, with success at each phase depending, in part, on the success of preceding phases. For example, the preliminary phase is designed to support the work of the beginning phase. It allows the counsellor to complete the preparations that will help welcome the client to the agency. As well, it works as a kind of warm-up, so counsellors can be ready and sensitive to the needs of their clients. Weak planning results in weak beginnings. Similarly, effective work in the action phase is easier when the beginning phase has been successful. A solid base of understanding permits counsellors and clients to set more pertinent goals, and a foundation of trust allows counsellors to be more challenging in their approach. In contrast, counsellors who attempt to challenge clients from a thin base of trust are likely to meet with resistance or rejection. Even in the

TABLE 1.4	Counselling Activities and Skills	
Phase	**Principal Activities**	**Priority Skills**
Preliminary	• Interview preplanning • Preparing the interview setting	• Planning • Establishing self-awareness
Beginning	• Establishing a working relationship • Interviewing for understanding • Evaluating	• Active listening • Promoting core conditions • Defining the relationship (relationship contracting) • Searching for strengths
Action	• Goal setting • Action planning • Helping clients change behaviour, manage feelings, change perceptions • Revising the contract, deepening the relationship, managing communication difficulties • Evaluating	• Teaching • Information giving • Supporting • Confronting • Action planning
Ending	• Ending the helping relationship • Referring to other resources • Evaluating	• Giving information • Supporting

action phase, it is important to try to sequence the steps. If clients try to develop action plans before they have set clear goals, their action plans are more likely to be vague and directionless.

Although counselling work tends to evolve sequentially through the four phases, usually it does not move forward in a neat and orderly manner:

> The logical progression of these phases makes the process appear to be a linear, step-by-step set of actitivities. In reality, change rarely proceeds in an orderly fashion; rather, it is more of a spiral, with frequent returns to prior phases for clarification or a reworking of various tasks and activities (Sheafor, Horesjsi, 2006:126)

The phases of counselling also provide a systematic and useful checklist of the key activities and logical steps that are part of the change or problem-solving process. By referring to the phases of counselling, counsellors and clients can remain clear on where they are in the counselling process, what has been done, what remains to be accomplished, and what options remain open. However, as any experienced counsellor will attest, "each counselling encounter is different, each relationship is uniquely complex, and the work may evolve in unpredictable ways." (Shebib, 1997:71)

Sometimes clear divisions between the phases of counselling are apparent. But more frequently, there are overlaps between the phases and shifts forward and back between one phase and another; and in some cases, phases may be skipped altogether. Some typical counselling scenarios are provided below.

> Jessica, a very private person, was distraught over the breakup of her marriage. Aware of her inability to cope and not knowing what to do, she attended several sessions with a counsellor. Her counsellor proceeded slowly, gently encouraging Jessica to talk about her feelings. Jessica was surprised that during the second counselling session, she began to weep. Afterward, she remarked that she felt as if a great weight had been lifted from her shoulders. She never felt the need to return for a third session.

> Clint was not interested in exploring his problem beyond a superficial level. Anxious to effect change in his life, he wanted to brainstorm ideas for dealing with his problems. Counselling work focused on helping him set goals. As this work progressed, Clint became more trusting, and the sessions began to focus on exploring his feelings.

> As Fernando talked about his problem, he suddenly realized that his situation was not as hopeless as he thought. Discovering another way to look at his problem, he identified several new ways to solve it.

> After a single session, Bob remarked to his counsellor, "My problem is the same as when I came in here, but somehow it doesn't seem to bother me as much."

CONVERSATION 1.2

HELPFUL FRIENDS AND COUNSELLORS

STUDENT: What is the difference between a conversation with a helpful friend and a counselling interview?

TEACHER: The goal of a friendship is to meet the needs of both people. Friends (and family) are important. If they are understanding, caring, and supportive, they can be an effective source of help. Much like a counselling relationship, just talking to a friend can be cathartic to the individual. But there may be limits in what friends can offer. Sometimes friends and families don't have specialized knowledge, or they may not know what resources or services are available to deal with specific problems. Friends and family may also be so emotionally involved with you that it is hard for them to be objective.

STUDENT: You're right. I find my family can't separate their feelings from mine, and they always end up giving me well intentioned but not very helpful advice.

TEACHER: Effective counsellors are comfortable discussing feelings, and they don't tell clients how they should feel. Good counsellors are excellent listeners, and they invest time to make sure they accurately understand clients' feelings and concerns. Counsellors know how to systematically explore problems, set goals, and develop plans for action. They assist clients in identifying and evaluating alternatives, while recognizing that the clients must choose for themselves. Therefore, counsellors do not impose advice or try to rescue clients by taking on their problems. Unlike friendships, counselling relationships are directed to meet the needs of one person only—the client.

The Preliminary Phase

The preliminary phase of counselling is essentially a time of planning with a focus on two central tasks. First, the agency setting is made attractive for clients so they are motivated to engage and remain with the agency. Second, counsellors prepare themselves for the interview.

The Agency Setting

Ideally, the agency is set up to appeal to the client groups that it serves. A drop-in counselling centre for teens should look different from a day program centre for seniors. Dim lighting and beanbag chairs meet the needs of teens but present a safety hazard for seniors. Tea is appropriate for seniors, but a soft drink makes more sense when the clients are teens. Ideally, the agency should:

- have uncrowded waiting rooms
- allow for reception and interview space that is private and confidential
- greet clients in a warm and friendly manner
- provide for the needs of children (e.g., by supplying a play area with age-appropriate toys)
- allow for wheelchair access
- have posters and other art that do not violate the values, religion, or culture of the agency's clients (generally, they should also be politically neutral)
- have up-to-date waiting-room reading material

But often, counsellors fail to ensure that their interviews are protected from phone calls and other interruptions that impede the flow of conversation. When interruptions are allowed, the message to clients is "I have other concerns that are more important than you. Hurry up and finish."

Moreover, flexible office arrangements are best. Some clients and many counsellors prefer an unobstructed arrangement without a desk between the participants, but others favour working over the desk. The office needs to be arranged with careful consideration to the messages that the design communicates. Chairs and desks should be arranged so that no psychological advantage or power is given to the counsellor. Seating arrangements should allow for adequate personal space between counsellors and clients. A comfort zone of about 1 to 2 m (4 to 7 feet) is adequate for most clients, but other factors might result in a need for more or less distance.

Counsellors also need to be careful in choosing personal items to display. Pictures and memorabilia that punctuate differences between counsellors and their clients should be avoided. Of course, clients may have different reactions. For example, some clients expect and appreciate seeing their counsellor's degrees or diplomas hung on the wall. For these clients, knowing something about the training and credentials of their counsellors helps to establish confidence and credibility. Other clients, however, may react negatively to such a display. For them, the display sets up social and intellectual barriers. Generally, counsellors should structure their offices with the needs and background of their clients in mind. In this respect, clients can be an invaluable source of consultation. Their opinions on office decor and layout should be solicited.

Interview Preparation

Counsellors can use the preliminary phase to predict how the interview time will be used and to make decisions related to the time, place, and structure of the interview. As well, counsellors can think about specific questions and responses for working with particular clients, without setting up a script or rigid agenda.

Shulman (1999) suggests that for a variety of reasons, clients often do not share feelings and concerns directly. They may be ambivalent about sharing, or they may hold back because of societal and cultural taboos about talking about sex, authority, and money. As a result, clients may raise these concerns indirectly, and counsellors must be alert to recognize clues about their clients' concerns. For example, a single parent who asks her welfare worker if he has ever been on welfare may be indirectly expressing her fear that the worker will be insensitive to the stress she faces in trying to cope with a limited budget. Sometimes, questions regarding personal background or circumstances may be indirect ways clients have of exploring concerns about trust.

Shulman (1999) recommends the preliminary phase skill of *tuning in* as a tool for anticipating the feelings and concerns that clients might bring to the interview. By tuning in, counsellors can think about what clients might express and how they will do so. The preliminary phase is also a time when counsellors examine their own readiness. For example, counsellors should take a few moments prior to each interview to self-examine through questions, such as the following:

- Am I dealing with personal stress or problems that might make me less effective or more vulnerable?
- Am I sufficiently disengaged from my last client to be open and objective?
- What personal biases do I need to manage in order to work effectively with this client?
- What reservations do I have about meeting this client?
- Do I have unfinished business with this client that I have not addressed?
- What feelings do I have toward this client that might impede my objectivity?

Client Files

The preliminary phase is also a time for fact-finding to help understand a client's situation. For example, a counsellor could research Tourette's syndrome as preparation for meeting a client with a child who has been diagnosed with this condition.

Typically, most agencies have files on each client which may contain considerable information regarding the client's age, place of birth, address, marital status, work history, educational background, prior experiences with counselling, and assessments of personality, values, past problems, ability to handle stress, communication patterns, and so on. Client files can also alert counsellors to any past incidents of violence and point out any need to take special precautions.

A review of client files can greatly speed the intake process, but it is important to maintain an open mind and avoid prejudgment, particularly with respect to the assessments other counsellors have made regarding manner and personality. Client reactions are influenced in part (and occasionally to a great extent) by the personality and behaviour of their counsellors, as shown in the following example:

> Russ waited for his counsellor, who was half an hour late for the scheduled interview. Russ was stressed because of personal problems and was anxious to get home to care for his sick children. Estelle, his counsellor, was also stressed owing to a difficult week of work. She was also aware that her next appointment was already waiting for her to finish with Russ. Determined to catch up, she moved quickly with questions to complete her assessment of Russ's situation. Russ, taken aback by Estelle's abrupt style, proceeded cautiously, hesitating to share personal information too quickly. Later, when completing her file notes on the interview, Estelle wrote: "Client was defensive and guarded. He appeared unusually resistant to exploring his feelings."

CONVERSATION 1.3

SHOULD I READ THE FILE?

STUDENT: If there's already a file on the client, should I read it before seeing the client for the first time?

TEACHER: There are pros and cons to prereading client files. It's important to be aware of the risks of either route. Some counsellors prefer to conduct their first interviews without reading their clients' files. They argue that by not reading the files, they are prevented from being unduly influenced (biased) by prior information. After a first interview, they feel more able to objectively evaluate the validity of previous records. In addition, they argue that clients can change, and approaching the interview with a fresh perspective makes it easier to relate to the client's present condition.

STUDENT: But suppose the client has a history of violence that is reported in the file. How would I be able to get that information in order to protect myself, but still keep an open mind? Is there a way of getting only the pertinent information from the file that would allow me to identify those problems?

TEACHER: That's one of the drawbacks of not reading the file. I like your idea of setting up some kind of process for identifying clients who might be dangerous. Clients who present safety concerns could be "red-flagged" in some way.

STUDENT: I think another drawback is that if you don't look at the file, you will miss out on knowing what's been done, what worked, what issues are key, and so forth. Is there a way of reading a file without being influenced by other writers?

TEACHER: Being aware of the potential for influence is crucial. It is important to remind ourselves that opinions in files are not those of the clients, but of the person writing the record. Ideally, records should be shared with clients and the conclusions jointly supported. Of course, this is not always possible.

STUDENT: Could I share the file with the client to get his or her reactions?

TEACHER: Probably not, at least not without the permission of the person who wrote the record. Depending on where you live, freedom of access to information legislation may give clients the right to petition for access to the file. Usually, the onus is on the agency or government department to provide a reason for withholding information. Counsellors need to be familiar with the regulations in their area.

The Beginning Phase

Successful preliminary phase work establishes a base for the first major task of the beginning phase—namely, developing a safe and trusting helping relationship for clients to work toward their goals. This relationship between counsellors and their clients influences whether clients will be willing to risk disclosure and is a significant variable that determines whether clients will continue with counselling. The counselling relationship is time-limited and based on a contract that outlines the objectives and terms of the relationship.

Some clients come willingly to counselling, perhaps as a result of an unresolved crisis or because they have been persuaded by others to seek help. Other clients are involuntary and in some cases overtly antagonistic to the counsellor. They may also be coming as a result of a current crisis or pressure from others. An employer, for example, may insist that a staff member seek counselling to address attitudinal or addiction problems.

Many clients are also under considerable stress, and this stress is intensified if the clients perceive counsellors negatively. Predictably, clients' past experiences with other agencies and counsellors shape their perceptions and expectations. Clients who have had bad experiences with counsellors will understandably be guarded against further disappointment. In addition, because counsellors are often in a position of authority, or clients see them in such a position, clients' past experiences with others in authority will come into play. Most clients, however strongly they may be motivated, will have some degree of resistance or ambivalence to change. Involuntary clients, in particular, may be especially resistant and in some cases hostile. They may perceive any initiative by their counsellors as a hostile act, however well meaning it was.

The counselling relationship is fundamental to counselling success. Even in short, one-session encounters, when a high level of intimacy is not crucial, clients will be more apt to engage and share when the counsellor gives some attention to developing the relationship. Chapter 3 more fully explores the importance of the helping relationship and specific skills for developing and maintaining it.

A second major task of the beginning phase is to acquire and deepen understanding of the client's situation or problem. In the beginning phases, clients are asked to tell their stories, describe their feelings, and explore their problems and dilemmas. For their part, counsellors must be prepared to listen, and this means being prepared to learn. Preliminary phase work may help counsellors predict possible themes, and experience may teach counsellors a great deal about common needs and issues. However, in the beginning phase, counsellors need to put aside all assumptions as they attempt to appreciate the unique nature of each client. The active listening skills of attending, using silence, summarizing, paraphrasing, questioning, and showing empathy are the basic tools for this exploration. These skills tend to motivate clients to gradually open up, organize their thoughts, and identify their feelings. They move the relationship beyond superficiality and help both the counsellor and the client achieve shared understanding. Active listening also enables counsellors to probe for details, definitions, and examples—information that is essential for preventing assumptions.

The Therapeutic Value of the Beginning Phase

The therapeutic value of counsellors listening without judgment can be enormous. Active listening enables what is often the most important part of any counselling encounter—the opportunity to tell one's story and express feelings without interference. Since intense listening is rare in everyday encounters, clients may be visibly moved when they feel heard. Moreover, when counsellors accept clients without judgment, clients become better able to accept themselves. Effective counsellors also encourage clients to explore the emotional components of their lives. When clients share emotions, counsellors need to be careful not to sabotage this sharing by rescuing, telling clients not to feel as they do, changing the subject, or conveying discomfort or judgment. In addition, as clients talk, they may release a flood of emotions. A client might remark, "I've told you things that no one else knows." As clients open up, they may begin to feel unburdened, a process that is known as **catharsis**, which Barker defines as a "verbalization and other expression of ideas, fears, past significant events, and associations, the expected result of which is a release of anxiety or tension, resulting in improved functioning; also called **ventilation**" (1995:49).

Effective counsellors probe for detail by asking questions systematically. They identify feelings and mirror them with empathic statements. This work enables clients to better organize their thinking and to explore and accept their feelings. When clients are confused or indecisive, orderly questioning helps them to categorize information and to pinpoint details or issues that they may have overlooked.

Cautions

For some clients, a single session may be sufficient to meet their needs, and they may not return for the next scheduled interview. Sometimes they decide not to return because they feel they don't need to. The cathartic release of emotions in a single session empowers them enough to deal with their problems.

Other clients may quickly respond to the power of the counselling relationship and disclose at a level they would not have predicted. Later, they may feel embarrassed, fearing that they have gone too far, or they may resent their counsellors for probing into areas they would have preferred to keep private. In response, clients may cut off the counselling relationship prematurely, or they may come to the next session but remain distant and guarded in order to protect themselves from overdisclosing.

One way to prevent problems is to be sensitive to individual pacing needs. Clients may give clues that the session is moving too quickly. The counsellor should watch for indicators such as hesitation, questions asking why the counsellor wants to know something, or statements that the client would rather not discuss particular issues.

Another strategy is to candidly discuss with clients how they feel about the session. The following excerpt illustrates this technique:

Counsellor: *Later tonight, when you think about our time together, how do you think you will feel?*

Client: *I think I'll have mixed feelings. It was really good to talk, but I wonder if I told you too much. I hope you won't think less of me.*

Counsellor: *You took a real risk with me in sharing your private thoughts and feelings. I think it's reasonable to worry about how I reacted. Would you like to know?*

Client: *Yes, very much.*

Counsellor: *Do you trust me enough to believe that I won't lie to you or tell you something just to make you feel better?*

If the client says *yes*, the counsellor might candidly share his or her reaction to the client disclosure:

I admire your courage to face such painful issues. As a result, I feel closer to you and better able to understand your struggle. No, I don't think less of you.

If the client says *no*, the counsellor initiates discussion of what work needs to be done to establish trust:

Perhaps we could talk a bit about what needs to happen between you and me in order for you to trust me.

In the above example, the counsellor helps the client anticipate feelings that might arise after the session. By doing so, the counsellor can help prevent the client from reaching false conclusions or making erroneous assumptions about what happened. In order for counsellors to have such discussions with clients, a high level of counsellor self-awareness is crucial. Counsellors need to be willing to examine how they are relating to their clients. They should be adept at identifying any personal biases (positive and negative) that they need to manage in order to work effectively with their client.

The Action Phase

In the beginning phase, counsellors work to understand their clients' perspectives, and clients organize their thinking and express their feelings. The action phase focuses on solving problems, managing feelings, setting goals, and exploring alternative strategies.

In practice, action-phase work may happen simultaneously with beginning-phase work, as clients may make discoveries or achieve insight from exploring issues, feelings, and problems. Skilled interviewers ask questions systematically, probing for detail as appropriate. This process alone helps clients organize their thoughts on complex issues. As well, summary, paraphrase, and empathy responses provide an important mirror for reflecting clients' feelings and ideas. As a result, clients may see their problems in a different light, or they may discover choices for action that they had overlooked.

In the action phase, counsellors play a key role by providing new information, ideas, or perspectives. This involves challenging distortions of problems and encouraging clients to consider issues they have overlooked. As well, counsellors need to encourage the work of change by ensuring that clients set clear and specific goals, which form the basis for the development of realistic action plans. Subsequently, counsellors may assist clients in implementing their plans. This assistance includes helping them to anticipate and address potential problems, as well as supporting them through the struggles of the change process. Counsellors also help clients develop new strategies for coping through skill acquisition strategies such as role playing or techniques for managing self-defeating thought patterns.

When clients experience the **core conditions** of congruence, empathy, and positive regard, they become better able to accept themselves, less defensive, and more open to experiencing and accepting their feelings. Client attitudes and feelings change as counselling progresses successfully. Some of the important signals that clients are changing and growing include the following:

- cues that they feel less apprehensive about counselling and the counselling relationship
- increased acceptance of feelings and more honest expression of previously denied feelings
- diminished negativism, self-doubt, and blaming of others and increased optimism and self-acceptance
- increased acceptance of responsibility for behaviours or choices
- reduced sense of responsibility for the actions and choices of others
- increased empathy for others (Gilliland & James, 1998:115)

As noted earlier, beginning- and action-phase activities can happen simultaneously. Shifts between beginning- and action-phase work are also common. For example, clients may explore a problem in depth, begin a change program, then revert to beginning-phase work to tackle another problem area. Some common scenarios are the following:

> Angelo's counsellor encouraged him to describe his situation. As he talked, he discovered aspects of his problem that he had overlooked and that suggested new possibilities for immediate action.

> Pari tended to keep her feelings so well hidden that she was unaware of their effect or intensity. With gentle encouragement from her counsellor, she began to open up. Talking about her feelings represented a dramatic shift in her behaviour. The therapeutic value of this change was enormous, as she unburdened herself from a lifetime of pent-up emotions.

Chapter 7 will explore how to assist clients through the work of the action phase.

The Ending Phase

Successful termination starts in the beginning phase, when the nature and limits of the counselling contract are defined. When counsellors and clients agree on the activities and goals of counselling, they have defined a point of termination. This point becomes the target of all counselling work; and though it may change as client needs and progress are reevaluated, counsellors should reinforce that termination is a reality of the counselling relationship.

Although evaluation is a component of all phases of counselling, the ending phase is a major opportunity to assess what was accomplished and what remains to be done. It is a time to help clients make the step to independence and to consider new directions and goals. It may also occasionally be a point of transition, such as when a counsellor refers a client to another service. The ending phase is also a time to evaluate the counselling relationship. This evaluation may involve addressing any unresolved concerns and expressing feelings about the ending of the relationship.

Counsellors need to be able to make intelligent decisions about when to terminate the relationship. Termination of counselling relationships may occur or be warranted for a number of reasons:

1. The relationship may be ended when the goals of counselling have been reached. Counselling relationships are time-limited; so when clients have developed a sufficient capacity to work on their own, it is time to end the relationship.
2. Counsellors may end the relationship if they do not have the time or competence to fulfill their clients' needs. In such cases, the ending will include referral to other counsellors or agencies.
3. Counsellors may determine that they are unable to work with sufficient objectivity. Here, again, referral is the preferred alternative.
4. Situational factors, such as illness, moving, or the end of a practicum, may necessitate termination or referral.
5. If evidence shows that counselling has not worked and that there is little potential for success, it is time to terminate or refer.
6. Clients may decide to opt out of future service and fail to show up for scheduled appointments. However, this does not necessarily mean that the work has been unsuccessful because "as many as two-thirds of dropouts report considerable progress" (Fortune, 2002:85).

Counselling relationships can be exceptionally intimate, and the termination of the relationship may evoke painful feelings of loss for both counsellors and clients. This sense of loss may be especially pronounced in long-term relationships. But even short-term relationships that have dealt with crises or intimate matters may arouse feelings of sadness as the relationship ends. Clients who have difficulty with transitions and who have become dependent on their counsellors may experience the ending as a crisis. Thus, counsellors must make sure that client overdependence is reduced to the point that they can function independently.

Young suggests that "a helper's feelings of loss at termination may also be due to a reliance on helping relationships to meet needs for intimacy (friendship) as well as a conscious or unconscious sexual attraction" (1998:286). The termination may also remind counsellors of other losses in their lives. When these losses remain unresolved, there is a risk that counsellors may be unable to appropriately handle termination with the client. They may feel guilty for leaving the client, and they might delay or avoid termination in order to elude their own feelings of pain.

But the ending phase can also be a time of continuing growth for clients; so it is important to involve clients in the process. As Brill and Levine (2005) suggest:

> In termination, as in the other steps of the problem-solving process, the client's participation is of maximum importance. If the helping relationship is at all significant, the way it ends will be important for the client's self-image and capacity for future relationships. The reason for termination should be clear in the minds of both client and worker and, whenever possible, feelings about it expressed and understood (pp. 140–141).

ASSESSING UNSUCCESSFUL COUNSELLING

Inevitably, counselling sometimes fails; so counsellors need to develop their capacity to systematically investigate and review failure. They need to be able to distinguish between failures that are beyond their control and those caused by their own mistakes. Failure may originate with the client; it may arise from personal issues associated with the counsellor, such as faulty technique or lack of skill; or it may come from factors that are outside both the client's and counsellor's control.

Client Variables

Client variables that could lead to failure include unrealistic expectations, poor motivation, unconscious self-sabotage, destructive personality, organic factors, and poor capacity for insight (Kottler, 1993:18). For example, substance abuse or mental disorders may make it difficult or impossible for clients to engage with the work of counselling. Or clients may resist or undermine counselling because of secondary gain, where the payoffs from maintaining the problem outweigh the benefits of change. Or clients may resist change because of an unconscious fear of success, because they expect to fail, or because the risks of change are too frightening to face.

At the same time, Kottler cautions against being too quick to blame failure on clients. "Many of us avoid dealing with our failures by blaming clients for not cooperating. If only they were more motivated and less ambivalent, if only they were willing to work harder and take greater risks, if only they did what we asked of them, if only they would act more like we would prefer, then counseling could work out quite nicely" (1993:17).

Counsellor Variables

Intellectually and emotionally secure counsellors are willing to examine their methods and attitudes, and they are willing to take their share of responsibility for poor counselling outcomes. Counsellor variables include mental attitudes, moods, and behaviours, all of which can dramatically affect how counsellors relate to and assess their clients. Some counsellor variables that affect counselling outcomes are burnout, personal problems, and loss of objectivity.

Burnout

A career working with people in crisis may be intensely satisfying, but it can also be emotionally stressful and draining. Counsellors may experience unrelenting pressure in workplace demands, including high caseloads, limited resources, and crushing paperwork. Counsellors can become depleted from trying to respond to the needs of their clients and the organization. In addition, counsellors are subject to their own family and economic stress and trauma. Counsellors may be resilient, but even the most sturdy person can become debilitated by stress.

Burnout is a state of emotional, mental, and physical exhaustion that hinders or prevents people from performing their jobs. Burnout may affect people in different ways, but certain symptoms are typical. The stress of burnout may show itself as a general state of physical exhaustion, including signs of diminished health, such as headaches, sleep disruptions, and digestive upset. Emotional and mental burnout may reveal itself as increased anxiety, inability to cope with the normal demands of work, depression, excessive worry, discouragement, pessimism toward clients, loss of a sense of purpose, general irritability, and inability to find joy in one's career or life.

Counsellors who suspect that they suffer from burnout should first consult a physician to rule out any medical condition that might be a factor. But the best way to deal with burnout is to prevent it from happening. For counsellors, this means balancing the demands of their work life by taking care of themselves. Counsellors need to develop personal wellness plans that address their own emotional, physical, and spiritual needs. An essential part of this plan is time away from the job. Counsellors need to avoid becoming over-involved by working unreasonably long hours and weekends or by skipping vacations. They need to make intelligent decisions about the limits of what they can do.

Counsellors can also prevent burnout by setting up and using a support system of family, friends, supervisors, and colleagues. By doing so, they ensure that they have people to whom they can turn for assistance and emotional support. Work colleagues and supervisors are essential for helping counsellors manage their emotional reactions to clients, such as fear and anger. Counsellors need to recognize that being able to accept help from others is a sign of strength and that they should model this belief in their own behaviour. Talking to others reduces isolation and allows for team participation and support with difficult decisions or situations. It is particularly important for counsellors to have someone to debrief with after stressful interviews, such as those with angry or assaultive clients.

Continued professional development is another important strategy for preventing burnout. Seminars, courses, and conferences expose counsellors to new ideas and the latest research and can help them renew their enthusiasm and creativity.

Personal Problems

Counsellors are subject to the same stresses in life as other people. They can become depressed, their children can become ill, their marriages can fail, or they can become responsible for caring for ailing and elderly parents. Responsible counsellors accept that there may be times when they need help too. They recognize the importance of having people in their lives to whom they can turn for assistance. When counsellors have healthy reciprocal relationships with others, they are less likely to subconsciously use their clients to meet these needs.

During acute periods of stress, counsellors need to recognize their vulnerability and take steps to protect their clients. These steps might include taking a temporary reduction in workload, shifting to a less demanding caseload, taking a "mental health" break, and seeking increased supervision or consultation to monitor their work. In extreme circumstances, they may choose to take extended leave or switch careers.

Loss of Objectivity

Objectivity is a measure of counsellors' capacity to relate to clients without allowing their own feelings and biases to distort their judgment (see Chapter 2 for a detailed discussion). A number of factors can lead to a loss of objectivity, including unresolved personal problems, difficulty dealing with particular emotions or topics, attraction or revulsion to clients, overidentification with clients, and excessive or unrealistic fear of particular clients.

Counsellors who are not aware of their values and beliefs and the impact of their behaviour on others are limited in their ability to monitor their level of objectivity. But counsellors who seek to increase their objectivity make themselves available for feedback or supervision. Moreover, they recognize their personal limitations and their inability to work objectively with every client. They know when to refer clients to other professionals.

Process or Technique Variables

Process variables that can lead to failure include pseudo-counselling, inappropriate advice giving, rescuing, and miscellaneous problems with technique or procedure.

Pseudo-Counselling

The goal of every counselling relationship is to improve the quality of life for the client. Achieving this goal may involve problem resolution, assistance with decision making, or management of painful feelings. Counsellors need to screen their responses and activities to ensure that their work supports the objectives of counselling.

Pseudo-counselling involves what Shulman (1999) describes as the **illusion of work**—counselling sessions are animated and active, but they are essentially empty and without real meaning. The illusion of work can be created through the following:

- interesting but irrelevant exploration of issues that do not contribute to problem solving, including an excessive focus on finding the root causes of problems
- use of clichés and patronizing platitudes
- overly intellectual exploration of issues
- avoidance of subjects or feelings that involve pain in favour of safe topics. Of course, it is sometimes appropriate to shift the focus to safe areas of discussion (for example, if the interview is almost over, or if clients are clearly unable to handle additional stress).

Inappropriate Advice Giving

Society conditions us to seek advice from experts, so it's not surprising that many clients come to counsellors expecting "expert advice" on how to manage their lives and solve their problems. Students and beginning counsellors often believe that counselling requires them to listen patiently to their clients' problems, then offer advice on what they should do. However, they need to learn that this approach is rarely helpful and is sometimes harmful for clients, particularly when such advice is based on values that are inconsistent with the client's lifestyle or culture.

Clients often seek advice even when they know what to do to manage their problems. Seeking advice can be a way of expressing dependency or transferring responsibility for decisions and outcomes to someone else. This dependency inhibits the right of clients to make choices, and it may leave clients feeling resentful or frustrated, particularly if the advice was unsolicited.

Advice giving may increase counsellors' self-esteem by underscoring their ability to be resourceful and helpful, but it may also undermine clients' self-esteem, leaving them feeling inadequate because they have been unable to figure out their problems for themselves or because they lack the will or resources to act on the "good advice." Counsellors who tend to give advice can become overly concerned about whether clients follow their advice, and if so, whether the advice is successful. They can also become disappointed when clients do not follow advice.

As Compton and Galaway (1999) conclude, "it is not your job to cure clients. Rather you assist them in recognizing and using strengths that they bring, as well as the resources of their environments... We are in a better position to empower and promote client **self-determination** if we refrain from giving advice and if we honour what clients bring to the relationship:

- knowledge regarding his situation
- knowledge as to how the problem emerged
- expectations regarding how you can help
- a network of social relationships
- views as to what she would like to have done
- strengths for use in reaching objectives" (Compton and Galaway, 1999:102-03)

   This injunction against advice giving does not mean that counsellors should withhold information or ideas that might benefit their clients. Here are some examples of information or advice that counsellors might provide:

- tentative suggestions regarding alternative courses of action that the client has over-looked. However, "when counsellors are unwilling or unable to present and explore all viable alternatives neutrally, they have an ethical responsibility to refer the client to another counsellor, or at the very least, to make their biases or limitations explicit" (Shebib, 1997:33).
- expert information based on research or knowledge (e.g., job search techniques, child-rearing principles)
- ideas for improving communication or problem solving
- suggestions regarding the process of problem resolution
- opinions and information that will help clients avoid unforeseen consequences (dangers) to themselves or impulsive or poorly considered action

   Where there is a range of individual choices, such as decisions related to marriage or career, advice giving is inappropriate. In such circumstances, the role of counsellors is to assist clients in identifying alternative courses of action, then to help them weigh the advantages and disadvantages of each alternative. Counsellors may suggest alternatives, but they should do this in such a way that clients feel free to reject their suggestions. As a rule, counsellors should probe for client ideas first with questions such as: What are your thoughts on what to do? What are your choices? What advice could you give yourself? What ideas have you considered but rejected?

Rescuing

Rescuing, or band-aiding, involves actions that prevent or protect clients from dealing with issues or feelings. Rescuing arises from the counsellor's need to avoid tension and keep the session cheerful, but it is misguided because rescuing diverts clients from addressing important though difficult issues in their lives. Rescuing is therefore a misuse of the support function of helping. Counsellors may become so preoccupied with avoiding or reducing tension that they interfere with their clients' ability to cope or solve problems. If problem situations are to be worked through successfully, clients must be allowed to experience and express painful emotions. For their part, counsellors must develop their ability to be present for such work without their own needs and anxiety interfering or becoming a burden to their clients.

There are three major types of rescue behaviour:

1. Responses that minimize tension, such as avoiding tough but otherwise timely and important topics and feelings by changing the subject, using humour to cut off discussion, or suggesting a coffee break.

> Rodney was finally willing to address his sadness over the death of his father. As he began to talk, he cried softly. As he did so, his counsellor reached out and put her hands on his shoulders, reassuring him that his grief would pass.

> Par hesitated for a moment as he struggled to collect his thoughts. Sensing that this might be a painful moment for him, his counsellor suggested that he might prefer to talk about something else.

> Counsellor responses such as these impede the work of counselling by preventing or discouraging clients from dealing with their feelings. For clients to learn to manage emotions, they must be allowed to experience their pain. If counsellors communicate discomfort or disapproval with expressed emotions, important opportunities for work may be lost.

2. Placating by withholding potentially helpful but critical confrontation or by offering false feedback and empty reassurance.

> Tara expressed fear about contacting her father, with whom she had not had contact for five years. Her counsellor offered support: "Everything is going to work out well. I'm sure your father will be ecstatic to see you."

> Shirley decided not to confront her client over an obvious hygiene problem. She concluded that it would be best not to upset her client and jeopardize a strong relationship.

3. Behaviours that impede independence, such as speaking for clients and doing for clients what they are able to do for themselves.

> Jessie's counsellor wanted to be seen as helpful and resourceful. She offered to rewrite her client's résumé and pick up application forms from local employers.

> José was having trouble understanding a school assignment. His childcare counsellor phoned his teacher to ask for clarification, even though José was capable of talking to the teacher himself.

For clients to become independent, they need to develop the skills and strength to deal with their lives. This may be a difficult process for clients, requiring counsellors to be supportive without stifling their clients' growth. Counsellors must avoid unduly protecting their clients by interfering with their opportunities and capacity to face their difficulties. This requires counsellors to be fully aware of their own need for power and control and to accept that successful counselling requires clients to be their own problem solvers. Furthermore, counsellors must rid themselves of any fantasy that only they can save their clients.

CONVERSATION 1.4

RESCUING AND SUPPORTING

STUDENT: What is the difference between supporting clients and rescuing them?

TEACHER: Rescuing robs clients of legitimate opportunities for growth. Supporting promotes self-determination by providing encouragement or resources to motivate clients toward growth and change. Timing is also a factor. Rescuing occurs when clients have the strength to deal with difficult areas or feelings, but their counsellors avoid the work or pain that this would entail. On the other hand, if clients are overwhelmed, some direct assistance by counsellors to lessen their burden is supportive. It may be wise to avoid excessive intimacy in the beginning of a relationship, and it may be hazardous to explore highly emotional topics near the end of an interview. An important question for counsellors to consider is "Whose needs are being met, mine or the client's?" Rescuing behaviour meets counsellors' needs under the guise of helping clients, but supportive behaviour helps clients to realize their objectives. In the long run, there are times when it is more supportive to allow clients to face their struggles and experience their pain. Effective counsellors are courageous enough to allow clients to express their pain and accept the reality that they cannot provide solutions to all problems.

Communication Stoppers

Some responses tend to bring communication to a halt. Rescuing and advice giving are two prime examples, but others that have the same effect include name calling, "playing psychologist" by offering clever, but unsolicited assessments, commanding, moralizing, minimizing the feelings or concerns of others, using platitudes or clichés, and excessive use of interrogating questions, especially *why* questions that tend to ask for justification or communicate subtle judgment.

Faulty Technique

Some of the problems that arise in counselling can be attributed to counsellors' inept use of skills. Poor technique can lead to missed opportunities and, in extreme cases, can be harmful to clients. For example, counsellors might fail to respond to individual differences (e.g., gender and culture), or they may cling to a rigid "one style fits all" approach to counselling. They may also be poor listeners, or they may lack empathy. They might push clients too quickly, or they might allow them to stagnate by neglecting to motivate them to make changes.

Uncontrollable Variables

Large caseloads may preclude counsellors from spending sufficient time with their clients. Resources may not be available to support clients in their change process, such as at a detox facility. In addition, unexpected events and crises, such as illness, death, or job loss, may frustrate progress. In some cases, client changes may be subverted by family and friends who are unprepared to support change.

SUMMARY

Counselling involves a time-limited relationship designed to help clients increase their capacity to deal with the demands of life. Counselling work may include many activities, such as helping clients deal with feelings, learn new skills, make decisions, and access resources.

Counselling is conducted by a wide range of people at various levels of education. Interviewing skills are imperative for effective counselling. Interviewing is essentially an information-gathering process; however, clients may experience some therapeutic relief from sharing their stories.

Counselling caseloads are characterized by diversity in culture, gender, age, religion, sexual orientation, language, education, economic ability, and so on. Working with diversity requires counsellors to be adaptive. Expert counsellors use research theory and experience as guides to determine which skills and procedures best meet the needs of their clients. Competent counsellors use a wide range of skills, know when to use skills, match the language of their clients, and adapt other variables, such as the time and place of the interview.

Four major skill clusters define the range of necessary skills: (1) relationship-building, (2) exploring/probing, (3) empowering, and (4) challenging skills. Counsellors use relationship-building skills to engage clients and develop trust. They use exploring/probing skills to gather information, clarify definitions, seek examples, and obtain necessary detail. They use empowering skills to help clients develop confidence, self-esteem, and control over their lives. Finally, counsellors use challenging skills to help clients manage anxiety and stress and to encourage them to critically evaluate their behaviour and ideas.

The four counselling phases are: (1) preliminary; (2) beginning; (3) action; and (4) ending. Each phase is characterized by unique tasks and skills. The preliminary phase focuses on preparing for the interview and setting up the right environment for counselling. The beginning phase is concerned with establishing the counselling relationship and with exploring for understanding. In the action phase, the focus shifts to goal setting and implementing change. In the ending phase, the relationship is concluded. During different phases of the relationship, different skill clusters assume priority.

Many variables can lead to poor outcomes in counselling. Client variables include unrealistic expectations and poor motivation. Counsellor factors such as burnout, personal problems, and loss of objectivity can also lead to failure. Process or faulty techniques, including pseudo-counselling, advice giving, and rescuing, can contribute to failure. Finally, failure may arise from factors outside the control of counsellors and clients.

EXERCISES

1. Assess the following statements as "true" or "false." Be prepared to defend your answers.

   a. It is important for counsellors to develop a personal style so that they treat all clients the same way.

   b. The counselling process has a lot in common with the process used by other professionals, such as doctors and lawyers; thus, competent counsellors gather information, diagnose the problem, and offer solutions or advice to their clients on the best resolution.

   c. Usually clients who seek help are in crisis, and their ability to make decisions is significantly impaired. Therefore, it is important that counsellors are comfortable with making important decisions on behalf of their clients.

   d. Application of skills or techniques detracts from spontaneity.

   e. Professional counsellors strive to be free of biases.

   f. Counsellors need personal experience with the same problem or issues their clients are experiencing in order to be effective.

   g. The counselling process evolves sequentially through a number of phases, with each phase having specific tasks and requiring specific skills.

    h. Effective counsellors are consistent, and they use the same skills in the same way throughout the counselling process.

    i. If the principles of counselling are applied effectively, all clients will be helped.

    j. Everything that happens in the counselling interview must be treated as confidential and must be shared with no one.

    k. Effective counselling involves blending the client's needs with those of the counsellor so that everyone involved is satisfied.

    l. The skills of counselling are also the skills of effective everyday communication.

2. Write a short essay supporting the following argument: The capacity to accept help from another person is a sign of strength.

3. Imagine that you are responding to the following client questions: What is counselling? How does it work?

4. Describe a situation in which you gave advice to or rescued someone. Do you have a tendency to give advice or rescue others? Seek feedback from others who know you to see if their perceptions agree with your self-evaluation.

5. In what ways might advice giving disempower clients?

6. Think of a recent or current problem that you are facing. Describe the ways that counselling might be used to assist you in addressing this problem. Using concepts from this chapter, identify what might be the major activities for each phase of counselling.

7. Review the tasks of each of the phases of helping. With which phase do you feel most comfortable? Least comfortable?

8. What do you think are the advantages and disadvantages of working from a four-phase model of counselling?

9. Identify and explore clients' legal rights to access file information in your jurisdiction.

10. List the pros and cons of displaying each of the following in your office:

    a. family portrait

    b. motivational posters

    c. degrees and diplomas

    d. bookcase with extensive professional books and journals

WEBLINKS

This site offers links to a wide range of psychology topics:
www.psywww.com/resource/bytopic.htm

A wide variety of counselling issues and links to professional organizations:
www.allaboutcounseling.com/aboutc.cfm

Links for people working in the social service field:
http://gwbweb.wustl.edu/library/websites.html#Counseling

Links to Canadian counselling associations and other counselling resources:
www.ccacc.ca/lto.htm

chapter two

Ethics, Values, and Self-Awareness

PREVIEW

After reading this chapter you should be able to:

- Describe professional ethics, including standards related to dual relationships and confidentiality.
- List and describe the core values of counselling.
- Identify principles for resolving ethical dilemmas.
- Understand the importance of counsellor objectivity and self-awareness.
- Know how to increase self-awareness.
- Understand and manage personal needs and values in counselling.

ETHICS

Ethics are the principles and rules of acceptable or proper conduct. All professions have ethical guidelines that define the limits of permissible behaviour and the sanctions or remedies for member violations of ethical standards. Codes of ethics serve the following broad purposes:

- Professionals can use their codes to assist them with decision making and as reference for their practice.
- Ethical codes help shelter clients from incompetent and unethical practice by members of the profession. Ethical codes recognize that clients may be vulnerable and subject to manipulation and abuse of power by professionals, so they constrain professionals from taking advantage of clients.
- Ethical codes also provide guidance on how counsellors can deal fairly with colleagues and their employers, including the responsibility to address the unethical conduct of colleagues
- Codes outline the philosophical and value principles of the profession. For example, the Canadian Association of Social Workers (CASW) code has six core social work values:

> Value 1: Respect for the Inherent Dignity and Worth of Persons
>
> Value 2: Pursuit of Social Justice
>
> Value 3: Service to Humanity
>
> Value 4: Integrity of Professional Practice
>
> Value 5: Confidentiality in Professional Practice
>
> Value 6: Competence in Professional Practice (CASW, 2005:4)

These ideals are echoed by the Canadian Counselling Association (CCA), which artic-ulates the following fundamental principles as the basis for ethical conduct:

a. respect for the dignity of persons

b. not wilfully harming others

c. integrity in relationships

d. responsible caring

e. responsibility to society

f. respect for self-determination (CCA, 1999:1)

Unethical behaviour typically arises from issues related to the following: breaking confi-dentiality; misrepresenting or working beyond one's level of expertise; conducting improper relationships, including sexual activity with clients; and causing conflicts of interest, such as entering into business or other **dual relationships** with clients.

Professional associations are responsible for monitoring their own policies and for investigating and resolving violations of ethical conduct. The CASW and CCA are exam-ples of professional bodies that can formally discipline members who violate their codes of ethics. As well, counsellors who are not members of professional associations may work with agencies that provide guidelines for ethical behaviour and decision making.

In addition, legislation defines and restricts the use of certain titles, such as social worker, psychologist, and psychiatrist, to those who have the appropriate degree or training.

The clients of these professionals can report misconduct or concerns to the appropriate professional association. However, there may be no legislation preventing people from offering counselling services under a wide range of other titles, such as counsellor, personal therapist, family and marital counsellor, and personal growth consultant. These practitioners may not have had formal preparation or training, and clients should be cautious when they seek their services.

The Canadian Counselling Association Code of Ethics and Standards of Practice (CCA, 1999) is included in this book as Appendix A, and the Canadian Association of Social Workers Code of Ethics (CASW, 1994) is included as Appendix B. Although the codes are the primary source for professional decision-making, counsellors should also consider relevant theory, research, laws, regulations, and agency policy. When faced with **ethical dilemmas**, they should consider consultation with colleagues, supervisors, professional associations and legal counsel. In addition, the CCA has published an ethics casebook (Shulz, 2000) designed to assist counsellors to clarify ethics and standards of practice. As well, the CASW has produced Guidelines for Ethical Practice (2005) as a reference point for social workers on ethical practice.

Dual Relationships

A **dual relationship** is a relationship in which there is both a counselling relationship and another type of relationship, such as business, friendship or sexual intimacy. The essential purpose of counselling is to meet the needs of clients; but dual relationships lead to the risk that counsellors could misuse (or be perceived to be misusing) their professional relationships for personal gain. Dual relationships "are problematic because they reduce the counselor's objectivity, confuse the issue, and often put the client in a position of diminished consent" (Cormier & Cormier, 1985:19). In dual relationships, the counsellor has a personal interest that may conflict with the client's interest. This may lead to intended or unintended exploitation, harm, manipulation, or coercion of clients. To prevent these problems and any conflict of interest, dual relationships should be avoided, particularly when they could potentially harm the client. Counsellors who are emotionally stable will not want or need to involve themselves in dual relationships to meet their own needs.

Not surprisingly, the codes of ethics for the various counselling professions strictly prohibit certain types of dual relationships, especially sexual involvement. Generally, they also prohibit sexual intimacies with former clients for a specified period after terminating the counselling relationship, but this injunction may extend indefinitely "if the client is clearly vulnerable, by reason of emotional or cognitive disorder, to exploitative influence by the counsellor. Counsellors, in all such circumstances, clearly bear the burden to ensure that no such exploitative influence has occurred, and to seek consultative assistance" (CCA, 1999:B12).

Despite these injunctions, abuses do occur. Reviewing the available research, Thoreson et al. (1993) found that the incidence of sexual contact between counsellors and clients ranges from 3.6 to 12.1 percent, with as many as 80 percent of counsellors who had sexual contact with clients engaging in it with more than one client. Conducting their own study, the researchers found after surveying 1000 randomly selected male members of the American Counselling Association (ACA) that 1.7 percent of the respondents reported engaging in sexual contact with a client during a professional relationship, and 7 percent reported engaging in sexual contact after a professional relationship (Thoreson et al., 1993).

While sexual intimacy is clearly unethical, other dual relationships are even more problematic. As Reamer (2002) observes:

> Other dual and multiple relationships are more ambiguous and require careful analysis and consultation. Examples include social workers in rural communities who cannot avoid contact with clients in social settings, social workers who are invited by clients to attend an important life event, social workers' relationships with former clients, and social workers' unanticipated encounters with clients at an Alcoholics Anonymous meeting when both parties are in recovery. (p. 66)

The CASW Guidelines for Ethical Practice (2005) offers this guidance on the issue of physical contact with clients:

> Social workers avoid engaging in physical contact with clients when there is a possibility of harm to the client as a result of the contact. Social workers who engage in appropriate physical contact with clients are responsible for setting clear, appropriate and culturally sensitive boundaries to govern such contact. (p. 12)

Reamer (1998) suggests that "comforting a distraught child who has been removed from his home because of parental neglect or holding the hand of a nursing home resident whose spouse has died" (p. 18) may be permissible.

Confidentiality

The rules regarding confidentiality are integral to every code of ethics. Ethical guidelines stress that the confidentiality of clients must be protected. Indeed, most clients enter counselling with an expectation that what they say will be kept private. For the most part, counsellors can assure clients that they will keep their disclosures confidential. However, often it is not so simple. **Absolute confidentiality** means that client disclosures are not shared with anyone. **Relative confidentiality** means that information is shared within the agency with supervisors or colleagues, outside the agency with the client's permission, or in courts of law owing to legal requirements, such as child abuse legislation. Usually, clients can be assured only of relative confidentiality.

In order to provide optimum service to clients, counsellors must share information about them within the agency. To monitor the quality of work and help counsellors improve their skills, supervisors need to review client files or consult with counsellors by reviewing audio and video recordings of their interviews. Other counsellors within the agency also have access to files.

Many people believe that counsellors and other professionals enjoy "privileged communication," i.e., that they are legally protected from having to share information that they have obtained while exercising their professional duties. However, the courts can subpoena counsellors' records, because Canada has no legislative protection for licensed or unlicensed psychotherapists.

There are valid reasons, including some legal requirements, for sharing information. For example, all jurisdictions in Canada have legislation that requires counsellors to report suspicions of child abuse and neglect to the appropriate authorities. Similarly, counsellors might have to break confidentiality when they believe that clients might harm themselves or others. Counsellors need to become familiar with the precise wording of relevant statutes in their area, since laws may vary significantly between jurisdictions.

One often-quoted legal precedent is the *Tarasoff* case, in which the client had told his counsellor of his intent to kill his girlfriend. The counsellor told the campus police of the threat, but he did not warn his client's girlfriend or her family. The client, a student at the school, subsequently carried out his threat and killed the young woman. The young woman's parents brought a successful lawsuit against the counsellor and the university. This litigation established that when counsellors believe that a client represents "a serious danger of violence to another" they have a **duty to warn** potential victims (*Tarasoff v. Regents of the University of California* [1976], cited in Woodside & McClam, 1990:267). Since the *Tarasoff* decision, there have been numerous applications to the Canadian context and legal precedents that address the duty-to-warn issue. The CASW Guidelines for Professional Practice (2005) allows for disclosure when "necessary to prevent serious, foreseeable, and imminent harm to a client or others" (p. 6). The CASW Guidelines also obligate social workers in such circumstance to notify "both the person who may be at risk (if possible) as well as the police" (p. 8). The CCA Code (1999) has a similar duty-to-warn obligation that requires counsellors to "use reasonable care to give threatened persons such warnings as are essential to avert foreseeable dangers" (p. 5).

Zastrow (1990) suggests that breaking confidentiality may be warranted or required in a range of circumstances, such as when a counsellor is summoned by the court in criminal, civil, or child welfare matters, when there are threats of suicide or violence towards others, or when a client's emotional or physical condition poses a danger to others (e.g., a pilot with a serious drinking problem).

Clients have a right to be fully informed regarding the limits of confidentiality, including any legal and ethical responsibilities that require counsellors to share information. Through discussions regarding confidentiality, counsellors can reassure clients that computer and file records are not shared indiscriminately.

Counsellors can take a number of steps to protect client confidentiality. They should discipline themselves not to discuss clients in public places and at parties or other social events. Counselling work is demanding, and an important part of dealing with the stress of the job is to unwind by talking about difficult cases and personal reactions with colleagues and supervisors. This is a healthy and necessary component of professional wellness. Unfortunately, time pressures and large caseloads may leave little or no time for this process during the working day, so it is easy to fall into the trap of discussing clients over lunch or in other settings where confidentiality cannot be ensured. The obvious risk is that the conversation will be overheard. Even when names are not used, accidental listeners may think that they know the person being discussed. In addition, they may decide that they would never go for counselling because what they say will soon be all over town.

Although it is tempting for counsellors to discuss clients with family and friends because they are available as supportive listeners, they should avoid doing so. Family and friends are not bound by the same ethics as counselling professionals and could accidentally disclose what they have heard, perhaps with a seemingly innocent observation or comment.

Sometimes counsellors breach confidentiality by failing to take simple precautions. For example, taking phone calls during a counselling session can lead to careless breaches of confidentiality and suggests to clients that the counsellor treats their private matters casually. In addition, counsellors should remove all case records, phone messages, and notes from their desk. This prevents clients from seeing the names of other clients and reinforces the fact that the counsellor will not leave private records in public places.

TABLE 2.1	Confidentiality Guidelines

- Review professional guidelines such as the CASW Code of Ethics and CCA Code of Ethics.
- Involve clients. Keep them informed and seek their permission to release information. Remember that freedom of information statutes may give clients the right to access your files.
- Become familiar with relevant legal statutes (e.g., child abuse or mental health legislation) that define and limit confidentiality. Disclose only that information that is required.
- Protect client records with secure filing systems. Do not leave files, notes, or phone messages about clients where they may be read by others. Insure that electronically stored data is protected.
- Ensure that consultations concerning clients with others are legitimate and conducted in a private and professional manner. This precludes conversations about clients at social gatherings or in a public place such as a restaurant.
- Ensure that interviews are private and free from interruptions.
- Discuss clients only with supervisors and use only support staff for processing necessary paperwork and documentation.

When counsellors leave phone messages for clients, they should leave only their first name and say nothing about their title or the nature of their call. Clients may not have informed roommates or family members that they are seeing a counsellor.

The interview itself should be conducted in private, not in the waiting room or where other staff or clients may overhear. When greeting a client in the waiting room, counsellors should refrain from using surnames. However, they need to be sensitive to the fact that many seniors and people from some cultures are insulted by the casual use of their first names.

Sometimes counsellors meet clients by chance in public places. When this happens, counsellors should ensure that they maintain confidentiality, even when the client appears unconcerned. They should gently shift the conversation to a neutral topic or suggest a private time and place to continue the discussion. At that time, counsellors can explain why they avoided public discussion.

VALUES FOR PROFESSIONAL PRACTICE

Values are principles or qualities that individuals and groups consider important or worthwhile. Ethics are derived from values. Values represent beliefs about what is desirable and good. Personal values describe what individuals consider desirable and what they believe is right and wrong. Professional values describe fundamental beliefs that the profession holds about people and ways the work of the profession ought to be conducted. Clearly, professional values (as reflected in ethical codes of conduct) and personal values have a major impact in shaping the practice of counselling professionals. Two key values of counselling are the belief in the dignity and worth of people and the client's right to self-determination.

The Belief in the Dignity and Worth of People

Belief in the dignity and worth of people is the core value of counselling. This value commits counsellors to ensuring that their clients are treated with regard for their rights. It obligates counsellors to demonstrate acceptance of the individual and to uphold confidentiality. Counsellors who value the dignity of their clients appreciate diversity and reject stereotyping, labelling, and other dehumanizing practices.

Counsellors must treat clients fairly, regardless of their personal feelings toward them. For example, they must resist the natural temptation to spend more time with clients they favour and less time with those whom they find difficult. Counsellors are expected to apply their skills and knowledge at an optimum level for each client, regardless of their personal reaction toward any client. Clients may have behaved in ways that counsellors perceive to be offensive, but this belief does not give counsellors licence to be disrespectful or to withhold service. Discriminatory practices are strictly prohibited by both major codes:

- Counsellors actively work to understand the diverse cultural background of the clients with whom they work, and do not condone or engage in discrimination based on age, colour, culture, ethnicity, disability, gender, religion, sexual orientation, marital, or socioeconomic status. (CCA, 1999:B9)
- Social workers recognize and respect the diversity of Canadian society, taking into account the breadth of differences that exist among individuals, families, groups and communities. (CASW, 2005:4)

These ethical guidelines underscore the need for professionals to actively engage in learning about other cultures in order to increase their sensitivity and their awareness of how their values and beliefs have affected their behaviour worldview and their way of relating to others. This topic will be explored in more depth in Chapter 10.

Counsellors, especially those who work with high-risk clients, such as those with chronic addiction problems, need to be careful that their view of and attitudes toward clients do not become jaded. Jaded counsellors often have a cynical and pessimistic perspective on the willingness and capacity of their clients to change and grow. Counsellors who believe that clients are incapable of growth are likely to invest less energy in supporting change. Moreover, they may be more prone to use controlling responses because of their expectation that the "clients cannot do it on their own." What would you predict to be the likely outcome of a counselling session when the counsellor labels the client "a hopeless alcoholic"? Conversely, belief in the dignity and worth of people is expressed through positive practices:

- involving clients in decision making, goal setting, and problem solving
- adopting a strengths approach
- maintaining an optimistic view of human nature, including the belief that people are capable of change and growth

Client Self-Determination

Self-determination is the principle that clients have a right to autonomy and freedom of choice to make their own decisions, insofar as possible. Counsellors have a duty to respect and promote this right even when they disagree with the decisions of their clients. Moreover, choice is an integral part of client self-determination. When clients have no choices or believe that they have none, self-determination is not possible. But adherence to the principle does not prevent counsellors from helping clients understand how their actions might violate the rights of others, nor does it prevent counsellors from helping clients appreciate the potential consequences of their actions. Some clients, such as people with mental disabilities and young children, may be unable to make competent choices. If so, counsellors may need to prevent them from acting in ways that are potentially harmful to themselves or others. But as Cottone and Tarvydas (1998) warn, expert knowledge does not give counsellors the moral authority to act on behalf of their clients with the assumption that only they know what is best for them.

The principle of self-determination also obligates counsellors to avoid behaviours that control and manipulate clients. Instead, they must employ strategies that empower clients to make independent and informed decisions. The counsellor's expertise lies not in knowing what is best for the client, but in being able to manage the process through which problems are solved, feelings managed, or decisions made. Empowerment is the process of assisting clients to discover personal strengths and capacities. In other words, through empowerment, counsellors seek to help clients take control of their lives and realize that they can improve their situation through their actions.

Sometimes, beginning counsellors are misinformed about the nature of counselling. They believe that their role is to listen to their clients' problems, then offer helpful advice or solutions. This gives rise to what Dumont describes as the *rescue fantasy*, a belief that the counsellor's role is to save people and put happiness back into their lives. He concludes that when this notion is communicated to clients, "they have no choice other than to rebel and leave or become even more helpless, dependent and sick" (1968:6).

Effective counsellors accept that clients have a right to be involved in counselling decision-making. They have the right to be treated as active partners in the counselling process and to participate in decisions affecting their lives. This right is underscored in the CCA code of ethics:

> **Clients' Rights and Informed Consent.** When counselling is initiated and throughout the counselling process, as necessary, counsellors inform clients of the purposes, goals, techniques, procedures, limitations, potential risks and benefits of services, and other pertinent information. Counsellors make sure that clients understand the implications of diagnosis, fees and fee collection arrangements, record keeping, and limits to confidentiality. Clients have the right to participate in the ongoing counselling plans, to refuse any recommended services, and to be advised of the consequences of such refusal. (1999:B4)

CONVERSATION 2.1

BLACK HUMOUR

STUDENT: I've just started my field placement, and I'm disturbed by what's happening. When the staff go for coffee, everyone jokes and makes fun of the clients. If they knew the way their counsellors talked about them, they would never come back. I didn't know that professionals could be so cold-hearted. Isn't their behaviour unethical?

TEACHER: Many professionals deal with the enormous stress of their jobs through "black humour" (also known as "gallows humour") by making jokes about tragic events or client

TABLE 2.2	Strategy Choices for Promoting Client Self-Determination

- Use advocacy skills to help clients access resources or to remove barriers to existing options.
- Avoid prescriptive advice and other controlling responses.
- Help clients identify, access, and explore options.
- Encourage clients to make their own decisions based on informed choice of the costs and benefits of any course of action.
- Assist clients to evaluate the consequences of their actions on others.
- Encourage clients to ask questions about counselling techniques and strategies, and provide access to information and records.
- Invite clients to evaluate the progress of counselling and the counselling relationship.
- When under court order or similar nonvoluntary conditions, provide information on the client's right to decline service, as well as the possible consequences of such denial. Whenever possible empower clients with choices.
- Adopt a mind-set that recognizes the client as the "expert" on his or her own problems, feelings, and preferred solutions.
- Avoid dependency-promoting behaviours, such as doing for clients what they can do for themselves, excessive involvement, and indiscriminate advice giving.
- Encourage optimism and foster a relationship climate of safety to help clients take risks.
- Honour client lifestyle choices.

misfortunes. It's one way that counsellors sustain their emotional well-being. It doesn't mean that they've become hardened or uncaring toward their clients; rather, it's a way of unwinding and relieving constant pressure. But as you've discovered, one of the dangers of black humour is that others will overhear it and draw conclusions about the person's attitudes. Is it unethical? What do you think?

ETHICAL DILEMMAS

An ethical dilemma exists when a choice must be made between competing values and potential courses of action. By virtue of their role, counsellors may have simultaneous obligations to different people and groups, including the agency that employs them, their clients, the community at large, and the legal system. When obligations conflict, an ethical dilemma is created, because there are costs and benefits to each potential solution. Ethics have their origin in the values of the profession; but "because people interpret abstract imperatives differently, they often disagree about what constitutes ethical behavior or 'appropriate actions'" (DuBois & Miley, 1996:123).

While ethical codes attempt to define acceptable behaviour, they usually do not offer answers about specific situations that arise for counselling professionals. But even though that they do not provide precise guidelines for resolving all dilemmas, codes are an important reference aid for decision making.

Types of Ethical Dilemmas

1. **Distribution of scarce resources (time, money, opportunity to participate in a program).**
   - An agency has limited funds available to assist clients with retraining. Who should get the money? The client with the greatest potential for success or the client who needs it most?

2. **Professional competence and ethical behaviour of colleagues.**
   - A student on internship (field placement) becomes aware that her supervisor is attending an AA meeting with one of her clients.
   - One of the staff informs you of his intention to phone in sick in order to extend his vacation a few more days.

3. **Policies and procedures of the agency setting that appear oppressive or insensitive to the cultural/diversity needs of the clients it serves**
   - A worker has information about a client that, if made known to the agency, would make her ineligible for service that she badly needs.
   - You become aware that your client, a single mother on welfare struggling to care for her four children on a meagre welfare budget, received a cheque from her mother to help with expenses. Legally, she is obliged to declare this income which will be fully deducted from her next welfare payment, thus depriving her and her children of much needed assistance.

4. **Behaviour of clients.**
   - A 17-year-old girl asks for your help to obtain an abortion without involving her parents.
   - Your client informs you that he has tested positive for HIV, but he hasn't informed his partner.
   - A 16-year-old boy tells you that he is working as a prostitute.
   - Your client casually mentions that he robbed a bank several months ago but was not caught.

5. **Competing values, needs, procedures or legal requirements.**
   - A 15-year-old girl discloses that her father has been abusive, but in recent weeks he seems to have changed. She asks that you do not make a report to the authorities. She says she knows her father will retaliate if he finds out that she told anyone.
   - A young 16-year-old Jehovah's Witness asserts her belief that she should not be given a blood transfusion to deal with a terminal illness.
   - An abused child says he will not cooperate with removal from his parents and says that he will run away from any foster home.

Cottone and Tarvydas (1998:135) identify five ethical rules or principles that can be used to help resolve ethical dilemmas: autonomy, beneficence, nonmaleficence, justice, and fidelity.

1. *Autonomy:* Honour clients' self-determination and their freedom to make their own decisions.

2. *Beneficence:* Pursue the welfare and benefit of others.

3. *Nonmaleficence:* In simple terms: Do no harm to others.
4. *Justice:* Be fair with equal distribution of resources, equitable effort among participants.
5. *Fidelity:* Be loyal, honest, and keep promises.

Under ideal conditions, counsellors can honour all five principles; but ethical dilemmas by nature represent competing principles, and each choice involves unique consequences. Ethical decision-making involves identifying and weighing which of the five principles ought to take priority in any given situation.

But application of any model for ethical decision-making does not mean that resolution of ethical dilemmas will be easy. When values and ethics compete, the decision as to which one should have priority can be painfully difficult. Hepworth, Rooney and Larsen (1997) propose the following four principles as guidelines:

1. The right to life, health, well-being, and necessities of life take precedence over rights to confidentiality and opportunities for additive 'goods' such as wealth, education, and recreation.

2. An individual's basic right to well-being takes precedence over another person's right to privacy, freedom, or self-determination.

3. People's right to self-determination takes precedence over their rights to basic well-being.

4. Person's rights to well-being may override laws, policies, and arrangements of organizations. (pp. 85–86).

Intimate knowledge of ethical principles and legal guidelines can make the decision-making process clearer, albeit no less difficult. For example, a client's right to confidentiality and self-determination must be given up when that client discloses child abuse; and the "duty to warn" principle means that professionals must break confidentiality to warn potential victims. However, it is not always clear the extent that a client's behaviour constitutes danger to the safety of others. Another example: Hepworth, Rooney and Larsen (1997) assert that people have a right "to carry out actions that appear contrary to their best interests, providing they are competent to make an informed and relevant decision" (p. 85). This would protect the rights of people to make errors and carry out actions that others might consider wrong. However, counsellors must consider when application of this principle must be abandoned because the individual's behaviour might result in death, such as in a case where clients threaten suicide. But while counsellors have a clear, legal and ethical responsibility to intervene to prevent suicide, their responsibilities are not as clear for other challenges. For example, homeless persons' lifestyles may reach the point where their hygiene, living, and eating habits become dangerous for them. The point at which their right to self-determination should yield to their right to health and well-being is not easy to establish.

A Model for Resolving Ethical Dilemmas

Step 1: Gather Facts

During this stage, it is important to control any tendency to act impulsively. Remember that assumptions and hearsay are not the same as fact. Most ethical codes require that professionals seek resolution with colleagues before proceeding. For example, the CCA code advises counsellors "to seek an informal resolution with the counsellor, when feasible and appropriate" (1999, A7). In many cases, frank discussion with colleagues reveals additional information or results in a satisfactory solution.

Step 2: Identify Ethical Issues and Violations

At this point, refer to the appropriate code of ethics (CASW, CCA, etc.) to identify whether the matter under question is addressed in the code. If the person in question is not governed by a professional code, then agency policies and procedures or local legislation may provide important reference points. For example, matters of discrimination in Canada are addressed under the Canadian Human Rights Act.

Step 3: Identify Possible Strategies

Here, the goal is to list the potential action strategies. Where appropriate, consultation with colleagues, professional organizations and supervisors can assist in generating alternatives.

Step 4: Ask Reflective Questions

Reflective questions help you consider the merits and ramifications of any action plan. Here are some sample questions:

- What are the advantages and disadvantages of not taking action?
- What are the advantages and disadvantages of taking action?
- What are the potential consequences (short-term and long-term) of action or inaction?
- Who might gain or lose?
- To what extent might other factors be influencing my judgment (e.g., unresolved relationship problems, bias, hidden agendas)?
- What values and principles have priority (e.g., right to confidentiality, duty to warn, self-determination, greater good vs. individual rights, etc.)?

A matrix chart, such as that illustrated by Table 2.3, can be used to compare benefits and risks.

Step 5: Take Action

While considering the risks and benefits of a chosen course of action, counsellors should carry out action plans in a way that minimizes risks and manages adverse outcomes.

TABLE 2.3	Decision-Making Chart		
Action Choices	**Benefits**	**Risks**	**Potential Outcomes**
Choice 1			
Choice 2			
Choice 3			

Objectivity

Effective counsellors may become intimately familiar with the lives of their clients; yet they are required to remain objective. **Objectivity** is defined as the capacity to understand situations and people without bias or distortion. When counsellors are objective, they understand their clients' feelings, thoughts, and behaviours without allowing their personal values, beliefs, and biases to contaminate that understanding. They also do not directly or subtly try to impose their preferred solutions on clients.

Counsellors can fail to be objective in a number of ways. The first is to make assumptions. Assumptions are distortions or false conclusions based on simplistic reasoning, incomplete information, or bias. Counsellors who have had similar experiences to their clients' may assume that their clients' problems and feelings are the same. Consequently, they do not take the time to investigate the distinctive viewpoints of their clients. Counsellors also may make assumptions about the meaning of words. But this danger can be avoided if counsellors remain alert to the need to probe for individual client definition and meaning, as in the following example:

Client (speaking to a First Nations counsellor): *I moved here about five years ago. I guess you know how tough it is for an Indian in this city.*

Counsellor (Choice 1): *I sure do. Prejudice is everywhere.*

Counsellor (Choice 2): *Like you say, it's not easy. But it's different for everyone. I need your help to understand better what it's been like for you.*

In this example, Choice 1 cuts off discussion, and the counsellor loses a valuable opportunity to appreciate his client's experience. Choice 2, on the other hand, offers gentle empathy, then probes for more detail. This second response reduces the risk that the counsellor will make errors of assumption.

A second way that counsellors can lose objectivity is by overidentifying with clients. When overidentification occurs, counsellors lose their capacity to keep sufficient emotional distance from their clients. Their own feelings and reactions become mixed up with those of their clients, clouding their judgment. Counsellors who find themselves in this position may find that personal counselling or consultation with a supervisor is sufficient to help them regain objectivity; or they may conclude that referral to another counsellor is necessary.

A third way that counsellors can lose objectivity is by becoming overly involved with clients. This overinvolvement includes dual relationships prohibited by ethical codes, as well as relationships in which counsellors rely on clients to meet their social and psychological needs. To prevent this from happening, counsellors need to make sure that they are meeting their personal needs in other ways. As well, counsellors should be alert to signs that they may be overinvolved with particular clients.

Table 2.4 summarizes protective strategies counsellors can use to avoid loss of objectivity.

CONVERSATION 2.2

PERSONAL INVOLVEMENT WITH CLIENTS

STUDENT: Is it ever okay to be sexually intimate with clients?

TEACHER: No! Universally, ethical codes of behaviour prohibit sexual intimacies with clients. For example, the CASW Guidelines for Ethical Practice (2005) succinctly states that "social

TABLE 2.4	Maintaining Objectivity
Loss of Objectivity	**Protective Strategies for Counsellors**
Making assumptions	Attempt to understand your prejudices and preferences.
	Listen to but don't be controlled by the opinions of others.
	Develop self-awareness regarding personal needs and values.
	Be inquisitive. Explore each client's situation to discover his or her unique perspective.
	Brainstorm other points of view or seek other opinions.
	Check your conclusions with clients to see if they match theirs—seek definition, detail, and example.
	Monitor cultural, gender and other biases.
Overidentification	Monitor reactions and discover areas of vulnerability; be alert to strong negative or positive reactions to clients.
	Refer clients when you cannot be impartial.
	Know why you want to be a counsellor—understand your needs.
	Use colleagues to critique your reactions and give you feedback.
	Use tools such as video recordings to review interviews for inappropriate attempts to influence or control.
Overinvolvement	Avoid promoting client dependency.
	Develop a wellness program to ensure that you are not relying on your clients to meet your needs for social and psychological involvement and acceptance.
	Recognize warning signs of overinvolvement (e.g., interviews that consistently run overtime, relief when a client does not show up for an interview, excessive worry about clients, reluctance to end a counselling relationship that has reached a point of termination).

workers do not engage in romantic relationships, sexual activities or sexual contact with clients, even if such contact is sought by clients" (p.12). A similar injunction is explicitly stated in the CCA code: "Counsellors avoid any type of sexual intimacies with clients, and they do not counsel persons with whom they have had a sexual relationship" (1999:7).

STUDENT: That seems straightforward. What about becoming involved with former clients?

TEACHER: That's a more difficult question. My opinion is that you never should, but you should consult individual codes of ethics for specific guidelines. For example, the CCA code requires a minimum of three years between the end of the counselling relationship and the beginning of a sexual relationship. The period is extended indefinitely if the client is clearly vulnerable. In any case, counsellors "clearly bear the burden to ensure that no such exploitative influence has occurred" (1999:B.12). A recent review of the literature concludes that harm to clients does occur when professionals have sexual contact with clients. including "denial, guilt, shame, isolation, anger, depression, impaired ability to trust, loss of self-esteem, difficulty expressing anger, emotional liability, psychosomatic disorders, sexual confusion, and increased risk of suicide" (Beckman, Turner, Cooper, Polnerow & Swartz, 2000:2).

STUDENT: What about other types of involvement? If you are a counsellor in a small town, it's impossible to avoid social contact with clients. Your client might be the owner of the only grocery store in town.

TEACHER: Codes of ethics for the various counselling professions (e.g., psychology or social work) frown upon dual relationships when there is a possibility of counsellors losing objectivity or where there is potential for client exploitation. In large cities, it's usually easy to refer clients in order to avoid the conflict of interest of dual relationships. As you point out, it's much more difficult in a small town, and some dual relationship arrangements may be inevitable. But relationships should never include sexual intimacy with current clients.

WORKING WITH COMPETENCE

High self-awareness enables counsellors to make important decisions regarding areas in which they are competent and those in which referral to other professionals is warranted. Counsellors must practise only within the range of their competence, and they should not misrepresent their training or experience. This helps to ensure that they do no harm to clients. As Mehr succinctly put it, "Do your best, do what you know how to do, do not get in—or stay in—over your head, and do not take advantage of a client for your own needs" (1998:190). The CASW and CCA codes provide references on practising within the boundaries of competence. The following list provides general guidelines for working with competence:

1. **Work within the limits of competence.** Counsellors should offer counselling services that are within the limits of their professional competence as measured by education and professional standards. Competent counsellors use only those techniques and strategies that they have been adequately trained to apply. They know that the support and assistance of other professionals is necessary for issues that exceed their expertise. Until counsellors have received the necessary training and supervised practice, they should not work in specialized areas of practice, such as interviewing children in abuse situations or administering or interpreting psychological tests. Untrained counsellors should not attempt to make psychiatric diagnoses.

   Counselling requires skilled interviewing but includes the additional goal of helping clients with such activities as problem solving, dealing with painful feelings, and developing new skills. Psychotherapy involves intensive counselling with emphasis on personality change or the treatment of more severe mental disorders. For example, attendance at a short seminar on hypnosis would not qualify counsellors to use hypnosis in their work. When access to other professionals is limited or unavailable, such as in rural settings or in urban areas with long waiting lists, counsellors must not conclude that "the provision of well-intentioned but unskilled service [is]... better than no service at all" (Daniluk & Haverkamp, 1993:18).

2. **Pursue professional training and development.** Counsellors should monitor their work and seek supervision, training, or consultation in order to evaluate their effectiveness.

They should pursue continued professional development in order to increase their competence and keep their knowledge current. Counsellors should also base their practice methods on accepted theory and empirical knowledge, using strategies that have a reasonable chance of success. People would not want to see a doctor whose most recent training was years ago in medical school. Similarly, clients should not be expected to work with counsellors who are not current in their field.

Professional counsellors need a core knowledge base, which typically requires two or more years of academic training, including supervised clinical experience in a recognized counselling or social service setting. Moreover, throughout their careers, counsellors should expect to spend time reading books and journals to increase their knowledge. As well, regular attendance of courses, seminars, and conferences should be a part of everyone's professional career.

By keeping their knowledge base current, counsellors are better able to be empathic because they are more aware of the issues and feelings that their clients face. Moreover, keeping up-to-date helps counsellors avoid judgmental responses that result from reacting from only their own frames of reference. The range of knowledge that counsellors need to pursue includes the following:

- Specific issues, problems, and challenges that their clients are facing. For example, counsellors working in corrections need to know something about finding a job if one has a criminal record and coping with the stigma of a criminal record. As another example, many clients are dealing with poverty, and counsellors need to be aware of its social and psychological effects.

- Relevant medical and psychiatric conditions (e.g., attention deficit disorder, multiple sclerosis, **schizophrenia**, bipolar disorder). Counsellor credibility and competence is greatly enhanced if their knowledge of these conditions is current.

- Lifestyle variation (e.g., same-sex relationships, single parents, extended families, and blended families).

- Cultural awareness about the values, beliefs, and customs of others.

- Lifespan development (i.e., developmental changes and milestones from birth to death). Life experience can greatly increase a counsellor's capacity for empathy and understanding. Of course, life experience may also cloud judgment and objectivity, so it is important that counsellors seek training and consultation to increase their understanding of others' experiences.

3. **Be aware of personal reactions and unresolved issues.** Counsellors need to be aware of situations where their clients' problems parallel unresolved issues in their own lives. This awareness is important to help them to know when to seek consultation or supervision, when to refer clients to other workers, and when to enter counselling to address their own needs. Clients have a right to expect that their counsellors are objective about the issues being discussed and that their judgment is not impaired by bias, unresolved personal problems,

or physical illness. If counsellors have emotional or physical problems that affect their ability to give competent services, they should discontinue service to the client.

In addition, large caseloads and the emotional demands of counselling work may result in emotional and physical fatigue, thereby weakening a counsellor's competence. "Counsellors must be cognizant of their own limits and must act to protect themselves and their clients from the consequences of burnout" (Daniluk & Haverkamp, 1993:18). Competent counsellors know how to set limits on the amount of work they are able to provide.

In general, interviewing is a process of gathering information without any expectation of influencing or changing clients. Competent interviewing requires an ability to explore and understand clients' attitudes, feelings, and perspectives. The basis for this competence is a nonjudgmental attitude and intelligent application of the active listening skills of attending, using silence, paraphrasing, summarizing, and asking questions (see Chapters 4 to 6). Yet although the principal goal of interviewing is information gathering, the process of interviewing may lead clients to unexpectedly release painful or forgotten feelings. Thus, adept interviewers are capable of dealing with unpredictable reactions that the interview promotes or of referring clients to appropriate alternative resources. Moreover, they know when and how to probe effectively.

CONVERSATION 2.3

I'M JUST A BEGINNER

STUDENT: I'm just a beginner. So if I'm supposed to work within the limits of my competence, I shouldn't do anything.

TEACHER: Like a lot of counsellors who are just starting, you may feel a bit overwhelmed.

STUDENT: I don't want to say or do the wrong thing. What if I don't know the right answers, or I don't say the right thing to clients?

TEACHER: First, there's rarely a single right way to respond. Most often, there is a range of choices of things to say or do in any situation. Second, no one knows all the right answers. Be honest with clients about the fact that you are still a student, and don't be afraid to admit your limitations, as this provides great modelling for clients. One goal of training is for you to expand your range of choices so that you can respond based on the needs of your clients and their situations. Remember, learning to be an effective counsellor is a lifelong process. At this stage, your professional responsibility is to make effective use of supervisors to monitor your work. Use them to develop your skills. Make it easy for them to give you feedback. Seek it out, and then try to be nondefensive. Look for opportunities to apply your developing knowledge base by taking some risks to learn new skills.

When I first started in the field I also feared saying the wrong thing. When I shared this feeling with one of my professors, he put it in perspective saying, "What makes you think you are so important to the client?"

SELF-AWARENESS

We live in a house of mirrors and think we're looking out.
—Fritz Perls

The Importance of Self-Awareness

Competent counsellors need to acquire a high level of awareness of who they are. Until counsellors develop self-awareness of their own needs, feelings, thoughts, and behaviours, including their personal problems and their areas of vulnerability, they will be unable to respond to their clients with objectivity.

Table 2.5 contrasts the characteristics of counsellors who have high levels of self-awareness with those who have low levels of self-awareness.

Counsellors who lack self-awareness and those who are not motivated to pursue it are destined to remain unaware of the ways they influence clients. For example, they may be unaware of how their nonverbal reactions to controversial topics betray their biases and discomfort. They may avoid particular topics, or they may behave in certain ways to mask their insecurities or to unconsciously meet their personal needs. As another example, counsellors with personal needs for control may meet this need through excessive and inappropriate advice-giving.

TABLE 2.5	Self-Awareness	
Counsellors with Self-Awareness	**Counsellors without Self-Awareness**
Identify and label their personal feelings.	Avoid or are unaware of their feelings.
Know where their feelings end and those of their clients begin.	Project personal feelings onto clients.
Recognize and accept areas of vulnerability and unresolved issues.	Respond inappropriately because unresolved problems interfere with their capacity to be objective.
Understand personal values and their influence on the counselling relationship.	React emotionally to their clients but don't understand why or how.
Recognize and manage internal dialogue (discussed later in this chapter).	Unconsciously use clients to work out their own personal difficulties.
Understand and control personal defence mechanisms.	Remain blind to defensive reactions.
Know how they influence clients and counselling outcomes.	Remain unaware how their behaviour influences others.
Modify behaviour based on reactions of clients.	Behave based on personal needs and style rather than in response to the needs and reactions of clients.
Set professional goals based on knowledge of personal and skill strengths and limitations.	Avoid or limit goal setting because they are unaware of personal and professional needs.

Increasing Self-Awareness

Counsellors who are serious about developing their self-awareness are secure enough to risk exploring their strengths and limitations. Self-awareness means becoming alert and knowledgeable about personal ways of thinking, acting, and feeling. Self-aware counsellors are strong enough to be open to discovering aspects of themselves that they might prefer to keep hidden. This is a continuing, career-long process. It requires counsellors to honestly look at themselves and how they relate to others. But as Harris and Maloney (1996) suggest, some behaviours, including racism, sexism, ageism, and heterosexism, operate unconsciously.

In the self-awareness process, colleagues, supervisors, and clients can be extremely helpful sources of information, but their feedback needs to be cultivated. Generally, people are reluctant to deliver critical feedback, however helpful it may be. Thus, the onus is on counsellors to create the conditions to encourage feedback. They can invite input from others through a number of strategies.

The first strategy is to create a safe climate. People balk at giving feedback to others because they fear how it will be received. One concern is the risk of retaliation. "If I say something, will I be attacked or made to feel guilty?" Another common worry is that feedback will damage the relationship. The major concern also might be that feedback will cripple the other person's self-esteem.

Therefore, counsellors must demonstrate that they are ready, willing, and able to respond nondefensively to feedback. The have a responsibility to consider feedback and when appropriate, to act on it. This means that they do not have to agree unconditionally with what has been said to them. But it does mean that they must listen and give nonaggressive responses, in other words, without blame or excuses. Sometimes, such control can be difficult to sustain, particularly if feedback is delivered in an uncaring and hostile manner. A general rule when dealing with clients is no matter what clients say or do, counsellors must maintain a professional role. Of course, this does not preclude setting appropriate limits, nor does it mean that counsellors have to tolerate personal or physical abuse. It means staying calm, being nondefensive, and refraining from retaliatory responses, such as name-calling or punishing statements.

The second strategy is to use active listening skills to ensure that feedback is concrete or specific. Counsellors can ask questions to get details, definitions, examples, and clarification. Summarizing and paraphrasing can also be used to confirm understanding.

Who Am I? How Do Others See Me?

Self-awareness for counsellors involves answering two basic questions: "Who am I?" and "How do others see me?" These questions require counsellors to explore and understand their personal feelings, thoughts, and behaviour.

Feelings

Effective counsellors are comfortable discussing a wide range of emotions. They don't avoid feelings; in fact, they recognize that for many clients, understanding and managing painful emotions is the greatest outcome of counselling. To understand client emotions, counsellors must be in tune with their own emotional reactions. Empathy, the basic tool for understanding the feelings of others, will be contaminated unless counsellors are fully in touch with their own feelings. This includes knowing where their feelings end and those of their clients begin.

Work and personal stress may also negatively affect a counsellor's capacity to relate effectively to clients. Counsellors must be aware of stressful situations and understand how they react to them. Self-aware counsellors avoid or reduce stressors by developing personal wellness plans for coping with the inevitable demands of the job.

Thoughts

Counsellors need to be aware of their own internal dialogue—the inner voices that evaluate their actions. Counsellors with low self-worth typically find that the inner voice is critical, issuing messages such as "I'm no good." Negative self-talk can lead to emotional distress and interfere with counselling performance in several ways:

- Counsellors may be reluctant to be assertive with clients and may be excessively gentle or nonconfrontational.
- Counsellors may be unable to objectively assess counselling relationship outcomes, since they tend to interpret problems as personal failures and to discount positive feedback or outcomes.

Significant research has been conducted regarding the ways that personal beliefs can influence performance and lead to maladaptive emotions and behaviour (Cormier & Cormier, 1985; Ellis, 2004). Counsellors need to become watchful of negative self-talk as a crucial first step in developing a program to combat its effects. Subsequently, systematic techniques such as thought-stopping can be used to replace depreciating self-talk with affirmations or positive statements. Negative thoughts can be interrupted by mentally saying, "Stop," or by snapping an elastic band on the wrist as a reminder to divert the self-talk (Young, 1998; Martin & Pear, 1992).

Behaviour

Counsellors need to take time to discover how clients are reacting to them. Personal needs and defence mechanisms may lead counsellors to blindly assume that problems in the counselling relationship arise from their clients' inadequacies or failings. Although effective counsellors have confidence in their own abilities, they have to accept that occasionally they may say or do the wrong thing. Counsellors need to be mature and open enough to evaluate their work and to take responsibility for their errors and insensitivities. For example, openminded counsellors consider the possibility that clients may be angry for good reason, perhaps because of oppressive agency routines.

Counsellors who lack self-awareness may fail to understand or accept the needs of their clients and are more likely to take their clients' behaviour too personally. As Wells and Masch remark, "Clients who should be open, confiding, and grateful for assistance often aren't—and often with good reason. The untrained worker, however, remains unaware of the reasons and ultimately feels like a failure, very angry, or even ill-used and burned-out" (1991:19). Ultimately, counsellors need to be self-aware enough to know which client reactions are reactions to their behaviour or personalities and which are the result of other variables beyond their control.

Sigmund Freud first described defence mechanisms in 1894; and over a period of 40 years, he identified most of the ones we talk about today (Vaillant, 1988). A defence mechanism is a mental process or reaction that shields a person from undesirable or unacceptable thoughts, feelings, or conclusions that, if accepted, would create anxiety or damage one's self-esteem. Significantly, defence mechanisms are unconscious and usually involve some distortion of reality (Corsini, 1984). All people, including counsellors, use defence mechanisms to protect themselves. Most people use one or more methods to defend themselves from perceived threats. Simple defences include blaming others or making excuses for their own failures. For example, counsellors might take credit for counselling successes but blame failure on their clients. Common defence mechanisms used by counsellors include the following:

- *Denial:* Refusing to acknowledge the existence of feelings or problems. When counsellors use denial, they fail to consider that their actions might be the reason for their clients' inappropriate behaviour.

- *Displacement:* Shift of emotions or desires from one person or object to another person or object. For example, counsellors deal with their own work stress by behaving aggressively with clients.

- *Rationalization:* Developing excuses or explanations to protect their self-image. For example, counsellors justify their inability to confront clients by concluding that it is best to offer only positive feedback.

- *Suppression:* Averting stressful thoughts by not thinking about them. For example, counsellors refuse to consider that personal biases might be affecting their decisions.

- *Regression:* Dealing with conflict or stress by returning to behaviour from an earlier stage of their lives. For example, counsellors deal with aggressive clients by becoming overly compliant or overly pleasing.

Counsellors should be alert to circumstances where they use defence mechanisms instead of confronting reality. Facing reality requires courage and taking risks, for to give up one's defences means sacrificing safety. Moreover, feedback from others can be threatening, because it challenges counsellors to let down their defences by addressing aspects of their situations that they might prefer to avoid.

When counsellors understand themselves, they recognize when their defences are up and can take steps to change their reactions and behaviour. They know when and where they are vulnerable, then use this knowledge to cue or trigger nondefensive alternatives. For example, when clients are angry or hostile, counsellors can discipline themselves to take time to empathize and encourage clients to ventilate, rather than respond more naturally by fighting back.

Self-aware counsellors know their skill strengths and limitations. This self-awareness enables them to consciously avoid overusing particular skills simply because they are strengths, and it helps them to know when it is appropriate to refer clients to other counsellors. It also helps them to set goals for professional skill development. Knowing the limits of one's ability is a measure of competence.

Personal Needs

Counsellors have the same basic needs as everyone else, including the need to be loved, respected, and valued by others. This is natural; but counsellors must understand how their personal needs can adversely affect counselling outcomes. Lack of self-awareness regarding personal needs can lead to unconscious structuring of the session to meet counsellors' needs instead of the clients' (Kell & Mueller, 1966; Brammer, 1985; D'Augelli, D'Augelli,

& Danish, 1981). "Sometimes helpers want to help themselves with their own problems through assisting others, or satisfaction is acquired through the power and influence over others afforded by the helping relationship" (Brammer, 1985:25). One student was told by her supervisor that her clients really liked her as a person; but when they had a problem, they would go to someone else because they did not believe she was capable of dealing with tough issues or giving critical feedback.

Corey and Corey warn that lack of self-awareness can impede counsellors from keeping their clients' remarks in proper perspective: "As a beginning helper, you are especially vulnerable to believing everything positive that your clients tell you about yourself. Thus, if clients tell you how sexually attractive you are, how understanding you are, and how different from anyone else they have met, it may be very difficult for you to resist believing what they tell you" (1989:192). Therefore, even positive feedback from clients must be interpreted cautiously. Clients may try to placate counsellors or use ingratiating tactics to manipulate, or it may be their way of relating to authority.

A range of counsellor needs may interfere with counselling, including the need to be liked; achieve status or prestige, control, and perfection; and cultivate social relationships. Table 2.6 summarizes the major warning signs and risks of these needs.

TABLE 2.6	Managing Personal Needs in Counselling
Personal Need	**Warning Signs and Risks**
To be liked and to be helpful	• Withholding potentially helpful but critical feedback • Inappropriately avoiding controversy or conflict • Trying to ingratiate (e.g., excessively praising, telling clients what they want to hear) • Acting with rescuing behaviour • Expecting or reaching for compliments from clients
Status or prestige	• Trying to impress with "exotic" techniques or brilliant interpretations • Taking credit for client success • Name-dropping • Bragging about successes
Control	• Advice-giving • Interfering with client self-determination (e.g., unnecessarily using authority, manipulating, dominating) • Imposing personal values • Stereotyping clients as needy and inadequate (which creates a role for someone to be "helpful")
Perfectionism	• Focusing on mistakes • Pushing clients toward unrealistic goals • Responding with self-depreciation to mistakes (e.g., "I'm a failure")
Social relationships	• Becoming overinvolved with clients (e.g., meeting clients socially, continuing counselling relationships beyond the normal point of closure) • Indiscriminate self-disclosure

Need to Be Liked

In the next chapter we will explore the importance of a warm and trusting counselling relationship. To a great extent, counselling depends on establishing and maintaining a safe environment, one in which clients feel safe enough to take risks. Obviously, this is easier if clients like their counsellors; but counsellors need to remember that having clients like them is not the primary goal of counselling. The aim of counselling is to support client change or problem management. This means that counsellors have to be assertive enough to risk making reasonable demands on their clients, which, in turn, may generate tension and anxiety. Otherwise, clients can easily stay locked into established but unhealthy patterns. The need to be liked becomes problematic when it becomes more important than achieving the goals of counselling. One beginning counsellor, a young male, wrote in his journal: "When a client says something negative or behaves in a self-destructive way, I realize I hold back. I don't say anything because I want to be liked. I want the client to like me, not see me as an authority figure. I'd rather be seen as a pal or a friend." This journal entry highlights the dangers and signals an important insight that will help the counsellor question some of his assumptions about counselling. He will need to reevaluate how his behaviour may be sabotaging client progress.

Need for Status or Prestige

Counsellors who have an excessive need to impress others, perhaps because of insecurity, may become technique-centred instead of client-centred. With this switch in priorities, the needs of the client may be overlooked as counsellors act to impress clients or others. The priority of counselling should be to bolster the self-esteem of clients.

Need for Control

Codes of ethics recognize that clients are vulnerable to exploitation. Consequently, counsellors need to give substantial attention to refraining from behaviours that result in undue control of clients. The principle of self-determination (introduced earlier in this chapter) is a basic value that upholds the right of clients to make independent decisions. Counsellors interfere with this right when they attempt to take over clients' problems and orchestrate their solutions.

In some settings, such as government agencies, counsellors may have the legal mandate to impose their services. This situation requires counsellors to be especially vigilant. As Brammer and MacDonald observe, helpers in these settings "must be wary of identifying too closely with the power of the agency under the guise of carrying out the agency's mission. Often the helpee becomes lost in such settings, and the helping services tend to support the power of the organization. The result may be an exaggerated emphasis on adjustment or pacification rather than on actualization and liberation" (1999:40).

Perfectionism

Perfectionism, an unrealistic pursuit of excellence, can negatively affect counselling. Counsellors who are perfectionists may be unable to realistically appraise their work, and they may have an unjustified tendency to blame themselves for client failures. Sometimes, counsellors who are perfectionists push clients toward unrealistic goals or challenge them to move at too fast a pace.

Need for Social Relationships

Counsellors with unmet social needs risk overinvolvement with clients. If counsellors do not have outlets in their own lives for social interaction, they may misuse the counselling relationship for that purpose.

Personal and Cultural Values

Counsellor self-knowledge of personal values and preferences is indispensable for effective counselling. Values constitute a frame of reference for understanding and assessing clients and for making decisions and choices.

Self-awareness of personal values is an important element of competence. All counsellors have personal values, and it is crucial that they understand what these values are in order to avoid imposing them on clients. Self-awareness of personal values is a first step for counsellors to manage the bias that comes from interpreting clients' behaviour from their own perspectives or cultures rather than from the clients'.

Cultural self-awareness refers to knowledge of the customs, traditions, role expectations, and values of one's culture of origin. Language is a particularly important variable. The word *authority* will have very different meaning for individuals who come from totalitarian countries and for those who come from democracies. Cultural self-awareness prepares counsellors to recognize and value the diversity of other cultures. Such awareness needs to be accompanied by a belief that one's own ethnic group is only one of many and that there are other appropriate beliefs and behaviours.

Inevitably, the personal values of counsellors influence the way they assess clients, the techniques and procedures they use, and the goals that they deem reasonable, including which topics will get more or less attention. Moreover, certain topics are more value-charged (e.g., abortion, assisted suicide, sexual orientation, religion, abuse), and the beliefs of counsellors may bias their work in these areas. For example, counsellors who find that they never discuss sexuality in their counselling work need to determine why. Are they avoiding this topic because of personal inhibitions? Are they unconsciously judging the sexual behaviour of their clients?

One way for counsellors to address this problem is to disclose their values to their clients. However, they should do this in such a way that clients do not feel pressured to adopt similar values. Clients should feel free to maintain their own values without fear that they are in some way disappointing their counsellors.

A counsellor's value system is an important variable that influences the methods and outcomes of counselling. In general, counsellors are most effective when their values reflect an optimistic and nonjudgmental view of people. Intellectually and emotionally, they accept and treasure the widest possible variations in lifestyle. They believe in the inherent strength and capacity of people and in their intrinsic right to freedom of choice. Table 2.7 examines some of the values that might impede or enhance counsellors' effectiveness. When counsellors have values that hinder effectiveness, they are more likely to find themselves behaving contrary to the ethics of the field, such as acting in ways that inhibit self-determination or failing to respect the dignity of their clients. Conversely, counsellors who have values that enhance their ability are more naturally inclined to support the ethics of the profession and are more likely to behave in ways that empower their clients.

TABLE 2.7	Values, Beliefs, and Attitudes That Help and Hinder Counsellors' Effectiveness	
Values That Hinder		**Values That Help**
To accept help from others is a sign of weakness.		To accept help is a sign of strength.
Some people are just not deserving of our respect or caring.		Everyone has intrinsic worth and the capacity to be productive.
People are inherently evil. Unless you are careful, they will take advantage of you.		People are essentially good.
I know what is best for my clients.		People are capable of finding their own answers and making decisions.
It is essential that my clients like me.		The purpose of counselling is to help clients exercise choice, not to make clients like me.
I've been there myself, so I know what my clients are feeling.		I can't know what my clients are feeling until I take the time to let them teach me.
People are incapable of changing.		People can and do change.
My religion/culture/viewpoint is the best.		I can accept a wide variety of cultures, religions, and viewpoints.
In this world, it's survival of the fittest.		We depend on one another and we have a responsibility to help others.
Counsellors have a right to impose service when it is in their clients' best interest.		Clients have a right to refuse service.

SUMMARY

Professional codes of ethics define the acceptable limits of behaviour for professionals. These codes recognize the potential vulnerability of clients and seek to protect them from misuse of position and power by professionals. Every counselling profession has its own code of ethics, but certain core principles are common. These principles put the needs of clients first and strictly prohibit sexual and exploitive relationships.

Ethics are the principles and rules of acceptable conduct. Ethical principles are derived from values, or what individuals and groups consider appropriate or worthwhile. The values of the counselling profession are rooted in a few basic principles: belief in the dignity and worth of people, respect for diversity, and respect for the client's right to self-determination. The principle of self-determination values the right of clients to have control and autonomy over matters that affect their lives. The needs of clients are foremost.

Confidentiality is an integral part of ethical practice. Confidentiality can be absolute, meaning that information is not shared with anyone, or it can be relative and shared for legal and operational reasons. Most client communication is subject to relative confidentiality, since legal constraints may require some degree of reporting. As well, the internal operation of the agency necessitates some sharing of information.

An ethical dilemma exists when a choice must be made between competing values. Five principles can help guide resolutions for ethical dilemmas: autonomy, beneficence, nonmaleficence, justice, and fidelity. Ethical decision-making involves weighing the five principles and deciding which ought to have priority in a given situation.

Although it is recognized that counsellors' values influence their work, counsellors need to be objective and to understand their clients without allowing their personal views, feelings, or preferences to contaminate their counselling role. Objectivity is the capacity to understand situations and people without bias or distortion. Counsellors can lose their objectivity by making assumptions, overidentifying with clients, and becoming overly involved with their clients.

Counsellors need to work at an optimum level for each client, regardless of their own feelings or reactions. They need to work within the limits of their competence by using techniques and strategies that they are qualified to deliver and that have a reasonable chance of success.

Self-awareness is essential in order for counsellors to work with objectivity. Self-aware counsellors know themselves—their feelings, thoughts, behaviour, personal needs, and areas of vulnerability. They understand how they affect clients, and they know the limits of their competence. They can answer the question "Who am I?"

EXERCISES

1. Can we promise our clients absolute confidentiality? Why or why not?
2. What are some advantages and disadvantages to allowing clients access to files?
3. Under what conditions would you make exceptions to the principle of self-determination?
4. Use the concepts in this chapter to explore ethical issues and strategies for each of the following situations.
   a. An elderly, frail woman suffering from inoperable cancer decides to kill herself.
   b. A client decides to give his life's savings to his church.
   c. A client boasts that if his girlfriend tries to leave him, he will kill her.
   d. A client from a counselling relationship that terminated six months ago phones to ask you for a date. (Assume that you are not in a current relationship.)
   e. Your client leaves your office in anger, determined to "teach my wife a lesson for the way she treated me."
   f. Knowing that you are in the market for a new car, your client, a used-car salesperson, offers to help you buy a car for wholesale price.
   g. A client inquires about your sexual orientation.
   h. Your client asks for your e-mail address so that he can keep in touch.
   i. Your client, a bisexual male, has tested HIV-positive but informs you that he does not wish to tell his wife. He says that he will practise safe sex.
   j. You receive a call from the client's wife. She says she is concerned about her husband and asks whether you think her husband might be gay.

k. Your colleagues begin to talk about a client. You are with them at a local restaurant.
l. One of your colleagues tells you that she has just returned from a one-day workshop on hypnosis. She says that she can hardly wait to try it on some clients.
m. You encounter one of your colleagues having lunch with a client. You notice that they are drinking a bottle of wine.
n. You have an erotic dream about one of your clients.
o. While you are counselling a student (in your role as school counsellor), he discloses that he is selling marijuana to classmates. (Would your answer be different if you were a counsellor in a community agency unconnected to the school?)
p. You are a counsellor working with a young, gay client. He has been socially isolated and is slow to trust anyone, but over time you have managed to form a strong working relationship. Imagine that he approaches you with a request that you walk with him in the annual gay pride parade. What variables would you consider in making your decision? What are the implications of going with him? What are the implications of not going?
q. Your client is down to her last two dollars. She offers to buy your coffee.
r. Your car is broken and requires an expensive repair. Your client has been struggling to set up a mobile repair service, but business has been slow. He offers to fix your car for a discounted price.

5. A good friend invites you to a small dinner party. When you arrive, you are introduced to the other guests, including a client who you have been working with for the past year. You note that her companion for the evening is not her husband. From observing their behaviour, there is no doubt that this is a romantic relationship. She has never mentioned this relationship in the past. What would you do for the rest of the evening? Should you disclose this relationship to the woman's husband? If she asks you to keep your knowledge of this relationship from her husband, could you continue to see them for marital counselling?

6. Assess the extent to which you believe that each of the following counsellor behaviours might be acceptable. Use the following rating scale:

5 = always
4 = often
3 = sometimes
2 = seldom
1 = never

Be prepared to defend your answer. How might your answer vary depending on the circumstances?

____ seeing a client after having had one alcoholic drink
____ accepting an invitation for dinner at a client's home
____ hugging a client
____ inviting a former client to a party at your home
____ dating a former client
____ having sex with a client
____ driving your client home
____ discussing your client with a supervisor

   ___ assisting a client to end his or her life

   ___ accepting a client's decision to commit suicide

   ___ allowing your teenager to babysit for your client

   ___ buying a car from your client

   ___ lending money to a client

   ___ reporting your client to the police (after the client tells you that he or she committed a crime)

   ___ reporting suspected child abuse by your client

   ___ sharing personal experiences, feelings, problems, and so on, with your client

   ___ getting angry with your client

   ___ discussing a client with your family or friends (without mentioning names)

   ___ giving a present to a client or receiving a present from a client

   ___ sharing information about clients with other counsellors

   ___ warning a person that your client has threatened to harm him- or herself

   ___ telling a client's partner that he or she is HIV-positive

   ___ advising a client to leave an abusive marriage

   ___ crying in the presence of a client

   ___ counselling a friend or neighbour at your agency

(adapted from Shebib, 1997)

7. Give examples of appropriate physical contact between social workers and clients. How might cultural, age, or gender variables affect your answer?

8. The case below is based on a case record completed by a social work student. Use the CCA and CASW codes to evaluate the appropriateness of the language used.

    I visited the Smith home to investigate allegations of child neglect. I was met at the door by Mrs. Smith, a single parent. I was surprised by her size; she was morbidly obese and smelled as if she hadn't showered in weeks. Rolls of fat hung out of Mrs. Smith's shirt, and portions of her legs were covered with dirt. Mrs Smith's slovenly appearance suggests she is unable to care for herself, much less her children (Reamer, 1998:93).

9. Explore the issues involved in discussing clients with friends and relatives. Is it acceptable to discuss clients if you change their names and other identifying data? Defend your answer.

10. Should some clients be forced to attend counselling?

11. Do you think black humour is ethical? Defend your answer.

12. What strong beliefs do members of your cultural/ethnic group hold?

13. Use the questions and situations below to examine your values related to sexual orientation issues.

   a. If your client were gay or lesbian, how might it influence the way you work with him or her?

   b. What would you do if a friend told you an antihomosexual joke or story? What if the person telling the joke were a client or a colleague?

   c. Do you have gay or lesbian friends?

   d. Do you think homosexuality is an illness?

  e. Your daughter discloses that she is lesbian. Predict how you might feel, think, and behave.

  f. Your best friend confides that he feels he is the wrong gender.

  g. What are your views on same-sex marriage?

14. Write an essay answering the question "Who am I?"

15. Explore your views regarding the following value-charged issues:

  a. Are people basically good or bad?

  b. Should people have the right to take their own lives?

  c. What religion(s) are acceptable?

  d. Should immigrants be required to speak the language of their new homeland?

16. The following questions will help you to examine your values and beliefs. Work in a small group to explore and debate your answers. Use this process as a tool to reevaluate your position on matters you deem important.

  a. What are the characteristics of the client you would most want to work with? (Be specific regarding as many variables as possible, such as age, gender, personality, culture, and religion.) Why would you choose these characteristics?

  b. What are the characteristics of the client you would least want to work with (e.g., age, gender, personality, culture, religion)?

  c. What topics or issues are likely to evoke strong personal reactions from you?

  d. What does authority mean to you? How do you behave and feel when you are relating to people in authority?

  e. In your opinion, what is the meaning of life?

  f. Where do you draw your strength?

  g. When you die, what do you most want to be remembered for?

17. Examine your reasons for wanting to become a counsellor. What needs do you expect to meet through your work? In what ways might your personal needs be an impediment?

18. What are your five most important values?

19. Work in a small group to explore your spiritual values through the following questions.

  a. Are religions basically good or bad?

  b. Are some religions better than others?

  c. Should cults be illegal?

  d. What does spirituality mean to you?

  e. Should spiritual issues be introduced by counsellors?

  f. When is it appropriate to discuss religion with clients?

  g. What are the implications of your religious views when working with someone with a similar perspective and when working with someone with radically different views?

20. Explore your personal strengths and limitations. Use the following topics to structure your assessment:

  • capacity to be assertive (as opposed to shyness or aggressiveness)
  • degree of self-confidence
  • comfort dealing with a wide range of emotions
  • need to control or be in charge
  • capacity to relate to diverse populations (age, gender, culture, religion, etc.)
  • ability to give and receive feedback (positive and critical)

- need to be helpful
- anxieties and fears
- competence in initiating relationships (beginnings)
- ability to deal with conflict
- self-awareness regarding how others see you
- overall awareness of personal strengths and limitations
- values and attitudes that will help or hinder your work as a counsellor
- capacity and willingness to change

Based on your answers, identify what you consider to be your five major strengths and your five major limitations.

21. Evaluate your capacity for handling feedback from others. Are you generally open and nondefensive when others critically evaluate your behaviour or performance? Do you tend to avoid asking for feedback, or do you actively solicit it? Interview friends and colleagues for their opinions.

22. Are you excessively dependent on your clients? Rate each statement below and rate yourself using the following scale:

    4 = always

    3 = frequently

    2 = sometimes

    1 = rarely

    0 = never

    a. I often feel responsible for the feelings, thoughts, and behaviour of my clients.
    b. I get angry when my help is rejected.
    c. I feel worthless and/or depressed when clients don't change.
    d. I feel compelled to help people solve problems by offering unwanted advice.
    e. I want to take care of my clients and protect them from painful feelings.
    f. When clients don't like me, I feel rejected or inadequate.
    g. I do things to make my clients like me, even if what I do is not helpful.
    h. I avoid confronting or challenging clients.
    i. I tell clients what they want to hear.
    j. I feel most safe when I'm giving to others.
    k. When clients fail, I take it personally.
    l. I spend too much time proving to myself and my clients that I'm good enough.
    m. I tend to be very controlling with clients.
    n. I tolerate abuse from clients to ensure they keep liking me.
    o. I feel responsible for solving my clients' problems.

    Interpretation: Carefully review any statements where you scored 4 or 3. Use your awareness of problem areas to develop a program of self-change.

23. Imagine that you are a client. What might your counsellor need to know about you (e.g., values, needs, preferences) in order to work effectively with you?

24. How do you deal with the demands of an increasingly diverse society?

25. Take an inventory of your friendship circle. To what extent do your friends come from the same cultural and values base as your own? Predict what might happen if you broadened your circle to include more diversity.

26. Develop a plan to learn about the cultures in your community.

27. Develop a plan to increase your understanding of world religions.

28. Research the codes of ethics for three or four different professional organizations. What common and unique features can you identify? Note: this website provides links to various codes: http://www.advocateweb.org/hope/codesofethics.asp.

 ## WEBLINKS

The Canadian Counselling Association site contains links to Canadian counselling and mental health professional associations as well as guidance and professional development information:
www.ccacc.ca/ccacc.htm

The Canadian Association of Social Workers website has links and information for social workers:
www.casw-acts.ca/default.htm

This site provides articles and links on the topic of ethics:
www.scu.edu/ethics/

chapter three

Relationship: The Foundation for Change

PREVIEW

After reading this chapter you should be able to:

- Define the characteristics of a counselling relationship.
- List the essential relationship-building objectives of each of the four phases of counselling.
- Explain the importance of the core conditions of warmth, empathy, and genuineness.
- Describe the core conditions.
- Describe relationship and sessional contract.
- Demonstrate the ability to negotiate counselling contracts.
- Define immediacy.
- Use basic immediacy skills.
- Explain how transference and countertransference influence counselling relationships.
- Describe the importance of empowering clients.
- Explain the importance of relationship endings.

WHAT IS A COUNSELLING RELATIONSHIP?

In my early professional years I was asking the question: How can I treat, or cure, or change this person? Now I would phrase the question in this way: How can I provide a relationship which this person may use for his own personal growth?
— *Carl Rogers*

A **counselling relationship** is a time-limited period of consultation between a counsellor and one or more clients in order to assist the client in achieving a defined goal. The expertise that counsellors bring to the relationship lies not so much in their ability to solve problems, but in their capacity to recognize and mobilize client strengths and resources. When strengths are revealed and resources identified, clients become empowered with new choices and revitalized optimism.

Counselling relationships have some of the same components of intimacy, caring, and support that characterize deep personal relationships. High-level communication skills are as important to friendships as they are to counselling. Moreover, many of the skills of counselling are also the skills of effective everyday communication. But friendships grow out of mutual attraction and common interest, whereas counselling relationships focus on helping clients achieve goals such as resolving crises, making decisions, and learning new skills. Counselling relationships are structured for the primary purpose of reaching these goals; and once the clients have achieved them, the counselling relationships are terminated.

Personal relationships can be terminated for personal reasons. However, counsellors are expected to persist in their efforts on behalf of clients even when they are frustrated by lack of progress or client resistance. Counselling may be ended when there is little likelihood of reaching its goals, but not simply because the counsellor prefers other clients. One measure of professionalism is the capacity of the practitioner to sustain commitment, patience, and caring despite frustrating obstacles.

Developing and sustaining an effective counselling relationship is widely accepted as critical to success in counselling (Kadushin, 1997; Shilling, 1984; Shulman, 1999; Rogers, 1980; Young, 1998). In fact, the relationship itself is often viewed as having primary importance (Kadushin, 1997). Capuzzi and Gross conclude that "specific procedures and techniques are much less important than the alliance between counselor and client" (1997:65). Almost 40 years ago, Rogers (1961) emphasized that a counsellor's attitudes and feelings are more important than technique and noted that the client's perception of the counsellor's attitudes is what is most crucial. Young echoes these sentiments: "Without a strong therapeutic alliance, the goals of therapy cannot be reached" (1998:155). Moreover, "even clients whose lives have predisposed them to distrust and suspicion often remain alert to clues that this professional relationship may hold promise (Miley, O'Melia, & Dubois, 2004:130).

Rogers' counselling classic, *Client-Centered Therapy* (1951), describes the experience of a client who successfully completed counselling following an unsuccessful experience with another counsellor. The second counsellor asked the client why he had been able to work through his problems on his second attempt. The client responded, "You did about the same things he did, but you seemed really interested in me" (Rogers, 1951:69).

Counselling relationships are not always comfortable. In fact, as Keith-Lucas proposes, "The attempt to keep the relationship on a pleasant level is the greatest source of ineffectual helping known" (1972:18). The helping relationship provides the necessary security for clients to disclose their feelings and ideas. As trust develops in relationships, so does the capacity of clients to become increasingly open to revealing themselves. Drawing from the strength of their relationships with counsellors, clients may risk new ways of thinking and behaving; and in this way, the relationship becomes the medium for change. In positive counselling relationships, clients perceive their counsellors as allies. They become increasingly willing to disclose because they do not fear that they will be rejected, judged, or coerced to change in ways that they find unacceptable. In its purest form, the counselling relationship becomes a collaborative endeavour.

COUNSELLING RELATIONSHIPS: CORE CONDITIONS

Rogers (1961) asserted the importance of seeing others as "becoming." This notion underscores a fundamental belief in the capacity of people to change. Clients are not bound by their past, and counsellors should not use diagnosis and classification as tools for depersonalizing clients and treating them as objects. In counselling, clients need to be seen for their potential, strength, inner power, and capacity to change. Rogers' philosophy suggests a number of introspective questions for counsellors to consider regarding their attitudes and behaviour in helping relationships:

- *How can I act so that clients will perceive me as trustworthy?* This means counsellors do what they say they will do and act in a way that is consistent with how they feel. It requires counsellors to communicate without ambiguity and contradiction.
- *Can I permit myself to experience positive attitudes of warmth, caring, liking, interest, and respect toward clients?*
- *Can I be strong enough as a person to be separate from my clients?* This requires a high level of maturity, self-awareness, and courage. Rogers summarizes this challenge: Am I strong enough in my own separateness that I will not be downcast by his depression, frightened by his fear, nor engulfed by his dependency? Is my inner self hardy enough to realize that I am not destroyed by his anger, taken over by his need for dependence, nor enslaved by his love, but that I exist separate from him with feelings and rights of my own (1961:52)?
- *Am I secure enough to permit clients their separateness?* Clients are not under counsellors' control, nor are they to be moulded as models of what counsellors feel they should be.
- *Can I let myself fully empathize with my clients' feelings and world perspectives without evaluating or judging?*

Truax and Carkhuff (1967) and others have built on the work of Carl Rogers (1951, 1961, 1980) to identify what have become known as the core conditions Core conditions are aspects of attitude that are prerequisites to forming and maintaining effective helping relationships. The essential core conditions are warmth, empathy, and genuineness. Although counsellors can use certain behaviours and skills to demonstrate core conditions, the conditions must represent the authentic values and attitudes of counsellors. When counsellors exhibit these core conditions, the potential for positive relationships with clients is increased.

However, there is no guarantee that clients will interpret warmth, genuineness, and empathy (or any communication) in the way that they were intended. Prior experiences and expectations, as well as cultural and individual differences, can easily lead to discrepancies in the way communication is perceived. Counsellors can expect to be rejected at least some of the time, despite their best efforts. Moreover, a client may perceive empathy as an intrusive attempt to "get into my head" and may interpret caring attitudes as manipulation. Secure professionals accept this reality, knowing that considerable resistance may be encountered as they work to develop the helping relationship.

Warmth

Rogers (1961) urged counsellors to shun any tendency to keep clients at a distance by treating them as objects with detailed diagnostic labels. Instead, he argued that counsellors need to learn that it is safe to express their **warmth** and to let clients know that they care. Warmth, although a difficult concept to define, is an expression of nonpossessive caring. As Mehr interprets it:

> People who lack warmth are described as cold, uncaring, or uninvolved. Thus, warmth implies involvement. The expression of warmth requires a nonjudgmental attitude and an avoidance of blaming. Warmth involves acceptance of the equal worth of others... Nonpossessive warmth entails a feeling of caring and concern without placing conditions on the relationship. (1998:182)

Warmth is a precursor to trust. It attracts clients to take risks because it indicates the goodwill and motivation of their counsellors. In the beginning, clients often come to counselling reluctantly, perhaps driven by external pressure or by the weight of their problems. Counsellors need to engage or connect with clients to help them find enough acceptance so that they return and sufficient safety so that they can take appropriate risks. Warmth says, "I'm approachable. You don't need to be afraid of me. I won't take advantage of your vulnerability. I'm a kind person." As a result, warmth is particularly important during the formative or beginning stage of the relationship. Warmth is also crucial for supporting clients during a crisis, and it is a necessary partner to caring confrontation. Clients will be more receptive to receiving feedback when they are persuaded that it originates from a caring attitude.

Although warmth can be defined behaviourally, it must arise from genuine feelings of caring for the client. Otherwise, the counsellor's actions will appear lacking in genuineness. Warmth is demonstrated by smiling appropriately and by showing sincere interest in the comfort of the client. Counsellors show warmth when they communicate nonverbally that they are totally focused on their clients. Simple courtesies, such as eliminating distractions from the interview, asking clients if they are physically comfortable, offering them a beverage, and making eye contact all convey warmth. Well-timed humour can also add a warm touch to the interview.

Brammer and MacDonald suggest flexibility in the amount of expressed warmth and caring, depending on the comfort level of clients. From their research, they conclude: "From a multicultural perspective, overt expression of emotion must be used sensitively. Asian American helpees might be quite uncomfortable receiving strongly emotional care, especially early in the relationship. In the Hispanic American culture, overt warmth might be more acceptable between female helpers and helpees, but not so for males" (1999:32).

Being warm doesn't preclude dealing with difficult topics. Nor does it imply that a great deal of the interview needs to be spent making small talk, as one might do during a social visit.

Sometimes in busy social service agencies, caseloads become unmanageable and the pace of the work frantic. Constant crises and unrelenting paperwork exhaust even the most energetic and caring workers, who may begin to lose the "spark" they had when they first entered the field. Unless controlled, the office routine can begin to feel more like an assembly line than a counselling service, as clients become numbers and the work becomes increasingly task-oriented. How does one continue to feel and express warmth under such conditions? The answer must be discovered individually, but we can learn something from the observations of one worker, a senior caseworker with over 25 years' experience:

> What works for me is to remind myself that no matter how overwhelmed I feel, it's worse for my clients. Often, they're broke, in crisis and not sure whether they want to live and die. They don't need me to be part of the problem. What doesn't work for me is to get caught up in cof-fee room negativism. You know what it's like—the ones who never have anything good to say and always expect things to get worse. It also helps if I take a few moments, sometimes precious seconds, between interviews to meditate. When I meet my client, I try to spend some time just being friendly.

Empathy

Empathy describes the capacity to understand the feelings and views of another person. Empathic attitudes and skills can generate powerful bonds of trust and rapport. Empathy communicates understanding and acceptance. An empathic attitude is characterized by one's willingness to learn about the world of another and begins with suspending judgment. "Without judging (or perhaps even liking) a client, the worker tries to understand the person's problem, accepting feelings without necessarily condoning his or her acts" (Schram & Mandell, 1997:123). But to be nonjudgmental requires considerable discipline in controlling personal biases, assumptions, and reactions that might contaminate understanding.

In addition, counsellors need to be able to enter the emotional world of their clients without fear of becoming trapped in their pain. Counsellors who are secure with themselves and their feelings have the capacity to enter their clients' worlds without fear of losing their own identity. Brill and Levine (2005) note that when a counsellor communicates acceptance, there is the "freedom to be oneself—to express one's fears, angers, joy, rage, to grow, develop, and change—without concern that doing so will jeopardize the relationship" (p. 118).

Chapter 6 explores the skills of communicating empathy, but a preview of the components of this important skill is provided here. Empathic skill has two components. First, counsellors must be able to perceive their clients' feelings and perspectives. This requires counsellors to have abundant self-awareness and emotional maturity so that they do not contaminate their clients' experience with their own. As Garvin and Seabury observe, "The concept of empathy relates to the act of experiencing something in a manner similar to another person while still retaining a sense of who one is and what one's separate responses may be" (1984:110).

The second component of empathy is to make an empathic response. This involves putting in words the feelings that the client has expressed. This task can be particularly difficult, since clients often communicate their feelings in abstract, ambiguous, or nonverbal ways. Empathic responses require a vocabulary of words and phrases that can be used to precisely define feelings. At a basic level, empathic responses acknowledge obvious and clearly expressed feelings. At a more advanced or inferred level, empathic responses are framed from hints and nonverbal cues. Empathic responses prove to clients that they have been heard, understood, and accepted.

Genuineness

Being genuine means one is authentic and real in a relationship. Counsellors who are genuine show high consistency between what they think and do, and between what they feel and express. Rogers (1961) used the term congruent to describe this quality and emphasized the importance of self-awareness to unambiguous communication. Counsellors need to be aware of how they are feeling and how they are transmitting their feelings in order to avoid giving contradictory messages.

Counsellors who are genuine are also highly trustworthy. They don't lie to clients. They are willing to provide feedback that is timely and helpful. They show respect for clients by being open and honest while maintaining warmth and empathy in the relationship. They do not work from hidden agendas, nor do they put on "masks" or play roles to hide their true feelings. As well, genuine counsellors are reliable. They do what they say they are going to do. Mehr offers this perspective: "Awareness is the first step toward achieving congruence between internal experiences and outward behavior. Genuineness also, however, requires the maturity and skills to be able to express these feelings in the context of a warm and empathic relationship" (1998:183).

Benjamin (1981) emphasizes the importance of being human in the interview and discarding false facades or professional equipment that might create distance and barriers in the relationship. "If the interviewer is remote and cold, can the interviewee be expected to come close and be warm? When the interviewer is cautious and wary, can the interviewee be unguarded? Will the latter be free to express openly his thoughts and feelings to someone barricaded behind a wall of professionalism?... We must be sincere, genuine, congruent—not act so, but be so" (53–54).

CONVERSATION 3.1

GENUINENESS

STUDENT: How far should I go with genuineness? What if I'm angry with my client? Should I say so? Or suppose I find my client disgusting. Should I express that too?

TEACHER: You've identified an important dilemma. On the one hand, the need for genuineness suggests that we should be open and honest with our clients. We shouldn't put on false fronts, lie to clients, or fake our feelings. But at the same time, ethical principles clearly prohibit us from doing harm. Being genuine doesn't entitle counsellors to "dump" on their clients. Moreover, genuine counsellors are truthful, but they are also timely. They share personal perceptions and feelings in an assertive way in order to meet their clients' needs. They might express their anger, but they do so without intending to punish, ridicule, or trap their clients. As for feeling disgust toward a client, I can't see how sharing that information would serve any purpose. On the other hand, it may be useful to the client if you explored the specific behaviours or attitudes that gave rise to those feelings. With sensitive feedback, your client can have the benefit of learning about his or her impact on others. One final point: Strong reactions toward our clients may hint at our own vulnerabilities. If you find a client disgusting, I'd want to ask you, "Where does that feeling come from? Are you sure it is related only to the client?"

STUDENT: Maybe the client "pushes my buttons" the same way my parents did.

TEACHER: Exactly.

Relationship and the Phases of Counselling

Each of the four phases of counselling—preliminary, beginning, action, and ending—has associated relationship tasks and challenges (Shebib, 1997). In all phases, counsellors need to develop effective skills and attitudes for engaging and retaining clients, including the following: sincerity, perceptiveness, honesty, respect for diversity, capacity to initiate conversations, ability to be a good listener, comfort with discussing feelings, empathy, ability to communicate confidence without conceit, and warmth.

Preliminary Phase

The goal of the preliminary phase is to create the necessary physical and psychological conditions for the relationship to begin. The counselling environment (e.g., agency setting, office layout, reception procedures) can have a dramatic impact on the client's mood and expectations even before the interview begins (Kadushin, 1997; Shebib, 1997). Preliminary phase work attempts to create first impressions that say to clients, "You will be respected here. You are important. This is a place where you will be supported."

Beginning Phase

The relationship goal in the beginning phase is to develop rapport, trust, and a working contract or agreement regarding the purpose of the work and the roles of the participants. The relationship at this phase must provide enough safety for clients that they will engage and continue with counselling. Counsellors create this environment of safety by communicating that they do not judge the client and that change can occur. The relationship enables clients to feel sufficiently free to take on the first risks of counselling—sharing their feelings and concerns.

Action Phase

In the action phase, the relationship continues to develop and strengthen, and new counselling risks are taken as clients find the courage and strength to change their ways of thinking, feeling, and behaving. During this phase, relationship work may need to focus on addressing communication problems, including, at times, tension, or conflict.

Ending Phase

Termination of the counselling relationship comes when counselling has served its purpose and clients have reached their goals. Termination focuses on reviewing the work accomplished, helping clients consolidate learning, and saying goodbye.

COUNSELLING CONTRACTS

A **contract** is a negotiated agreement between the counsellor and the client regarding important variables that define the work. Counsellors typically begin contracting early in the first interview; however, contracting is continuous throughout the life of the helping relationship. It not a single event task that once completed is finished. Moreover, rigid adherence to negotiated contract is hazardous. Counselling contracts need to be periodically revisited and updated as necessary, sometimes even several times during a single session.

Clients may develop fresh insight that changes their priorities. Increased trust may enable clients to address more difficult topics and feelings that they were unwilling to consider at the beginning of the relationship. As well, new problems and issues may emerge as a result of changing circumstances.

Since clients and counsellors often have different ideas about the objectives and methods of counselling, it is important for them to reach understanding regarding the nature of the work (Gladding, 1996). Such understanding results in a contract that "helps clarify the counselor-client relationship and give it direction; protect the rights, roles, and obligations of both counsellors and clients; and ensure the success of counselling" (Gladding, 1996:117).

The contract is like a road map that provides general directions on how to get from A to B. It confirms that all parties are working toward the same ends. When counsellors and their clients are working toward agreed-upon objectives, it is much more likely that clients will "own" the work, rather than see it as something that has been imposed on them. Contracting reduces suspicions that counsellors may have hidden agendas.

A counselling contract also predicts an end point to the relationship. Defining tasks and goals makes it clear when the relationship should be ended. In this way, the counselling relationship is clearly distinguished from a friendship, which may last for a lifetime.

Shulman's 1999 research confirmed the importance of contracting for counselling success. In particular, his findings supported the relevance of helping clients participate in setting the contract. Egan (1998) underscores the empowering nature of contracting. He describes the contract as a kind of charter that can "give clients a flavour of the mechanics of the helping process, diminish initial client anxiety and reluctance, provide a sense of direction, and enhance clients' freedom of choice" (p. 56).

Contracts may be formal and signed by both the counsellor and the client. But more frequently they are informal and ratified with verbal agreement or a handshake. There are two broad types of contracts, engagement or relationship contracts and sessional contracts.

Relationship Contract

The relationship contract process is designed to answer two critical questions: What are the goals and objectives of our work? And how will we work together? Here are the essential elements of the relationship contract.

1. **Definition of the Objective or Purpose of the Counselling Relationship**

If there is no agreement on the purpose of counselling, the work is apt to be directionless. Without agreed-upon purpose, counsellors tend to make assumptions about the needs and wants of their clients. The problem with assumptions is that they are so frequently wrong. The multiple purposes of counselling can include helping clients with problem solving, decision making, and managing feelings. They can also provide support, give information, and foster skill acquisition.

Every counselling agency has a purpose that defines and limits its service. Specialty agencies, such as employment counselling centres, may focus on career testing and job search skills, while a transition home may provide crisis counselling and shelter. A community centre might provide a broad range of counselling, education, and group support services.

Counsellors define and limit their role based on their position in the agency and their training. An intake worker, for example, may be restricted to initial screening and assessments, while a community outreach worker may specialize in reaching clients who do not voluntarily seek service.

But clients may have specific wants and needs that do not mesh with the mandate of the agency or its workers. Abraham Maslow's (1954) famous hierarchy of needs can be a useful way of understanding client priorities. Maslow suggested that people normally seek to fulfill their basic needs before pursuing higher order needs. He arranged his hierarchy in the following order:

1. physiological or basic survival needs (air, water, and food)
2. safety needs (personal security, stability, protection, and freedom from fear)
3. belonging/love needs (relationships)
4. self-esteem needs (sense of worth and importance)
5. self-actualization needs (achieving one's full potential)

Maslow's theory can be a useful reference for counsellors. As one counsellor put it: "You can't counsel a client who hasn't eaten." In simplest terms, counsellors need to begin by ascertaining where clients are in terms of unmet needs. As basic and higher-order needs are met, the goals of counselling need to be adjusted accordingly.

Contracting also explores three variables: agency, counsellor, and client. Contracting works well when the client's needs match the agency's mandate and the counsellor's competence. But when the service the client needs is beyond the mandate of the agency or the competence of the counsellor, referral to another counsellor or agency is appropriate.

In addition, the contracting process aspires to establish a relationship of equality between clients and counsellors, while recognizing each person's role. Zastrow's observation about social workers is relevant to understanding this role:

> The expertise of the social worker does not lie in knowing or recommending what is best for the client. Rather, the expertise lies in assisting clients to define their problems, to develop and examine the alternatives for resolving the problems, to maximize the client's capacities and opportunities to make decisions for themselves, and to help clients to implement the decisions they make. (1990:62)

2. **Discussion of the Roles and Expectations of the Participants**

Counsellors should know something about what clients want from them. Do clients expect them to provide advice on how to manage their problems? Do they want to be challenged with new information and new perspectives? Are they looking for someone who is warm, gentle, and supportive, or someone who will just listen? Similarly, counsellors need to tell clients about any expectations they have. Role discussion may also address issues such as how the participants might address conflict and how they can provide feedback to each other.

Moreover, clients may be aware of their pain and recognize and accept the need for change and help, but they may have no idea what form this help might take. In such situations, counsellors need to be able to help them understand the potential assistance that counselling can provide.

Some clients also have unrealistic expectations of their counsellors and the process. They may believe that counsellors will tell them what to do and solve all their problems. Or they may have no faith in the process whatsoever. According to Wicks and Parsons, when people enter counselling, they often anticipate "either a miracle or complete failure" (1984:175). Contracting is a significant opportunity for demystifying the process and for challenging unreasonable positive or negative expectations.

The following example is taken from the midpoint of a second interview. It illustrates how the counsellor gently encourages the client to reexamine some self-imposed restrictions on the relationship:

Client: *Let's keep my feelings out of this. I simply want to look at ways to improve my relationship with my son. If you could teach me some techniques, I'd be most grateful.*

Counsellor: *Of course, you're entitled to privacy on issues or feelings that you don't want to share with me. At the same time, I wonder if you might be too hasty in restricting what we can discuss.*

Client: *I don't get it. What do you mean?*

Counsellor: *Well, you've been through a lot. With your son's arrest and his disappearance for over a month, I'd be surprised if you weren't feeling stress.*

Client: *Who wouldn't?*

Counsellor: *That's exactly my point. When I don't talk about feelings that are bothering me, I have to keep them inside or pretend they're not there. I've found that doesn't work. Sooner or later, I have to face my feelings.*

Client: *I'm just afraid that if I start crying, I won't be able to stop.*

Counsellor: *That tells me that the pain must be very deep. (silence as the client tears up)*

Counsellor: *I won't push you, but I hope our relationship can become a safe place for you. It's okay with me if you cry.*

Many clients are slow to develop trust, perhaps for good reason. They may have life-long experiences of betrayal or abuse by people they trusted. Why should it be any different with a counsellor? As a result, it is understandable that they approach counselling with a degree of mistrust. Wicks and Parsons provide a compelling observation: "Though there may seem to be a great distance between counsellors and their clients during the beginning phase of counselling, they should not be discouraged because at that point their clients may be closer to them than anyone else" (1984:168). In fact, counsellors can foster relationship development if they try to match their responses to their clients (Huber & Backlund, 1991):

Client: *I really don't see the point in being here. My situation is hopeless. I've been to other counsellors and nothing worked. I'm only here because my wife insisted. She thought you might be able to help.*

Counsellor (Choice 1): *You certainly do sound discouraged. But I think you should give counselling a chance. Maybe by talking about your problems we can discover some solutions you've overlooked.*

Counsellor (Choice 2): *Given your past experiences, I can see why you're pessimistic. You're wise to be skeptical until you find out if you can trust me. In the end, the results will be the most important thing.*

In this example, Choice 1 is well meaning but ill timed. Responses such as this may "impede the client's cooperation... especially if the client has already been discouraged by previous counselors who began treatment on a positive, optimistic note, only to end counseling efforts with no improvement" (Huber & Backlund, 1991:24). Choice 2, however, is not condescending and does not provide false hope.

Homebuilders usually prewire new homes so that future installation of services like cable television will be easy. In the same way, relationships can be "prewired" to make resolution of communication difficulties easier. Contracting strategies, such as discussing in advance how conflict will be addressed and working to develop and refine open communication, are the tools for prewiring relationships. If conflicts occur, a mechanism is already in place for resolving them.

3. **Discussion of the Methods and Routines of Counselling**

Counsellors should not work from a secret script with mysterious techniques that they hide from clients. Instead, they should be willing and able to describe their work in simple, nonjargonistic language. In this way, clients can know something about what is happening as well as what remains to be done.

Shulman (1999) emphasizes the need for workers to provide clear, nonjargonistic statements that describe the range of services available. This is particularly important in settings where the counsellor may be the one who initiates first contact. When the purpose of the meeting is explicit, clients do not have to worry about workers' hidden agendas, and they are in a more informed position to take advantage of assistance. In the example below, a school counsellor is making an excellent attempt to engage with an 11-year-old boy who has transferred to the school in the middle of the academic year and seems depressed and alone:

> **Counsellor:** *My name is Mr. Smith. I'm here because your teacher thought I might be able to help you with some of the problems you're having at school. I know that it can be tough to be the new kid. Sometimes it's just not much fun. Maybe we could meet and see if we can figure out a way to make things better. What do you think?*

Similarly, Interview 3.1 illustrates part of the contracting process. It is taken from about the 15-minute mark of a first session with a parent of a teen who is abusing drugs. Sometimes, contracting can start very early in the interview. At other times, such as in this example, it is helpful to give clients some space to describe their feelings and problems before proceeding to contracting.

4. **Practical Details**

Practical details in the contracting process include issues such as the time and place of meetings and any fees for service. Ethical issues, including the limitations of confidentiality, are also part of the contract.

Sessional Contracts

Whereas the relationship contract concerns broad issues that define the overall direction of the work and the respective roles and expectations of the participants, the sessional contract defines the focus for the current session. Although the importance of defining sessional focus seems self-evident, it is surprising how often counsellors proceed without a clear sense of direction or purpose. Or, they assume that their clients understand and are working with the same purpose in mind. When clients are involved in negotiating the contract, they are respected and empowered as active partners, not passive recipients of service.

Sessional contracts can direct attention to one or more of the three major domains: behaviour, thinking, and feeling. Sessional contracts based on behaviour target objectives such as skill development, problem solution (what to do or say), decision making, exploring options, and goal setting. Sessional contracts based on thinking are concerned with helping clients explore values, assumptions, beliefs (including spiritual beliefs) and self-esteem issues. When feeling is the focus of the contract, the work is on clients' emotions.

Contracting Leads

Counsellors are sometimes too quick to assume that clients need to work on solutions when their primary need may be to "unwind" with a sympathetic listener. Through contracting, counsellors ensure that what is done in the interview is explicit and relevant. Here are some examples of counsellor leads that might be used in contracting.

- What are you hoping to accomplish as a result of our work today?
- What brings you here?
- If you wish, we could explore...
- Here's an idea of where we might go from here.
- In my experience I have found that it is very helpful, sometimes crucial, to talk about feelings before working on problem solutions. Does this make sense to you, or not?
- Here's some choices. We could work on finding a solution. Or perhaps it might be better to just spend time talking about how your feel.
- I wonder if it makes sense to talk a bit about...
- What do you need to get out of today?
- What do you need from me?
- Let's talk about how we can use our time here.
- Finish this sentence. When I leave here today I hope that....
- What do you want to talk about today? (Note: this lead will require a follow-up regarding expected outcome)
- Several times you've hinted at.... Perhaps it might be important to focus on this a bit.
- (To an involuntary client) You feel forced to come. Nevertheless, you could have chosen not to. So, I wonder if we could talk about how you could make the best use of the time we have together.

IMMEDIACY

Immediacy is a tool for exploring, evaluating, and deepening counselling relationships. The goal of immediacy is to strengthen the counselling relationship. Egan (1998) describes two major types of immediacy: relationship immediacy and here-and-now immediacy.

Relationship Immediacy

Relationship immediacy refers to the process of evaluating the general working climate of the counsellor–client relationship. The focus is not on a particular incident but on the way the relationship has developed and how it is helping or standing in the way of progress. "The relationship is evaluated or reviewed, and relationship strengths and weaknesses are examined by exploring the respective feelings, hopes, and frustrations of the parties involved" (Shebib, 1997:114).

Relationship immediacy might be used effectively when feelings such as anger, resentment, or resistance to the work seem to be adversely affecting the relationship. Similarly, positive feelings of liking or attraction might also need to be addressed if these feelings are clouding objectivity or progress. The example below illustrates how a counsellor might initiate relationship immediacy.

> **Counsellor:** *I want to put aside what we've been talking about and take a look at what's happening between us. I think we have great rapport, and we both seem relaxed when we're together. But I believe I've become reluctant to be totally honest. Maybe it's because I don't want the relationship to become unpleasant. If I'm not mistaken, you seem to hold back too.*

DIALOGUE	ANALYSIS
Counsellor: This might be a good time to pause and talk about how we might work together. Then we'll both have a shared sense of direction.	A simple, nonjargonistic statement initiates the contracting process. The importance of contracting is identified.
Client: Yes, I was wondering where we go from here.	
Counsellor: Perhaps you have some ideas on what you'd like to achieve. I'd like to hear them. Then, if you wish, I can add some of my own.	By seeking input, the counsellor communicates respect for the client's needs and signals that the counsellor is not going to take control and make all the decisions. This helps to empower the client and minimize any tendency for the client to become overly dependent.
Client: As I told you, my big goal is to keep my son alive. I don't want to receive a call from the hospital saying he has overdosed.	
Counsellor: Whether your son uses drugs is not under your control. But we could talk about some of the ways you could deal with his behaviour, such as how to handle when he breaks curfew or what to do when you think he's high.	The counsellor attempts to gently contain the work within areas that the client can control, namely her behaviour.
Client: That would be great! Those are two of my biggest problems.	The client's reaction confirms understanding and provides agreement on one target for work.
Counsellor: Obviously, this is a time of stress for you. One of the ways I may be able to work with you is to help you deal with your feelings. Sometimes you might feel overwhelmed by everything that's happening, and I'd be happy just to listen or to help you sort out your feelings.	Counsellors can use statements of purpose to suggest additional ideas to help clients make the best use of the services available. In this statement, the counsellor attempts to introduce feelings as one of the areas on which counselling might focus.
Client: You have no idea how tough this has been for me as a single parent. My father was addicted to alcohol, and my son brings back all those memories.	The client's willingness to begin to share some of her feelings signals to the counsellor that she has accepted the offer to explore feelings.
Counsellor: So, you're no stranger to the pain that is caused by addiction.	Empathy is the preferred response to strong feelings.
(five minutes later)	*(continued)*

Counsellor: What do you need and want from our relationship?

Client: I want you to be honest with me.

Counsellor: What do you mean?

Client: Don't try to spare my feelings. If you think I'm wrong, say so. Don't sugarcoat the truth.

Counsellor: So, if I have some ideas about how you might do things differently or another way of looking at things, I'll just tell you.

Client: Exactly.

Counsellor: Can I expect the same from you?

Client (hesitates): I guess so.

Counsellor: You seem unsure. Would it be tough to confront me if you thought I was wrong?

Client: I'm the kind of person who likes to keep those kinds of things inside.

Counsellor: Sometimes it makes sense to hold back. But it's better to have choices. I'd like to convince you to risk telling me the truth. Then you can decide if that works better, at least in dealing with me.

(a few minutes later)

Client: About a year ago, I went to a family counsellor for help. That was a disaster.

Counsellor: You might be worried that this will turn out the same way.

Client: Yes.

Counsellor: Now I'm worried too. (counsellor and client laugh) Tell me what went wrong; then

This work sets the stage for feedback. It gives the counsellor a clear picture of the client's preferred style. Knowing this, the counsellor can tailor any feedback to fit the client's expectations.

Notice that the counsellor makes no assumptions of meaning and asks the client to define the vague term "honest." Later, if the counsellor wishes to challenge the client, he or she can use an introductory statement such as the following to remind the client of the contract: "Remember when we agreed that if I had some ideas that were different from yours, I should be honest?" Because there has been prior agreement, the client is more likely to support the process and to be open to feedback or challenges.

Some clients have trouble dealing with persons in authority. Others are simply shy and have habitual patterns of taking a passive approach to relationship problems. The counselling relationship can be an opportunity to experiment with new ways of relating. When counsellors create conditions of safety for risk taking, clients can learn skills that they can transfer to other relationships.

The purpose of this process is not to engage the client in a gossip session about the mistakes of colleagues. Candid discussions about what was effective and ineffective provide important information on the client's expectations and fears for the current relationship. This gives the counsellor a chance to customize counselling to

(continued)

we can talk about how we can avoid the same problems here. Just tell me what happened, but don't tell me who your counsellor was.

Client: Well, for one thing, he never gave me any information. If I asked for a brochure or something on heroin, he'd always say sure, then he'd forget.

(a few minutes later)

Counsellor: Do you have any questions?

Client: Who gets to see my file?

meet the needs and wants of the client. Reviewing the client's counselling history may enable both the client and the counsellor to learn and build on the mistakes of the past. Of course, this discussion must be conducted in a professional manner that does not involve maligning colleagues.

A little shared humour adds warmth to the relationship.

Discussion regarding the limits of confidentiality and any other ethical concerns that the client has can now be addressed.

Remember that the counselling contract should be reviewed on a regular basis. Exploration of problems may promote insight, and this may lead to changed expectations and revised goals. As the counselling relationship matures, the roles of counsellors and their clients must also evolve.

Here-and-Now Immediacy

Here-and-now immediacy focuses on counsellor–client interactions as they occur within the interview. With here-and-now immediacy, counsellors reveal their current feelings and perspectives. Here-and-now immediacy addresses and deals with relationship issues such as tension, lack of trust, and lack of direction in the session (Egan, 1998; Young 1998).

All relationships, including the counselling relationship, are occasionally tested with minor or serious personality conflicts and communication breakdowns. Describing the counselling relationship, Compton and Galaway conclude that "it is not necessarily pleasant or friendly. Sometimes the problem is worked out in reaction and anger (1999:175). Handled wisely, these conflicts have the potential to deepen rather than impair relationships.

Here-and-now immediacy is a tool for preventing communication breakdowns. By addressing relationship difficulties as they arise, more serious problems are prevented from developing from the build-up of unresolved feelings. This does not imply that every relationship issue must be explored. Here-and-now immediacy should address significant feelings and issues that affect the relationship as they occur, but it is important for counsellors to be sensitive to timing and pacing. Generally, here-and-now immediacy should **not** be introduced when a session is ending, when there is no time for resolution, or before sufficient trust has developed. However, immediacy has the potential to build trust.

Counsellors can ensure the appropriateness of using here-and-now immediacy by asking: Would immediacy be useful for the client? Does the client have the capacity (personal strength and resources) to profit from immediacy at this time? Immediacy is a way to get closer to clients.

In the following example, the counsellor uses here-and-now immediacy to identify a sharp change in the mood of the interview.

Example 1:

Counsellor: *You seem to have become somewhat quiet. When I ask a question, you give me one- or two-word answers. Usually, you're quite expressive. Is something wrong?*

Client: *Now that you mention it, yes. I'm just not sure how much I'm willing to trust you. At first it was okay, but now you seem intent on pushing me to deal with things I'd rather keep private.*

Counsellor: *Perhaps I'm moving too fast or bringing up issues we haven't agreed to talk about.*

Client: *Mostly, you don't take no for an answer. When I say I don't want to talk about something, I mean it.*

Counsellor: *Like earlier today when I kept coming back to how you felt when you broke up with your wife.*

Client: *That's a perfect example.*

Counsellor: *I guess I was pushy. I knew you would rather avoid the topic. At the same time, I could see that there was so much pain involved that I thought it might be useful to talk about your feelings.*

Client: *You're probably right. I should face it, but I'm afraid.*

When responding with immediacy, it is important to use **I-statements** to underscore responsibility and ownership of feelings. In general, the emphasis should be on statements such as "I'm uncomfortable," not "You make me feel uncomfortable."

Example 2:

Counsellor: *Let's stop for a moment. I'm feeling confused, and I'm not sure where we're headed. What's happening for you?*

Client: *We do seem to be headed in circles. I'm lost too.*

Counsellor: *All right, let's talk about how we can get back on track.*

In Interview 3.2, the counsellor uses immediacy to address concerns that his client has become dependent. Initially, the client is reluctant to discuss this issue, but the counsellor's persistence sets the stage for the client to emerge with some important feedback. Changes in the relationship can then be negotiated. Moreover, the process models communication and relationship problem-solving skills that are transferable to other situations.

Transference

Transference is a concept first introduced by Freud to describe the tendency of clients to communicate with their counsellors in the same way that they communicated with significant people in the past. Transference can include reactions of both attraction and aversion. When transference is strong, clients have intense feelings and reactions that are unconnected to experiences with their counsellors. Transference is likely present when there are strong feelings of liking or disliking another person on the basis of first impressions (Young, 1998). For example, a client might relate to the authority of a counsellor with the same withdrawal and inner anger that characterized earlier relationships with parents. In addition, as Egan notes, "Some of the difficulties clients have in their day-to-day relationships are also reflected in their relationships to helpers. For instance, if they are compliant outside, they are often compliant in the helping process. If they become aggressive and angry with authority figures outside, they often do the same with helpers" (1998:180).

INTERVIEW 3.2	IMMEDIACY

DIALOGUE	ANALYSIS
Counsellor: I'd like to suggest that we take a few minutes to talk about you and me. I think it might be useful to look at what's working and what's not working.	The counsellor signals an interest in looking at the relationship and provides a brief rationale (relationship immediacy).
Client: I think it's been great. You always seem to know what to say. I don't know if I could cope if it weren't for you.	Many clients are uncomfortable with immediacy discussions, perhaps because of past failures. The client's praise of the counsellor may be justified, or it may be an attempt to avoid the issue.
Counsellor: Thanks. To be honest, I have mixed reactions to what you're saying. It's nice to be appreciated, but I'm also concerned. I wonder if by relying on me so much, it's becoming harder for you to do it on your own.	The counsellor discloses feelings (here-and-now immediacy).
Client: I can't do it on my own.	Without attempting to argue with the client, the counsellor gently persists in encouraging the client to look at the issue. The client is able to identify an important parallel to her relationship with her father (transference).
Counsellor: Okay, so you need help. Being able to seek and accept help is a sign of strength. My concern is that I may be doing things for you that you need to do yourself.	
Client: Now you sound like my father. He's always saying that I should stand on my own two feet more and not rely on him so much. But every time I try to be independent, he interferes.	
Counsellor: Does that happen between you and me?	
Client (hesitates): A little.	
Counsellor: Can you elaborate?	The counsellor uses a simple probe to make sure that he understands. An empathic response recognizes the client's **ambivalence**, or mixed feelings. Asking for an example is important to confirm that both counsellor and client have the same reference point.
Client: Don't get me wrong, I really want your help, but sometimes it seems like you've already decided what I should do. I figure that you probably know what is best, so I just go along with your plan.	
Counsellor: It sounds as though you have mixed feelings. On the one hand, you value my help,	*(continued)*

but at the same time, I also sense some reluctance. I wonder if part of you knows it isn't good for you if you don't have the freedom to make your own decisions.

Client: That's right.

Counsellor: Can you think of a recent example? I want to make sure I understand.

Client: Earlier today when I mentioned that I wanted to go back to school, you were really supportive, and I appreciated that. But it seemed like you were bulldozing me to take art. I like to paint, but it's a hobby, not something I want to pursue as a career.

Counsellor: That's a good point. Thanks for the feedback. Let's talk about how we can change our relationship to avoid similar problems. I'll try to be more sensitive to interfering. I'll need your help. If you think I'm pushing, will you tell me?

Client: I promise to do that.

Immediacy enables the counsellor and the client to negotiate changes in their relationship.

Below are some examples of relationships in which client transference is apparent:

- Kevin desperately wants to be liked. He gives his counsellor unsolicited praise and gifts. Increasingly, he begins to act and talk like his counsellor.
- Claire suffered abuse from her father and both of her brothers. In the first session with a male counsellor, she immediately begins to cry, despite the fact that she felt optimistic and self-confident before she entered his office.
- Amar has a strong need for approval. He withholds information that he thinks might provoke the counsellor's disagreement.
- Jaimie, a six-year-old who has been abused, behaves in a sexually provocative way.
- Toby, age eighteen, has had a very strained relationship with his father. His counsellor notes how easily he becomes angry during the interview at the slightest provocation.

With transference, unresolved issues result in distortions in the way that others are perceived. Consequently, successful examination and resolution of counsellor–client relationship difficulties helps clients develop communication and problem resolution skills that will be useful to them in their daily lives. It is important that counsellors distinguish client reactions and feelings that arise from the current relationship from those that arise from transference. Counsellors should not be too quick to rationalize clients' feelings and behaviours as transference. Their clients' responses may be valid reactions to what has transpired in the counselling session.

Countertransference

Countertransference is the tendency of counsellors to inappropriately transfer feelings and behaviours to clients. Young views countertransference as an ethical issue that should be addressed by supervision so counsellors can get help to "monitor the tendency to be too helpful, and to deal with feelings of sexual attraction as well as anger, fear, and insecurity" (1998:169). Corey and Corey warn of the dangers of countertransference: "The emotionally intense relationships that develop with your clients can be expected to bring your unresolved conflicts to the surface. Because countertransference may be a form of identification with your client, you can easily get lost in the client's world, and thus your value as a helper becomes limited" (1989:94).

Countertransference issues are emotional reactions to clients, whereby counsellors come to see clients as projects, sexual objects, friends, or even extensions of themselves (Young, 1998:169). Below are some signs that countertransference is happening or that a risk for countertransference is present for counsellors:

- having intense feelings (e.g., irritation, anger, boredom, sexual attraction) for clients you hardly know
- feeling attraction or repulsion
- being reluctant to confront or tending to avoid sensitive issues or feelings
- continually running overtime with certain clients and wishing that others would not show up for scheduled appointments
- acting with rescuing behaviour, such as by wanting to lend money, adopt abused children, or protect clients
- thinking about client similarities to other people you know
- dealing with clients who have problems or personal histories similar to your own
- employing unnecessary or excessive self-disclosure
- feeling reluctant to end the counselling relationship

CONVERSATION 3.2

SELF-DISCLOSURE

STUDENT: I think that many counsellors misunderstand self-disclosure. Some of my colleagues make a point of telling their clients about their past, whereas others share little or nothing about their private lives.

TEACHER: Counsellor self-disclosure can be an important part of effective counselling. The problem is knowing what to share, how much to share, and when to share it.

STUDENT: I agree. I think some disclosure conveys that the counsellor is warm and human, and it helps clients overcome the common mistaken belief that they are the only ones with problems.

TEACHER: Self-disclosure models appropriate sharing of feelings and gives clients the courage to open up. Some clients may feel reassured knowing that their counsellors have faced similar problems. But unless it's handled carefully, clients may see their counsellors as needy.

STUDENT: Back to your earlier statement. What do you share? How much? When?

TEACHER: The answers vary depending on the client and the situation. In general, a moderate level of self-disclosure is appropriate (Cormier & Cormier, 1985). But some situations may warrant a great deal of self-disclosure, and some none at all. Depending on the situation, too much self-disclosure may be as bad as too little.

STUDENT: As I see it, the most important principle is that self-disclosure should be an option, not a compulsion. Counsellors need to be able to self-disclose, but they also should be able to constrain themselves from always disclosing. If the session is moving smoothly without self-disclosure, then it's probably unnecessary. Self-disclosure must strengthen the relationship or otherwise contribute to the work. The primary goal is to meet the client's needs.

TEACHER: That's right. For me, the most important principle is to avoid letting counsellor self-disclosure shift the focus of the interview from clients to counsellors. That leads to role reversal, with clients counselling counsellors. As I said earlier, too much self-disclosure leads clients to see counsellors as incapable and lose confidence in the process and the capacity of their counsellors to help. The counselling relationship is not mutual, with each person taking turns sharing a problem. What's often forgotten is the fact that self-disclosure involves more than sharing details of your past or your personal problems. Sharing your feelings with clients about the relationship or the work is also self-disclosure and a key element of the skill of immediacy. Rogers (1961; 1980), a central figure in counselling and the founder of client-centred (person-centred) therapy, emphasized the importance of being transparent and real in the relationship by sharing moment-to-moment feelings that are relevant to the relationship. After all, if we can't be open about our feelings, how can we expect clients to be?

Dependent Relationships

A **dependent relationship** arises when clients become overly reliant on their counsellors for decision making. Common indicators that a dependent relationship exists include excessive permission seeking, frequent phone calls or office visits for information, and an inability to make simple decisions or take action without consulting the counsellor. A dependent relationship undermines the principle of self-determination by shifting power away from clients and preventing them from developing independence.

Reactions to Power and Authority

Transference happens to some degree in all relationships, but it is much more likely to occur in relationships in which authority is present. However, to some extent, all counselling relationships involve power and authority. Counsellors may have roles of authority when clients have clear social control issues. Moreover, counsellors such as probation and parole officers have formal power, or they work with clients as part of a court order. Counsellors may also have power because clients perceive them as having superior or expert knowledge. Some counsellors, such as those in welfare settings, have control over services and benefits that clients are seeking. Clients also may react to other variables, such as age, socioeconomic status, position, gender, marital status, appearance, size, intelligence, and social demeanour.

Need for Empowerment

Often, clients come to counselling with low self-esteem and confidence. Seligman's (1975) concept of **learned helplessness** is a useful perspective for understanding. He suggests that individuals can become demoralized through failure to the point that they give up trying to alter their circumstances, even in situations in which change is possible. Persons with learned helplessness can be difficult and frustrating to work with because "to initiate changes, you must envision that your actions are possible and your effort will make a difference. You must believe that you are capable of taking action and garnering resources to augment your own" (DuBois & Miley, 1996:24). Persons who have learned helplessness do not believe that their efforts will make a difference.

In addition, if clients are locked into seeing themselves as victims, they are likely to resist change; or they may enter into dependency relationships in which they relinquish power and control to others, including their counsellors. In working with clients who show signs of learned helplessness, counsellors must remember that "helplessness is a perception and not an accurate description of an individual" (Arnhold & Razak, 1991:102). The reality is that "many who are afflicted with crippling low self-esteem are in fact quite capable in some respects—the problem is that they think and feel otherwise about themselves" (p. 102).

Counsellors need to be self-aware so that they may take steps to manage their own unmet needs that might impede their capacity to be helpful. For example, if they have a high need for control, they can potentially take power from clients, who for their part, may freely give it away. The concept of **empowerment** gives priority to assisting clients to maintain or assume control over their lives. Empowerment is concerned with giving clients access to resources and enabling clients to achieve a sense of control over matters that affect their lives. As clients become empowered, there is an increase in their self-respect, confidence, knowledge, and skills.

Strategies for Empowering Clients

Counsellors who are committed to empowering their clients must start with a basic belief that their clients are capable of managing their own lives. They must relinquish the mistaken notion that clients depend on them for advice, decision making, and problem solving. Clients are empowered when they participate in decisions about counselling goals and procedures.

An empowerment attitude gives priority to clients' capacities and strengths. Thus, counsellors should search for and recognize their clients' strengths and resources. Questions and statements can be used to shift the focus of the interview in this direction, such as "What's working well for you?" "Let's talk about how you were able to cope with this problem for so long." "When you were able to manage, what were you doing that helped you succeed?" "Why don't we take an inventory of your strengths?" Sometimes counsellors can offer other perspectives that empower. For example, responding to a woman who has struggled for six months to find work and get off welfare, a counsellor might say, "I'm impressed with your ability to hang in there. Many people would have given up." Ignoring or questioning self-depreciating remarks that reinforce low self-esteem are other choices for focusing on strength.

The principle of self-determination introduced in Chapter 2 promotes empowerment by helping clients recognize choices and encouraging them to make independent decisions. To avoid promoting unhealthy client dependency, counsellors should not do for clients what clients can and should do for themselves. Furthermore, when clients are successful as a result of their actions, their confidence and self-esteem increase. Counsellors should acknowledge and give clients credit for their success.

Strengths Approach

Clients are often besieged by debilitating problems and chaos. Counsellors cannot ignore real problems; but in the process, they should not focus all their attention on problem situations and what is dysfunctional in their clients' lives. Counsellors should adopt a strengths approach to clients in order to acquire a balanced perspective. The strengths approach assumes the inherent capacity of people. Individuals and communities are seen to have assets and resources that can be mobilized for problem solving. Sheafor and Horejsi (2006), Saleeby (2002), Glicken (2004) and others have discussed techniques and guidelines for maintaining a focus on client strengths. Their work suggests the following guidelines for the strengths approach:

1. Trust that clients have the capacity to change, and that they can learn to cope with their problems and challenges. Every experienced counsellor can relate amazing stories of people who have recovered from adversity and overwhelming odds.

2. Stay interested in strengths. Acknowledge clients' skills, resourcefulness, motivation, and virtues. When workers value their clients' strengths, clients learn to value themselves. Discovering overlooked abilities, knowledge, and experience can also energize counsellors and clients. Look for strengths in the way clients have handled adversity with comments and questions such as: You've been through a lot in your life, but somehow you've managed to survive. How have you been able to do this? Or you might say: In what ways have your problems made you stronger?

3. Ask questions or make statements that uncover strengths, such as: Think of a time when you were able to handle problems such as this. What skills and resources enabled you to cope? What are the things in your life that you feel good about? What's working well for you? What would your friends say are your best qualities?

4. Negotiate a partnership with clients where they share responsibility for identifying priorities, goals, and preferred ways of proceeding. Accept that they are the "experts" on their own lives, and with encouragement, they can make decisions on what will and will not work. Counsellors need to be flexible and accept that every intervention plan will be individualized to the unique needs and attributes of each client. What works with one client may be counterproductive with another.

5. Avoid diagnostic labels as a way of describing clients. Labels tend to ignore strengths by focusing on pathology and deficits.

6. Focus on problem solving and goal setting rather that on discussions of blame or on finding the root causes of current behaviour or problems. There may be cathartic benefit to discussing history, but once this purpose is achieved the focus of the work should shift to present and future events. Goal setting energizes clients to action and mobilizes their resources and motivation for change.

7. Keep in mind that families, neighbourhoods, and communities have formal and informal resources that are potential sources of help and strength for clients. Challenge clients to identify and discover these resources. Ask questions such as: Who do you trust? Who supports you when you need help? Use community directories to pinpoint agencies, services, and self-help groups that could be supportive.

ENDING THE COUNSELLING RELATIONSHIP

Counselling relationships vary in length from a single interview or a short encounter to many years. Some are superficial, with minimal emotional investment by the participants, while others result in considerable intimacy and emotional involvement. But all relationships, regardless of their length, have the potential to be intimate. The counselling relationship is not designed to be permanent; but owing to its intimacy, the ending of the relationship may trigger powerful feelings and behaviours in both clients and counsellors. For some clients, intense satisfaction and feelings of accomplishment punctuate their success, but others may feel abandoned and deserted. The ending may remind them of the pain and sadness of other endings, and they may need help dealing with their loss and grief (Shebib, 1997; Shulman, 1999). Hess and McCartt Hess note that the end of the helping relationship brings attention to the fact that "the impending separation is a violation of the wish intrinsic in most meaningful attachments that the relationship would remain permanently active" (1984:561).

The initial reaction of both clients and counsellors to a pending termination of an intimate counselling relationship is often denial (Hess & McCartt Hess, 1984; Shulman, 1999). Counsellors need to be sensitive to signals that clients are having trouble with endings. Some clients who have shown progress might regress to previous ways of coping, or they may present new and complex concerns that seem to say, "I'm not ready for this to end."

Other clients might express their pain about the ending by expressing unfounded anger and resentment (in effect, avoiding the pain of the ending or denying the importance of the relationship). Still others fail to show up for the final meeting as another way to avoid dealing with the pain of the ending.

Counsellors who have invested heavily in the relationship also have to deal with their own feelings about the ending. This may result in a variety of denial reactions:

- Denial of the ending by allowing or encouraging clients to remain in counselling longer than necessary. The counselling relationship is not designed to be lifelong. The counselling contract should include defining an end point to the relationship. As well, individual interviews should be structured within a time frame. A defined time frame helps to focus and contain the work. Excessively long interviews without time controls can lead to fatigue, unnecessary repetition, and inattention.

- Denial of the ending by making false or unrealistic concessions or promises (for example, by promising to visit or correspond with clients)

- Denial of feelings by behaving apathetically or avoiding discussion of feelings about the ending

- Denial of feelings by abruptly ending without warning

Dealing with Endings

One way to assist clients in dealing with endings, including denial responses, is to teach them about "the predictable reactions to loss and to aid them in identifying those reactions when either directly or indirectly expressed" (Hess & McCartt Hess, 1984:561). The ending phase, when handled effectively, offers rich potential for work. Surprisingly, many books on counselling do not examine the therapeutic possibilities of the ending phase.

DIALOGUE	ANALYSIS
Counsellor: If I'm not mistaken, you look a little glum today.	The counsellor risks empathy by picking up on nonverbal cues from the client. The counsellor suspects that the client's anger may be connected to the ending of the relationship.
Client: Can't you ever let anything pass? Why don't you just get off my back?	The client's first reaction is to deny his feelings by discounting the value and importance of the relationship.
Counsellor: Tomorrow, you will be leaving the centre to return home. Maybe we could talk about that. I'm wondering how you feel about it. I wouldn't be surprised if you had mixed feelings of being happy to be leaving, but also sad to be leaving your friends here.	
Client: It's no big deal, but why should you care?	
Counsellor: I feel sad knowing you're leaving. We've become very close, and I'll miss our time together.	By sharing her own feelings, the counsellor communicates her willingness to deal with emotions. This acts as a model for the client. Of course, any feelings the counsellor shares must be genuine.
Client: It's been all right. I guess you're okay.	
Counsellor: Thanks, and you're okay with me too. (ten seconds of silence) How do you feel about us not seeing each other anymore?	Although his anger softens, he is still reluctant to acknowledge his feelings. The counsellor persists.
Client: I wish it wasn't happening. I don't know if I'm ready to go.	Although the client has trouble labelling his feelings, he begins to open up. The counsellor uses empathy to acknowledge the feelings suggested by the client's remark.
Counsellor: It's very scary thinking about leaving.	
Client: I want to go home, but my mother and I always seem to end up fighting. You and I can talk and not fight. Why can't it be that way with my mother?	The client risks talking about his feelings about going home. The counsellor tries to get the client to accept credit for success in the counselling relationship. She challenges him to consider how he can transfer some of his behaviour in the client–counsellor relationship to his relationship with his mother.
Counsellor: Maybe you have more control than you think. What do you do differently with me than with your mother?	

With trust firmly established in the relationship and the urgency of the end approaching, clients may broach significant themes and topics in the ending phase (Shulman, 1999). Shulman (1999) describes the phenomenon of **doorknob communication**, whereby clients bring up important issues at the end of the interview/relationship when there is little or no time to address them. Clients are typically ambivalent about dealing with the issues, but their need to address them finally overcomes their need to avoid them.

A second strategy is for counsellors to honestly express their feelings about the termination of the relationship. This models appropriate sharing for clients, and it stimulates them to risk sharing their reactions and feelings. Of course, this discussion requires counsellors to be open to strong feelings, such as sadness and anger. Shulman (1999) underscores the importance of counsellors sharing their own feelings, but he acknowledges that this is a difficult skill to develop. In part, this difficulty arises from the fact that counsellors may be struggling with their own sense of loss as they prepare to end their relationship with a valued client. Continued self-examination can help counsellors develop self-awareness about their own behaviours and feelings regarding endings and separations.

Interview 3.3 illustrates how the ending process can be used to address feelings. The client is a young adolescent about to be discharged from a residential treatment centre. For the last six weeks, he and his counsellor have been actively planning for his return home. The client has been looking forward to more freedom and release from the rules and restrictions of the centre. As part of his prerelease planning, he has spent two weekends with his family.

SUMMARY

The counselling relationship is negotiated in order to assist clients to achieve defined goals. Developing and sustaining an effective counselling relationship is widely accepted as critical to success in counselling. It is characterized by some of the same elements of a deep friendship; but it differs in important ways, such as its time-limited nature and its emphasis on goal achievement.

Over the four phases of counselling—preliminary, beginning, action, and ending—the counselling relationship needs to be developed, sustained, and then ended. Throughout all phases, counsellor warmth, empathy, and genuineness are essential.

The counselling contract is an important tool that enables counsellors and their clients to agree on their respective roles and the purpose of the counselling relationship. There are two types of contracts, relationship or engagement contract and sessional contract. Contracting is a continuous process throughout the helping relationship, with periodic revisions based on changing client needs and priorities. Counselling relationships are formed for one or more broad purposes, such as to offer support, assist with problem solving, help clients learn skills, or help them deal with painful feelings.

Immediacy is a tool for exploring, evaluating, and deepening counselling relationships. Relationship immediacy refers to the process of evaluating the general working climate of the counsellor–client relationship. Here-and-now immediacy focuses on counsellor–client interactions as they occur within the interview.

Counsellor self-disclosure has an important place in counselling. But counsellors must use it intelligently to ensure that it meets the needs of their clients and that it does not move the focus of the interview away from their clients.

Transference is the tendency of clients to communicate with their counsellors in the same way that they communicated with significant people in their past. Countertransference is the tendency of counsellors to inappropriately transfer feelings and behaviours to clients. It is important that counsellors are able to distinguish between client reactions and feelings that arise from the current relationship and those that arise from transference. All counselling relationships involve power and authority; thus, clients are particularly vulnerable to transference reactions.

Persons with learned helplessness believe that change is not possible through their own efforts. Counsellors need to look for ways to empower such individuals so that they can assume control over their lives. The strengths approach assumes the inherent capacity of people, individuals, and communities as having assets and resources that can be mobilized for problem solving.

The inevitable ending of the counselling relationship may trigger powerful feelings in both clients and counsellors. The ending phase, when handled effectively, offers rich potential for work.

EXERCISES

1. What were (or are) the attributes of your most positive relationship with another person? The most negative? How can you use this information to be a more effective counsellor?

2. Interview friends and colleagues on the topics of warmth, empathy, and genuineness. Ask them to describe how they know when someone exhibits these inner qualities.

3. Talk to people who are happy in their work. Ask them to describe how they sustain their energy and enthusiasm.

4. Pay attention to the people you see and meet over the next week. Who evokes strong emotional reactions? Who seems most similar to your parents or other authority figures? Now examine your feelings and try to identify transference reactions—feelings that you carry over from prior relationships and that are not based on objective reactions to the current relationship.

5. Orchestrate an immediacy encounter. Contract with a colleague with whom you have a working relationship to spend one hour evaluating and strengthening your relationship. Use the following open-ended statements to develop themes for your discussion, but be sure to explore your ideas and responses:
   - The thing I value most in this relationship is…
   - The one thing that is missing in our relationship is…
   - When I first met you, my reaction was…
   - You are most like…
   - When I think about sharing feelings with you…
   - In order for us to become closer, I would have to…
   - What I want most from you is…
   - When I think of the future of our relationship, I…

   Periodically, share how you are feeling using a statement such as "Right now I am feeling…" You are free to add other significant themes in your relationship that are not suggested in the above list. When you are finished, discuss what changes you would like to make in your relationship.

6. Imagine that you wished to use immediacy in each of the following situations. Develop an introductory response to begin the encounter.

   a. You are dealing with a client who hints that he or she is sexually attracted to you.
   b. You are counselling a client who has become demanding.
   c. You are feeling confused and you are not sure what to do next in the interview.
   d. Your client continually questions your training.

7. Do you agree with the observation made by Keith-Lucas (1972:18) that "the attempt to keep the relationship on a pleasant level is the greatest source of ineffectual helping known"? Examine your own needs with respect to keeping the counselling relationship warm and pleasant. How far would you go to ensure this as an outcome? Under what conditions might you need to sacrifice pleasantness?

8. Imagine that you are the designated counsellor in each of the following situations and that you are about to see each client for the first time. What barriers might you anticipate in developing a relationship with each client? Develop a relationship-building strategy.

   a. Hospital setting: A man, age 64, has just learned that he has terminal lung cancer. The ward nurses tell you that he is angry with his doctor and that he blames him for not making an earlier diagnosis.
   b. A young woman (age 21) has just been released from prison and is about to see you, her probation officer. Reports from the prison note that she has considerable difficulty dealing with persons in authority.
   c. Employment counselling setting: A man with 25 years' experience and four university degrees has been laid off after 15 years with the same company. As you walk to your office, he remarks, "I don't see the point of this. I think this is a big waste of time, but the company is paying for it, so I might as well get all I can."
   d. School counselling office: A teenager is referred by her teacher, who suspects that she might be using drugs.
   e. Crisis line: A man, age 33, is threatening suicide.
   f. Health clinic, working with a physician colleague: A woman is HIV positive. Your task is to tell her about her HIV-positive diagnosis.
   g. Home visit: You are a social worker interviewing parents to investigate anonymous allegations that their children are suffering physical abuse.
   h. Mediation centre: You are working with a couple who have sought mediation assistance to work out custody and visiting rights.
   i. Community counselling agency: The client, age 35, has a long history at the agency. Other counsellors have noted that the client has a tendency to become dependent and makes daily phone calls for advice.
   j. Transition home: A woman is returning to the house for the third time after being severely abused by her husband. On previous occasions, she has vowed never to go back to her husband, but each time she has reconciled.
   k. A mental health counselling centre: A man is seeking assistance for depression. He has considerable difficulty relating to women.

9. What are the issues (pros and cons) involved in counselling friends?

10. This exercise is designed to expand your self-awareness regarding issues that might affect your counselling relationships. Complete each sentence quickly, without attempting to edit your thoughts.

   - The one thing I have to have from other people is...
   - What's missing in my personal life is...
   - Something that people do that bothers me is...
   - The one type of person I'd hate to work with is...
   - Relationships would be better if...
   - What I like most about people is...
   - What I dislike most about people is...

11. Most of us tend to repeat established patterns when we begin new relationships. Seek feedback from others who know you and explore questions such as the following:

   - What first impressions are you likely to leave with others?
   - How do their perceptions compare with your intentions or inner feelings?
   - Now consider the following questions:
   - What are your typical feelings, thoughts, and behaviours as you begin new relationships?
   - How are beginnings the same or different for you when you are relating to different individuals or groups (for example, clients, colleagues, or supervisors)?
   - What works for you?
   - What doesn't?

12. Based on your observations and insights from the previous question, begin the process of developing a range of different skills and strategies for beginning relationships. This will help you avoid becoming locked into established patterns. Define personal goals for development related to how you handle beginnings. As part of this, detail three different beginning styles you wish to add to your skill repertoire. Describe when and how you will experiment with these three approaches. What problems do you anticipate might interfere with achievement of these goals?

13. Think about significant relationships in your life that have ended because of separation, death, or other reasons. How did you respond emotionally and behaviourally to these endings? In retrospect, are there things you wish you had said or not said? What remains unresolved in these relationships? (Suggestion: If this exercise evokes strong emotions, you may find it useful to debrief with a friend or colleague.)

14. In your answer to the previous question, what behavioural patterns are evident? What are the implications of your insights for your work as a counsellor?

15. Rate the extent to which you think it would be appropriate for you to disclose the information listed below. Use the following scale:

   5 = always appropriate

   4 = usually appropriate

   3 = sometimes appropriate

   2 = usually not appropriate

   1 = never appropriate

Be prepared to defend your answers with examples.

___ a. details of your education and training

___ b. your philosophy of counselling

___ c. information about your age, marital status, and number of children

___ d. your sexual orientation

___ e. particulars about your life, such as personal problems that you have faced

___ f. details about your everyday life, such as your hobbies, reading preferences, and vacation plans

___ g. intimate details about your personal life, such as marital problems and recovery from addictions

___ h. feelings such as anger, boredom, confusion, or sexual attraction that are influencing the interview

To what extent were your answers influenced by your comfort level with each of the categories?

16. Under what conditions do you think it would be wise for a counsellor to avoid self-disclosure?

17. Evaluate your general comfort with self-disclosure. What areas of your life are you reluctant or unwilling to talk about? To what extent would your friends and colleagues describe you as open or closed? Do you tend to be guarded about sharing information, or do you generally disclose a great deal to others? How does your comfort with disclosure vary depending on whom you are talking with (e.g., family, friends, authority figures, clients, colleagues, strangers)?

18. What are the implications of your answers to the previous question for your work as a counsellor?

19. Evaluate the potential appropriateness of each of the following counsellor self-disclosures (the counsellor is speaking to a client).

a. Your situation reminds me of my own problems. Maybe we can pool our energies and find a solution that works for both of us.

b. I'm sorry to say that it's none of your business whether I have children.

c. When my husband abused me for the first time, I knew the marriage was over and I left.

d. Addictions treatment centre, meeting a client for the first time: Hi, I'm John and I'm a recovering alcoholic, so I know what you're going through.

e. I'm feeling confused. I think we need to stop for a minute and decide where we're going.

f. Your problems are really getting to me. They remind me so much of my own struggles. They bring back all my pain.

g. You have the most beautiful eyes.

h. I like what you're wearing today. It's really sexy.

i. Generally, I like to try to establish open communication in my relationships, so I push myself to be open with my feelings even when it's difficult.

j. Your attitude really makes me want to just give up on you.

k. This has been a bad day for me. There have been some cutbacks at the agency and I'm worried about losing my job, so if I seem a little preoccupied today I hope you'll understand.

l. What a weekend! We partied all night. I could hardly make it to work today.

20. Describe how counsellor self-disclosure might be appropriate in response to each of the following client statements or questions. Suggest a response.

   a. Have you ever felt so angry that you wanted to kill someone?
   b. My mother never gives me the support I need.
   c. I began using drugs when I was 11.
   d. Are you gay?
   e. I'm terrified about going back to school. I don't think I can handle it. It's been so many years since I wrote an essay or read a book.
   f. My teenage son is driving me crazy.
   g. I think this counselling session is a waste of time.
   h. I really like you.
   i. I don't think anyone has ever been as depressed as I am.

 WEBLINKS

"The Foundation of Person-Centered Therapy" by Jerold D. Bozarth:
http://personcentered.com/therapist.html

This site contains links to major personality theorists including Carl Rogers:
www.ship.edu/~cgboeree/perscontents.html

chapter four

Listening: The Basis for Understanding

PREVIEW

After reading this chapter you should be able to:

- Define the components and importance of effective listening.
- List common obstacles to listening.
- Describe techniques for overcoming listening obstacles.
- Explain the importance of active listening.
- Describe and demonstrate the components of attending.
- List and explain the multiple meanings of silence in counselling.
- Identify a range of choices for dealing with silence.
- Define and demonstrate paraphrasing skills.
- Define and demonstrate summarizing skills.

THE NATURE OF LISTENING

Listening is defined in Webster's dictionary as "hearing with thoughtful attention." Competent listening involves hearing, observing and responding; it's a complex process that requires sensory, mental, and behavioural competence. Obviously, effective listeners need to hear; but simply hearing words is insufficient for listening. Skilled listeners are sensitive to nonverbal information, such as voice tone and gestures, which support, repeat, enhance, or contradict verbal messages. As a mental process, listening involves separating relevant information from irrelevant information, assigning meaning to words and experiences, remembering, and linking related data. Put simply, listening is making sense of what has been heard. Behaviourally, proficient listeners are dynamic and responsive. They use questions to get clarification, definitions, and examples to ensure that they have enough information to hear what the sender meant for them to hear. They also use summaries and pharaphrases to ensure the accuracy of their observations and conclusions.

The Importance of Listening

Listening is a cornerstone of counselling and is essential to understanding and relationship development. Often clients come to counselling with considerable experience of not being heard. They may have turned to family and friends for help but found that their concerns were discounted or were met with simplistic advice by people who were so anxious to help that they failed to listen with attention. In contrast, effective counsellors and interviewers have a cultivated ability to listen.

As a fundamental building block for the counselling relationship, listening communicates to clients that their ideas and feelings are important. Listening also educates counsellors about the uniqueness of their clients, thus minimizing any tendency to make erroneous assumptions. Moreover, listening encourages clients to tell their stories and disclose their feelings. In the process, they may gain enormous therapeutic value from releasing pent-up emotions. Also, when counsellors listen to clients, clients become better able to listen to themselves. In general, systematic listening, punctuated with appropriate probes, clarification responses, and summaries, helps clients organize confusing and contradictory thoughts.

Listening is an act of acceptance and caring that says, "Your feelings are precious and unique. I won't insult you by assuming that I know what you're going to say before you say it. I won't judge or ridicule what you say. I won't try to change you to fit my idea of what you should be." Listening means joining our clients in understanding their world, their perceptions, and their feelings.

Ironically, while listening requires counsellors to be silent, being silent does not necessarily mean that one is listening. A silent person may hear the words and even be able to repeat verbatim what has been said, but a tape recorder or a clever parrot can do the same thing. Egan (1977) introduced the term *hollow listening* to mean listening without responding. Hollow listeners are silent or use clichés such as "I know just what you mean." Hollow listeners may be attentive to the speaker, nod their heads to signal approval, and look as though they're involved; yet there is very little intimacy to the encounter. As Egan concludes, "The ultimate proof of good listening is good responding" (1977:137).

Listening in its purest form is a search for meaning. Kadushin says:

> Listening is the dynamic process of attaching meaning to what we hear, making sense of aurally received, raw verbal-vocal symbols. It is a purposive and selective process in which the hearer screens, gives attention to, recognizes, comprehends, and interprets sounds communicated by a speaker (1997:50).

Therefore, listening is not a passive act. Effective listeners are busy with the task of trying to comprehend what is happening for their clients. Sometimes, counsellors are patiently quiet as they respectfully yield the right to speak to their clients. At other times, they are vocal, with questions and directives for more detail, example, or clarification. But at all times, they should carefully observe and try to understand nonverbal behaviour. Daly's distinction between perceived listening and actual listening underscores the importance of active involvement in listening: "No matter how effective, skilled, or competent an individual is in listening, unless he or she is perceived as listening by the other interactants, little may be accomplished" (cited in Wolvin & Coakley, 1996:31). Active listening, a collection of skills discussed in this and subsequent chapters, is the way that counsellors show their clients that they are listening. This is possible because they are, in fact, mentally and physically committed to the task of listening.

Good listening can be physically and emotionally exhausting. Nichols noted: "Listening is hard work. It is characterized by faster heart action, quicker circulation of the blood, a small rise in bodily temperature" (cited in Wolvin & Coakley, 1996:29). It requires counsellors to focus all their intellectual and physical attention on clients so that they have the counsellors' unwavering commitment. Listening is the client's reward for talking.

Overcoming Listening Obstacles

Close-minded listeners respect only those who agree with them. Since they already have the "right" answers, there is no need to consider new thoughts and ideas, nor is there any reason to seek additional information. In contrast, open-minded listeners are willing to explore new ideas and are secure enough to hear different opinions without distortion. Open-minded listeners use the following methods:

Being Patient

In order to make themselves understood, people need to be able to frame their ideas. Clients who lack the ability to express themselves, perhaps because they have a limited vocabulary or capacity to articulate in precise terms, use words that are vague, ambiguous, or contradictory. Others may not have sufficient awareness or insight to describe their feelings. In such circumstances, counsellors can become impatient, and this becomes an obstacle to listening. They may try to hurry the process by finishing sentences for clients who are struggling to express themselves. Or they can become lazy and assign their own meanings to words and phrases.

Encouraging Trust

Client messages can be incomplete or missing because of trust issues, particularly in the beginning phase, where the client may be reluctant to share. This is understandable, since the counselling relationship has yet to be tested. Consequently, the client may hold back information or feelings that are ultimately vital for understanding and instead present "safe" issues to test the relationship or only hint at more important concerns. Ideally, as counselling progresses, clients learn that they can depend on their counsellors to respond with respect and understanding. Unfortunately, in some cases, they may learn that their counsellor cannot be trusted with feelings.

Controlling Noise and Staying Focused

Once messages are sent, they must be received and interpreted accurately; hence the importance of a counselling environment that is free from distraction and interruption. Counsellors never discontinue an interview to answer the phone since that may breach confidentiality, impede relationship rapport, and stop the flow of information. Similarly, pagers, fax machines, cell phones, and even an unanswered ringing phone can destroy the ambience of a meeting. Ideally, all such equipment should be turned off.

Good listening is difficult work that requires effort to stay focused. Since we can think many times faster than others can talk, it's easy to allow our thoughts to wander. The trick is to keep our minds busy with listening. Active involvement in listening, through summarizing, paraphrasing, and asking questions, helps counsellors stay alert and focused. Mental involvement helps counsellors concentrate and understand what's being said. For example, as they listen, they can ask themselves, "What does the client mean by that? What are the key points in that explanation?" However, counsellors should avoid trying to figure out what clients are going to say next, since this will only divert their attention from listening.

Internal noise can also interfere with listening. Counsellors might be preoccupied with their own needs or ideas. They could be looking forward to their vacation and imagining their break. They may be under personal stress, suffering from fatigue, or thinking about other clients. A counsellor who is tired might deliberately neglect to explore or define important ideas.

Controlling Assumptions

If counsellors believe that they already know what others are going to say and are not open to new information, then listening is not possible. Apparent patient attention and silence could give the illusion of listening, but assumptions and preconceptions quickly become obvious to astute clients. Typically, clients are guarded and defensive with people who have opinions different from their own. In the example below, a high-school student has just told her counsellor that she has been offered a scholarship at a prestigious university.

> Student: *It's one of the finest universities in the area. It's really quite an honour to have been chosen from all the applicants. My father, who never had a chance to go to university, is ecstatic.*
>
> Counsellor (Choice 1): *Wow! That's terrific. You must be so proud of yourself. This is really an outstanding opportunity.*
>
> Counsellor (Choice 2): *How do you feel about it?*

Choice 1 in this example assumes feelings and meaning. As a result, further exploration is discouraged or cut off. Choice 2 is a listening response that encourages more information. It allows for the possibility that the client might say, "I'm depressed about it. I've been going to school for 12 years, and I really wanted to take a year off." Choice 2 illustrates a basic principle of effective listening: Good listeners are open to learning.

Managing Personal Reactions

What clients say and how they say it may arouse a counsellor's tension and anxiety. Emotions in the client can trigger emotions in the counsellor, which, if unchecked, can lessen the counsellor's capacity to listen. For example, an angry client might stimulate fear in a counsellor who then becomes preoccupied with fear or insecurity and begins to act defensively. A depressed client can have a contagious effect and cause a counsellor to become similarly despondent. Certain words or messages might act as emotional triggers for counsellors and lead to faulty listening and understanding.

Many beginning counsellors react strongly to clients who have been abusive, and they erect listening barriers. They get so trapped in their own need to condemn the abhorrent behaviour that they have no room left to become aware of their clients' frames of reference. Consequently, they fail to establish any base for understanding and any credibility to promote change. Entering into the private world of clients whose behaviour and attitudes differ sharply from one's own requires emotional maturity, skill, and, often, abundant courage. Such capacities distinguish and define competent counsellors.

Sometimes counsellors become bored (for example, when dealing with clients who speak in a monotone, or those who are repetitious and long winded). There are more than a few anecdotes in the field about counsellors who fell asleep during interviews. To stay alert during an interview, counsellors must arrive alert. They should get enough sleep and exercise, and avoid heavy lunches that might lead to drowsiness. Short breaks to take a walk, stretch, or clear the mind are important ways of sustaining energy.

When clients present difficult feelings and topics, some counsellors handle their own discomfort by becoming inappropriately quiet or silent, becoming excessively talkative, changing the subject, or offering premature advice or reassurance. Such responses may communicate that the counsellor does not understand or is not listening or, in the case of inappropriate silence, that the counsellor does not care. Counsellors need to become confident in their skills and abilities so that they can tolerate clients' feelings, reactions and even verbal assaults with a minimum of defensive reactions that obscure listening and understanding.

Knowing That Listening Does Not Mean Agreeing

A common misconception occurs when people confuse listening with agreeing. For example, a person might say, "I told him what I want. Why doesn't he listen to me?" Failure to comply with one's wants and needs is used as evidence that the other person isn't listening. Moreover, some people don't listen because they are afraid that listening will be misconstrued as consent. If each party to an argument clings to his or her own beliefs without hearing the other side, then how is communication possible? Counsellors need to be careful not to succumb to this fallacy. One new counsellor remarked, "If I listen to someone who abuses children, am I not condoning it?" But listening does not mean agreeing. Weaver provides a useful perspective:

> We may listen carefully and at length to the presentation of our opponent. We may question; we may explore; we may do our best to hold our own biases in abeyance as we try to see the world through his eyes. And we may, after all this, decide that our own position is the better and cling to it still. This does not mean that we did not listen (1972:22).

Exemplary counsellors are vigilant when they are dealing with clients who test their values and beliefs. They discipline themselves by taking extra precautions to ensure they are listening accurately. They also try to become alert to any internal noise that might impair their capacity to hear. They know they are vulnerable, and they take preventive measures.

Being Aware of Blind Spots

Since everyone's frame of reference is different, we can never perfectly understand how other people are experiencing their world. Our understanding is always clouded to some extent by the meanings we assign to events and by our own thoughts and feelings. So counsellors may have blind spots that prevent them from hearing or understanding their clients. Blind spots are especially a risk if counsellors have unrecognized or unresolved problems parallel to those of their clients. For example, one counsellor experienced unusual discomfort when trying to work with a client who was dealing with an unwanted pregnancy. Ten years ago, the counsellor had placed her own child for adoption, but she had never addressed the emotions she felt over the decision. Whenever her client focused on her options, the counsellor's own feelings made it tough for her to separate her feelings from the client's.

Table 4.1 summarizes strategies for overcoming common listening problems. But these strategies are intended as ideas, rather than as recipes for responding. Each interview situation requires individualized and creative responses.

ACTIVE LISTENING

Understanding is always tentative; hence the importance of allowing clients to confirm or correct our understanding. Active listening describes a cluster of skills used to increase the accuracy of meaning. Attending, being silent, summarizing, paraphrasing, questioning, and empathizing are the essential skills of active listening. They breathe life into listening so that it becomes a continuous process of paying attention, hearing, exploring, and deepening. Active listening involves hearing what is said, as well as what is left unsaid. Counsellors need to use both their eyes and ears to ascertain meaning. Careful attention to such cues as word choice, voice tone, posture, and verbal hesitations is necessary to discover confirming or conflicting messages in the verbal and nonverbal messages. Subtle changes in voice tone or sudden shifts in the topic may signal important areas for the counsellor to explore. In one case, a 28-year-old woman who was describing her career goals happened to mention her sister. But as she did so, the counsellor noticed that she avoided eye contact and her voice dipped slightly. He asked how she felt about her sister. The woman began crying as she related how her sister had always been the favoured one in the family and how she had felt rejected by her mother. Subsequently, this relationship became a central issue in the counselling, and the client developed insight into how she was using her career as a desperate attempt to gain her mother's acceptance.

Active listening skills can also be used to defuse critical incidents. The FBI, for example, has trained negotiators to use active listening skills to handle situations involving hostages or barricaded subjects (Noesner & Webster, 1997). They found that active listening, particularly the skills of paraphrasing, empathizing, and open-ended questioning, helps subjects (i.e., hostage-takers) release frustration, despair, anger, and other powerful feelings, with the result that they return to a more normal level of arousal and rational thinking. One of the reasons active listening is so effective is that it does not

TABLE 4.1	Overcoming Listening Obstacles
Problem	**Counsellor Choices**
The client has problems with language, e.g., misleading word choice and difficulty communication verbalizing ideas.	Ask questions to clarify meaning. Pay careful attention to nonverbal communication for clues to meaning.
Messages are incomplete, ambiguous, or unclear.	Probe for detail and examples. Paraphrase to confirm understanding. Ask for definition.
Relationship problems/trust issues are resulting in client censorship of feelings and ideas.	Show empathy. Provoke candid discussion of trust or relationship issues. Go at a slower pace and reduce questions. Communicate openness through nondefensive responses.
There is outside interference, e.g., noise and lack of privacy.	Hold phone calls and move interviews to a private setting.
There is internal interference, e.g., counsellor fatigue, difficulty concentrating, boredom, hearing impairment.	Start a personal wellness plan. Improve time management skills. Defer the interview. Use self-discipline to increase concentration (e.g., mentally summarize key details) Summarize, paraphrase, empathize.
The counsellor has a loss of objectivity when dealing with ideas that are contrary to his or her values.	Use supervision or consultation to address personal issues that cloud objectivity. Discipline yourself to explore ideas that are different.
There are cultural barriers between counsellor and client.	Enlist the client's help to understand cultural values and issues, then adapt the interview style to fit. Use translators or refer the client to a counsellor of the same culture.
Content is overwhelming for the counsellor, e.g., when the client rambles or is long-winded.	Summarize to identify themes and priorities. Selectively interrupt to control the flow of the interview.
The client is inappropriately silent.	Attempt to understand the meaning of silence, then respond appropriately.
The client has speech problems (e.g., mumbling, stuttering, whispering).	Remember that problems may decrease as the counsellor becomes more familiar with the client's style. Ask the client to speak up.

threaten people with an overt attempt to change them. Active listening builds rapport because it shows that the listener is nonjudgmental and is interested in understanding. Individuals in crisis may erect heavy psychological defences, but "because active listening poses no threat to an individual's self-image, it can help a subject become less defensive. Thus, active listening creates fertile ground for negotiation and, eventually, change" (Noesner & Webster, 1997:16). In short, active listening is critical for nonviolent crisis intervention.

Attending, using silence, summarizing, and paraphrasing will be explored in the following sections. Subsequent chapters will address the skills of questioning and empathy.

Attending

Attending is a term used to describe the way that counsellors communicate to their clients that they are ready, willing, and able to listen. When coupled with understanding and appropriate verbal responses, attending promotes exploration. As a basic active listening skill, attending conveys physical and psychological commitment and openness to the helping interview. Attending says to clients, "I'm here for you. You have my undivided attention. I'm not afraid of your feelings and what you have to say." Wolvin and Coakley (1996) use the term *energetic attention* to underscore the importance of bringing both effort and desire to listening.

Certain core attending skills are universally applicable, and counsellors can use them with confidence. First, counsellors need to ensure that their feelings, attitudes, and commitment to clients are genuine. Egan describes attending as a learned set of skills; however, he cautions that counsellors cannot fake it: "Your mind-set, what's in your heart, is as important as your visible presence. If you are not 'for' your client, if you resent working with a client, this will ooze out into your behavior" (1998:62). If a counsellor has negative feelings about a particular client, then referral to another counsellor may be warranted. On the other hand, if such negative feelings permeate a counsellor's attitude toward many clients, then additional remedies may be necessary, such as personal counselling, assistance to deal with burnout, consultation and supervision to manage feelings, or career change.

Second, providing space to clients so that they can speak begins the active listening process. This includes efforts by counsellors to control physical noise and curb internal distractions. Self-discipline to suspend hasty assumptions and judgments is also essential. Counsellors must work to avoid reacting with verbal or nonverbal messages that express impatience, disagreement, or judgment. But as noted earlier in this chapter, this may be difficult when clients present ideas that are offensive or conflict with one's values and beliefs.

Third, counsellors can show that they are attending by being on time for the interview, remembering important details, and following through with agreed-on plans. There is a certain physical and verbal presence that conveys commitment. Verbal and nonverbal behaviours, such as head nods and encouraging probes, convey interest. Counsellors need to bring a certain warmth to the interview, which is communicated through appropriate smiling, changes in voice tone, and expressions of caring and support. An unemployed client who reports with glee to his counsellor that he has found work has a right to expect more than a monotone "That's great."

There is general agreement that the following behaviours convey appropriate attending, particularly when they match the client's nonverbal behaviour: keeping an open posture, maintaining eye contact, leaning forward, using responsive facial expressions, giving brief encouraging comments, and speaking in a warm and pleasant tone (Egan, 1998; Kadushin, 1997; Wolvin & Coakley, 1996). Counsellors should avoid displaying a "poker face," which can easily be mistaken as a "don't care" attitude. Wolvin and Coakley reviewed the research and reached a number of conclusions that have implications for counsellors:

- Individuals whose shoulders and legs are turned toward rather than away from the other person are perceived to be more empathic.
- Individuals with open body positions (e.g., arms and legs uncrossed) are perceived more positively than those with closed body positions.
- Individuals who lean toward others are perceived to possess more warmth and empathy.
- Listeners who engage in head nodding provide positive reinforcement for speakers.
- The smile is the best indicator of interpersonal warmth.
- People who engage in eye contact and gazing (looking at another person) project more attentiveness, interest, warmth, empathy, intimacy, truthfulness, sincerity, and credibility than those who do not engage in eye contact.
- Individuals who are embarrassed, ashamed, sad, submissive, guilty, or deceptive tend to have less gazing behaviour. (1996:176–83)

As with any counselling skill or procedure, attending must be applied intelligently relative to diversity and cultural variables. For example, among Middle-Easterners, six to twelve inches is a comfortable conversational distance; but "arms length" is most comfortable for Westerners (Hackney & Cormier, 2005). Counsellors should also avoid rigid adherence to one style of attending. For example, the needs of a client who is embarrassed may be best served by averted or less intensive eye contact until more trust and comfort develops.

Careful attention to words, phrases, and nonverbal communication opens counsellors to learning. Counsellors need to hear what is said, as well as what is not said. They need to reflect on how ideas are communicated, through tone of voice, posture, and other clues, and listen carefully for confirming or conflicting messages. As well, they need to sift through what may be complex and sometimes confusing information to identify patterns, priorities, and areas of relevance. This work may involve the major senses of hearing, sight, smell, and touch. Although counselling work generally centres on hearing and sight, significant information can be gleaned from our other senses. For example, alcohol and some other drug use may be detected by smell.

When counsellors are patient, they give clients space to confront painful emotions and to gather their thoughts. When counsellors sit still, maintain culturally appropriate eye contact, and avoid needless questions, they do much to convey to their clients their unwavering attention. These actions focus the attention of the interview completely on clients. To accomplish this, counsellors must develop their ability to be comfortable with silence.

However, it is important to remember that effective listening involves more than silence. As Garrett points out, "One who frequently interrupts to say what he would have done under similar circumstances is not a good listener, but neither is he who sits quietly and says nothing" (1982:29). Knowing how and when to continue or interrupt silent moments during interviews is a core skill that will be explored in the next section of this chapter.

CONVERSATION 4.1

PROBLEMS WITH LISTENING AND RESPONDING

STUDENT: I find that I'm so busy trying to think of what to say next that I miss what the client is saying.

TEACHER: Yes, it is tough. That's a common problem, even for experienced counsellors. It is hard to stay focused on what's being said without some thought of what to do next. But with practice it can be done. One trick is to think about what is being said before thinking about what to say. As you reflect on what is being said, try to identify major themes and feelings. Often, your response will emerge naturally out of this effort.

Remember that listening is hard work and you need to be "in shape" for the interview. One essential component of this is to address your psychological needs by dealing with your own issues that might make it difficult to hear clients. If you have unresolved difficulties, especially if they mirror those of your client, it will be particularly difficult to listen effectively. A second component is to make sure you fully disengage from your last client before engaging with the next. Finally, make sure you understand before you move on. Summarize, paraphrase, and ask defining questions to enhance and confirm your understanding. As a rule, the more you occupy yourself with the active demands of listening, the less you will be tempted to let your thoughts wander.

Silence

We should not break silence unless we can improve on it!
—Elbourne, 1997

Drawing on my fine command of language, I said nothing.
—Benchley, cited in Kadushin, 1990:254

The Personal Meaning of Silence

The second major active listening skill is silence. One distinguishing quality of effective counsellors is their mastery of language to communicate ideas and promote change. However, language fluency alone is insufficient. Counsellors also need to understand the importance of silence in communication. They need to balance their verbal agility with an equally strong capacity for silence.

Individuals and cultural groups show considerable differences in their comfort with silence. In some cultures, silence is a sign of respect. But for many counsellors, silence is unnatural; and if pauses occur in the conversation, they become anxious and fear that their clients will see them as incompetent. They also often burden themselves with pressure to fill the silent void with words. A silent pause, even as short as a few seconds, may lead to inner panic. Almost on reflex, they act to fill silent moments with questions and interpretations.

Some people judge silence harshly. They see quieter people as unmotivated, uninterested, aloof, rejecting, and ignorant. In a discussion with a group of students in a counselling class, I asked members who rated themselves as "more verbal" to talk to "less verbal" members about their typical reactions to silence. The more verbal members made statements such as "I feel judged," "I don't think you are very interested," "I am boring you," and "I wonder if you care about what we are doing?" Their comments clearly indicated that they felt threatened by silence or viewed it as evidence of judgment or lack of interest.

In contrast, the members who rated themselves as quieter noted that they often did not have enough time to respond and revealed that they were fearful or felt inadequate. Sample comments from this group were: "You don't give me enough time to speak," "I'm scared to talk," "I worry about making a fool of myself," and "By the time I think of what to say, someone else has already said it."

Many philosophers, poets, spiritual leaders, and writers have reflected on the meaning of silence. Typically, they extol its virtues and its power, as the following samples illustrate:

"Silence is the perfect herald of joy." (William Shakespeare)

"Let thy speech be better than silence, or be silent." (Dionysius)

"I have often regretted my speech, never my silence." (Syrus)

"Silence is golden." (Carlyle)

"Observe silence and refrain from idle talk." (Bahá'u'lláh)

"I'll speak to thee in silence." (William Shakespeare)

"Silence gives consent." (Oliver Goldsmith)

"There is no reply so sharp as silent contempt." (Montaigne)

"Silence is one great art of conversation." (William Hazlitt)

"The world would be happier if men had the same capacity to be silent that they have to speak." (Spinoza)

"Silence is the most perfect expression of scorn." (George Bernard Shaw)

"There is an eloquent silence; it serves sometimes to approve, sometimes to condemn; there is a mocking silence; there is a respectful silence." (La Rochefoucauld)

Silence in Counselling

Counsellors may have the same anxieties about silence as other people have. Silence may heighten their sense of inadequacy as counsellors and lead to uncertainty in the interview. As a result, counsellors may become impulsive and try to fill silences too quickly.

However, counsellors who discipline themselves to allow silence in their interviews may find that their relationships take on an entirely different tone, with their clients answering their own questions and discovering their own solutions. A repertoire of skills positions counsellors for dealing with silence in an interview. Counsellors should become comfortable permitting silence, as well as knowing when to interrupt silences appropriately. Knowing when to speak and when not to requires some understanding of the various meanings of silence. A recent survey of the use of silence in counselling suggested that counsellors use silence "primarily to facilitate reflection, encourage responsibility, facilitate expression of feelings, not interrupt session flow, and convey empathy" (Hill, Thompson, & Ladany 2003:513). But silence may be ill advised with clients who are psychotic or with those who are likely to view the silence as punishment.

During silence, workers need to do more than just keep quiet; they also need to *attend* to the silence. **Attended silence** is characterized by eye contact, physical and psychological focus on the client, and self-discipline to minimize internal and external distraction. Silence is not golden if it communicates lack of interest or preoccupation, or if it says, "I'm not listening." This means refraining from fidgeting and from other digressions, such as taking notes or answering the phone. At the same time, counsellors should not stare or turn the silence into a contest to see who is the first to break it. Counsellors should not automatically assume that silence is a measure of failure, nor should they think that a few moments of silence means that the work of counselling has stopped. Passive clients may be busy with thought, or they may be seeking to gain control or understanding of painful and forgotten feelings.

Every silent interlude has a different meaning, and counsellors need to be astute to discover the significance of each quiet moment and the most appropriate response. Understanding different types of silence helps counsellors look for cues and consider appropriate responses. Here are the six common meanings of silence in counselling:

1. **The client is thinking.**

Although all clients need time to process information and frame their responses, some need more time than others. Some clients talk with only a momentary pause to catch their breath, but others punctuate their speech with periods of reflection. If counsellors do not allow this time for contemplation, their clients may feel disempowered or inadequate. Clients may be formulating their thoughts or feelings, only to be prematurely cut off by counsellors whose own anxiety with silence does not permit them to wait.

When clients need time to reflect, counsellors can simply remain attentive and nonverbally show their interest and involvement through eye contact, open posture, and so on. They can also verbally indicate their willingness to listen by using simple phrases, such as "I sense you need some time to think. That's okay. I'll wait." and "It's okay with me if you just need to think without speaking."

2. **The client is confused and unsure of what to say or do.**

Sometimes questions are unclear, the focus of the interview is ambiguous, or clients do not know what is expected of them. Clients may sit in silence, shifting uncomfortably and attempting to sort out what to do next.

When clients become quiet because they are confused, allowing the silence to continue sustains or increases the clients' anxiety. These circumstances warrant interrupting the silence to clarify meaning, direction, or expectations. Rephrasing, summarizing, paraphrasing, and even repetition can help in such situations.

Counsellor: *Perhaps you're confused.*

(client nods)

Counsellor (Choice 1): *I think I might have confused you with my last question. It didn't make sense to me either. Let me reword it.*

Counsellor (Choice 2): *Let's slow down a bit. Help me to understand what's unclear or confusing.*

In addition, clients may have difficulty expressing their ideas, or language problems may be a barrier. Sometimes clients just need a little more time to find the right word or phrase. At other times, counsellors need to tentatively suggest ideas or help clients label feelings.

Clients are more likely to be silent during the beginning phase of counselling and during first interviews. This is normal and usually indicates that clients are unsure of what to say or do. Consequently, they depend on the counsellor to take the lead to clarify role and direction.

3. **The client is encountering painful feelings.**

Interviewing and counselling can stimulate powerful feelings and memories. Counsellors who can tolerate silence give space to their clients so that they can experience and deal with pain or anxiety. In some cases, clients may be ambivalent about facing their feelings. They may be afraid of their intensity, or they may be unwilling to face their feelings, at least at this time. Silence is a chance for clients to examine the merits of continuing further or retreating to safety. Usually, such moments are obvious because the discussion is intense immediately before the silence.

When clients are struggling with powerful feelings, counsellors may need to use multiple responses. First, you can allow this type of silence to continue. Responding with attentive silence can be very therapeutic and supportive. It says, "I am here. I understand. I have the courage to be with you as you deal with your pain."

Second, you can support silence with empathy when dealing with powerful client feelings. Otherwise, clients might feel ignored or misunderstood. Empathy confirms that feelings have been heard, and subsequent silence gives the client time to process. Empathy might be used to let clients know that they have been understood. As well, empathy tells clients that they have not been abandoned and that their counsellors are ready, willing, and able to be with them while they consider their feelings. Once the counsellor has expressed empathy, silence may be appropriate. In the following example, empathy frames two long, silent moments:

> Counsellor: *As I listen to you, I'm beginning to sense your feeling of resentment that your mother continually tries to run your life.*
>
> *(15 seconds of silence)*
>
> Client:*(tears in her eyes) Resentment. That's only part of it. I don't think I could ever live up to her expectations.*
>
> *(counsellor maintains eye contact, faces client)*
>
> *(10 seconds of silence)*
>
> Client: *But it's going to be okay. I realize that I have my own expectations to meet. It's me I have to face in the mirror.*
>
> Counsellor: *Sounds like you're beginning to accept that your mother is not going to change, and that only you have control over who you are and how you act.*

4. **The client is dealing with issues of trust.**

Before trust develops in the counselling relationship, clients may be hesitant to share personal information, and they may communicate this reluctance through silence. This is a normal and self-protective way for people to avoid rejection and maintain a sense of control over private matters. But a different trust issue may arise with involuntary clients who use silence as a way to control or sabotage the interview or demonstrate hostility. Their silence says what the client may want to express: "I'm here, but you can't make me talk." Silence becomes a way of retaining dignity and control in a situation in which they feel disempowered.

Generally, counsellors will want to gently move the interview toward more openness and intimacy. One way to proceed is to acknowledge the risk in sharing and to candidly discuss issues of trust. You can open the door with a comment like this: "I know it's not easy to share your feelings with a stranger. You don't know me yet and you can't be sure how I might respond." Another strategy is to move at the client's pace and discuss less threatening content until trust in the relationship develops.

Sometimes it is preferable to put trust issues on the table, rather than trying to proceed when there is so much obvious resistance. Consider using a lead such as the following:

> Counsellor: *I'd like to share a perception with you. I've noticed that whenever I ask a question, you answer me quickly, then you become rather silent. I'm worried that there might be some problems between you and me that we should discuss. Or perhaps you see it differently. In any case, I think it would help if we could discuss it. I'm certainly willing to listen to any of your concerns or feelings.*
>
> *(client is silent)*
>
> Counsellor: *I'm not you, and without your help I can't understand how you feel. But I suspect you'd rather not be here. That's how I'd feel in the same circumstances.*

In the example above, the counsellor's invitations do not guarantee that the client will open up to discuss feelings about being forced to attend the interview. However, such openness to discuss the issue frequently works. In any case, clients will have heard the invitation, and it may help to build trust.

5. **Silence is the client's usual way.**

Some clients are quiet by nature. They are unused to giving long or spontaneous responses, and they may be more comfortable keeping their ideas to themselves. It is important that counsellors do not consider clients' silence a sign of counselling failure and that they avoid the temptation to end any silence prematurely. Sometimes counsellors need to modify their own expectations and ways of relating to allow for the extended silences of some individuals.

As we will see in the next chapter, some interview techniques are effective in drawing out quieter clients. For example, open-ended questions that cannot easily be answered with a simple yes or no may help overcome patterns of continued silence. Another technique is to discuss with clients how silence is affecting the counselling work, then to explore ways for them to become more expressive. Sometimes clients don't understand the expectations of their counsellors but once they do, they are willing to cooperate. Professionals should reflect on the fact that whereas they have had training on the skills and process of counselling, their clients have not. Clients may be inaccurately seen as resistant when they are just unsure what to say. This underscores the importance of workers keeping clients fully informed by taking advantage of opportunities to explain their intent and procedures. Simple statements such as the following help demystify the counselling process:

> Counsellor: *I'm sure there's more that you can tell me. It will help me to understand better if you tell me more details and perhaps give me a few examples.*

Counsellors can also adapt their methods by using strategies that require less verbal interaction. Children, for example, may respond more to play, art, music, and drama. Adolescent males may be more motivated to talk if the interview is conducted in conjunction with an activity, such as a walk in the park or a game of pool. Counsellors are wise to remember that while they tend to be most comfortable with verbal interaction, their clients might favour other methods. For example, some clients like to write in journals, which gives them a chance to think introspectively without time pressures. With these clients, counsellors might seek agreement to use relevant journal entries as reference for discussion. In the following case, a counsellor relates how poetry was used:

> The client was a 20-year-old woman who seemed, at first, reluctant to talk about her depression. Her usual responses were one-word or short answers. I remembered that she had mentioned that she liked poetry, so I asked her if she would be willing to bring some of it to our meeting. She was willing and, in fact, eager to share her work. She brought a short poem to the next session which she read to me. The poem revealed her deep depression and her preoccupation with death. Afterward, we talked about her torment at a level that would not have been otherwise possible. Each week she brought a new poem, and these poems became our starting point. As she began to feel better about herself, her poems became more buoyant and optimistic, and they became one measure of her progress.

6. **The client has reached closure.**

Silence happens when there is nothing more to say about a particular topic or idea. Silence is a way of saying, "I'm finished. Let's talk about something else."

When counselling topics reach natural and appropriate closure, counsellors need to move on to a new subject. They may break such silence by seeking confirmation that an end point has indeed been reached. One strategy for preventing premature closure is to acknowledge the possibility of closure, as well as the possibility that the client may need time to formulate more ideas. A comment such as the following acknowledges both alternatives:

> Counsellor: *I'm thinking that we might have gone as far as we can with that idea. Or perhaps there's more you'd like to say.*

Subsequently, a transition to a new topic is appropriate. It may also be valuable to take a few moments to summarize before moving to a new area of discussion.

CONVERSATION 4.2

LEARNING TO DEAL WITH SILENCE

STUDENT: How long is a reasonable time to allow a silence to continue?

TEACHER: Without knowing the context, I cannot answer your question. Sometimes after a few seconds of silence, it is appropriate to break in and say something. But in other circumstances, an extended silence of several minutes is okay. Each situation must be looked at individually.

STUDENT: I agree, but my problem is that I get uncomfortable after a few seconds. I get so anxious that I usually rush to say something, even when I know I should keep quiet.

TEACHER: Try paying attention to what you are saying to yourself during silent moments. Watch for depreciating self-talk, such as "If I don't say something, the client will think I'm incompetent." Counter this by reminding yourself that silence has its place in counselling. If you interrupt too soon, you rob clients of important opportunities to reflect. Remember that comfort with silence can be learned; but like all skills, learning requires practice. It may help to have a glass of water so that you can take a long, slow sip to prevent speaking prematurely. Deep breathing may also help. Finally, don't overcompensate. Some silences should be interrupted.

Nonverbal Cues and Silence

Sometimes, nonverbal cues can reveal the meaning of silence. Presenting the open palms of one's hands may say, "Wait; I need time." Looking away and clenching a fist may signal an angry silence. At other times, the meaning of silence is unclear. In such situations, counsellors may choose to let the silence continue for a while to see if its meaning becomes apparent, or they may wish to seek help from their clients to understand it. Below are some sample responses that counsellors can use:

- You've (We've) become very quiet. I'm wondering what that means.
- Help me understand the meaning of your silence.
- Perhaps you're hesitant to tell me, or maybe you just need some time to think.

Although silence is often ambiguous, and understanding its meaning is difficult, some clues help counsellors interpret silence. Table 4.2 presents some of the messages of client silence. The table includes a range of nonverbal clues and ideas about how to respond to each. However, all nonverbal behaviour needs to be interpreted with extreme caution. The same behaviour may have multiple meanings. Crossed arms may suggest defensiveness but may also signal that the client is physically cold, or the client may be both defensive and cold. You need to interpret all nonverbal behaviour by considering the individual client and the overall context in which the behaviour occurs, and then check it out with the client to confirm accuracy.

Encouraging Silence

Silence can serve a number of useful purposes in counselling. It provides time to experience feelings and contemplate. Insight may emerge from moments of uninterrupted thought. Therefore, it makes sense for counsellors to promote periodic silence in their interviews with clients. This may be particularly useful when working with clients who are impulsive and clients who seem afraid of silence. The following are examples of counsellor leads:

- I think it might be useful if we each took a quiet minute or two to think about this idea.
- Let's pause for a moment.
- It's okay with me if you want to think about it for a while.
- When you're ready, we can talk about it. In the meantime, I'm comfortable if we don't say anything.
- Occasional silence is something that may occur during our time together. Sometimes one or both of us will need time to think.

Paraphrasing

Paraphrasing means restating the client's words and ideas in your own words. But paraphrasing is not the same as repeating what the client says. Repetition confirms memorization, but it does not mean that the words and ideas have been understood. Paraphrasing is a way of stating thoughts from a different angle. The defining feature of an accurate paraphrase is its interchangeability with the client's ideas. In the process, paraphrasing can help clients organize disjointed thoughts.

TABLE 4.2	Responding to Silence: Nonverbal Cues	
Client Actions	**Intended Message**	**Counsellor Response Choices**
One palm of hand raised 90 degrees, squinting, furrowed brow, eye movement, smiling (positive or pleasing thought).	"Please be patient. I need time to think."	Verbalize willingness to wait. Indicate attended silence with eye contact and other nonverbal expressions of support.
Shoulder shrugging, raised palms, rapid eye movement.	"Help—I'm confused and don't know what to do next."	Set the direction; clarify instructions. Rephrase the last response.
Ignoring or providing inappropriately short answer, moving the chair back.	"You can't make me talk." "I don't want to be here."	Communicate that it's okay not to talk. Empathize with resistance. Describe your feelings when forced to talk.
Starting to talk, abruptly stopping, shaking head, stuttering.	"I don't know whether to talk or not."	Empathize with ambivalence. Discuss the risks of sharing and not sharing.
Physical withdrawal, averted eye contact, carefully measured words, whispering.	"I'm scared of what you might think of me."	Reassure and convey a non-judgmental attitude.
Tears, covering eyes, quivering lips, flushed face, looking at the floor, trembling.	"I'm overwhelmed with these feelings."	Show empathy, use attended silence, then reveal further empathy.
Low voice tone, a pattern of short answers.	"This is the way I am. I don't say much."	Accept it as a cultural/individual norm. Gently encourage with open-ended questions. Explain the importance of sharing.
Leaning back, smiling, saying, "That's it."	"I'm finished."	Summarize. Change the topic and move on.

Paraphrasing is an important active listening skill that serves two purposes. First, paraphrasing confirms that counsellors have been listening and have understood clients. Second, paraphrasing gives clients an opportunity to correct inaccuracies. In the beginning phase of counselling, paraphrasing is particularly important because the counsellor is just starting to understand how the client thinks and feels. Paraphrasing helps the counsellor "get on board." Paraphrasing, together with summarizing and empathizing, assists in developing the counselling relationship. As well, it helps clients explore their problems in a way that is less forceful and directive than direct questioning techniques.

Paraphrasing concentrates on immediate client statements; it is presented without judgment and without an attempt to solve problems. The important point to remember is that paraphrasing does not add to or alter the meaning of a client's statement. In the example below, notice how the counsellor's paraphrase responses capture the essence of what the client has said.

> Client: *Losing my job was just the start of a bad year. I've had big marriage problems too, and now my daughter is on the street.*
>
> Counsellor: *You've had a number of serious things go wrong this year.*
>
> Client: *Right now the most urgent thing is to find some way to get my daughter back home. I need to know she's safe.*
>
> Counsellor: *So the focus of your attention is seeing that your daughter is out of danger.*
>
> Client: *I'd love to be able to leave my husband and move to a new city, but what would happen to my daughter? I can't be selfish.*
>
> Counsellor: *If it were just you, you'd know what to do. But your daughter really is your priority.*
>
> Client: *You're absolutely right. Once she's okay, then I'll take care of myself.*

Counsellors can add variety to their interviews by using a range of different lead-ins for paraphrasing. Some examples are listed below:

- Put a different way, you seem to be saying...
- As I understand it...
- Is this right? You're saying...
- In other words...
- It seems as if...
- It sounds a bit like...
- As I hear it...
- The picture I get is...

But it is always preferable for counsellors to present paraphrases tentatively. This provides the opportunity for clients to correct errors, confirm accuracy, or provide more detail. A tentative paraphrase opens discussion for deeper exploration. Statements such as "Correct me if I'm wrong" and "Would it be fair to say...?" suggest tentativeness.

Sometimes counsellors move too quickly by doing two things at once. In the example below, the counsellor offers a potentially useful paraphrase, then abruptly switches to a question that will move the interview in a different direction.

> Counsellor: *As I see it, you've reached a point in your life where you're not going to take any more abuse. What do you see as your options?*

In this example, a vocal pause or short silence should have been given to allow the client the chance to confirm that the paraphrase was correct. Client confirmation may come from both verbal and nonverbal channels.

Paraphrasing and Empathy

Paraphrasing differs from empathy because it concentrates on the content of messages—information, facts, details, and descriptions—whereas empathy focuses on feelings.

Paraphrasing may be less threatening to clients who have trouble discussing feelings. Paraphrasing can be used as a prelude to empathy, with empathy being introduced as clients become more trusting and willing to address their feelings.

In general, paraphrasing arises from words that the client has actually said, whereas empathy builds on verbal and nonverbal cues, responding to feelings that the client may never have identified. Paraphrasing is more closely related to summarizing. Both paraphrasing and summarizing condense content, and both highlight key ideas in the client's communication.

The following example shows the difference between paraphrasing and empathy:

Client: *Not having a job is getting me down. I know it doesn't help to sit in front of the TV all day hoping someone will call with my dream job.*

Counsellor paraphrase: *You're aware that you have to become more active in searching for a job in order to stop the downward slide.*

Counsellor empathy: *You're aware that wishing for a job offer is making you depressed.*

In the paraphrase response the counsellor paid attention to the key message (content) in the client's statement, then restated it in different words. In the empathy response the counsellor picked up on the emotional component. Counsellors often find that simple paraphrases such as the one above have a powerful, positive effect. Paraphrasing helps clients realize that counsellors are listening and that they are interested. Subsequently, clients who feel heard and understood often release their defensiveness and fears about sharing. In turn, the process of sharing and exploring may generate new understanding or insight for clients regarding their feelings and problem situations.

CONVERSATION 4.3

EFFECTIVE PARAPHRASING

STUDENT: If the client has just said something, what's the point in restating it? I think that a client might find paraphrasing very irritating.

TEACHER: You're saying why anger your client by repeating what's obvious?

STUDENT: That's right.

TEACHER: Notice that I just paraphrased what you said and you seemed okay with it.

(student nods in agreement)

TEACHER: An effective paraphrase is more than just mechanical restatement or parroting of the client's words. Verbatim restatements may irritate clients because they don't add anything to the interview. A useful paraphrase considers client ideas from a different perspective. Paraphrases are most potent when they invite or stimulate further elaboration and discussion. Nevertheless, I think it's best to avoid excessive use of paraphrasing or any other skill. Use paraphrasing when you need to check your perceptions and when it seems important to let a client know that you understand.

Summarizing

Summarizing is an active interviewing skill that can serve a number of purposes. First, summarizing confirms understanding and checks assumptions. Since client messages may be complex and ambiguous, it is crucial that counsellors validate their interpretations. When they summarize content, counsellors present a snapshot of their clients' main ideas in condensed format for verification.

> Counsellor: *So far you seem to be saying that you don't see any point in trying the same old strategies. Talking to her didn't seem to work. Ignoring her was even worse. Now you're not sure what else you can do. Does that seem like an accurate summary?*

Second, summarizing is a way of organizing complex data and content by tying disjointed but related ideas together. This may help clients look at existing problems differently, thus permitting new insights. Such summaries can also significantly reduce a client's confusion by ordering ideas in a more coherent sequence. The example below is excerpted from the mid-point of an hour-long counselling session. Prior to this point, the client had been talking about a variety of ways to manage his depression:

> Counsellor: *Let me see if I can sum up what we've been talking about. Essentially, as you see it, you need to work on long-term solutions, some related to improving your fitness, others targeting your social life. As well, you want to look at things you can do immediately to reduce your depression, including getting a medical and looking for some fun things to do. Is that a fair way to outline our discussion?*

The counsellor's summary helps the client systematize his action plan. Summaries such as this help clients and counsellors identify priorities. By summarizing, counsellors configure their clients' problems and issues in a way that gives precedence to certain ideas.

Third, summarizing can be helpful in working with clients who are verbose—who introduce irrelevant material and wander from topic to topic. Summarizing separates what is important from what is irrelevant by focusing the interview on particular themes and content.

> Counsellor: *From what you've been saying, it seems that your problems at work with your supervisor are your top priority. Do you agree?*

Summarizing may focus on a short time within an interview, or it can encompass a broader period, including the whole interview or the entire helping relationship. Two types of summaries are content (or simple) summaries and theme summaries. A **content summary** focuses on content and is an unedited condensing of the client's words. All ideas are included. A **theme summary** edits unnecessary detail and attempts to identify key patterns and areas of urgency. The following examples illustrate the two types of summaries:

The client, a 45-year-old male, has been describing how unhappy he has been as a welder.

> Client: *From the first day on the job, I knew that welding wasn't for me. Even as a child, I always wanted to work with people. As a welder, I spend most of my time on my own. Last week was a good example. From Monday to Thursday, I was in the shop basement, and the only time I had any human interaction was when I went to lunch. It's not much better at home. My wife has gone back to school, so she's busy with homework every night. The kids are grown and we don't see them that often. All I seem to do is work and watch TV. With the junk on TV, that's not much of a life. The only thing worth watching is CNN.*

CONTENT OR SIMPLE SUMMARY *From the beginning, you were aware that your welding career didn't meet your long-standing need to work with people. It seems that your work, with last week as a typical example, leaves you on your own. With your wife studying and your children gone, TV offers little comfort.*

THEME SUMMARY *You're feeling isolated. Neither your job nor your home life gives you much opportunity to fulfill your long-standing need to work with people.*

Content summaries make little or no judgment about relevance. The major goal of the content summary is to organize ideas and sum up data. But theme summaries are more risky. They require interviewers to judge which information is relevant and which is irrelevant. In the above example, different interviewers might focus on different themes, depending on their mandate. A researcher investigating television programming would hear this client's statement differently than would a career counsellor or a marriage counsellor.

Good summarizing involves four essential steps that you can remember with the acronym LIVE: listen, identify, verbalize, evaluate.

STEP 1: LISTEN In this step, the task is to listen carefully to verbal and nonverbal messages that provide clues to content and meaning. Counsellors must exercise a great deal of self-discipline to avoid contaminating clients' ideas with personal bias and definition. Counsellors can ask questions, request examples, and probe for definition as ways to reduce any risk of imposing their own bias and assumptions. But at the same time, they need to control distractions, including outside noise, daydreaming, attending to other activities, or becoming preoccupied with what to say next. In general, active involvement in what is being said diverts counsellors from any temptation to become distracted. Another technique to avoid distraction is to silently repeat or review client messages.

Listening means paying attention to the five Ws: Who? What? Where? When? Why? and How? Sample questions to consider are: Whom are clients talking about? What are they saying? What are they feeling? What are they thinking? When does this happen? Where does it occur? Why does it happen? How are clients saying it?

STEP 2: IDENTIFY The primary goal of this step is to make sense of all that has been said and heard. This involves distinguishing important information from irrelevant information, identifying underlying themes and patterns, and setting priorities. It also means hearing what has been said in context, and avoiding a common pitfall in listening: not seeing the forest for the trees. The counsellor's goal is to attach as similar a meaning as possible to the meaning the client intended. But at this step, counsellors need to remember that their perspectives are biased. What they deem significant and what their clients view as important may differ sharply. This reality underscores the importance of discussing these differences openly within the interview.

One technique that counsellors can use is to listen for key words indicating how clients are thinking. Use of the words *should* and *must* may signal self-imposed unrealistic or irrational expectations. Ellis (1993a) believes that individuals may develop excessive needs for certain things, such as achievement, approval, and love. Problems develop when these needs become translated into dogmatic "musts," and "shoulds." For example, a client might say, "I have to get my master's degree in order to be happy." In the same manner, use of the word *can't* might suggest feelings of inadequacy or self-esteem problems.

STEP 3: VERBALIZE The goal of this step is to verbalize your understanding of what the client has said in a summarization response, using words and phrases that the client can understand. Understanding is always tentative, at least until clients have an opportunity to confirm or challenge counsellors' perceptions. So this step is crucial to test the accuracy of comprehension.

The move to a summarizing statement can be flagged by counsellor leads:

- To summarize what you have been saying...
- If I may offer a summary...
- To be sure I understand...
- Let's summarize.
- Summing up...
- Let's pause for a moment to recap.

STEP 4: EVALUATE After summarizing for clients, the next step is to watch and listen carefully for signs that the summary is correct. Accurate summaries may be signalled nonverbally by the client's head nods, smiles, and relaxed posture, and verbally with short statements, such as "that's right" and "exactly." Disagreement may be direct, with expressions like "No, that's not right," or it may be nonverbal, with clients moving back, hesitating, or looking away. But lukewarm responses, such as "kind of," are subtle clues that your summary is incomplete or inaccurate. In addition, paralinguistic cues, such as speech that is drawn out, may indicate a lukewarm response, even though the words may appear to confirm understanding. When dealing with lukewarm response, counsellors need to use questions and statements to invite confirmation. This reinforces the notion that the client's right to be heard accurately will be respected, and it empowers clients to take an active role in evaluation. Leads such as the following can be used:

- Does my summary capture the important points?
- I'm wondering if you agree with my summary.
- Is that accurate?
- How does that sound to you?
- What have I missed?

SELECTIVE PERCEPTION **Selective perception** is a term used to describe the natural tendency to screen out irrelevant information to avoid being overwhelmed. But in counselling, what clients consider relevant may differ from what counsellors consider relevant. What a person deems important is likely to be influenced by one's frame of reference, which is uniquely defined through influences such as past experiences, personal values, current mood, interests, concerns, fears, prejudices, health, culture, and context. For example, a tow-truck driver looks very different depending whether you have a flat tire on a dark and stormy night or whether you're being towed for illegal parking. As well, the word *mother* may call up images of love and support or memories of abuse and pain. But selective perception can affect counsellor objectivity. In a famous counselling anecdote, a social worker was surprised to discover how many of his clients developed sexual problems after he took a course on sexual counselling! Johnson underscores the dangers of selective perception: "There is evidence that you will be more sensitive to perceiving messages that are consistent with your opinions and attitudes. You will tend to misperceive or fail to perceive messages that are opposite to your opinions, beliefs, and attitudes" (1997:129).

Counsellors need to be alert to the dangers of selective perception in their own thinking and responses. They must be vigilant to make sure they understand how and when prior learning, values, and current expectations influence their interpretations. They also need to be careful that they don't impose their own sense of what's important.

Of necessity, counsellors must ignore some parts of a client's communication and selectively attend to others. Typically, it is not possible to respond to everything a client says. Consider how many ways a counsellor might respond to the following statement:

> Client: *You could say my life is complicated. Six months ago, I started a new job, and it's terrific. I'm making more money than ever. But I don't have much time to enjoy it, given that I'm working six days a week. Maybe I should just force myself to take a vacation. With my wife working too, I think it's been hard on the kids. My youngest daughter's not doing too well in school, and she seems very depressed. Most nights, she just goes to her room right after supper and shuts the door. Maybe it's just a stage, and she's like all teenagers. Now I've just heard that my father can't live on his own anymore. I don't know whether to take him in with us, arrange home care, or place him in a senior's centre.*

In this example, there are many areas of potential importance (financial management, work pressures, stress, daughter, caring for parents). Let's look at some counsellor response choices:

> Counsellor (Choice 1): *Sounds like the most urgent need is to deal with your dad. Why don't we spend some time looking at the options?*

> Counsellor (Choice 2): *Sounds like you've got a lot on your plate. How do you manage your work stress? How do you support your daughter? What can you do with your father? Have I missed anything? (client says no) What's most important to you?*

Choice 1 illustrates the danger of selective perception. The counsellor assumes that caring for the father is the most urgent concern. In contrast, Choice 2 avoids this pitfall. The counsellor uses summarizing skills to identify major themes, then checks for accuracy. Partialization is another useful skill in this type of situation. Partialization involves helping the client to set priorities (Brill & Levine, 2005). Once the most urgent problem is addressed, other problems become more manageable. In general, it is usually neither necessary nor desirable for counsellors to try to work with everything at one time. Note that clients are also prone to selective perception, which may impair their ability to see all parts of a problem or available solutions that are within their grasp. Summarizing can be used to bring these overlooked aspects to the foreground:

> Counsellor: *You've told me many times that you don't see any way out of your situation. At the same time you've mentioned a couple of strategies that have worked for you in similar conditions.*

INTERVIEW 4.1   LISTENING, SILENCE, AND SUMMARIZING SKILLS

The following interview excerpt illustrates some important concepts from this chapter. This is the second interview with a client who is seeking help with anger management. The excerpt begins about five minutes into the interview.

DIALOGUE	ANALYSIS
Counsellor: Maybe we could take a minute to review the key points we discussed last week. (three seconds of silence; client smiles and nods her head)	This opening comment sets the stage for a review of the last interview. This is important for reestablishing the contract. It confirms that issues important in the last session still remain priorities. After offering a summary, it is important to confirm its accuracy. In this case, the counsellor uses the brief silence to confirm the client's (nonverbal) agreement.
Counsellor: I remember two points. First, you indicated that you wanted to find out what your triggers are—the things that lead you to lose control. Second, you wanted to explore some ideas for staying in control. Have I missed anything?	This theme summary focuses on what the counsellor considers to have been the priority of the last session. Checking for client agreement is an important adjunct.
Client: Yes, that about sums it up. But I don't want to become a pushover.	The client confirms partial accuracy, then adds a point that the interviewer's summary has missed. This should alert the interviewer to the client's priorities.
Counsellor: So, anger management, but not at the expense of giving up your rights. (ten seconds of silence)	A succinct paraphrase acknowledges the client's priority.
Counsellor: You've become very quiet. I'm struggling to understand what that means. (ten seconds of silence; client looks at the floor, tears in her eyes)	Initially, there is not enough information for the counsellor to understand the meaning of the client's silence. It might be tempting to move on with further questions, but the counsellor suspects that the silence is significant. A gentle statement invites the client to give meaning to her silence. Nonverbal clues (looking away, tears) suggest that the client is encountering strong feelings. The counsellor now focuses on feelings.
Counsellor: Perhaps this is painful for you to think about.	
Client: In every relationship I've ever had, I end up being the underdog. I do everything to	

(continued)

please my partner, but nothing for me. I always give in. But inside, it's a different story. I'm full of rage and resentment.

The client's comments suggest that she is willing to take a trust risk. This is a critical moment in the interview. The client will be watching carefully for signs of rejection.

Counsellor: Tell me more. (leans toward client, maintains eye contact)

This directive encourages the client to go on with her story. It confirms direction and is short enough not to interfere with the momentum that the client has established. Attending behaviour shows that the counsellor is interested and open to hearing the client's ideas and feelings.

Client: That's the essence of the problem. I let things build up inside, then I explode. Once, I was even fired when I blew up at my boss.

The client continues to risk. This signals that trust is growing, but the connection may still be very fragile. As we will see in Chapter 6, it is now important for the counsellor to make an empathic connection with the client's feelings.

Counsellor: So your anger is a bit like a time bomb, ticking away until you explode.

Here the counsellor paraphrases using a simile that is consistent with the client's phrasing.

Client: Exactly. (short silence)

This silence may be a simple pause that allows the client to decide what to talk about next.

Client: But, as I think about it, it's not just my anger. I guess what I'm really afraid of is never having things go my way.

The client does not accept the counsellor's paraphrase as accurate. Secure counsellors need not fear such mistakes or corrections. The client's willingness to correct the counsellor indicates her trust.

Counsellor: As I hear it, you seem to need to have more control over your life.

Client: No, that's not it. It's not control so much as validation.

SUMMARY

Listening is the basis for understanding and a prerequisite for relationship development. But understanding others requires considerable effort and patience. One useful skill is active listening: attending, summarizing, paraphrasing, questioning, and empathizing. Verbal and nonverbal attending behaviours also demonstrate a capacity and willingness to listen. Moreover, communication requires counsellors to shift between speaking and listening while attempting to understand. A wide range of problems, such as cultural and language barriers, difficulty in framing ideas, outside noise, ambiguity, loss of objectivity, and speech problems, can interfere with this listening process. So competent counsellors remain sensitive to these problems and take steps to overcome them.

In addition, active listening skills are tools for increasing understanding, communicating interest to clients, and letting clients know that they have been heard. Active listening involves counsellors in an ongoing process of paying attention, listening, exploring, and deepening.

Attending is the way that counsellors communicate that they are physically and psychologically committed to the helping relationship. Attending begins with a positive attitude and a genuine desire to get involved. This attitude is confirmed with behaviours such as making eye contact, assuming an open posture, and leaning toward others, if culturally appropriate.

Effective counsellors are comfortable with silence, but they also have the wisdom to know when to interrupt silence. An important part of this skill is understanding the different types of silence. Nonverbal cues are important indicators of the meaning of silence. In addition, counsellors can seek help from their clients to understand silence. Since silence can serve useful purposes in counselling, counsellors may wish to encourage periodic silent moments of reflection.

Paraphrasing is a way of restating someone's words and ideas in your own words. Paraphrasing is important in counselling because it confirms to clients that counsellors have heard and understood them. Summarizing helps clients to organize complex thoughts and is used to focus on relevant themes and content. The acronym LIVE can be used to describe the process of summarizing: listen, identify, verbalize, and evaluate. Counsellors need to summarize and paraphrase without judging or giving advice.

EXERCISES

1. List words, phrases, and situations that you think are your emotional triggers.

2. Over the next week or so, pay attention to the vocal pauses and silences that you and others use in everyday and professional communication. What indicators suggest comfort with silence? Discomfort?

3. Deliberately alter your response time to experiment with silence.

4. Ask a colleague to observe your use of silence during an interview (e.g., attended silence, appropriate interruptions, length, etc.)

5. Explain how silence can be used effectively in counselling.

6. During interviews with some colleagues or clients, find opportune moments for brief periods of reflective silence, then continue the interview. Discuss with your colleague/client what the impact of the silence was on the interview.

7. Videotape an interview and/or ask a colleague to observe your attending behaviour.

8. Work with a colleague to explore the effects of poor listening. As an exercise, deliberately (but subtly) violate the principles of effective listening and attending. For example, interrupt inappropriately, ask unrelated questions, switch topics prematurely, and avoid eye contact and other indicators of interest. When you are finished, discuss how it feels to not have others listen to you.

9. Paraphrase each of the following clients' statements.

- At a party the other night, I finally met someone with whom I can carry on an intelligent conversation. He seemed interested too, but he didn't ask for my phone number.
- It's a dilemma! I don't know whether to finish the school year or drop out and get a handle on some of my debts.
- My supervisor wants to see me today. I know she wants to talk to me because I've been late for work over the last few weeks.
- If she wanted me to call her, why didn't she say something?
- First my car broke down, then the fridge. Now it's the plumbing. I should marry someone who is good at fixing things.
- I think that with AIDS and all the other diseases you can catch, we should all take precautions. You never know who might be infected.
- Well, to put it bluntly, I think my partner has a lover. But I could forgive that. I just want our relationship to be the way it was when we first met.
- I've tried everything. I have a great résumé. I've called everyone I know. I look for a job five to six hours a day. Still, I can't find work.
- Lately, I've been thinking that there has to be more to life than work and play. I'm not even sure if I believe in God, but I need to find some meaning for my life.
- I just lost it. My anger built up and I hit her. She got so upset that she packed up and left with the kids. I've never done anything like that in my whole life. I realize that I didn't solve anything by losing my temper. Now I may have ruined my marriage and turned my kids against me.
- I guess I'm going to have to find some way of dealing with my drinking problem. The other day I was so sick from drinking that I couldn't even get out of bed. I just can't let booze continue to jeopardize my work and my family.

10. Conduct an interview with a colleague on any topic of interest. As interviewer, your job is to practise paraphrasing. Watch for verbal and nonverbal indicators that your paraphrase was correct.

11. Conduct a five- or ten-minute interview with a colleague on any topic of interest. As interviewer, you should practise summarizing skills. Try to offer both content and theme summaries. At the conclusion of the interview, offer a complete summary of the session. Ask your partner for feedback.

WEBLINKS

Quotations and links on listening form the International Listening Association:
www.listen.org/Templates/quotes_main.htm

"Tips on Effective Listening," by Larry Alan Nadig:
www.drnadig.com/listening.htm

"Listening—With Your Heart as Well as Your Ears," by Herbert G. Lingren:
www.ianr.unl.edu/pubs/family/g1092.htm

Major child and youth care website. Click on "reading" for access to practice hints, reference library and other useful connections:
http://cyc-net.org

chapter five

Interviewing Skills:

The Search for Meaning

PREVIEW

After reading this chapter you should be able to:

- Describe the importance of asking questions.
- Identify and describe common questioning errors.
- Explain why clients might not answer questions.
- Define open, closed, and indirect questions.
- Describe the advantages and disadvantages of open, closed, and indirect questions.
- Demonstrate the capacity to formulate open, closed, and indirect questions.
- Explain the importance of concreteness in counselling.
- Demonstrate the ability to probe for appropriate concreteness.
- Identify key questions for every interview.
- Recognize the five different types of interview transitions.

THE ART OF ASKING QUESTIONS

Asking questions is a cornerstone of active listening and counselling. Purposeful and well-timed questioning considers variables such as the current interview phase, the type of sessional contract, level of trust, and the capacity of the client to handle that level of questioning. When used effectively, questions can serve three very powerful purposes:

- **Information Gathering.** Questions provide an opportunity for clients to share relevant details, definitions and examples. As an adjunct to empathy, questions explore, clarify, and define emotions, thus lessening the possibility that counsellors will make erroneous assumptions.
- **Providing Focus.** The sessional contract defines the objectives of the interview, and this purpose determines the nature and type of questions that will be used. Focussed questions insure that the interview remains on track. Moreover, a series of questions can systematically lead clients through problem exploration, goal setting, and problem solving.
- **Promoting Insight.** Asking thought-provoking questions stimulates clients to begin a reflective process that can promote insight. Asking the right questions can promote awareness by leading clients to examine issues, ideas, and feelings that they might have otherwise overlooked. By sequencing questions, counsellors can teach clients to analyze and respond to problems. Effective questioning can also help clients make connections and uncover patterns in their thinking and problem solving.

Structured interviews follow a defined sequence of predetermined standard questions. Examples include interviews that require counsellors to complete forms to establish clients' eligibility or to make assessments. In structured interviews, there is little or no freedom of choice regarding the focus and pace of the interview.

Unstructured interviews permit interviewers and clients freedom to go in any direction without predetermined control or set questions. In these types of interviews, the tone is more conversational in tone and the pace and style of questioning is less rigid. In general, the contract remains flexible.

No single approach to questioning works with every client. Counsellors must consider numerous factors, such as the goals for the session, the context in which questions are asked, and the individual needs of clients, and then adapt their questioning techniques accordingly. Therefore, the best counsellors use a repertoire of techniques. They use questions to engage clients in higher-order thinking, kindle their curiosity, and prompt them to consider new possibilities.

Questioning Pitfalls

Asking questions is a skill. Faulty questioning may bias answers, antagonize clients, or keep the interview at a superficial level. In addition, insensitive questions that disregard clients' feelings or culture can leave them feeling judged or abandoned. Moreover, poorly timed questions may rush the interview or frighten clients with demands for disclosure before trust has been established.

Jargon

Questions must be clear and understandable to the client. But like many other professionals, counsellors have their own words and language (jargon) to describe their activities. Furthermore, each office has abbreviations, distinctive words, and phrases that are commonly understood by the people who work there. This jargon allows for streamlined communication and helps to define activities and routines precisely. Unfortunately, jargon is often used inappropriately with clients who do not understand it, as in the following example:

> Counsellor: *I'm assuming that this is the first time that you've gone through the intake process. After we complete your app., I can refer you to an appropriate community resource.*

A new client may have no idea what is meant by the terms *intake process* and *community resource* or the abbreviation *app.* Too embarrassed to ask, these clients may be left feeling demoralized, stupid, and incapable. Nonassertive clients frequently respond to jargon by acquiescing or pretending that they understand when, in fact. they have no idea what has been said. One woman phoned an immigrant services centre in a state of panic. She had been to the local welfare office and signed a form but had no idea what she had endorsed. Now she feared that she had made some mistake, since her monthly welfare cheque was $100 less than usual.

Leading (Biased) Questions

Leading questions manipulate clients to choose what appears to be the preferred answer. For example, both "Don't you believe it's time you took care of yourself instead of putting your husband first?" and "You like school, don't you?" bias the answers. Clients who have a high need to be liked by their counsellors and clients who tend to be compliant are especially vulnerable to leading questions. These clients are less likely to be assertive by disagreeing with their counsellors.

How a question is worded can dramatically affect the answer. Asking your spiritual leader, "Is it all right to smoke while praying?" may get a very different answer than asking, "Is it all right to pray while smoking?" (Sudman & Bradburn, 1983:1).

Counsellors may use leading questions to camouflage their own ideas. For example, the counsellor who asks, "Do you think you should be doing that?" is probably saying, "I don't think you should be doing that." Leading questions tend to corner clients, as in the following interview excerpt, in which a counsellor talks to a man about his mother.

> Counsellor: *Given what you've been saying, it's time for action. Wouldn't you agree that allowing your mother to live alone at home is not in anyone's best interest?*
>
> Client: *I suppose you're right.*
>
> Counsellor: *Would you prefer to put her in a seniors' home?*
>
> Client: *I really don't want to put her in a home. That wouldn't be right.*
>
> Counsellor: *Don't you think this might be easier on your family than taking on the enormous problems involved in moving her in with you?*
>
> Client: *(hesitates) I suppose you're right. But...*
>
> Counsellor: *(interrupts) I have a list of possible placements. Do you want to make some calls now?*

It's easy to see how the counsellor's agenda in the above encounter discounted the views and needs of the client. By selectively emphasizing one alternative, the counsellor allowed the client little freedom of choice. Consider how the outcome might have been different had the counsellor used the lead below.

> Counsellor: *Given what you've been saying, it's time for action. What do you see as your options?*

Such a lead would have allowed the client to identify alternatives, such as arranging for in-home care for his mother or inviting her to live with him. The counsellor's favoured alternative is not out on the discussion table to contaminate the discussion.

Excessive Questioning

Although questions are an indispensable part of most interviews, excessive questioning can leave clients feeling interrogated and bombarded. As a response to intense questioning, some clients fail to return for a second interview. Others become increasingly defensive and terse with their responses, particularly if they are unsure of the purpose of the questions. Excessive questioning can overwhelm clients, leaving them frustrated, confused, and exhausted.

Benjamin offers this warning about relying on questions to conduct the counselling interview: "By initiating the question-answer pattern, we are telling the interviewee as plainly as if we put it into words that we are the authority, the expert, and that only we know what is important and relevant" (1981:72). He suggests that the client may submit to the "humiliation" of questions "only because he expects you to come up with a solution to his problem or because he feels that this is the only way you have of helping him" (72). Martin (1983) warns that counsellors need to be careful not to ask too any questions, as if they are conducting an investigation. He suggests that this behaviour locks clients and counsellors into set roles. Moreover, relying on questions results in the interview digressing to "a question-and-answer interrogation in which the client waits for the counsellor to come up with the next topic" (George & Cristiani, 1986:147). Consequently, "it is not reasonable of the therapist to expect to ask a lot of questions and then have the client suddenly start self-exploration" (Martin, 1983:81).

Some clients simply do not respond well to questions. For example, involuntary clients may experience questions as an invasion of their privacy. As well, clients from some cultures may react unfavourably to questions. In such circumstances, reliance on questions will frustrate the goals of the interview. Counsellors may find that rather than getting more information, they are obtaining less. Counsellors should be alert to signs that their clients are reacting poorly to questions. For example, their clients' answers may become briefer, signalling their intention to be less cooperative. Clients also may communicate their displeasure nonverbally by shifting uncomfortably, grimacing, or averting eye contact. Some clients may refuse to answer by becoming silent, but others may be more outspoken with their disapproval, saying, "I don't see the point of all these questions." If counsellors continue with questions when it is clear that their clients are rejecting this approach, serious damage to the counselling relationship may result.

In addition, questions put counsellors in control. To some extent, counsellors need to have control of the interview in order to establish its focus and structure. However, clients may be left feeling that they have lost control. As Leeds argues, "Because the other person is compelled to answer, the power goes to the person asking the question. Just watch the power shift when someone asks, 'Where are you going?' and you answer, 'Why do you ask?'" (1993:58).

Consequently, it is important that counsellors are able to modify their approaches to reduce or eliminate questions. Sometimes, for example, an empathic response can achieve the same purpose as a question:

Client: *I just don't know what I'm going to do. Since she left, I've felt lost and unsure of what I should do with my life.*

Counsellor (Choice 1): *What are some possibilities?*

Counsellor (Choice 2): *Sounds as if you feel all alone and uncertain of what to do next.*

Choice 1 seeks more information from the client about what alternatives he sees for himself. This question moves the interview away from feelings to problem solving and decision making. In Choice 2, the counsellor acknowledges the client's feelings, as well as his indecision and the response is much more likely to be perceived as supportive and sensitive.

Sometimes counsellors have to ask a lot of questions, such as in determining eligibility for service or completing an intake (first) interview. But one way to lessen the impact of excessive questions is to have periodic pauses to check how their clients are doing. For example, they might say, "I'm asking a lot of questions. How are you doing? I know it can be a bit overwhelming." Respectful comments such as these empower and involve clients in the process.

It is important for counsellors to remember to balance questions with responses that confirm understanding (summaries) and empathic responses that affirm sensitivity to feelings. Benjamin's terse observation is worth remembering: "We ask too many questions, often meaningless ones. We ask questions that confuse the interviewee, that interrupt him. We ask questions the interviewee cannot possibly answer. We even ask questions we don't want the answers to, and, consequently, we do not hear the answers when forthcoming" (1981:71).

Multiple Questions

Multiple questions are two or more questions asked at the same time. If the questions are complementary, they are not problematic. A second question may be asked simultaneously that embellishes or clarifies the first:

> Counsellor: *How did you feel about it? How did you feel when he rejected you?*

In this example, the second question does not detract from or contradict the first. Of course, the second question alone would have sufficed. In contrast, the example below illustrates how multiple questions can be confusing:

> Counsellor: *How did you feel about it? Did you see any other way of handling the situation?*

In this example, both questions are potentially useful, but not when they are asked simultaneously. The client has to decide which question to answer. Each will take the interview in a different direction. At their worst, multiple questions can bombard and assault clients with complex and conflicting demands. Imagine if you were the client in the following interview:

> Counsellor: *So, is there anything you can do? Do you think you might have told her how you felt? Or maybe you see it differently. How long do you think you can continue to hang on?*

The counsellor may be well meaning, but responses such as these complicate matters and may add to the client's confusion. Generally, counsellors need to curb any impulse to ask more than one question at a time. When they ask a question, they should wait for the answer before proceeding to another question or topic.

Irrelevant and Poorly Timed Questions

One way that counselling interviews are distinguished from everyday conversations is that interviews have a definite purpose or intent. When counsellors know the purpose of the interview, they are able to frame questions that support that purpose. Conversely, counsellors who are unsure of the purpose are more likely to ask random questions.

Counsellors should have a purpose for questioning and they should be prepared to share this purpose with their clients. They might offer a brief explanation: for example, "It would help me to understand your situation better if I asked you some questions. This will give me an idea of how you see things." Preambles such as this inform the client of the counsellor's motives and procedures. When clients know what is happening, they are less likely to be defensive and more likely to support the process.

Sometimes counsellors ask excellent questions but ask them at the wrong time, which leads to inappropriate topic change. A common error of this type occurs when counsellors ask content questions after clients have expressed their feelings:

Client: *I was furious with her. I never imagined that my best friend would be having an affair with my husband. We've been married for 10 years, and I thought I could trust him. I feel like a complete fool.*

Counsellor: *How did you find out they were seeing each other?*

In the example above, the counsellor's question is valid, but it is timed insensitively. Since the client has just risked expressing strong feelings, the counsellor should consider empathy as the preferred response. The next chapter addresses this critical skill.

A second common error occurs when counsellors shift the topic without exploring beyond a superficial level. This can happen for several reasons. First, counsellors may be unskilled at probing a topic. Second, they may be overly cautious about probing, perhaps fearing that they will be invading their clients' privacy. Third, they may be fixated on problem solving, as in the following example:

Client: *We fight all the time.*

Counsellor: *How do you think you might cut down on the fighting?*

In this example, the counsellor jumps to problem solving far too quickly. A better choice would have been questions to find meaning and empathy to connect with feelings. For example, the counsellor needs to learn what the client meant by "fight." Do they yell and scream? Do they refuse to talk to each other? Or is there physical conflict?

Why Questions

Why questions should be used cautiously, since they tend to be more threatening for clients because they ask for justification; and their tone often suggests judgment, disapproval, or embedded advice. The question "Why don't you leave him?" may put a client on the defensive with the implied message "You should leave." *Why* questions ask people to explain and justify their behaviour. Frequently, this requires a degree of insight that they simply do not have. In response, clients may make up answers or feel exposed and stupid for being unable to answer the question.

Even when judgment is not intended, "when someone asks why you did something, you might feel she or he is judging you for not being able to handle the situation more effectively" (Hill, 2004:121). *Why* questions may provoke defensive reactions, including avoidance and attack. The following excerpt illustrates:

Client: *I can't relate to my father anymore. He can't see that I need my independence.*

Counsellor: *Why don't you just move out and be on your own?*

Client: *Impossible. I've got two more years of college and I can't afford it.*

Counsellor: *Why not just tell him how you feel?*

Client: *It's easy for you say, but you just don't understand.*

Kadushin (1997) suggests asking *what* instead of *why* questions. For example, "What prevents you from sharing your feelings?" is more helpful than "Why don't you share your feelings?" The first question seems to accept that there are explanations and reasons for the client's behaviour, whereas the second question seems to demand justification.

When Clients Do Not Answer Questions

Sometimes clients do not answer questions, or their answers are superficial. To decide how to proceed in such cases, counsellors need to consider some of the reasons why clients might be reluctant to respond.

Questions Are Not Understood

Clients may not understand questions because they have not heard them. For example, clients may be hard of hearing or deaf, or counsellors may be speaking too softly. As well, clients may not have been listening. In addition, counsellors may be using words, phrases, metaphors, and expressions that are not part of their clients' repertoire. But effective counsellors are able to adapt their idiomatic language and voice volume to meet their clients' needs and expectations. They avoid technical terms and jargon, particularly when communicating with clients from different cultures. Furthermore, counsellors are role models for their clients, and one of the interesting and positive outcomes of counselling is that clients may learn how to listen. When counsellors demonstrate effective listening and responding skills, clients tend to imitate them. Alternatively, counsellors can teach clients to use listening tools. For example, to encourage clients to summarize, leads such as this can be used: "Please tell me in your own words what your understanding of our agreement is. I want to make sure we both have the same understanding."

The Purpose of Questioning Is Unclear

Clients have a right to know why questions are being asked, and they are more apt to respond when the purpose is clear. Counsellors may simply state the purpose in an explanatory sentence: "The reason I am asking this question is..." But if counsellors don't have a valid reason for asking particular questions, they should not ask them. Questions are crucial for accomplishing the goals of counselling; but they must be used cautiously, either to obtain important information or to direct the interview to relevant channels.

The Answers to Questions Are Unknown

Some questions are difficult for clients to answer. For example, the questions may call for insight and explanations that are beyond the clients' current level of understanding. Sometimes, clients are unable to articulate their ideas and inner feelings. Learning disabilities also are a factor for some clients. Counsellors need to be observant to notice situations where clients don't know answers to questions.

Client Privacy Is an Issue

If clients are concerned about their privacy, they may say, "That's not an issue I care to explore." They may change the topic abruptly, or they may respond with silence. Some clients resist questions because of prior experiences of being embarrassed, interrogated, or put on the spot. Moreover, their cultural norms may discourage questions of any type, or they may restrict the areas in which questioning is appropriate. In some cases, clients withhold answers because they fear that their answers will not be understood or that they will be judged. At other times, they are simply not ready or able to address the issues the questions raise.

Counsellors can use a number of strategies to handle situations where clients do not answer questions. First, counsellors should honour the rights of clients to control areas of discussion and levels of intimacy during any phase of the relationship. Using the contracting process, counsellors can respect their wishes not to explore the particular area and shift the discussion to less threatening content.

Second, counsellors can evaluate whether they have given their clients enough time to answer. Some clients are slower to respond, and counsellors may misinterpret their silence as reluctance to speak.

Third, they might tactfully ask clients what prevented them from answering. Sometimes, trust issues impede candour. But candid discussion of barriers to trust usually increases trust, provided that counsellors are nondefensive. Moreover, by remaining nondefensive, counsellors demonstrate their capacity to be open and nonjudgmental. They show their ability to handle tough issues without retaliating. As well, when questions target sensitive or private information, counsellors can express empathy regarding how hard it might be to share such personal material.

Fourth, counsellors can simply stop asking questions. If they continue to ask questions even though clients refuse or dismiss them, unfortunate consequences will likely result. Moreover, under persistent questioning, clients may become increasingly frustrated, angry, and resistant, or they may feel inadequate because they have been unable to successfully meet their counsellors' expectations.

Cross-Cultural Interviewing

Counsellors need to be careful that their counselling and questioning methods are not culturally biased. For example, cultural groups differ profoundly in the way they react to questions. In a book on effective cross-cultural interviewing, McDonald makes this important observation:

> In [caucasian] society, a person being interviewed will barely wait before responding to a question. Aboriginal people, however, may pause before answering a question. Culturally, the pause may be related to thinking about the answer, considering whether the answer may affect the relationship between the interviewee and the interviewer, or wondering whether the question even requires an answer at all, especially if the answer appears obvious. The question of "small" talk which is so prevalent is also related to this point. Traditionally, native people do not engage in this kind of exchange. They may be judged as shy, reticent, or uncooperative by an interviewer when, in fact, the behaviour may actually indicate they feel that there is nothing worthwhile to say, so there is simply no reason to comment. (1993:19)

But when attempting to relate effectively to members of other cultures, counsellors need to avoid stereotyping and overgeneralizing. Within a culture, an individual may subscribe to all, some, or none of the cultural norms. Table 5.1 summarizes considerations for using questions appropriately.

TABLE 5.1	Guidelines for Questioning	
Don't:		**Do:**
Bombard clients with questions.		Balance and add variety to the interview with a range of other skills.
Ask more than one question at a time.		Pause after each question to give clients time to answer.
Use leading questions to control clients and their answers.		Remember that summary and empathy responses are important to confirm understanding.
Use *why* questions, as they usually imply blame or convey judgment.		Ask questions one at a time.
Ask questions unless you have a reason to need or a right to have the answer.		Respect cultural norms and individual styles that may make certain questions inappropriate. Ask questions for a specific purpose. Ask open questions. Ask a long series of closed questions.

Types of Questions

When counsellors vary the way they ask questions, the interview takes on more vitality and use of time becomes more effective. But an effective questioning technique depends on a number of factors, including timing, the nature of the relationship, the purpose of the interview, and the mood of the participants. Moreover, questions that are surprisingly useful with one client may generate hostility in another. Perhaps the most important point to keep in mind is that there is an art to asking questions that precludes any attempt to structure questioning in the same way for each client.

Closed Questions

Closed questions can easily be answered with a *yes* or *no*, and they are useful for confirming facts and obtaining specific information. Since closed questions do not invite detailed responses, they can effectively bring closure to an interview or slow the pace of clients who are overly verbose. On the other hand, closed questions should be avoided with clients who tend to be succinct. For example, clients can easily dismiss the question "Do you have anything you want to talk about today?" with the answer "No." Typically, closed questions begin with words such as *can, did, are, have, is, will, would,* and *do,* as in the examples below:

- Can you tell me what you've done about it?
- Did you have an opportunity to call the school?
- Are you feeling depressed?
- Have you thought about taking your own life?
- Is my understanding correct?
- Do you agree that the most important problem right now is...?

In general, when counsellors want a definite *yes* or *no* answer to an important question, a closed question is preferable. In the example below, the client hints that suicide might be an issue. This possibility is too significant to be ignored, so the counsellor uses a closed question to see if this is a risk.

> Client: *Lately, I've been so down, I wonder what's the point of going on.*
>
> Counsellor: *Have you been thinking about killing yourself?*

Sometimes, organizations require an intake interview that requires a great deal of information. A series of closed questions is an efficient way to quickly gather data. Unfortunately, too many closed questions may irritate clients and leave them feeling interrogated and restricted. To minimize these effects, counsellors should blend closed questions with various interview strategies—in particular, other active listening skills. Garrett suggests that "when considerable information is desired, it is often best obtained by encouraging the client to talk freely" (1982:22). This perspective is echoed by Kadushin (1997), who contends that clients are grateful when given freedom to explain themselves in their own way.

Open Questions

Open questions are distinct from closed questions because they are difficult to answer with a simple *yes* or *no*. For this reason, open questions are usually preferable to closed questions. They provide a great deal of freedom for clients to answer the questions in the way they choose, with as much or as little depth as they wish. Open questions may be used to begin an interview: for example, "What brings you here today?" They may also be used to explore thoughts, feelings, or behaviour: "What were you thinking?" "How did you feel?" "How did you respond?"

The vast majority of open questions are "five W" questions, which ask *who, what, where, when,* and *why,* and *how* questions, such as those listed below:

- Who knows about your situation besides your wife?
- What have you been able to do to cope with this problem?
- Where do you see this relationship going?
- When did this begin?
- Why do you think it has been difficult for you to cope? (As noted earlier, *why* questions should be used cautiously.)
- How do you see it?
- At what point do you think you might be ready to make a decision?

Keep in mind that with some clients, both open and closed questions yield the same result. With these clients, the closed question "Did you have any feelings about what happened?" and the open alternative "How did you feel?" will generate the same response. Thus, counsellors should avoid using the closed alternative with less verbal clients. Moreover, if counsellors want an expansive answer, they should avoid using closed questions, particularly when dealing with clients who tend to provide single-word or short answers to questions. For example, instead of asking, "Did you come here for help with your résumé?" counsellors might ask questions that convey a greater expectation for detail, such as "What were your reasons for coming in today?"

Moreover, closed questions become leading questions when they suggest the right or expected answer to the client. In the example below, a single mother describes her situation:

Client: *I often think that my kids don't give me enough respect. Just once, I'd like them to ask me how my day went. When I'm tired, they could help out more.*

Counsellor: *Do you feel angry?*

Client: *Sure I do. Who wouldn't?*

In this example, the client hints at strong but undefined feelings. Even though the client affirms anger, this may not be her main feeling. The client may indeed be angry, but other feelings may be dominant. Yet many clients find it easier to go in the direction suggested by the counsellor's question than it is to shift the answer. A less biased question might be "How do you feel about this?"

Kadushin suggests that open-ended questions can be intimidating for inexperienced clients who are unsure of their expected role: "For such interviewees, open-ended questions provide little structure, little guidance for what they are supposed to talk about and how they are supposed to talk about it" (1997:241). But straightforward relationship contracting with such clients about counselling routines and expectations can be a useful way to reduce their embarrassment and increase their control.

Indirect Questions

Indirect questions, or embedded questions, are statements that act as questions. Indirect questions are a softer way of seeking information. Their wording tends to be less intimidating than more direct open and closed questions. Indirect questions are effective for breaking up the monotony and threat of constant questioning, particularly when they are combined with other skills, especially empathy. The following are some examples of indirect questions:

- I wonder whether you believe that it is possible.
- Perhaps you're feeling confused over her response.
- I'm curious about your opinion.
- Given what you've said, I would not be surprised if you decided to accept the offer.
- I have no idea what you might be thinking.
- I would not be surprised to find that you have strong feelings on the matter.
- You may have already reached a conclusion.
- Your views on this are very important to me.

CONVERSATION 5.1

ALTERNATIVES TO QUESTIONS

STUDENT: Sometimes, it feels as if all I do is ask questions. I can't help thinking that if I were the client, I'd be really irritated. I don't want to leave clients feeling interrogated. But questions seem to be the only way to get the information I need. Do you agree?

TEACHER: You're right. There is a real danger that clients will become defensive if they feel cross-examined. But by paying attention to the needs, feelings, and responses of individual clients, you will be able to see if you are alienating them with too much questioning. Sometimes counselling works best if you avoid or minimize questions. For example, clients who have not yet developed trust in their counsellors may respond better in interviews when questions are minimized.

Another drawback to asking too many questions is that too much responsibility for the direction and content of the interview can be left on your shoulders. This can be disempowering for clients and can lead them to become overly dependent.

STUDENT: But are there ways to explore and get information without asking questions?

TEACHER: Yes, there are a number of skill alternatives to questions for gathering information and making assessments. Techniques such as showing empathy, summarizing, using silence, and self-disclosing may be more effective ways of getting details, facts, and examples. Empathy, for example, is a powerful counselling tool that tells clients that we understand or are trying to appreciate their feelings and perspectives. Empathic responses and summaries create an essential base of trust by showing that counsellors are nonjudgmental and capable of listening and understanding. In response, clients often become more courageous and motivated to share and explore. Appropriate use of silence creates space for clients to speak. Questions are important for effective interviewing; but you should try to add variety to your interviews by using a range of skills.

TABLE 5.2	Types of Questions			
Type	**Description**	**Advantages**	**Disadvantages**	**Examples**
Closed questions	Questions that can be answered *yes* or *no*	• Provide specific information. • Confirm facts, conclusions, or agreements. • Slow the pace of the interview by limiting focus. • Are easy for clients to answer.	• Restrict answers. • Repetitive closed questions can leave clients feeling interrogated.	• Will you be going to the parents' group tonight? • Did you say everything that you wanted to say?
Open questions	Questions that promote a more expansive answer.	• Allow for an unrestricted range of responses. • Empower clients by giving them increased control of answers.	• Client answers may be more time-consuming. • Are more challenging for clients to answer.	• What are your plans for this evening? • How are you feeling?
Indirect questions	Statements that act as questions.	• Are less threatening than traditional questions.	• Client may choose not to respond.	• I am interested in knowing if you have plans for the evening.

CONCRETENESS

Concreteness means the clarity and specific nature of messages. When communication is concrete, all participants share understanding of words, phrases, ideas, feelings, and behaviours. Counsellors should assume that all clients define common experiences and emotions in their own way. So if counsellors do not probe for idiosyncratic meaning on key ideas, and feelings, there is significant risk that their understanding of their clients will be incomplete and subject to error and distortion. At the same time, counsellors need to ensure that their expressed ideas and feelings are concrete. They can do this by offering defining detail and examples and by remaining alert to signs (verbal and nonverbal) that their clients may be assigning different meanings that those intended.

Table 5.3 rates concreteness on a continuum scale of 1 to 3. Probes for increased concreteness are essential at levels 1 and 2. At level 3, concreteness can be increased by asking for additional details and examples.

Unclear or Ambiguous Messages

Concreteness is necessary because messages are often unclear or ambiguous. Shared understanding between two people is possible only when each participant understands a message in the way that the sender intended. This is an exceedingly complex task, with considerable potential for distortion. But probing for concreteness can reduce or eliminate distortion.

People may lack the vocabulary and self-awareness to express their ideas precisely, and their messages may be incomplete, superficial, or ambiguous. If a client says, "I feel strongly

TABLE 5.3	Levels of Concreteness		
Level	**Description**	**Examples of Client Statements**	**Sample Responses to Increase Concreteness**
1	Minimal detail, definition or example	There are some things I could comment on. I know exactly how you feel.	What do you mean? How exactly do you feel?
2	Meaning is suggested, but content is vague, ambiguous, or inadequate.	I have the usual share of problems with my kids. I have strong feelings about my relationship with him. We'll have to get together soon.	Problems? Perhaps you might tell me more about the challenges you are facing. When you say "strong feelings, I'm not sure what you mean
3	Language is precise and there is shared understanding of ideas.	My eldest child has been absent from school for two of the last three weeks. I feel disappointed and rejected when my husband forgets my birthday	What has prevented him from going? Tell me more.

about it," the counsellor has been given an opportunity to help the client become more specific. Let's look at the choices:

> Client: *I feel strongly about it.*
>
> Counsellor (Choice 1): *I'm not surprised. From what you've been saying, who wouldn't feel that way?*
>
> Counsellor (Choice 2): *Perhaps you could be more specific. What exactly are your feelings?*

In Choice 1, the counsellor is supportive but does not probe to find out how the client is feeling. This client hints at feelings but gives no information about their precise nature. Unless the counsellor probes further, as in Choice 2, assumptions and misunderstanding are the likely outcomes.

Information Gaps and Missing Data

Counsellors should consider probing for concrete details whenever clients don't give key information or defining details, such that understanding is compromised. Probing can help obtain examples, quantify data, or check the client's frame of reference.

When someone describes a problem or shares a feeling, there is a natural tendency to make assumptions based on our own prior learning and experience. So when clients ask if counsellors know how they feel, the counsellors may automatically answer *yes* without further inquiry or clarification. But even though personal experience can help them appreciate the problems and feelings of clients, counsellors risk communication breakdowns if they neglect to openly explore their assumptions for accuracy. Active listening enables them to understand the experiences of others without contamination.

Moreover, a counsellor can miss important information by failing to notice the underlying emotional or personal content in the words. Although people may have links and similarities in their experiences and common human needs, everyone is unique. All people have different frames of reference based on their learning and experience. Consider the images that a word such as *anger* might evoke for various people. One person might vividly recall an abusive childhood, in which anger always led to someone getting hurt. Another might visualize screaming and hurtful words, while someone else thinks of withdrawing and saying nothing. As another example, consider what "old" means. To a 12-year-old, 30 might seem like old age; but to a man in his late 80s, 70 is young. Similarly, a joke may be perceived as humorous by some people, or as provocative, insulting, or sexist by others.

Using Simple Encouragers and Directives

The simplest way to probe for more information is to use short phrases and gestures that encourage clients to continue with their stories. Nonverbal gestures, such as head nods, sustained eye contact, and attended silence, convey such support and interest. Short statements and directives, such as "Tell me more," "Yes, go on," "What else?" "Please expand on that," and "Uh huh, hmm," can be used to sustain client sharing without interrupting the flow of the interview. A short example will illustrate.

> Client: *I guess I'm pretty angry.*
>
> Counsellor: *Meaning?*
>
> Client: *Our relationship is on the rocks.*

Counsellor: *Tell me more.*

Client: *My brother always puts me down. It's got to the point where I don't want to be around him.*

(counsellor nods, attentive silence)

Client: *We used to be so close. We were inseparable. But in the last year, it's become so competitive.*

Using Questions

Questions are the primary tool for seeking information. Intelligent questioning can be used to get examples, define terms, or probe for detail. The interview excerpt below demonstrates this process.

Counsellor: *I want to make sure I understand. What do you mean when you say "competitive"?*

Client: *It's something ugly. Not just wanting to win, but needing to win. It's as if everything rides on winning.*

Counsellor: *Is that true for both of you?*

Client: *At first, it was just him. Now I'm just as bad.*

Counsellor: *What's a typical example?*

Counsellors can use series of questions to explore vague statements beyond a superficial level. The following excerpt illustrates:

Client: *I know there are many times when I let my feelings get the better of me.*

Counsellor: *What kinds of feelings?*

Client: *Sometimes I let my anger build to the point where I'm ready to explode.*

Counsellor: *"Ready to explode"—what does that mean?*

Client: *I would never become physical and hurt someone. I'm just afraid of getting really mean and saying hurtful things.*

Counsellor: *Has that happened?*

Client: *Yes. (hesitates) A lot.*

Counsellor: *Can you think of a good example?*

Client: *My mother. She's always trying to control my life. Most of the time, I just try to ignore her constant nagging. But lately it seems that every second day she phones with advice. I don't want it and I don't need it. Yesterday, I blew up at her.*

Counsellor: *What did you do or say?*

Client: *I told her in no uncertain terms to butt out of my life. She started to cry, then I felt guilty.*

Opening Up Sensitive Areas for Discussion

One distinguishing characteristic of exemplary professional interviewers and counsellors is their capacity to be comfortable with any topic. Skilled counsellors take the initiative to open sensitive areas for discussion. Often, clients hint at a concern, which provides counsellors with a natural opportunity to probe for more detail and to open the discussion to a greater level of intimacy.

Client: *(avoiding eye contact) It's not easy to open up to a stranger.*

Counsellor: *It is tough. You might wonder how I'm going to react or whether I will hold what you say against you.*

Client: *It's just so embarrassing.*

Counsellor: *One way to overcome that is to take a chance on me. I'm open to anything you have to say. I find that when I avoid talking about a tough area, it becomes even more difficult to deal with later.*

Client: *Lately, I can't sleep at night because I'm wondering if I might be gay.*

Probes for concreteness are invitations to clients to trust their counsellors by revealing thoughts that they might prefer to keep hidden. Embarrassment, fear, uncertainty, taboos about taking help, and simple mistrust of the interview process, including suspicion about the motives of the interviewer, present natural barriers to sharing information. Shulman (1999) suggests that the same societal taboos that inhibit open discussion of sensitive topics also affect helping relationships. Among the taboos that Shulman identifies is reluctance to talk about sex, money, dependency, and authority. To Shulman's list of common taboos could be added discussions of death, spiritual issues, and health, as well as others that vary between people and between cultures.

For some people, taking help from someone else suggests dependency and weakness, which may result in feelings of inadequacy. Thus, one challenge for counsellors is to convince their clients that asking for help is a sign of strength, not weakness.

In addition, clients often view counsellors and interviewers as authority figures, and they tend to relate to them based on their prior experiences and images of people in power. Shulman (1999) suggests: "As one enters a helping relationship, problems with the authority theme should be anticipated as a normal part of the work. In fact, the energy flow between worker and client can provide the driving force that helps to power the work" (p. 179).

In addition, probes for concreteness propel the interview from a superficial level of discussion to an intimate level that requires a deeper investment from everyone involved in the interview. Chapter 1 defined the illusion of work concept as a kind of implicit partnership between workers and clients. In this arrangement, counsellors permit clients to avoid the pain and struggle that are often associated with growth, while counsellors avoid the risk that purposeful challenge entails:

> We have all developed the capacity to engage in conversations which are empty and which have no meaning... Workers have reported helping relationships with clients that have spanned months, even years, in which the worker always knew, deep down inside, that it was all illusion. (Shulman 1999:175)

Appropriate probes for concreteness are one way to avoid this illusion of work. (See Table 5.4 for more information.) Skilled counsellors continually work toward understanding the perspective and feelings of their clients. Moreover, effective interviewers and counsellors are learners, and they recognize that the best teachers are their clients. This means having the courage and assertiveness to ask difficult questions about private matters. At the same time, it means behaving responsibly by treating client responses with care. To be ethical, counsellors must question wisely, exploring only those matters that are relevant to the work and fit their competence and training. Thus, asking clients for more concreteness requires that counsellors are willing to invest time and energy to listen.

But some thoughts may be private, and lack of relationship trust may preclude full disclosure. For example, people fearing judgment or ridicule may tell others what they think they want to hear or what they believe will result in acceptance. Individuals also may distort or exaggerate messages because of past experiences. For this reason, counsellors need

TABLE 5.4	Promoting Concreteness	
Client Response	**Analysis**	**Counsellor Choices**
I have strong feelings about abortion.	The client does not provide enough information for the interviewer to understand the precise emotional reaction or point of view.	Describe those feelings. Tell me about those feelings.
I feel angry.	Further inquiry is necessary to prevent any natural tendency for the counsellor to attribute personal meaning to the word angry.	Angry? What does angry mean to you?
I hope you understand what it's like to be a single mother on welfare.	Personal experience or work with other clients could leave the counsellor open to making assumptions.	Everyone's experience is different. I need to hear what it's like for you.
There are several things missing in our relationship. My family is weird. I've learned a great deal.	Detail is lacking.	What's missing? In what ways are they weird? What are some things you have learned?
I'm fed up.	The target is missing (i.e., whom or what the person is angry with).	What are you fed up with? Whom are you fed up with?
She's really quite old.	The speaker's perspective is unclear.	How old is she?
I wish he'd show some respect.	The desired behavioural response is not detailed.	If he showed respect, what specifically would he be doing?
I have a right to my views.	The client's views are not personalized.	What are your views?
Sometimes, I feel like giving up.	"Sometimes" is a vague modifier. Giving up is not defined.	When you say "sometimes," how often do you mean?

to know when to back off and respect their clients' right to declare some topics off limits. Probing too deeply or moving too fast may result in clients revealing a great deal; but having done so, they may react adversely. They might feel violated and not return to future sessions, or they might put up barriers to protect against further unwanted inquiries.

But none of this means that the interview relationship is dysfunctional. In relationships, everyone must decide how much, when, and with whom they are willing to reveal personal thoughts and feelings. Restraint and self-censorship of some ideas and feelings are normal and necessary. Moreover, everyone differs in the degree to which they are comfortable with disclosing intimate thoughts and feelings. Some people prefer to remain private, sharing little or nothing. Others open up very slowly and only with people whom they deeply trust. Cultural norms may also influence what individuals are willing to share. Counsellors need to be alert to signs of client resistance, such as requests to change the subject or nonverbal cues signalling reluctance to continue. Then they can work with the client to make an intelligent decision on whether to continue, as in the following example:

Counsellor: *How did you feel when your father said that?*

Client: *(shifts uncomfortably, averts eye contact) I don't know if I'm ready to discuss it.*

Counsellor (Choice 1): *Okay. Let's talk about something else.*

Counsellor (Choice 2): *This is a difficult area for you, and you have mixed feelings about continuing.*

In Choice 1, the counsellor moves quickly to change the subject. This will lessen the client's anxiety, but it also robs the client of the opportunity to deal with a difficult yet potentially important topic. Here, the counsellor decides how to proceed. In Choice 2, the counsellor is more patient and attempts to empathize with the client's ambivalence toward continuing. In response, the client may say, "You're right, it is tough. But I can handle it." Or the client might say, "I'd rather we talked about something else." With either client response, the counsellor has respected the client's right to self-determination.

Counsellors need to have the time to deal with the results of any probe for concreteness. Concreteness opens new avenues of inquiry, stimulates feelings, and invites clients to share at a deeper level. Consequently, the end of the interview is a poor time to begin probing.

CONVERSATION 5.2

INCREASING YOUR ABILITY TO BE CONCRETE

STUDENT: Do you need a large vocabulary to help clients express themselves concretely?

TEACHER: It helps, but it's probably more important that you use the vocabulary you already have. Be curious. Ask questions. Express interest in hearing more. Seek definition of unfamiliar words or familiar words that are open to misinterpretation. Listen. These are the essential steps to concrete understanding.

Making Choices

A theme throughout this book is that effective counsellors have a broad range of alternatives for responding. When they have choices, counsellors are not locked into repetitive patterns, and interviews are more interesting and vibrant for both clients and counsellors. The following example demonstrates some of the many ways that a counsellor might respond to a client:

Client: *I suppose I should have expected it. My girlfriend said she needed time to think, to "reevaluate our relationship," as she put it. It was tough, but I gave her some time alone.*

Counsellor (Choice 1): *How did you feel about what was happening? [an open question that focuses the discussion on the client's feelings]*

Counsellor (Choice 2): *What was your plan? [an open question concentrating on the client's behaviour and thoughts]*

Counsellor (Choice 3): *Tell me what you planned to do (felt) (thought) (wanted to do). [directives]*

Counsellor (Choice 4): *Sounds like this was a painful time for you. [empathic response directed to the client's feelings]*

Counsellor (Choice 5): *I'd be interested in knowing how you handled it. [indirect question]*

Counsellor (Choice 6): *(silence) [silence used to give the client an opportunity to continue sharing]*

Counsellor (Choice 7): *It was hard, but you were able to give her time to reassess your relationship. [paraphrase]*

KEY QUESTIONS FOR EVERY INTERVIEW

Some interviews are highly structured with a series of questions to answer, such as a survey or a standardized assessment tool. Others are much less predictable, and the discussion may take unexpected detours. Whatever the nature of the interview, counsellors can use the following six key questions and their variations as reference points for most interviews:

- What brings you here today?
- What are your expectations of me?
- What do I need to know about your situation?
- What do you mean by...?
- What did we accomplish?
- What have we missed?

It is important to remember that these questions are starting points. Additional interviewing and counselling skills are probably required before the targeted topic area can be considered complete.

Key Question One: What brings you here today?

Counselling relationships are purposeful, and this question helps to begin the process of defining the sessional contract. As noted in Chapter 3, the sessional contract may shift as trust and insight develop in the relationship Therefore, counsellors need to be alert to shifts in focus and willing to negotiate changes in the contract when appropriate.

In addition, it is always preferable to have a repertoire of ideas (choices) for accomplishing the same task. A repertoire permits flexibility and contributes to keeping the interview interesting and individualized. Listed below are some alternative ways of asking the question "What brings you here today?"

- How would you like to spend our time together? (Because this type of open question gives maximum control to clients, it is useful for working with some reluctant clients.)
- Perhaps you might bring me up to date on what has happened since we last met.
- Do you have feelings and concerns from our last session that you want to address?
- What do you think would be a good starting point?
- There are a number of things we could do. For example...
- What would you like to talk about?

Key Question Two: What are your expectations of me?

This question and its variations initiate relationship contracting. Clients may come to counselling with clear ideas of what they want from their counsellors, or they may be aware only of their pain and be hopeful that some help will be forthcoming. In any case, it is important that both clients and counsellors understand their respective roles in the process. Of course, this agreement is always open to modification.

Key Question Three: What do I need to know about your situation?

At the beginning of an interview or when a new topic is introduced, an open-ended question such as "What do I need to know about your situation?" empowers clients to identify areas of immediate concern or willingness to explore. This question communicates to clients that counsellors will respect their needs and wants without making assumptions. It seems to say, "I am willing to listen and learn. I will treat you as a person, not as a number or a category." At least initially, clients may not put forward their most urgent need. They may start with a safe topic to test the waters for understanding and acceptance. But once they feel more trust, they may present more serious matters.

Sample variations of this question are "What are the important things I need to understand about you and your problem?" and "Can you tell me the key points we need to explore?" Questions designed to learn about a client's situation generally target three important areas:

1. how the client *feels* about the problem—**affective area**
2. how the client *thinks* about the problem—**cognitive area**
3. what the client *is doing* about the problem—**behavioural area**

Affective Area

Sometimes solutions to problems are obvious to clients, and they do not need help with decision making or problem solving but still lack the capacity to cope with their dilemmas. Often this is because their struggles to deal with painful feelings detract from their power to solve the problem. So in many circumstances, management of emotions is a prerequisite to problem solving. The question "How do you feel?" is one way to introduce feelings and to encourage clients to explore the emotional components of their problems.

Counsellors who are task-oriented with a focus on problem solving may move the counselling interview prematurely to problem solving or, worse still, may ignore feelings that are at the heart of their client's struggle. While questions can encourage expressions of emotions, the active listening skill of empathy is the foundation for working with feelings. (See Chapter 6.)

Cognitive Area

How people think about their difficulties is often more important than the problem itself. An event that may be no big deal to one client may represent a life-threatening crisis to another. Counsellors need to be aware of a client's subconscious self-talk, which refers to the mental messages we give ourselves. Golden and Lesh (1997) use the acronym MOANS for five words that often signal negative self-talk: *must, ought, always, never,* and *should.*

- I *must* succeed or I am worthless.
- I *ought* to be able to do it.

- I *always* screw up.
- I will *never* be able to get a job.
- I *should* feel differently.
- Everything *must* be perfect.

In contrast, positive self-talk builds confidence and is self-empowering. It moves people away from a victim mentality of feeling powerless. It also enables individuals to deal with crises realistically, without self-imposed rigid and punishing demands.

By seeking to understand how clients think about problems, counsellors can get valuable clues regarding important issues, such as self-esteem, motivation, and irrational thinking. Subsequently, counsellors can directly challenge clients' negative self-talk.

Sometimes, counsellors can achieve quick and dramatic counselling interventions by challenging the rationality of the worrier. By offering facts, challenging assumptions, and inviting clients to consider the real probabilities of dreaded events, counsellors introduce much-needed critical thinking that may interrupt the worry cycle (Shebib, 1997:81). Questions that can prompt exploration of the cognitive area include:

- What do you say to yourself about this problem?
- What does your "inner voice" say?
- What messages do you give yourself that are self-defeating?
- What are you telling yourself?

Behavioural Area

Although it is important not to move too quickly to work on problem solving, an important part of work in the beginning phase involves interviewing clients to learn what they are doing and not doing about their problems. Such information is important for assessment. It tells counsellors whether their clients are active in seeking and working on solutions or whether they have become withdrawn and have given up. Some questions for exploring the behavioural area are the following:

- What have you been doing?
- What do you do just before the problem occurs?
- How do you respond?
- What did you do?
- What did you say?
- Has the way you have been handling your problem changed?
- What are some of the ways you have been coping with this issue?

4. What do you mean?

This question is a basic concreteness probe that can be used during all phases of the interview to ensure clarity. It moves the interview from superficial understanding to specific or concrete exploration.

5. What did we accomplish?

This question ensures that evaluation becomes part of the work, thus enabling counsellors and their clients to review progress and identify accomplishments. Evaluation reviews the counselling relationship and assists with making changes to the contract. Evaluative questions include:

- How has our work met your expectations?
- Looking back on our session, what were the things that you found helpful? Unhelpful?
- How would you like things to be the same or different next time we meet?
- What remains to be done?
- How would you evaluate the work?

CONVERSATION 5.3

WORKING WITH CHILDREN

STUDENT: Do you need to modify basic counselling and interviewing skills when working with children?

TEACHER: Yes, you have to modify your approach when working with children. But this is also true for every client. Having said that, there are some basic principles for working with children. First, you have to speak in words appropriate to the child's age and developmental level. A young child, for example, may not understand the concept of time. When my kids were young, a half-hour was "one Mr. Rogers show" and three days were "three sleeps." Second, play and art are often better ways to engage children than interviewing. Children often act out their problems during play. Third, children may not respond well to questioning, particularly to *why* questions. Listening, empathy, and gentle encouragement to talk are more effective. Fourth, you need to recognize that children have unique ways of expressing their feelings. As Erdman and Lampe observe, "Pouting, crying, remaining silent, laughing, fidgeting, and fighting are some of the natural means children use to express their needs and feelings, and counsellors need to recognize these as such" (1996:375).

6. What have we missed?

At the end of an interview (or as a significant topic draws to a close), the question "What have we missed?" often yields surprisingly rich information. This question provides a last-chance opportunity for clients to talk about unexpressed issues and feelings. In addition, when clients have been ambivalent about sharing some details, this question may tip the scales in favour of sharing. It also empowers clients by giving them control of content and a final chance to make sure their needs are on the table for discussion. Some variations of this question are:

- What else do we need to talk about?
- What's left to explore?
- Have we covered all that is important?
- What questions haven't I asked?

In the following example, the counsellor prompts the client to examine the session:

Counsellor: *Our time is almost up, and I want to make sure I haven't overlooked anything that is important to you. What have we missed?*

Client: *Well, we haven't even begun to talk about how my divorce has changed my kids. In many ways, they have been the real victims.*

Counsellor: *I agree with you. It's very important that we don't overlook them. Does it make sense to you to make that discussion part of our next meeting? I want to make sure there is enough time.*

Client: *Yes, that makes sense.*

Counsellor: *Then let's make that Number 1 on our list for next time.*

But there are some risks to opening up new areas at the end of an interview, particularly if the topic involves strong emotions for the client. In the above example, the counsellor suspected that this was a topic that needed a lot of time, so she suggested deferral to the next session. In such circumstances, the counsellor might have been tempted to ask further questions or to empathize. But these responses might have prolonged the interview beyond the time available. It is important to end the interview without leaving the client in a state of distress.

INTERVIEW TRANSITIONS

An **interview transition** occurs when the topic of conversation shifts from one subject to another. Such shifts may occur spontaneously in the course of the interview, or they may be orchestrated in order to further the objectives of the interview. The need for a transition arises in the following situations:

1. Discussion of a particular issue is finished, and it is time to move on.
2. Discussion triggers ideas in another area or links to earlier areas of discussion.
3. The topic is too threatening or painful, and a topic change is needed to reduce tension.
4. The subject has limited relevance or has lost its relevance to the goals of the interview.
5. A change from one phase of the interview to another is necessary. (Shebib, 1997:156)

There are five types of transitions: natural, strategic, control, phase, and connect, or linking (Shebib, 1997:156).

Natural Transitions

Natural transitions arise as the discussion flows seamlessly from one topic to another, with clear links between the two topics. The most common natural transition occurs when clients mention new themes as part of the interview, and counsellors use this information to jump to the new topic.

Client: *As I talk about my dissatisfaction with my job, I realize that the same could also be said about my marriage.*

Counsellor: *Perhaps we could address that now. Tell me what's happening in your marriage.*

Clients are unlikely to resist natural transitions since the interview moves clearly in the direction they have suggested. The topic change is not abrupt, and transition responses indicate that counsellors have heard what their clients have just stated.

Strategic Transitions

Strategic transitions arise when counsellors make choices among topic alternatives. Imagine that a client makes a statement such as the following:

> Client: *This has been the worst year on record for me. My finances were a disaster anyway, and now that I've lost my job, I think I'll go under. Needless to say, this hasn't been good for my marriage. I can see how hard it is on my kids. My eldest daughter seems to avoid me entirely, and I'm sure my son is on drugs. What's the point in living?*

How should counsellors respond to this revelation? Should they select finances as a priority for follow-up? Or go with one of the other problems: marriage, relationships with children, drug abuse, or unemployment? Should they focus on problems or feelings or both? How a counsellor responds is a strategic decision that affects the direction of the interview, at least for the moment. But as much as possible, clients should be involved in decisions to make a strategic transition.

Control Transitions

Because counsellors have to orchestrate the flow of the interview, they sometimes use control transitions to manage the direction of the interview. Redirecting the flow of an interview is warranted when the discussion topic is irrelevant or when it prevents dialogue on more important issues. Preventing premature subject changes is crucial for ensuring concreteness or full exploration of content and feelings. Moving too quickly from topic to topic may render the interview superficial (Shebib, 1997).

Control transitions are used not to dominate clients, but rather to exercise professional duty to ensure that the interview time is productive. In practice, counsellors and their clients should share control, with counsellors giving clients as much power as possible to set the course of counselling based on their needs. Commenting on the role of counsellors, Kadushin notes that "skillful control of the interview involves giving direction without restriction; it implies stimulation and guidance without bias or pressure" (1990:356). Skilled counsellors are sensitive to the following elements of the interview that are open to control:

1. specific topics that are the subject of focus
2. the extent that the interview focuses on each of the three domains: feelings (including control on level of emotionality), behaviour, and thinking
3. sequence in which topics are discussed, including decisions to move the interview from one phase to another
4. use of time, including depth of discussion as well as interview starting and end times

The example below illustrates a control transition:

> Counsellor: *I think we might be moving too quickly here. We haven't had a chance to talk about your feelings. I wonder if you'd agree that we should do that before we move on to a different topic. It might help us both to understand why it's been so difficult for you to make a decision.*

In this example, the counsellor gives a brief reason for slowing down the interview and focusing on feelings. Clients who understand what is happening are much more likely to support the process.

But clients themselves may suddenly change the subject of the interview for a variety of reasons. For example, perhaps they were revealing too much, or the material was too painful or personal to discuss. Because of issues of client trust and readiness, counsellors need to use control transitions wisely and be mindful of the underlying feelings that client-initiated shifts signal. One way for counsellors to deal with a topic shift is to openly acknowledge the shift, then gently explore its meaning.

> Counsellor: *Am I right in thinking that you seemed uncomfortable talking about your relationship with your father?*

> Client: *It's not something I want to get into right now.*

> Counsellor: *That's okay. I won't force you. On the other hand, you might decide later that you're ready.*

Counsellors can use summaries as a way to introduce control transitions. As the example below illustrates, summarizing makes the topic switch seem less abrupt. This is important because abrupt transitions, such as the one below, may appear harsh to clients and accentuate their feelings of being cross-examined.

> Counsellor: *So, as I understand it, drug abuse has had a significant impact on your work. Your boss has reached a point where he will support you, but only if you enter rehab. Let's shift our focus for a minute and talk about problems with your family.*

Directives

Directives are short statements that provide direction to clients. Using directives is another way of controlling the flow of an interview. Directives such as "Describe your feelings," "List your main reasons," "Give an example," "Tell me what you did," "Share your thoughts," "Tell me more," "Expand on that," "Don't move too quickly," "Describe your feelings," and "Put it in your own words" are used to control the pace of the interview and to get more information. But since overuse of directives may leave clients feeling controlled, they should be used sparingly.

Phase Transitions

Counsellors also use topic changes to help move the counselling process into the next phase. For example, in the beginning phase, relationship building and problem exploration are paramount. However, at some point, it becomes clear that sufficient time has been spent on problem exploration, and it is time to move on to the challenges of the action phase, where the activity shifts to problem solving and sessional contract work on feelings, thinking, or behaviour. Thus, phase transitions are needed to bridge the work of one phase to another, as illustrated by the following example:

> Counsellor: *I wonder if we've reached a point where it makes sense to begin talking about the changes you want to make. We could begin to discuss some of your goals, then think about how to achieve them.*

In the example below, the counsellor uses a phase transition to end the interview and to establish a link to the next session.

> Counsellor: *I'm impressed with your insights about how you tend to put yourself down. It seems to me that the next logical step might be to explore how to combat this tendency. If you agree, we can start with that next time.*

Pacing

Generally, interviewers should proceed at a pace that their clients can manage. This does not mean that clients must always be 100 percent comfortable with the intensity of the interview. Indeed, the work of interviewing and counselling can be demanding, and exploring difficult topics can be exhausting. Here are some general guidelines for pacing:

- Move more slowly in new relationships and first encounters.
- Expect differences between clients.
- Don't expect to maintain the same intensity or an ever-increasing intensity throughout the interview. Periodic "rest" periods with nonthreatening or less demanding topics can energize clients.
- End interviews with less demanding questions and responses.

Moreover, counsellors need to carefully manage interview transitions between one topic and another. As well, they should avoid rigid agendas, such as might be followed in a formal meeting and instead allow some freedom of movement between topics. As well, counsellors also need to be careful not to sprint from one topic to another without adequate exploration or completion.

Connect (Linking) Transitions

Connect or linking transitions are used to join or blend ideas from recurrent themes. For example, a client may make continual subtle references to a need to have everything just right. The counsellor might use a connect transition to bring this theme to the foreground:

> Counsellor: *In all your examples, you talk about how you make sure that you pay attention to every little detail. Then you seem to berate yourself if everything isn't perfect.*

Connect transitions can have a powerful effect on clients by stimulating them to think about issues in new ways. Clients who have felt stuck and hopeless may find new energy. By connecting apparently discrete events, connect transitions allow them to understand problems from new perspectives, recognize different sources for pressures, and take new actions to lessen the pressures (Middleman & Wood, 1990:80).

CONVERSATION 5.4

NOTE-TAKING

STUDENT: What are your thoughts on taking notes during an interview?

TEACHER: You first.

STUDENT: I have mixed feelings. On the one hand, I don't want to forget anything. But it seems so cold and clinical to be writing when clients are talking. It seems to take away from the intimacy of the relationship.

TEACHER: Suppose you were the client and I were taking notes.

STUDENT: I'd wonder about what you were writing about me. I'd be really scared that someone else might see the notes. I'd probably be really careful about what I said.

TEACHER: What if I told you that you could see the notes?

STUDENT: That would help. Then I'd be able to correct any mistakes. I'd really want to know who would have access to the file.

TEACHER: All clients have a right to that information. They may not ask, but, as a rule, you should tell them. You raised a good point earlier about how note-taking can detract from rapport in the interview. I agree. I think it's particularly important to put the pen down when clients are talking about feelings or other private matters. On the other hand, most clients expect that you'll write down information such as phone numbers and addresses.

STUDENT: I'd prefer not to take notes at all during the interview and just write up a summary after the client leaves.

TEACHER: That would be ideal. Of course, that's not always possible. There may be forms or computerized questionnaires to complete that can't be delayed until after the interview. Or you may have clients waiting, so there may be no time after the interview.

INTERVIEW 5.1   INTERVIEWING SKILLS

The following excerpt illustrates some of the important concepts from this chapter. This is the first interview with the client. The counsellor works in a community service centre that offers a variety of programs.

DIALOGUE	ANALYSIS
(During the first five minutes of the interview, the counsellor and the client engage in small talk.)	Interview openings establish first impressions. A few minutes spent on small talk helps clients relax, and it should not be considered time wasted.
Counsellor: Perhaps you can tell me what brings you here today. You did not tell me much on the phone, but I had the impression that you felt some urgency.	A simple phase transition begins the process of establishing the purpose of the interview. By making a link to the intake phone call, the counsellor demonstrates that the client's sense of emergency was heard. This lets the client know that the counsellor is sensitive to feelings.
Client: I've been on welfare for six months, and I just can't make ends meet.	
Counsellor: Sounds rough. Tell me more.	A supportive and sympathetic reaction communicates warmth and concern. The counsellor uses a directive to seek more concreteness.
Client: It's not just the money—it's what it's doing to my kids.	
Counsellor: What do you mean?	It would be easy to assume what the client is talking about. Instead, the counsellor probes for definition.
Client: My oldest is 18. He doesn't seem to have any motivation. Sometimes he says he can hardly wait until he's 19 so he can go on welfare too.	

(continued)

Counsellor: I wonder if it seems to you that being on welfare somehow connects with your son's attitude.

The counsellor uses an indirect question to ask for clarification.

Client: Sure it does. It's all he's known for the last five years.

Counsellor: I need your help to understand what you were hoping would happen when you came here today.

The counsellor's statement initiates the working contract.

(The client explains that she would like some help to get into retraining.)

(20 minutes later)

Client: I'm willing to work anywhere, but eventually, I want to find something that fits.

The counsellor's response accents a key word. This is yet another way to seek more concrete information. Accenting encourages clients to say more.

Counsellor: Fits?

Client: I'd really like to work with people.

Counsellor: I noticed earlier that as you described your volunteer work with kids, you seemed really happy.

A linking transition connects two parts of the interview.

Client: I'd love to do it full-time, but there's no way.

Counsellor: What prevents you?

The counsellor uses an open question to probe for concreteness. This will help the counsellor understand the real or imagined barriers that this client foresees.

Client: I need to earn a living. Volunteers don't get paid. To get hired full-time, I'd need to get a diploma.

Counsellor: Sounds as if you've already looked into it. Have you thought about going back to school?

The counsellor uses a closed question to check if the client is prepared to go to school. Since the client has introduced the idea, the counsellor's question is not leading. In other circumstances, such a question might need to be avoided or approached cautiously, since it sounds like advice.

Client: Yes. Like I said earlier, I'm determined to get out of this rut. I suppose I should do something about it.

SUMMARY

Asking questions is an art. Faulty questioning may bias answers, antagonize clients, or keep the interview at a superficial level. But good questioning can systematically lead clients through problem solving and can help clients examine areas that they might otherwise overlook. It is important to balance questions with responses that confirm understanding (summaries) and empathic responses that confirm sensitivity to feelings. So experienced counsellors use a broad repertoire of skills all the time.

The type of interview also determines the type of questioning. Structured interviews follow a defined sequence of predetermined questions. Unstructured interviews permit interviewers and clients freedom to go in any direction without any predetermined control.

Faulty, insensitive, and poorly timed questioning may bias clients' answers, antagonize them, or keep the interview at a superficial level. Common errors include jargon, leading questions, excessive questioning, multiple questions, irrelevant or poorly timed questions, and *why* questions.

Moreover, clients may not answer questions for a variety of reasons. For example, they may not understand the questions or their purpose, they may not know the answers, they may want privacy, or cultural norms may be influencing their response.

In addition, questions can either be closed or open. Closed questions can be easily answered *yes* or *no*. Open questions are difficult to answer with a simple *yes* or *no*. The vast majority of open questions will be "five W" questions. Another effective questioning tool is indirect questions, which are statements that function as questions.

Concreteness concerns the extent to which the discussion conveys clear and specific meaning. When communication is concrete, all participants share understanding of language, ideas, and feelings. Probes for concreteness propel the interview from a superficial level of discussion to an intimate level that requires a deeper investment from everyone involved in the interview. A number of strategies are important for promoting concreteness, including recognizing the need for concreteness, demonstrating comfort and willingness to communicate at a deeper level, knowing when to pursue concreteness, using simple encouragers, and probing for detail with questions and directives.

Interview transitions occur when the topic of the interview shifts from one subject to another. Such shifts may occur spontaneously in the course of the interview, or counsellors may orchestrate them in order to further the objectives of the interview. There are five different types of transitions: natural, strategic, control, phase, and connect, or linking. Key questions can also be used as a rough template for interviews in order to establish sessional and relationship contracts, explore meaning and evaluate results.

EXERCISES

1. Classify each of the following questions as open, closed, or indirect.
   a. How do you feel about your brother?
   b. I'm puzzled over your reaction.
   c. Do you have time to see me next week?
   d. I'd like to know something about your strategy.

2. Reword the following closed questions as (a) open questions and (b) indirect questions.

   a. Are you enrolled in the secretarial program?
   b. Were you referred by the principal?
   c. Are you feeling sad?
   d. Do you want to talk about your feelings?
   e. Did you tell her how you felt?

3. Conduct an interview with a colleague. Use questions inappropriately (e.g., ask irrelevant questions, change the topic frequently, bombard with questions, and ask leading questions). After the interview is completed, discuss how it felt to be in both the interviewer and the client role.

4. Conduct a 10-minute focused interview with a colleague. Your task is to explore one topic in as much depth as possible. However, in this interview, you are not allowed to ask questions. Use a range of skills other than questions. (Note to the client: Try not to be overly cooperative.) After the interview is over, discuss the experience.

5. As a conditioning exercise for interviewing quiet clients, conduct an interview with a colleague. Set up the interview so that your colleague does not respond verbally. Use a variety of techniques other than questions.

6. Imagine that you are responding to the following client statements. Suggest follow-up responses that are open questions, closed questions, indirect or embedded questions, and directives.

   a. I have mixed feelings.
   b. The next step is to solve the bloody problem.
   c. It's been a long time.
   d. I know exactly what she means.
   e. You have no idea how I feel.
   f. I'm really angry with you.
   g. There are some significant things happening in my life right now.
   h. I'm not sure I can handle this problem. I need help.

7. Each of the following client statements has one or more problems with concreteness. First, identify the concreteness problem. Second, suggest a possible counsellor response to promote concreteness.

   a. I still have feelings for her.
   b. I've given it a lot of thought.
   c. I hardly sleep at night.
   d. I've tried to control my kids, but nothing seems to work.
   e. She's an elderly person.
   f. I feel bad.

8. Each of the following counsellor statements contains phrases or jargon that may be unfamiliar to clients. Reword each, using everyday language.

   a. It seems as though your son has a lot of interpersonal difficulty, and it is generating acting-out behaviour.
   b. Cognitively, he seems well within the mean.
   c. It appears to me that you are feeling ambivalent.
   d. After intake, it seems appropriate to make a referral to one of our community resources.

9. Work in a small group to brainstorm jargon that is used in a setting that you know. Next, reword these terms and phrases so that they are easily understandable.

10. Pick an issue that you have very strong feelings about (e.g., abortion, capital punishment, increases in tuition fees). Conduct a five- to ten-minute interview with a colleague to explore his or her views on the same topic. However, do not reveal any of your feelings or thoughts on the topic. After the interview is over, discuss the experience.

11. Watch a talk show. See if you can identify the interviewing skills that are used. Look for evidence of improper interviewing technique.

12. Videotape an extended interview with a colleague. Classify each response that the counsellor makes in terms of type—open question, closed question, summary, and so on. Identify patterns. Are there skills that are overused or underused?

13. **Interview Aerobics**

    Prepare flash cards with the names of various skills on each card (e.g., open question, closed question, paraphrase, summary, empathy, indirect question, directive, silence, wild card [any skill], self-disclosure, contracting). Then use them in an interview with a colleague.

    Note: The exercises below are designed to help you develop a range of skills. The more comfortable you are with a wide array of responses, the more you will be able to respond based on the needs of the client and the situation.

    Exercise 1: Shuffle the cards. The counsellor listens carefully to what the client says, then selects the first card in the stack and follows the directions on that card. For example, if the next card reads "closed question," the counsellor must ask a closed question, even if that might not be the best response.

    Exercise 2: Work with a partner who will choose an appropriate skill card for you to use.

    Exercise 3: Conduct an interview using the cards in any order that you choose. Continue interviewing until all of the cards are used. Cards may be used more than one time.

    Exercise 4: Conduct an interview using the cards in any order that you wish. However, you can use each card only once.

    Exercise 5: Develop your own strategy for using the cards.

    (Adapted from Shebib, 1997:161)

WEBLINKS

"The Art of Questioning," by Dennis Palmer Wolf (1987). *Academic Connections* (Winter 1987), p. 1-7. Article about how teachers can use questions to stimulate thinking and inquiry: **www.exploratorium.edu/IFI/resources/workshops/artofquestioning.html**

"What is motivational interviewing?" by Stephen Rollnick, Ph.D., & William R. Miller, Ph.D. (1995). *Behavioural and Cognitive Psychotherapy*, 23, 325-334: **www.motivationalinterview.org/clinical/whatismi.html**

"Questions for Problem Solving," by Rick Sheridan. A short article offering sample questions to assist in the problem solving process: **www.csuchico.edu/~csu/site/questions.htm**

chapter six

The Pursuit of Empathic Understanding

PREVIEW

After reading this chapter you should be able to:

- Explain the importance of emotions.
- Name the basic families of emotions.
- Describe how to recognize clients' emotions from nonverbal behaviour.
- Define what is meant by empathy.
- Define the three types of empathy: invitational, basic, and inferred.
- Explain when not to use empathy.
- Identify what to avoid when responding with empathy.
- Demonstrate the basic ability to formulate empathic responses.
- Explain the importance of "tough empathy."

EMOTIONS

Feeling and longing are the motive force behind all human endeavor.—Albert Einstein

Emotions define and shape the course of our lives. They remind us that we are alive, but sometimes they make us long for death. Some emotions—such as the joy at the birth of a child—demand to be expressed. But some are too frightening to acknowledge and are destined to remain forever hidden, perhaps even from ourselves.

Because the human experience is so closely connected with emotions (feelings), we can expect counselling work to frequently focus on helping clients identify, explore, manage, or accept their emotions. **Emotions** are defined by Barker as a "state of mind usually accompanied by concurrent physiological and behavioral changes and based on the perception of some internal or external object" (1995:110). Emotional responses also trigger unique physiological responses in our bodies. Historically, these responses have helped humans respond to important situations:

- *Anger*—the hands swell with blood, making it easier to use weapons or strike back; increased heart rate and adrenalin serve to increase energy and power.
- *Fear*—blood flow to the legs increases, making it easier to escape; the body may freeze for a moment, giving time to gauge whether hiding is a better response.
- *Happiness*—brain activity inhibits negative thoughts and fosters increased energy.
- *Love*—general bodily responses promote well-being and a general state of calm and contentment.
- *Surprise*—raising the eyebrows expands the field of vision, thus making it easier to figure out what is going on and to plan the best action.
- *Sadness*—a general drop in energy and enthusiasm creates an opportunity to mourn. (Goleman, 1995)

Counsellors work with clients' emotions in a number of ways. The counselling relationship provides safety for clients to explore and understand their feelings. Friends and family may be well meaning but poorly equipped to deal with complex emotions. They may be prone to simplistic advice giving, or they may try to change the subject when painful feelings are revealed. Counsellors, on the other hand, are able to deal with feelings. They don't tell clients how they should feel, nor do they insult or frustrate clients with quick-fix solutions. Instead, they allow clients to express emotions without needing to censor what they reveal. Nonjudgmental responses and permissive encouragement from counsellors can be enormously therapeutic for those clients who have struggled on their own to cope with their emotions.

The overall goal of this kind of counsellings is to help clients gain **emotional literacy**, "the ability to experience all of one's emotions with appropriate intensity and to understand what is causing these feelings " (Parrott, 1997:260). Goleman (1995) suggests that the ability to recognize feelings as they happen is the cornerstone of emotional intelligence and that people who are more in touch with their feelings are better able to navigate their lives and are more competent decision makers.

Weisinger (1998) argues that understanding emotions comes from appreciating the interactions of three components: thoughts, physiological changes, and behaviour. Johnson provides a perspective:

> Feelings are internal physiological reactions to your experiences. You may begin to tremble, sweat, or have a surge of energy. Your heart may beat faster. Tears may come. Although feelings are internal reactions, they do have outward signs. Sadness is inside you, but you cry or frown on the outside. Anger is inside you. But you may stare and shout at the person you are angry with. Feelings are always internal states, but you use overt behaviors to communicate your feelings to other people. (1997:134)

Black gives perspective on the nature of joy:

> Joy may be looked on as anxiety's opposite. It, too, is a composite of feelings: delight, fulfillment, and refreshment, along with the warm glow that comes with an increased heart rate, deeper breathing, and a general relaxation of muscular tension. When we are in the midst of an experience as pleasantly exhilarating as joy, we are likely to identify it in an inner conversation with ourselves as a wonderful feeling. (1983:35)

Counsellors can help clients consider how their emotions might be interfering with decision making or everyday life. Decision making, for example, may be difficult when the clients' emotions pull them in different directions. But many unhappy feelings, such as sadness, anger, grief, and disappointment, are part of everyone's life. In fact, feelings like grief are healing responses, and they are not usually pathological or in need of treatment.

Diversity and Emotions

As one might expect, there are wide variations in the extent to which various cultures and individuals express emotions. While underscoring the importance of exceptions, Dodd offers the following generalizations:

> Asian cultures generally practice reserve and emotional restraint. The idea of extreme emotion, such as loud sobs during a funeral or boisterous laughter on festive occasions, would be considered too emotional. To a lesser extent, some Scandinavian cultures appear publicly reserved. Britons and Germans appear more reserved than Italians, Greeks and Czechs. (1995:121)

Ivey, Ivey, and Simek-Downing offer this interesting perspective: "There may be four participants in the interview: the counselor/therapist and his or her cultural/historical background and the client and his or her cultural/historical background" (1987:94). But counsellors can lessen their natural tendency to be ethnocentric (the sense that their values and lifestyle are superior) through willingness to explore and understand the culture and history of their clients. By working on cultural self-awareness, counsellors can better understand how their background influences their perceptions and interactions.

Classifying and Understanding Emotions

Our language has wisely sensed the two sides of being alone. It has created the word "loneliness" to express the pain of being alone. And it has created the word "solitude" to express the glory of being alone.
— *Paul Tillich*

Although there are hundreds of words for emotions in the English language, most fall into one of ten categories or families of emotions as listed in Table 6.1. As with any classification system, the categories are arbitrary tools designed to organize our thinking. Specific words for

TABLE 6.1	Feeling Inventory		
	Intensity		
Feelings	**Low Level**	**Medium Level**	**High Level**
Anger	annoyed, irritated, miffed, offended, resentful, provoked, displeased, aggravated, put off, ticked, upset, disturbed	angry, mad, hostile, hateful, disgusted, inflamed, in a tiff, fed up, sore, agitated	outraged, furious, vengeful, repulsed, boiling, in a rage
Fear	alarmed, nervous, anxious, teased, uneasy, timid, bothered, apprehensive, intimidated, butterflies	frightened, scared, worried, distressed, fearful, jumpy, uptight	shocked, horrified, panicked, terrified, mortified, terrorized, cold sweat
Strength	adequate, up to the challenge, able to cope, stable	confident, capable, adept, healthy, qualified, whole, energized, dynamic, tough, strong, brave, determined, secure	invulnerable, in control, bold, potent, courageous, unbeatable
Weakness	delicate, insecure, timid, shy, small, fragile, tired, weary	weak, vulnerable, falling apart, burnt out, cowardly, helpless, useless, sick, incompetent, inadequate, unprotected, frail	defenceless, impotent, worthless, no good, powerless, exhausted, lifeless, useless
Joy	satisfied, glad, good, pleased, comfortable	happy, contented, joyful, loved, excited, optimistic, cheerful	euphoric, ecstatic, thrilled, delighted, passionate, elated, marvellous, full of life, terrific, overjoyed
Sadness	disappointed, hurt, troubled, downcast, upset, bothered	unhappy, glum, sad, depressed, melancholy, blue, lonely, dismal, pessimistic	agonized, dejected, despairing, despondent, hopeless, miserable
Confusion	distracted, muddled, uncertain, doubtful, hesitant, mixed up, unsure, indecisive	confused, baffled, perplexed, puzzled, ambivalent, stumped, jumbled, disjointed, frustrated	(in a state of) pandemonium or chaos, mystified, swamped
Shame	embarrassed, humbled, regretful	belittled, discredited, guilty, shamed, remorseful, ashamed	disgraced, scandalized, humiliated, mortified
Surprise	startled, puzzled	surprised, stunned, shocked	astonished, astounded, flabbergasted, amazed, overwhelmed, awed
Love	attracted, friendly	close, intimate, warm, tender, cherished, smitten with, doting on	loved, adored, raptured, crazy about, wild about, flip over, idolize, worship

emotions within the categories are used to more precisely define emotional states and to provide some information about the intensity or strength of the emotion. Similar attempts may be found in Carkhuff (1981), Young (1998), and Cormier and Cormier (1985). Counsellors need to respond to the range of subtle feelings that clients express and in language that clients can understand. But this table should be interpreted with caution, as word choice alone is an insufficient indicator of emotional intensity. A client who says, "I'd kill for a chocolate ice cream" is clearly exaggerating. Another might minimize a problem, saying, "It doesn't bother me," but context and other cues might reveal evidence of profound pain.

Sometimes people confuse feelings and thoughts. For example, the statement "I feel that this is the best alternative" expresses a point of view (thought), but it does not convey any information about the emotions involved. On the other hand, the statement "I feel confident that this is the best alternative" does express an emotion.

Word Modifiers

Word modifiers (e.g., *very, extremely, somewhat, mostly, little*) serve to limit, quantify and add further precision to the level and type of emotion expressed. We can expect some difference in emotional level between people who describe themselves as somewhat happy and others who say they are incredibly happy. Other examples of modifiers that are commonly used with emotional expression are *serious, never, constant,* and *mostly.*

Metaphors

Metaphors describe a state by using a symbol in a direct comparison. For example, a client who says he is "going around in circles" is using a metaphor to describe his feelings of confusion.

Here are some metaphors with the possible feeling that each suggests:

- tied up in knots, in a pressure cooker (stressed)
- about to blow up, bent out of shape (furious, anger)
- on a sinking ship, down in the dumps (hopeless)
- tearing my hair out (swamped)
- in a sticky situation (vulnerable)
- between a rock and a hard place (helpless, confused)
- butterflies in my stomach (fear, excitement)
- on top of the world, on cloud nine (happy, ecstatic)
- taken for granted (devalued)
- going around in circles, feeling pulled apart (confused)
- egg on face, like two cents (embarrassed)

In addition, sometimes people use metaphoric phrases to describe ways of dealing with emotions, such as "rising above it."

Nonverbal Behaviour

Most people are familiar with the physiological reactions that occur in moments of great fear. Powered by increased adrenal secretion, our bodies respond automatically with elevated heart rate, rapid breathing, dry mouth, and other symptoms. Many of these reactions are clearly visible to any observer, even before any verbal declaration of fear. Nonverbal behaviour is usually outside our conscious control and is less likely to be censored. Consequently, counsellors can often trust nonverbal communication as a more reliable indicator of feelings than verbal communication. Moreover, the visual channel of nonverbal communication is the most significant. In general, research has shown that often more than 55 percent of the meaning of a message is conveyed nonverbally, accentuating the importance of understanding nonverbal communication (Wolvin & Coakley, 1996). Peoples' emotions may be conveyed much more accurately by their body posture and eye contact than by their words. Furthermore, counsellors who are able to respond to nonverbal as well as verbal messages "project an unusual warmth, sensitivity, and perceptiveness that enhances the intimacy of the relationship" (George & Cristiani, 1986:145).

In addition, counsellors can learn a great deal about their clients' feelings from carefully observing their manner and the way they present their ideas. Nonverbal cues act to confirm, contradict, or even substitute for verbal expressions of emotions. For example, a client might say, "I'm ecstatic," but saying it in a sarcastic manner conveys the opposite. Another common example occurs when people say, "I'm interested in what you have to say," but at the same time they continue with another activity, which underscores their lack of interest. Below are additional examples:

Confirmation:

a. Client says, "I'm happy," accompanied by a smile.

b. Client expresses anger by shaking a fist.

Contradiction:

a. Client says "Yes," while shaking head.

b. Client says, "I'm not angry," while shouting or avoiding eye contact.

c. Client says, "It's not a big deal," while crying.

Substitution:

a. Client cries, looks away, moves chair back, glares, frowns, shifts uncomfortably.

b. Client uses gestures, such as pointing.

But counsellors need to interpret nonverbal behaviour cautiously. Typically, each nonverbal behaviour can have many meanings, each of which can vary according to culture, context, and individual comfort level. For example, people from some cultures interact at very close personal distance, but others experience the same personal distance as intrusive or even aggressive. Some people consider direct eye contact rude, while others view avoidance of eye contact as cold or as evidence that people are lying. In fact, in some cultural groups, lack of eye contact is considered a sign of respect and courtesy (Corey & Corey, 1989:84).

BODY LANGUAGE *Kinesics* is the study of body language, including such variables as posture, facial expressions, gestures, and eye motion. Sometimes body language is easily interpreted, such as when people use gestures that have direct verbal equivalents. For example, people might point to indicate direction or use their fingers and hands to signify size or numbers. But at other times, body language is ambiguous and more difficult to interpret, particularly when people communicate contradictory messages. For example, a person might appear to be listening intently and making appropriate eye contact; but if this is accompanied by fidgeting and rapid finger tapping, then the real message is: "I'm bored." Johnson offers a perspective on this difficulty:

> For one thing, the same feeling can be expressed nonverbally in several different ways. Anger, for example, can be expressed by jumping up and down or by a frozen stillness. Happiness can be expressed through laughter or tears. Any single nonverbal message, furthermore, can arise from a variety of feelings. A blush may show embarrassment, pleasure, nervousness, or even anger. Crying can be caused by sadness, happiness, excitement, grief, pain, or confusion. (1997:173)

Even a simple smile may have multiple meanings: (1) it may show warmth, pleasure, or amusement; (2) it may be an attempt to appease or humour someone in order to reduce threat or obtain approval; (3) it may reveal nervousness; or (4) it may simply be a habit with no particular meaning (Wolvin & Coakley, 1996:180). Consequently, counsellors should look for multiple indicators of meaning, rather than for a single signal.

VOICE Counsellors can learn a great deal from voice tone, volume, and pitch. These variables can reveal if clients are depressed, euphoric, angry, or sad. For example, Kadushin (1990) concluded that anger tends to be expressed with speech that is more rapid and loud, whereas sadness is characterized by more pauses and slowness of speech. Silence is also an important component of nonverbal communication (see Chapter 4). Counsellors need to be able to read nonverbal cues to decide how, when, and if they should interrupt a silent moment.

SPATIAL DISTANCE *Proxemics* is a term used to describe how people use space and distance. Hall's model (1959) is widely used to describe the four main distances:

1. Intimate distance is a zone of up to 0.5 m (2 feet) reserved for private exchanges of intimate thoughts and feelings.
2. Personal distance is a zone of about 0.5 to 1 m (2 to 4 feet) that is used for less intense exchanges with friends and family.
3. Social distance is a zone of approximately 1 to 3.5 m (4 to 12 feet) used for more impersonal meetings and social contact.
4. Public distance beyond 3.5 m (12 feet) is used for casual exchanges, such as giving a speech or lecture.

How an individual uses space is influenced by many variables, including gender, age, culture, physical characteristics, status, various personality traits, and the nature of the relationship. For example, people tend to want more space as they become older (Wolvin & Coakley, 1996:186). Thus, counsellors should adapt their seating to meet the needs of individual clients and situations and remember that angry clients may need more personal distance. Moreover, in such situations, counsellors need more space for safety reasons. Counsellors should also be mindful of spatial shifts during the interview. Often these changes are subtle, such as when a client shifts his or her chair back, as if to say, "I'm not comfortable with what we're talking about." Similarly, as clients lean in and move toward them, counsellors can conclude that intimacy and trust are increasing. If a client seems to be physically and psychologically withdrawing, this may be the wrong time to confront or to introduce more sensitive topics.

Finally, counsellors need to be aware of their own nonverbal behaviour and the subtle ways it might influence their clients. Counsellors may inadvertently communicate displeasure by frowning, turning away from clients, or increasing the physical distance between them. Alternatively, they may disclose that they like clients by smiling, using a pleasant voice tone, increasing eye contact, and leaning toward clients (Mehrabian, 1981:162). Some counsellors might even laugh nervously when they are anxious or scared, thereby confusing their clients. But counsellors can review videotapes of real or mock counselling sessions to increase their sensitivity to appropriate and inappropriate nonverbal communication habits.

Individual Differences and Cultural Context

All feelings can be experienced as positive or negative at varying levels of intensity, but this subjective determination is individually defined. For some people, anxiety can be debilitating, seriously affecting the quality of their lives. However, for an athlete, the same emotion may arouse a competitive spirit, and the individual might thrive on its physiological consequences. Counsellors need to remember that their clients may respond with emotional reactions very different from their own—with similar feelings, sharply different feelings, without significant emotional reactions, or with markedly increased or decreased intensity. Therefore, counsellors should avoid using their own measuring criteria to interpret the emotions of others. For example, if they expect that people in crisis will be verbal and declare their pain, then they might miss the fact that the quiet child is much more needy than the one who is acting out.

But circumstances and context are not always good predictors of feelings. One person might be anxious about public speaking but find the experience exhilarating, while another person is terrified by the prospect. One individual might enjoy parties and be stimulated by the chance to meet new people, but a second person looks for any excuse to avoid the panic brought on by crowded social events. Consequently, when the meaning is not obvious, counsellors should ask clients to explain their emotional experiences.

In the following example, the counsellor makes erroneous assumptions, then, sensitive to the client's nonverbal message, works to correct the error. This models openness to the client and serves to reinforce the reality that counsellors are not perfect:

> Client: *My mother is coming to visit me next week.*
>
> Counsellor: *Oh, that's nice. It's always great when you have a chance to see your folks.*
>
> Client: *(hesitating) I guess so.*
>
> Counsellor: *(picking up on the client's hesitation) Perhaps I was too hasty in assuming you would be happy that she was coming. I should have waited until you told me how you felt. How do you feel about her visit?*
>
> Client: *I dread it. My mother always wants to tell me how to run my life.*

Individuals are also often governed by cultural norms, and there are wide variances in the extent and manner to which they express emotions. Some cultures value emotional expression, whereas others favour emotional restraint. Cultural empathy (Cormier & Hackney, 2005) requires counsellors to pay attention to both cultural as well as contextual considerations. Note that empathic responses should be culturally appropriate with consideration of issues of pride and shame. For some clients, empathic responses may lead to embarrassment and "loss of face." Client receptivity to empathic responses should be considered.

Mixed Feelings

Clients interpret their own problems and experiences and find them frequently complicated by multiple and seemingly contradictory feelings from two or more emotional families (see Table 6.2). A great deal of stress and confusion can arise from the pushes and pulls of competing feelings that, if unmanaged, can disrupt a client's life. The terms *ambivalence* and *of two minds* are often used. But ambivalence is normal, and it can be a valuable help to decision making.

> Example: *A woman describes the joy she felt when her son left home to begin training as a counsellor, but as she talks her eyes well up with tears. Clearly, she is experiencing a strong sense of loss, despite the fact that words speak to her pride and happiness. More accurately, both feelings exist simultaneously.*

People also have feelings about the emotions they experience. Sometimes they are very aware of these mixed feelings, sometimes not. Try this simple experiment. Close your eyes and recall a recent strong emotion, such as anger or joy. Take a moment to get in touch with your feelings. Now try to complete this sentence, "I feel _____ about feeling (your recent strong emotion)." Many readers will find that this simple exercise leads to a deeper understanding of their emotions. Some may find guilt behind their joy; others, fear.

TABLE 6.2	Common Mixed Feelings
happy/scared	This often arises in conjunction with a lifestyle change (e.g., getting married, returning to school, starting a new job, sending children to daycare, experiencing the "empty nest" when children leave home).
happy/sad	Some transitional life events, such as leaving one job for another or seeing a child off to college (kindergarten, etc.), elicit these feelings. A sense of loss as well as gain is often present.
depressed/fed up	These feelings suggest that the person has "bottomed out." Significantly, being fed up may be used as a strong motivator for change (e.g., deciding to change a self-destructive drug habit).
angry/afraid	Fear is often the most significant emotion, but anger is more commonly expressed (e.g., a parent facing a teenager who is two hours late for curfew).
hopeful/despairing	Many clients fluctuate between believing that change is possible and life will get better and that nothing will improve and further effort is futile. Developing and sustaining motivation is crucial in such situations (e.g., a person coping with a life-threatening illness).
attracted/repulsed	Many people who are considering changes in their lives experience these feelings. Part of them wants things to be different, and part wants the security of their present situation, however distressful (e.g., a person contemplating leaving an abusive relationship).
love/hate	This usually arises in the face of contradictory evidence (e.g., a friend whose behaviour is erratic—sometimes loving, sometimes abusive).

Mixed feelings are often associated with anxiety and stress, especially when the feelings require opposing responses. If a person is both attracted to and repelled by a particular choice, anxiety is likely to continue until he or she resolves the dilemma.

Affect

Affect is a term counsellors use to describe how people express emotions like sadness, excitement, and anger. Culture and context help to define what is considered within the "normal range" of affect. Moreover, affect is communicated through voice tone and quality, posture, facial expressions, and other nonverbal cues. These terms are often used to describe affect:

- *Blunted:* Emotional expression is less than one might expect.
- *Flat:* There is an absence or near absence of any signs of emotional expression.
- *Inappropriate:* The person's manner and mood contradict what one might expect. For example, a client might laugh while describing the death of his mother.
- *Labile:* There is abnormal variability in affect, with repeated, rapid, and abrupt shifts in affective expression.
- *Restricted or constricted:* There is a mild reduction in the range and intensity of emotional expression. (For more information, see American Psychiatric Association, *Diagnostic and Statistical Manual of Mental Disorders, 4th ed.,* 2000.)

Psychologists and other mental health professionals use the terms **affective disorder** or **mood disorder** to describe a variety of disturbances in mood. The most common mood disorders are depression and bipolar disorder. Clients with depression are likely to experience many of the following symptoms: a depressed mood; inability to experience pleasure; loss of energy and interest in life and work; changes in appetite; sleep disturbances (especially insomnia); decrease in sexual energy; feelings of worthlessness, helplessness, guilt, anxiety, or pessimism; and thoughts of death or suicide. With bipolar disorder, clients have alternate depressive and manic episodes. Manic episodes include these symptoms: abnormally elevated mood, irritability, hostility, grandiosity, overactivity, flight of ideas, decreased need for sleep, and buying sprees or other indicators of poor judgment (Nicholi, 1988:315; American Psychiatric Association, 2000). In these situations, referral to a physician should be considered as an adjunct to counselling (see Chapter 8 for more in-depth discussion).

EMPATHY

The Nature of Empathy

In everyday terms, empathy means seeing the world through someone else's eyes. For purposes of counselling, empathy is defined as "the process of accurately understanding the emotional perspective of another person and the communication of this understanding" (Shebib, 1997:177). This definition underscores the twin components of empathy: understanding and communication. A counsellor who is perceptive and adept at understanding the client's major feelings but cannot communicate that understanding is a limited helper (Gladding, 1996:130). The primary target of empathy is to reply to feelings; but in the process, counsellors typically capture elements of their clients' thoughts and situations.

Responses that deal primarily with clients' thoughts may be more appropriately described as reflective responses (Garvin & Seabury, 1984).

Empathy is a powerful helping tool and a core condition for all helping relationships, regardless of the counselling or therapeutic model adopted (Walrond-Skinner, 1986:113). Empathy is a fundamental building block for the helping relationship, and empathy is clearly connected to positive outcomes in counselling (Rogers, 1980). Appropriate empathy communicates understanding, builds trust, and assists in establishing the counsellor's credibility. It is widely ranked as among the highest qualities that a counsellor can possess (Shulman, 1999; Egan, 1998; Walrond-Skinner, 1986). Miller and Rollnick (2002) conclude that the degree of empathy expressed by counsellors is a significant determinant of the success of clients in addictions treatment, whereas confrontational counselling leads to high dropout rates and poor outcomes.

In addition, when counsellors are empathic, they are less likely to oversimplify complex problems. Because they understand more, they are also less prone to insult their clients with well-meaning but unusable advice. Egan puts it bluntly when he says that empathy restrains the counsellor: "Empathy keeps helpers from doing useless, things such as asking too many questions and giving premature and inept advice. Empathy puts the ball back into the client's court and thus in its own way encourages the client to act" (1990:135). Counsellors need to remember that clients have real and rational reasons for feeling as they do.

Counsellors who accept the feelings of their clients help them accept themselves and their feelings. As Parrott observes, "Empathy communicates to clients that they are worth understanding, that their inner hopes and private fears have value" (1997:196). Rogers notes, "True empathy is always free of any evaluative or diagnostic quality. The recipient perceives this with some surprise: 'If I am not being judged, perhaps I am not so evil or abnormal as I have thought. Perhaps I don't have to judge myself so harshly.' Thus, the possibility of self-acceptance is gradually increased" (1980:154).

Rogers further suggests that empathy is more than just a skill—it is a way of being with another person. As he succinctly put it, "The ideal therapist is, first of all, empathic" (1980:146). Empathy is essential for understanding, and some clients "cannot even begin to think about changing their painful situations until they are satisfied that the essence of their pain has been communicated" (Middleman & Wood, 1990:59).

Empathy also assists clients in identifying and labelling feelings, which allows them to deal with the feelings. Moreover, with strong and supportive counsellors, clients can find the courage to deal with feelings that may have been too painful or overwhelming to address on their own. In this sense, empathy contributes to therapeutic change.

Furthermore, clients often adopt the communication patterns of their counsellors. Thus, counsellors who use empathic communication and other active listening skills are modelling skills that clients can use to improve their relationships with others. Counsellor empathy models a healthy way and effective way of communicating.

But in order to effectively empathize, counsellors need to be able to demonstrate comfort with a wide range of feelings. For instance, they need to be able to openly talk about painful feelings like grief. Just as doctors and nurses need to be able to deal with catastrophic injury without losing control or running away, counsellors must develop their capacity to work with intense feelings without needing to change the subject, intellectualize, or offer quick fixes. Sometimes, counsellors misinterpret this capacity as meaning that they need to be emotionally detached and coldly indifferent. In fact, empathic counsellors are deeply involved with their clients. But they put aside or suspend their own reactions to their clients' feelings and adopt an accepting and nonjudgmental attitude. Hancock describes the importance of **controlled emotional involvement**, which she defines as "the empathic sensitivity of the worker to the client's feelings, disciplined by self-awareness, such that the worker's feelings do not inappropriately affect his or her understanding and purposeful response" (1997:131).

Rogers emphasizes the need to "sense the client's private world as if it were your own, but without ever losing the 'as if' quality... To sense the client's anger, fear, or confusion as if it were your own, yet without your own anger, fear, or confusion getting bound up in it" (1961:284). Rogers also provides this important observation about empathy:

> You lay aside your own views and values in order to enter another's world without prejudice. In some sense, it means that you lay aside your self; this can only be done by persons who are secure enough in themselves that they know they will not get lost in what may turn out to be the strange or bizarre world of the other, and that they can comfortably return to their own world when they wish. (1980:143)

However, empathic understanding does not necessarily mean that we endorse our clients' views or behaviour. As Miller and Rollnick (2002) note, "It is possible to accept and understand a person's perspective while not agreeing with or endorsing it. Neither does an attitude of acceptance prohibit the counselor from differing with the client's views and expressing that divergence" (p. 37).

CONVERSATION 6.1

INCREASING EMPATHIC VOCABULARY

STUDENT: I would really like to increase my empathy skills, but my vocabulary is so limited. I seem to know only a few feeling words, such as happy, sad, and angry. How can I increase my feeling word choice?

TEACHER: It's not necessary to have an encyclopedic vocabulary. But you should have enough word choice to capture a broad range of feelings. Study Table 6.1 for new feeling words; then take advantage of every opportunity to practise empathy and use these words. The Internet has many sites that feature feeling word inventories and these can be useful. But remember that feelings are often mixed. Read books and watch TV with a special ear for discerning how people are feeling. One of the best ways is to use invitational empathy to ask others how they feel, then to listen carefully to their words. This will help sensitize you to their unique vocabulary. By adopting at attitude of interest and curiosity and focusing on feelings, you can dramatically increase your vocabulary.

Types of Empathy

The three types of empathy are basic empathy, inferred empathy, and invitational empathy. With invitational empathy, a counsellor uses strategies to encourage clients to talk about their feelings. With basic empathy, a counsellor mirrors what the client has explicitly said. And with inferred empathy, a counsellor reaches empathic understanding by interpreting subtle clues. At any point in an interview, counsellors can use empathy to explore a client's behaviour, thinking, or feelings. When they focus on behaviour, they explore what clients are doing or saying, or they shift attention to problem solving. When they pursue thinking, they are interested in their clients' beliefs and assumptions, including their inner dialogue and self-esteem. But empathy enables counsellors to pay primary attention to the third area—feelings. Frequently counsellors are too anxious to solve problems, and they move the interview focus prematurely to this area, ignoring or discounting what may be more important than solutions—their clients' feelings.

Invitational Empathy

Invitational empathy encourages clients to explore emotions. It can also be used to move the interview away from a focus on problem solving. Invitational empathy is initiated with a simple question such as, "How do you feel?" Invitational empathy says to the client that the counsellor is ready and able to talk about difficult feelings.

To do this, counsellors can draw on their knowledge of human growth and development, such as ways that people tend to deal with particular life events and crises. Some clients are reluctant to share their feelings for fear of judgment, or they may believe that they shouldn't feel a particular way. Others may think they are the "only one" or that they are "crazy," "evil," or "abnormal." For example, it is common to feel some relief, even happiness (as well as grief) when a loved one who has been struggling with a painful illness dies; but a client may feel guilty for feeling this way. Invitational empathy normalizes the experience, making it easier for the client to talk about it and to accept it: "It's normal at a time like this to struggle with mixed feelings—grief, pain, comfort, and perhaps joy that her suffering is at an end."

By encouraging clients to talk about feelings, then responding nonjudgementally, the counsellor is saying, "It's okay to feel this way." In the following example, the counsellor uses invitational empathy to "give permission" to a client who might otherwise suppress or ignore his pain to experience and verbalize his emotions.

Client: *I guess it's no big deal. So what if they know the scoop on my marital problems?*

Counsellor: *A lot of people in the same situation might feel embarrassed and perhaps disappointed or angry that a friend could be so indiscreet about something said in confidence.*

In the example below, the counsellor uses nonverbal cues as a basis for invitational empathy to encourage the client to explore a difficult topic.

Counsellor: *Would you mind if I shared an observation with you? I may be wrong, so I'd like your opinion.*

Client: *Sure, go ahead. Say it.*

Counsellor: *I notice that whenever mention of your father comes up, you seem keen to change the topic.*

(long silence, client stares at the floor)

Counsellor: *Some memories are painful—maybe even too painful to talk about.*

Client: *(softly, tears in his eyes) It's just that his death was so unexpected. We had a fight that morning, and I didn't even get a chance to say goodbye.*

Invitational empathy begins with questions and responses targeted at encouraging clients to express feelings. The choice of strategy is influenced by the usual variables, including the amount of trust in the relationship, time constraints, culture, and the counsellor's role. Timing, for example, is one of the most important variables. Since the exploration of feelings can be time consuming, it is important for counsellors to make sure that they have enough time to complete the process. Intelligent use of silence is another important variable. Clients may need their counsellors to patiently listen and restrain themselves from filling every silent moment with words.

One way to bridge the interview into a discussion of feelings is to use invitational statements, such as "I do not know how you feel, but if you are feeling pain or loneliness, I am ready to listen." Comments such as "I need your help in understanding your feelings" can also move the interview into the affective—or feeling—area.

Frequently, clients provide natural opportunities when they give hints about how they are feeling. Then the counsellor can use questions to encourage further sharing. Open questions promote clients to share feelings: "How are you feeling?" "What feelings best describe how you reacted?" Closed questions target specific information about feelings: "Did you feel angry?" "Is this something you feel strongly about?"

Helping clients understand the importance of addressing feelings is an important step that keeps clients involved in decision making (contracting). When counsellors inform clients and solicit their support for the process, clients' motivation is higher. Here are some sample leads:

- I think it might help if we shift our focus and talk a bit about how you feel. This might help us both to understand why your decision is so difficult.
- We haven't yet talked about your feelings. In my experience, feelings often present one of the biggest barriers.
- Until feelings are understood and accepted, they can distort our thinking and even reduce the amount of control we have over our behaviour. So you might find it useful if we spend some time exploring how you feel.

In addition, directives can be used to move the interview into the feeling area: "Tell me how you feel." "Let's switch our focus and talk about your feelings." Directives are one way to manage the flow and focus of the interview.

Moreover, with some clients, counsellor self-disclosure is a powerful tool if used sparingly: "I don't know how it is for you, but I know that for many months after my marriage ended, I was in a state of shock."

Another tool for exploring feelings is the sentence completion statement. Sentence completion statements give counsellors a way to focus feelings on a particular area, and they give freedom to clients to control the answer:

- When I think about all my problems, I feel...
- If I could use one feeling to describe my situation it would be...
- When I first came for counselling I felt...
- The feelings that I most need to deal with are...

But invitational empathy should always respect clients' rights to privacy. Compton and Galaway point out:

> It is questionable whether any client wants to be fully and totally known. There is something very frightening about someone's knowing everything about us as an individual for in knowledge lies control; so in the ordinary course of living people reveal their intimate selves only to those they trust. Without the pain of the problem and the hope that the worker can offer some help toward coping with it, few clients would be willing to share themselves with an unknown other person. (1984:238)

Basic Empathy

With **basic empathy**, counsellors perceive and respond to feelings that are explicitly communicated. Basic empathy may involve labelling feelings or summarizing expressed feelings. Frequently, clients want to talk about feelings, particularly those closely related to their problem situations. When they take the initiative to introduce feelings, it is relatively easy and nonthreatening for counsellors to respond with basic empathy. Basic empathy simply says, "I have heard how you feel, and I accept your feelings without judgment." With basic empathy, no attempt is made to interpret, judge, or promote greater awareness or insight beyond that which the client has already articulated.

Despite its apparent simplicity, basic empathy can be a powerful helping tool. When people express feelings in everyday communication, they may be blocked or discouraged when others react by judging, ignoring, or giving advice. For example, one common but extremely unhelpful response is "You shouldn't feel that way." In contrast, basic empathy creates a climate in which clients do not have to defend or hide their feelings. For many people, basic empathy responses are an unusual and satisfying experience. As one client described it, "For the first time, I felt safe. Someone had finally listened and heard me." Hancock states that "empathy helps to establish an atmosphere that gives each client a secure feeling that this is a place where 'it's safe to be me, this me, here and now'" (1997:167).

Furthermore, counsellors who punctuate their work with frequent empathy are more likely to build rapport and evoke further information from clients (Egan, 1998). Simple logic suggests that when people believe that they are accepted and understood, they are more likely to feel secure and less likely to raise defences. As a result, clients are more inclined to share and explore at a deeper level of intimacy than they would under more threatening conditions. The example below illustrates basic empathy:

Client: *I was ready to kill her. How could she embarrass me in front of all those people?*

Counsellor: *So you are angry that she didn't have enough sense to keep quiet.*

Client: *Angry, but also hurt. After all, she was supposed to be my best friend. How could she double-cross me?*

Counsellor: *Sounds as if you feel betrayed.*

But empathic responses also need to be presented with an air of tentativeness in order to give clients an opportunity to offer corrections. A simple pause or a question such as "Have I got it right?" can be used to this end.

Inferred Empathy

Inferred empathy, sometimes called *advanced accurate empathy* (Egan, 1998), includes attempts to identify clients' feelings based on nonverbal cues, themes, and hints. Counsellors should also pay careful attention to what their clients don't say, including topics they avoid and sudden shifts in focus. Inferred empathy is a powerful counselling tool that enables clients to deal with feelings at a level deeper than expressed emotions.

Some clients find that their trust level increases when counsellors identify their hidden feelings: "My worker seemed to know how I felt without my saying so. Finally, I felt understood. In fact, I began to understand myself better." Moreover, inferred empathy may be particularly useful with clients who lack feeling vocabulary or are unaccustomed to expressing feelings. Inferred empathy seems to say, "I have the courage and the ability to hear your feelings."

Client: *It was a tough situation. Here I was in front of all those people with my private life laid bare.*

Counsellor: *From the tears in your eyes, I suspect this was a painful and embarrassing moment for you.*

In the above example, the client seems willing to explore her experience, yet she stops short of verbally identifying her feelings. The counsellor takes a mild empathic risk and considers context and nonverbal cues to infer empathy. Inferred empathy should always be presented tentatively to allow room for correction and further exploration.

With inferred empathy, some speculation based on the evidence of feelings is necessary. Consequently, there is more risk involved than with basic empathy. There are two significant risks. First, because the information base for inferred empathy is more ambiguous, more errors are likely. Hence, counsellors should be especially tentative with inferred empathy. As well, counsellors should avoid becoming overly speculative to the point where they are simply guessing at their clients' feelings. Second, inferred empathy may be met with resistance from clients who are unwilling or unable to acknowledge their feelings. Inferred empathy picks up on subtle cues, and clients may be surprised to hear that their feelings have been communicated. They may react with anger and resentment that their feelings have been uncovered. In addition, some clients are afraid of the intensity of their feelings, whereas others have strong needs for privacy. Thus, inferred empathy must be timed appropriately. The counselling relationship should have a reasonable level of trust, and the counselling session should have sufficient time left to process any reactions. Otherwise, it is best to defer inferred empathic responses till later.

Since inferred empathy involves "reading" the clients, counsellors need to develop skills in this area. First, clients provide clues to their feelings in a number of ways. They might be embarrassed about sharing their feelings or reluctant to ask for help, so they talk about a "friend who has a problem." Second, as stressed above, understanding nonverbal behaviour is crucial. Astute counsellors learn a great deal about their clients' feelings by carefully observing changes in voice tone, sudden shifts in posture, nervous behaviour, tears, grimaces, clenched fists, finger tapping, and smiling. As well, certain behaviours can suggest feelings. For example, a boy who runs away from a group home just before a visit from his mother may be saying something about his fear or anger. A client who arrives late, refuses to take his coat off, and sits with arms folded across his chest might be saying, "I don't want to be here."

But another way that many clients share feelings is through analogies. For example, a client who compares his life to a speeding train may be expressing his fears of being out of control. Some clients hint at their feelings by asking questions, such as "Do you worry about your kids when they are out late at night?" In addition, clients who minimize problems, as in "I have a bit of a problem. Do you have a minute?" or "This is probably not important" may be signalling that they have significant issues and feelings that they need to discuss.

Tuning in, or **preparatory empathy** (Shulman, 1999), is another useful way to prepare for inferred empathy. Preparatory empathy is a preliminary phase skill that involves trying to anticipate the feelings and concerns that clients might bring up in the interview. Since clients often do not directly reveal their feelings, tuning in helps workers anticipate how clients might communicate feelings indirectly. Shulman (1999) illustrates tuning in with a common example involving an encounter between a new 22-year-old worker meeting with a 38-year-old mother of seven children. The mother asked the worker, "Do you have any children?" The worker responded defensively by talking about her training in child psychology. Shulman suggests that the worker missed the implicit feelings expressed by the mother—the fear that the worker will not understand her. Had she used the tuning-in skill, the worker might have been able to consider in advance the range of feelings that a mother of seven kids might have when meeting with a young counsellor who has no children. With such advance preparation, the worker might have been more sensitive to the mother's real question, perhaps responding, "No, I don't have any children. Why do you ask? Are you wondering if I'm going to be able to understand what it's like for you having to raise so many? I'm concerned about that as well. If I'm to help you, I'm going to have to understand, and you are going to have to help me to understand" (Shulman, 1999:45). This response might have set the stage for a discussion of the mother's feelings about workers and given the worker a chance to share her own feelings. Similar counsellor strategies might be appropriate for client questions, such as, "Have you ever been to jail?" "Do you know what it's like to live on the street?" and "How old are you?"

CONVERSATION 6.2

WHEN NOT TO USE EMPATHY

STUDENT: I don't think empathy is always such a good thing. I watched one taped interview of Carl Rogers and two other therapists interviewing the same client, Gloria. If I had been Rogers' client, I would have been irritated. He seemed to continually regurgitate what the client had just said.

TEACHER: You've raised a good point. Too much empathy, particularly when you get stuck at a basic level, might leave you and your client going in circles. It's also true that if you move too fast with empathy, your clients can feel threatened and put up their defences. This is particularly true with clients who have strong needs for privacy. They may view your empathic statements as an unwanted intrusion into their feelings. Empathy invites greater relationship intimacy, and some clients are not ready for the risks that this entails. Some clients open up to empathic responses only to later regret having revealed too much. They may "clam up" in future sessions, never return to counselling, or they may resent their counsellors for allowing that to happen. But even though you might have been irritated, it's interesting to note that years later, Roger's client Gloria described how her short time with Roger's was life-changing for her. This reminds us that clients respond differently to the same technique. Be careful that your perception of the Roger's tape doesn't deter you from using empathy. It may be exactly what your client needs. Other clients who may not be ready for empathy are those who are so caught up in their own talking that they do not even hear empathic statements. As Shea (1988) suggests, attempts to empathize with this group may actually be counterproductive because empathy interferes with what they want most—an audience to listen.

STUDENT: I think one way to handle that is to test your client's capacity for empathy with a few basic empathic statements. If they are not well received, you can back off by switching to less demanding content or more basic empathy.

Teacher: I agree, back off, but not forever! As trust develops, the client may welcome that same empathic response that he or she first rejected. To continue the list of times when empathy may not be a good idea, I'd add the following:

- when your clients reject empathy
- when it's clearly time to move on to problem solving or another activity
- when empathy is continuously misinterpreted by clients (for example, as controlling).

We should always remember that counselling techniques will not work the same with all clients. Cultural norms, trust level, mood, and personal resiliency are all variables that influence how empathy is received.

Four Generalizations about Empathy

Generalization One

When clients share feelings, empathy is often the preferred response. The **principle of positive reinforcement** states that "if in a given situation, somebody does something that is followed immediately by a positive reinforcer, then that person is more likely to do the same thing again" (Martin & Pear, 1992:26). Moreover, clients take an interpersonal risk when they share their feelings. Empathy acknowledges this risk by conveying recognition and acceptance of the clients' feelings. In this way, it reinforces the wisdom of the risk and motivates clients to continue sharing feelings. On the other hand, when clients share feelings and they are not rewarded (or reinforced) with empathy, then they tend to keep their feelings more private. This underscores the importance of expressing empathy early in the relationship.

Generalization Two

Counsellors should risk expressing empathy early in the relationship. Norms, once established are difficult to alter. Early empathy helps form the norm that the counselling relationship is a safe place to express feelings. To become comfortable with empathy, counsellors need to overcome their own fears about bringing emotions into the foreground. Many workers fear that by encouraging clients to express emotions, they might trigger extreme reactions, particularly suicide. But this fear is not substantiated. In fact, it takes energy to suppress emotions; therefore, by helping clients express and get in touch with their feelings, counsellors can help them decrease the negative effects of these feelings.

Invitational empathy is useful for working with clients who are reluctant or unable to articulate feelings. Counsellor timing is critical, and counsellors should present invitational empathy in a gentle and tentative manner.

Early in the counselling relationship, counsellors should give priority to acquiring, maintaining, and deepening empathic understanding by remaining alert to empathic opportunities. One obvious opportunity arises whenever clients verbalize feelings. In such moments, counsellors can use basic empathy to confirm understanding. Sometimes clients reveal feelings nonverbally, and counsellors can use inferred empathy. When clients have not shared feelings, counsellors can adopt invitational empathy to encourage them to share their emotions.

TABLE 6.3	Types of Empathy Type		
Type	**Description**	**Major Use**	**Comments**
Basic	Response to clearly articulated feelings	To encourage continued expression of feelings To confirm capacity to hear feelings	Basic empathy contributes to the development of trust. It signals to clients that counsellors are willing and able to deal with feelings.
Inferred	Response to nonverbal cues and other indicators of feelings	To move feelings into the verbal channel of communication	Inferred empathy may generate more anxiety in some clients if feelings that they avoided, suppressed, or wanted to keep hidden are made visible.
Invitational	Encouragement of clients to talk about feelings	To stimulate discussion of feelings To normalize feelings	Inferred empathy may promote client insight.

Generalization Three

Counsellors should express empathy tentatively. Counsellors need to refrain from using empathy as a weapon by insisting that their clients must feel a particular way. Counsellors should also look for indicators that clients have accepted their empathy and that it is accurate. Clients provide confirmation through head nods, smiles, reduction in anxiety, and verbal confirmation (for example, "That's right" or "You seem to know exactly how I'm feeling even before I tell you"). Clients also implicitly confirm willingness to accept empathy when they continue to share feelings at a deeper level. Moreover, sometimes clients correct counsellors. This is an important and positive outcome of empathic risk. It enables counsellors to adjust and refine their understanding and helps them reach a point of shared meaning with their clients. Thus, empathy should be seen as an active process of developing understanding.

Generalization Four

Empathy requires flexibility in its use, including the ability to refrain from using it. Empathy is an important and powerful skill, but counsellors need to use it intelligently. When clients are willing to address feelings, empathic responses are effective (see Table 6.4 for suggestions). But with some clients, empathic statements result in the opposite of what was intended. Instead of deepening trust and encouraging clients to open up, empathy arouses defences. This may happen when empathy targets feelings that clients would prefer to hide, or when clients experience empathy as invading their personal space. When clients resist empathy by withdrawing or becoming defensive, counsellors should discontinue using it for a while.

Moreover, situational differences influence how the work of empathy unfolds. Some clients are very verbal and open with their feelings and respond positively to empathy. Others need gentle encouragement to talk about feelings, and they open up discussion of feelings gradually and in a very controlled manner. Counsellors will generally find that they encounter less resistance when they match their clients' pace.

TABLE 6.4	The Empathic Communication Process

- Listen for or probe for feelings.
- Observe nonverbal indicators of emotion.
- Consider context—problem, phase, setting, relationship.
- Identify the general category of feeling (e.g., anger, sadness, etc.), including mixed or ambivalent feelings.
- Identify the level or intensity of emotion (i.e., low, medium, high).
- Choose an appropriate specific feeling word, phrase or metaphor.
- Formulate a tentative empathic response.
- Wait for or encourage the client to confirm or correct your empathic perception.
- Correct or offer a deeper empathic response based on the client's response.

Empathic Response Leads

Using a range of different responses adds interest and variety to the interview. But using the same words and phrases too often can irritate clients and reduce the energy and vitality of the interview. Having a range of leads for empathic response prevents the interview from sounding artificial. The following list provides some variations:

- So, you feel...
- My sense is that you might be feeling...
- From your point of view...
- As you see it...
- I wonder if what you're saying is...
- Perhaps you feel...
- I gather that...
- It seems to you that...
- What I understand from what you have said is...
- It sounds like...
- You appear to be feeling...

Why Achieving Empathic Understanding Is So Difficult

Empathic errors are generally unlikely when counsellors are similar to their clients (in age, gender, race, etc.) and when they have had similar problems and experiences. But even in these situations, empathic errors can happen if counsellors do not separate their own experiences from those of their clients. Counsellors need to remember to allow for individual differences by remembering that, however similar their own experiences might be, they can never fully understand how their clients feel. Through empathy, they can get a sense of their clients' feelings, but this understanding will never be perfect. The challenge is to "see beyond conventional facades, refrain from imposing personal interpretations and judgments, and be willing to risk understanding another person's private logic and feelings, which in superficial daily contacts the counsellor might see as weak, foolish, or undesirable" (Hammond, Hepworth, & Smith, 1977:3).

Empathy is perhaps the most difficult counselling skill to master. As Egan notes, "Although many people 'feel' empathy for others, the truth is that few know how to put it into words" (1998:83). Moreover, empathy demands a lot of mental energy from counsellors. First, they must manage their own emotional and judgmental reactions. Then they have to find meaning and discover feelings from their clients' verbal and nonverbal communication. But this can be exceptionally demanding, since clients may keep feelings hidden, suppress feelings, or lack understanding or awareness of their emotions. As well, relationship issues, including lack of trust, embarrassment, and fear of being judged, can inhibit clients from disclosing. For example, there may be societal, cultural, or personal norms that prohibit sharing of feelings. Or clients may not have the ability (language) to adequately communicate their emotions.

Further complicating the empathic process is the fact that counsellors must respond right away. In an interview, there is no time to use a thesaurus or dictionary and no opportunity to consult others, rehearse their empathy, or ponder the feeling state of their clients. Empathic risk means daring to share perceived understanding with clients using concrete words and phrases that are accessible in the situation.

Responses to Avoid

When attempting to express empathy, counsellors need to avoid certain responses. In particular, they need to be aware of the effect of cutoffs, empty responses, and sympathy.

Cutoffs

Cutoffs are phrases that inhibit the further expression of feeling. Counsellors who make statements such as "Don't feel" and "You should feel" are demonstrating a low level of understanding and acceptance of how their clients feel. Although such statements have some limited supportive value, they generally force clients to defend their feelings. Similarly, when counsellors ask clients questions such as "Why do you feel like that?" a judgmental tone is present that can leave clients feeling defensive (see Chapter 5).

Another response that may inhibit clients is silence. When clients risk sharing feelings, some response (empathy) is appropriate. But when counsellors fail to acknowledge feelings, they may be saying, "This is not important" or "I'm not capable of dealing with your emotions." In response, clients might feel abandoned, embarrassed, or judged.

Counsellors can also make the mistake of cutting clients off by changing the subject or offering advice. A subject change gives the message "Let's not talk about that," and advice trivializes feelings.

Empty Responses

Empty responses are devoid of content. Phrases such as "I hear what you are saying" and "I understand what you mean" convey no confirmation that the counsellor has understood. Another empty response is parroting, or repeating, what the client has said. Egan describes parroting as "a parody of empathy" (1998:96). In contrast, empathy communicates the counsellor's effort to go beyond merely hearing the words to understanding the client's feelings and perspectives. Using empathy, the counsellor rephrases the client's statements and assigns labels to feelings that the client expressed but did not name.

Be aware that clichés and platitudes, such as "Everybody has to have a little pain in their life," patronize and reject clients' feelings. As Egan puts it, clichéd responses say, "You don't really have a problem at all, at least not a serious one" (1998:96).

Sympathy

Sympathy refers to concern for other people's problems and emotions and is related to our own emotional and behavioural reactions. Sympathy is the counsellor's personal reaction; and though it is intimately connected to the client's feelings, it is not the same as empathy. It might be helpful to think of sympathetic responses as self-disclosures and empathy as a process of seeking to understand another's feelings. However, counsellors are human, and it is normal for them to have emotional responses when listening to their clients. In fact, their reactions are the basis for compassion, an indispensable component of a caring counselling relationship. Clearly, there are moments when it is appropriate to express sympathy, letting clients know that counsellors support them and are moved by their pain. At the same time, it is essential for counsellors to develop the ability to separate their emotional reactions (sympathy and compassion) from those of their clients. Counsellors also need to ensure that their sympathy does not detract from the client's feelings by interfering with their need to express feelings, tell their stories, and face the reality of their problems.

> Client: *I'm really worried about telling my dad that I've dropped out of college. Even when I was a little girl, my father kept saying, "You've got to get an education, or you'll never get anywhere in life."*

> Counsellor (Choice 1—sympathetic reaction): *I don't think it was very fair for him to have laid such a heavy burden on you. It always makes me kind of angry when I hear about parents pushing their kids.*

> Counsellor (Choice 2—empathic reaction): *So you fear that you've let your father down.*

In the above example, Choice 1 is a misguided attempt to offer support. Judgmental in tone, it shifts the focus from the client's feelings to those of the counsellor. Choice 2 expresses basic empathy, setting the stage for further exploration.

Empathy Substitutes

When counsellors express empathy, they need to acknowledge the feelings that clients have expressed (verbally and/or non verbally). They can include a brief "because" clause that summarizes content. In most situations, they will stop there. This gives clients a chance to process what they have heard and to offer corrections. But when clients experience this kind of empathy, they may be motivated to share at a deeper level. At this point, counsellors should avoid subject changes, cutoff responses, content questions, sympathy, or any other response that diverts attention away from empathy. Below are some examples of appropriate and inappropriate empathic responses.

> Client: *Sometimes when he speaks to me that way, I just want to go hide in a corner.*

> Counsellor 1 (appropriate empathy): *It sounds like maybe you're feeling embarrassed.*

> Counsellor 2 (inappropriate empathy—subject shift): *It sounds like maybe you're feeling embarrassed. Would you like to talk about ways of overcoming it?*

Counsellor 3 (sympathy confused with empathy): *I feel sorry for you that he treats you that way.*

Counsellor 4 (non-empathy): *There's no reason why you should have to put up with such treatment.*

Counsellor 5 (non-empathy—failure to identify feelings): *You're feeling that he should stop doing that.*

Tough Empathy

It's not hard to feel caring and compassion for most people in pain, such as the aging client who loses his job, the young mother who has had a second miscarriage, and the single parent who is trying to raise children on a limited income. However, some clients may challenge a counsellor's tolerance. Even the most accepting counsellors occasionally find it difficult to lay aside personal reaction, suspend judgment, and respond with empathy to clients such as the following:

- Bob, an angry 20-year-old who savagely attacked an elderly woman
- Pernell, a father who argues for the morality of sex with his children
- Eileen, an HIV-positive prostitute who asserts her right to have unprotected sex with her customers
- Ruby, a woman who rejects and attacks efforts to help

Counsellors working with clients such as these are likely to experience strong emotional reactions, and they may find it difficult to put aside their personal feelings in order to feel and express empathy. Often, these are clients who appear to lack empathy and feelings for others in their lives. In fact, "the blotting out of empathy as these people inflict damage on victims is almost always part of an emotional cycle that precipitates their cruel acts" (Goleman, 1995:106).

Why then should counsellors respond with empathy to such people? First, empathy is a way for counsellors to understand how their clients think and feel. Second, as noted earlier, empathy is instrumental in forming the helping relationship, the prerequisite condition for the contract between client and counsellor. One outcome of empathy is that clients come to feel valued and understood. As a result of the empathic relationship, clients begin to reveal more, make discoveries about themselves, and alter their perspectives about themselves and others. With clients who lack empathy for others, counsellor use of empathy obliges them to face their feelings and those of their victims.

In situations in which it is difficult to respond with empathy, counsellors may need to work on their own issues. For example, they can ask themselves, "What is it about this particular client that makes it difficult for me to be empathic?" "Does this client remind me of someone else (e.g., parent, former partner)?" "To what extent do I have unresolved feelings and issues that this client triggers?"

Another strategy for counsellors is to spend time getting to know the client. Usually, familiarity increases empathy.

Carl, an employment counsellor, carefully read Antonio's file. Antonio was a 19-year-old unemployed male. From all indications, Antonio was not very interested in finding a job. His mother complained that he usually slept until noon and that he rarely even read the newspaper want ads. Antonio arrived for his appointment 20 minutes late and gave out a clear message that he didn't want to be there. "How long will this take?" he asked bluntly.

Carl's natural reaction was anger and disgust at Antonio's attitude. He wondered to himself why he should spend time with this client, who was clearly unmotivated. Putting his personal feelings aside, Carl decided to respond with empathy, and he gently replied, "My hunch is that you don't see much point in being here. Maybe you're even a little angry at being forced to come." Antonio, a bit surprised at Carl's perceptiveness, told him how much he resented everyone trying to run his life.

Gradually, Antonio began to let down his defences, and a very different picture emerged. Antonio talked about the rejection he felt from countless employers who turned him away. Soon, it was clear to Carl that Antonio was deeply depressed. He slept late because he couldn't sleep at night. He had stopped looking for work because it was the only way he knew to deal with the pain.

Sometimes counsellors fear expressing empathy because they mistakenly believe that empathy endorses their clients' beliefs or lifestyles. But keep in mind that being empathic does not mean agreeing with client feelings or perspectives. Empathy simply attempts to say, "I understand how you feel and how you see things." In fact, clients must feel understood before they will respond to any efforts to promote change. Empathy is one of the ways that counsellors establish credibility and win the trust of their clients. When a trusting relationship exists, clients may be willing to consider other perspectives and look at the consequences of their choices.

INTERVIEW 6.1   POOR SUBSTITUTES FOR EMPATHY

The following excerpt illustrates some of the inappropriate responses that counsellors sometimes use instead of empathy. Ignoring feelings and offering empty responses, simplistic advice, and sympathy are inadequate substitutes for empathy.

DIALOGUE	ANALYSIS
Client (softly, with tears in her eyes): I just haven't been the same since he left. I still look out the door and expect him to come home.	Inappropriate topic shift: The client is clearly experiencing some pain, perhaps grief, and she trusts the counsellor enough to share these feelings. Generally, when clients share feelings, particularly feelings that are strong, empathy is the preferred response.
Counsellor: How old was he when he ran away?	
	The counsellor's response shifts the focus away from feelings to content. This may subtly signal to the client that the counsellor is uncomfortable with feelings. Continual shifts such as this will "train" the client not to share feelings.
Client: He was just 16. I still thought of him as my baby. Now I go to sleep at night wondering whether he's dead or alive.	
Counsellor: You thought of him as your baby. Now you go to sleep at night wondering whether he's dead or alive.	Parroting: Repetition at this point serves no purpose. Sometimes key words or phrases can be emphasized as a way to focus attention, but this type of parroting is inappropriate here.
(silence)	
Counsellor: I understand how you feel.	*(continued)*

Client (buries her face in her hands): Sometimes I just don't know whether I can go on living. If something doesn't happen soon, then... (counsellor interrupts)

Counsellor: You have to think of your husband and your other children.

Client: Yes, I know, but do you have any idea what I'm going through, how tough it is just to get out of bed in the morning?

Counsellor: My guess is that you feel very angry at the world, maybe even some guilt that you are somehow responsible for your son's running away.

Client: No! I don't feel guilty. I was always a good mother. I think if my son were here, he'd say that too. When he became addicted to drugs, it was more than either of us knew how to handle.

Counsellor: I hear what you are saying.

Client: So what am I supposed to do? I feel so empty and useless.

Counsellor: It's a very bad feeling.

(brief silence)

Counsellor: You shouldn't feel that way. One day your son might walk in the door. You have to go on living.

Client: I suppose you're right. Thanks for listening. It felt good to get it off my chest.

Counsellor: I'm glad I was able to help.

Superficial response: The counsellor tries to be supportive, but the response is empty. Until the counsellor risks empathy with specific feeling words and phrases, the client cannot know whether she has, in fact, been heard.

Rescuing, ignoring feelings: It seems obvious that this counsellor is unable to deal with the powerful feelings that the client presents. After an ill-timed interruption, the counsellor offers a misguided and simplistic solution, while ignoring the emotions the client expressed.

Inaccurate empathy: The counsellor attempts invitational empathy. Unfortunately, there is insufficient evidence to support the counsellor's conclusion that the client feels angry or guilty. The counsellor may be right, but as suggested, it is merely a guess, a poor substitute for empathy. Moreover, the counsellor is not attending to the feelings that the client has already expressed.

Superficial response: This counsellor's response has the same problems as her earlier one, "I understand how you feel."

Inaccurate empathy, lack of specificity: The counsellor attempts empathy but misses the intensity of the client's feelings. Then the counsellor quickly shifts the focus without giving the client time to respond.

One important requirement is to accept clients' feelings without judgment and without trying to tell them how they should feel.

Sometimes clients benefit from the interview, even when the counsellor's responses are as poor as those depicted in this encounter. Simply telling one's story and verbalizing feelings can help people deal with pain or problems. However, it is much more likely that this client is ready to dismiss the counsellor. The counsellor may be just as relieved that the interview is over.

Counsellors may find wisdom in Nicholi's observation that "whether the patient is young or old, neatly groomed or dishevelled, outgoing or withdrawn, articulate or inarticulate, highly integrated or totally disintegrated, of high or low socioeconomic status, the skilled clinician realizes that the patient, as a fellow human being, is considerably more like himself than he is different" (1988:8).

INTERVIEW 6.2   EFFECTIVE USE OF EMPATHY

DIALOGUE	ANALYSIS
Client: For as long as I can remember, I've been drinking on a daily basis. It's no big deal.	The counsellor tries to proceed cautiously with basic paraphrasing. Mirroring the client's thoughts conveys that he has been heard. Suspending verbal and nonverbal judgment helps to develop trust.
Counsellor (softly, while maintaining eye contact): Drinking has been part of your life, and you don't see a problem with it.	
(client nods)	The counsellor uses an open question to encourage the client to talk about his feelings. Such statements also say to the client that the counsellor is willing to listen.
Counsellor: You mentioned that your family gives you a hard time about drinking. How do you feel about that?	
Client: Yeah. I work hard all day. If I want to have a drink, no one has a right to tell me to stop. Drinking helps me to relax.	The counsellor uses inferred empathy. Although the client does not directly label his feelings, from the words, context, and nonverbal messages, the counsellor speculates that resentment might be the predominant feeling.
Counsellor: Sounds as though you resent it when others interfere with something that gives you pleasure.	The client's response suggests that he is responsive to the counsellor's empathy. He signals this by continuing to share at a deeper level. This is a significant event in the interview, which should give the counsellor confidence to continue to risk empathy.
Client (loudly): They should back off and mind their own business. I don't tell them how to live.	
Counsellor: It's more than just resentment. Perhaps you're angry that they don't respect your right to live your life as you see fit.	Here again, the counsellor infers anger from the client's nonverbal expression. By labelling the anger, the counsellor gives the client "permission" to discuss his anger.
Client: I guess I shouldn't be so ticked off. After all, my father was an alcoholic, and I know firsthand what it's like to live with a drunk.	Since the counsellor accepts his anger, the client may feel less that he has to defend it.
Counsellor: To some extent your feelings are mixed—you feel anger because you think they should mind their own business. But you also	The counsellor picks up and identifies the client's mixed feelings. Mixed feelings can often be a
(continued)

see where they are coming from, and you are sympathetic to their fears.

Client: Well, to be perfectly honest, it's not just their fear. I don't want to drink myself to death like my father did.

Counsellor: You've done some thinking about how you'd like your life to be different. When your wife confronts you, it really touches a nerve, and you're reminded of fears you'd rather not have.

Client: No way I'm going to let that happen to me.

Counsellor: You're determined to control your drinking.

Client: I'm not going to be like my father.

Counsellor: Correct me if I'm off base, but as you talk, I wonder if a part of you is afraid that your drinking could get out of hand.

source of anxiety for clients, particularly if they pull their emotions in different directions.

This client was initially guarded and defensive, quick to defend his right to drink. As he finds acceptance from the counsellor, he begins to let his guard down. In some interviews, such as this one, trust can develop quickly, but more often, the counsellor requires extended patience.

The counsellor responds with inferred empathy.

The counsellor uses a basic empathic response. A return to basic empathy gives the client some breathing room. Counsellors should avoid constant pressure on clients to move to a higher level of intimacy. The counsellor needs to move deeper, but caution is critical to avoid moving too quickly.

The counsellor uses both confrontation and invitational empathy in this statement. Presenting the ideas in a tentative manner softens the confrontation.

SUMMARY

Because of the central role that emotions play in our lives, counsellors must give priority to exploring and understanding clients' feelings. Emotions are characterized by physiological as well as psychological and behavioural reactions. Learning about the ten families of emotions—anger, fear, strength, weakness, joy, sadness, confusion, shame, surprise, and love—provides counsellors with a starting point for organizing their thoughts about emotions. But clients may describe their emotions using specific feeling words and modifiers or through metaphors and nonverbal channels of communication.

Body language, or kinesics, includes variables such as posture, facial expressions, gestures, and eye motion. Sometimes body language is easily interpreted, but at other times it is ambiguous and thus needs to be interpreted with caution.

Voice tone, volume, and pitch can help counsellors identify emotions. Voice variables can reveal if clients are depressed, euphoric, angry, or sad.

Proxemics describes the use of space and distance. Counsellors should adapt their seating to meet the proxemics needs of individual clients. They should also observe spatial shifts during the interview.

Feelings can be experienced as positive or negative, but this subjective determination is individually defined. The same emotion may be debilitating for some but exhilarating for others. Moreover, circumstances and context may not always be good predictors of feelings.

In addition, mixed feelings, including contradictory emotions, are common. A great deal of client stress and confusion can arise from the pushes and pulls of competing feelings, which, if unmanaged, can control a client's life.

Empathy is a core skill for all helping relationships. Empathy helps build the helping relationship, assists clients in identifying and labelling feelings, models a healthy way of relating to others, and helps clients to accept their own feelings. Although counsellors can never know exactly how their clients feel, empathy enables them to move closer to understanding how they think and feel.

The three types of empathy are basic, inferred, and invitational. Basic empathy mirrors what the client has explicitly said, while inferred empathy attempts to reach empathic understanding from less obvious clues. Invitational empathy involves strategies to encourage clients to talk about their feelings.

Tuning in, or preparatory empathy, is a way for counsellors to prepare for inferred empathy. Preparatory empathy involves trying to estimate the feelings and concerns that clients may bring to the interview.

A variety of strategies can be used to encourage clients to express feelings, including invitational statements, questions targeted at feelings, explanations of the importance of addressing feelings, directives, self-disclosures, and sentence completion statements.

Finally, there are four key generalizations about empathy: (1) When clients share feelings, empathy is often the preferred response. (2) Counsellors should risk expressing empathy early in the relationship. (3) Counsellors should express empathy tentatively. And (4) empathy requires flexibility in its use, including the ability to refrain from using it.

EXERCISES

1. Begin a log to track your feelings. At periodic intervals (e.g., every hour), record words and phrases that best describe how you are feeling at that moment. Try to be as precise as possible, using terms that capture the essence and intensity of how you feel. Maintain your log for at least one week.

   a. What patterns or cycles are apparent? Are there times of the day or week when you are more likely to feel particular emotions?

   b. How were your emotions linked to events or people?

   c. How could you have altered your emotions (for example, to increase pleasurable feelings and decrease negative feelings)?

   d. What have you learned about yourself from this exercise that will assist you in your work as a counsellor?

2. Recall the 10 families of emotions: anger, fear, strength, weakness, joy, sadness, confusion, shame, surprise, and love. Rate your ability to show or express each one on a scale of 1 to 5. (5=strong, 1=unable to express)

   a. What are the emotions that you have more difficulty expressing? Are there feelings you would never express?

   b. How do your ability and willingness to share emotions vary depending on the person you are with?

3. Would you find it easier to tell your friends (your parents, family, etc.) that you love them or that you are angry with them?

4. What did you learn about expressing emotions when you were growing up? Discuss and compare your experiences with a colleague.

5. Describe in detail how you feel, think, and act when you experience specific emotions. For example, you might write, "When I feel scared, I want to escape. My breathing is shallow. I tend to look away. I become quiet. I think I might vomit." Hint: use your imagination to visualize situations where you might experience the specific emotion.

6. Share the details of an intense emotional experience with a partner. What was easy and difficult about sharing your feelings? What responses from your partner were helpful? Unhelpful?

7. For each of the following situations, predict and describe the emotions that the individual might experience. Remember that there may be many possibilities and that some experiences (although apparently negative) may result in positive emotions. What nonverbal cues might you observe in each case?

   a. a man whose wife of 60 years has just died
   b. a young teenager on a first date
   c. a middle-aged man fired from his job
   d. a student denied admission to a training program
   e. a mother discovering her teenage daughter using drugs
   f. a student about to take an exam
   g. a teacher on the first day of class
   h. a person who lost a friend in the 2005 Asian Tsunami
   i. a prisoner about to be sentenced
   j. a 16-year-old with sexual identity problems
   k. a job applicant
   l. a job interviewer
   m. an angry client
   n. a client seeing a counsellor for the first time
   o. a client seeing a counsellor for the last time (e.g., counselling may be at an end or the counsellor may be leaving the agency)
   p. a patient in hospital waiting for major surgery
   q. a child entering a foster home
   r. a man who has just abused his wife
   s. a person dealing with depression
   t. a parent dealing with a child who has ADD (attention deficit disorder)
   u. a couple on the day of their marriage
   v. a couple on the day their divorce becomes final
   w. a serial killer
   x. a compulsive gambler
   y. a 12-year-old boy coming to a new school
   z. an 11-year-old girl who has been sexually abused by her father

8. Identify feeling words and phrases that best describe how each of the following clients may be feeling:

   a. "Everyone in my life keeps putting me down. Even my own children constantly criticize me."
   b. *(shaking)* "Fifteen hard years with the same company and what do they do? They dump me with three weeks' notice."

c. (*a 6-year-old boy, crying while speaking to recreation staff*) "No one wants to play with me. No one likes me."

d. "When I saw the pictures from the Tsunami in 2005, I just couldn't stop crying."

e. (*an ex-offender to parole officer*) "Have you ever been to jail?"

f. (*a 16-year-old boy*) "I'd rather live on the street than go to another foster home. Five foster homes in five years. I've had enough!"

g. "I didn't expect to live to see forty."

h. "Why do you want me to go to see a psychiatrist? Do you think I'm crazy? You're that one that's crazy."

9. Assume that the clients below are speaking to you and that an empathic response is appropriate.

a. (*youth speaking to a youth justice worker*) "You don't care about me. All you guys are the same. You tell me that you want what's best for me. Well, if that's true, then why do you force me to come to these counselling sessions when I don't want to?

b. (*client, smiling*) "For the first time, things are really starting to come together for me. My kids are all doing well in school, my marital problems are on the upswing, and I finally put some money aside for a rainy day."

c. (*parent to a teacher*) "I don't know what to do. I know you said I should try to help my son with his homework and show some interest in his work. But he comes home from school and goes straight to his room. When I ask about his homework, he always says that there wasn't any. When I offer to help, he makes it clear he'd rather do it on his own."

d. (*teenager, crying*) "I'm pregnant. This will kill my dad, but first he'll kill me."

e. "Everyone always says how together I am. But I don't feel together. Sometimes I get so wound up that I think I'm going to burst."

f. (*man, 57, talking about his family problems*) "I have to make every decision. I can never count on my wife or kids for help."

g. (*parent to a teacher*) "My son does not have ADD. I don't care what you say. I'm not going to put him on drugs."

10. Each of the following client statements expresses more than one feeling. Identify feeling words and phrases that best describe the mixed feelings. Next, formulate an empathic response.

a. "Thanks for seeing me today. It really felt good to get things off my chest. No one has ever listened to me the way you did. I hope you don't think I'm crazy or stupid."

b. (*eyes welling up with tears*) "It's over. I don't care to be with him any more."

c. (*shouting*) "I am calm."

d. "To tell you the truth, I'd like to just march right in, look him in the eye, and tell him exactly where to go. I don't know what to do."

e. "Finding out that my former girlfriend had my baby was totally shocking. After we broke up, she didn't even tell me she was pregnant. I'd love to be a father, but I don't want a relationship with her. Maybe it would be best if I just forget the whole thing. But I want to do what's right."

f. "Living on your own is the pits. Now I don't even know where my next meal is coming from. I used to love being married. I felt as if life really had meaning. But at least now, I don't have to worry about being beat up by my husband every time he gets drunk. It's just so difficult. Maybe I should give him another chance."

g. (*woman, 79 years old, crying*) "My daughter keeps saying that she is coming for a visit, but it has been weeks since I have seen her. (*wipes away the tears*) It's not that important. I really do not want to be a bother. Just feeling sorry for myself this morning."

11. Tough empathy. The statements below may evoke strong personal reactions. Assume that the person is speaking to you and that you are responding with empathy, even though empathy may not be the preferred response.

   a. "This country was much better when it was white and Christian. With such high unemployment, don't you think it's time to stop letting every damn immigrant into the country? No wonder I can't get a job."

   b. "I'm not ashamed to admit it. Once in a while, I hit my wife. It's no big deal."

   c. "I don't care what you say. I won't give up on you until you convert and save your soul."

   d. (*employer*) "This is really hard for me to do. I've tried everything possible to cut costs, but unfortunately I'm going to have to make some major changes. I just don't know what else I can do. I have to lay you off."

   e. (*applicant for welfare*) "Don't you even think about turning me down. I'm not leaving this office without a cheque."

   f. (*student to teacher*) "I suppose this course is going to be like all the others. Lots of reading, a bunch of papers. I only hope there's some relevance to it all."

   g. (*client, 35 years old*) "I had no idea she was only 15. She was the one who wanted to have sex. From the look in her eyes, I could tell she was begging for it. It's really unfair that I'm now charged with rape. Besides, 15 is old enough for someone to make up their own mind."

   h. "This counselling isn't very helpful. So why don't we just forget it and do what both of us really want? How about it, sweetheart? Let's go out for dinner."

   i. "I really don't worry too much about AIDS. What can I do about it? If I'm meant to get it, then I'll get it. So what? We all have to die sometime."

   j. "I'm not stupid. I know that he shouldn't hit me. But I guess I deserved it, the way I put him down. I should learn to keep my mouth shut. When I see him, I'll apologize."

   j. (*client, with angry tone*) "No one is willing to talk to me about the fact that I might be dying. I can accept it, but every time I ask the big question, people change the topic."

12. In question 11 above, what do you think are the advantages of responding with empathy?

13. Videotape a television program. While taping it, turn off the sound. Pay attention to the nonverbal communication of the actors. Watch the tape, this time with the sound turned on. How successful were you in correctly reading the nonverbal cues?

14. Interview people from different cultures, preferably people who have been in this country for only a short time. What are the differences between their use of nonverbal communication (e.g., eye contact, spatial distance, touching) and yours?

15. Conduct practice interviews with a colleague to experiment with spatial distance. Deliberately increase or decrease the distance between the two of you to learn about the effect of space. At what point did your space become violated? How did physical distance affect the quality of your verbal exchange?

16. The following is the typescript of a portion of a worker's interview. The setting is a social service agency, and the worker is an employment counsellor. Critically evaluate the counsellor's responses (e.g., appropriateness of questions, use of empathy, etc.) What attitude do you think the counsellor converys to his client? Suggest alternate responses based on empathy.

Counsellor: Hello. Are you Leah? I'm Mr. Short. Won't you come into my office? *(brief small talk in office)*

Counsellor: So what is your problem? How can I help you?

Client: Well, I don't really know where to begin. Right now, my life is a mess. I've gotten along well so far, but lately... well, I'm just not coping very well. *(client pauses, wipes tears with a tissue)*

Counsellor: Okay, calm down. Try not to cry. Have you been to this agency before? By the way, how old are you?

Client: No, this is the first time. I wonder if anyone will ever give me a chance. Sometimes I feel why not give up? I feel so scared all the time. Don't get me wrong—I really want to work, to be independent, to buy my kids all the things I haven't been able to afford. I just don't know if I can do it. I haven't worked in 10 years. Plus, there's the problem of daycare... the things you read... it's hard to know whom to trust. Things just seemed so much easier when my husband was alive.

Counsellor: You say you haven't worked in 10 years. What was the last job you held? What did you do? What are your job skills?

Client: Mostly, I've worked as a secretary. It was okay, but I don't want to do that anymore. I really don't have a clue what I'd like.

Counsellor: So you know you want to get out of clerical work, but you're unsure what else you might do or like.

Client: Yes, exactly.

Counsellor: Have you considered social services? There are lots of good programs that you could complete in a short time.

Client: No, I don't think I'd like that.

Counsellor: How can you be sure until you give it a try? Sometimes volunteer work is a really good way to find out if you like it.

Client (hesitates): Well... I guess so.

Counsellor: Actually, I was in the same boat as you. Then I volunteered. Next thing I knew I was back in school. Now I'm working full time and loving it. I have a friend who works at the volunteer bureau. Why don't I give her a call and set up an appointment for you?

Client (hesitates): Okay... thanks.

Counsellor: No problem. I was glad to be of help. I'll phone her, then I'll give you a call. It'll probably be next week or so.

17. The purpose of this exercise is to develop your ability to "track" the flow of an interview including identifying the use of particular interviewing and counselling skills. Work with student colleagues. One student will be the counsellor, another the client,

with the others as observers. Videotape a fifteen-minute segment of a counselling interview and/or use a verbatim transcript of the session to assist your review. Classify each counsellor response (e.g., open question, closed question, silence, empathy, self-disclosure, or mixed response). Use the following table to compile interview statistics. Place a check in the box each time a particular skill is used. Notice that the table is organized to divide the interview into time segments.

	0–5 minutes	6–10 minutes	11–15 minutes
Open question			
Closed question			
Indirect question			
Silence			
Empathy			
Self-disclosure			
Directive			
Summary			
Paraphrase			
Other (specify)			

Some questions to consider:
a. Did the counsellor use a variety of different responses?
b. To what extent did the counsellor vary his or her approach as the session progressed?
c. What interview transitions were apparent? Were they appropriate? Consider, for example, whether the transition occurred prematurely before concrete understanding or exploration was completed.
d. What skills were overused or underused?
e. Which responses were productive? Which responses were counterproductive?

18. By interviewing colleagues or friends from diverse ethnic groups, investigate how different individuals from varying cultures express emotions.

WEBLINKS

Comprehensive list of emotions and feeling words:
www.preciousheart.net/empathy/Feeling-Words.htm

Empathy and listening skills for emotional intimacy:
www.touch-another-heart.com/index.htm

Emotional intelligence: comprehensive list of website links on the topic of EQ:
www.eq.org/

chapter seven

Empowerment: The Purpose of Counselling

PREVIEW

After reading this chapter you should be able to:

- Describe the elements of empowering clients.
- Identify motivation principles and skills.
- Explain the use of confrontation.
- Identify different types of thinking errors.
- Be aware of strategies for confronting thinking errors.
- Demonstrate the ability to assist clients by reframing.
- Explain the principles of effective goal setting.
- Demonstrate the ability to help clients set goals.
- Identify the steps of action planning and implementation.
- Describe principles and techniques for brief counselling.

EMPOWERMENT: MOBILIZING STRENGTHS FOR CHANGE

In Chapter 3, the concept of empowerment was described as the process of helping clients discover personal strengths and capacities so that they are able to take control of their lives. The foundation for empowerment in counselling is the belief that clients are capable and have a right to manage their own lives. Thus, an empowerment attitude focuses on the capacities and strengths of clients. But empowerment values and methods require counsellors to forgo any need to control clients by taking on an "expert" role that puts clients in positions of dependency. Giving priority to empowerment constrains counsellors from hiding behind professional jargon. Moreover, counsellors who empower demystify the counselling process through open and nonjargonistic discussion with clients of their methods and assumptions.

Self-determination, an important component of client empowerment, is promoted by helping clients recognize choices and by encouraging them to make independent decisions. Counsellors should not do for clients what they can and should do for themselves. Furthermore, when empowerment is the priority, clients become the experts, and there is "collaboration and shared decision making within the professional relationship (Sheafor & Horejsi, 2006:79).

McWhirter asserts that the potentially empowering aspects of counselling include "an underlying belief in basic human potential and in clients' ability to cope with their life problems, a collaborative definition of the problem and therapeutic goals, skill enhancement and development, recognition and analysis of systemic power dynamics and an emphasis on group and community identity" (1991:226).

Often clients come from disadvantaged and marginalized groups where they "have been 'beaten down' by oppression, poverty, abuse, and other harmful life experiences. They want better lives for themselves and their families, but they feel powerless to make the necessary changes. Some clients have a pervasive sense of failure and feel different from and rejected by other people" (Sheafor & Horejsi, 2006:422).

Sometimes powerlessness arises from negative self-evaluation and low self-esteem or from lack of confidence in one's ability to alter one's life. But sometimes the systems that are set up to assist clients are themselves oppressive and contribute to powerlessness. Describing the welfare system, Carniol observes, "As for the clients, evidence shows that they often find themselves blamed for the problems they face. They find they don't get the help they need or they don't get nearly enough to make a difference—or they get 'cut off'" (1995:3).

Racism and other prejudices may also deny clients access to jobs and resources such as adequate housing. A full discussion of these realities is beyond the scope of this book, but they serve as a reminder to counsellors that they have some responsibility to advocate for progressive changes within the systems that serve clients. As well, counsellors' work involves them in advocating for clients by assisting them in accessing services and resources that will help them meet their needs. Shulman (1999) stresses the need for workers to have faith in the capacity of systems to change, and he argues that they have a responsibility not just to work with the problems of individuals but also to promote social change. His view is echoed by Carniol, who offers this challenge: "Social justice demands a transformation of power, including a basic redistribution of wealth—so that the practice of democracy comes within the reach of everyone, rather than being manipulated by those who now dominate the heights of our political and social structures" (1995:153).

This perspective draws counsellors into broader activities, including working to identify and remove gaps and barriers to service and encouraging more humane and accessible policies and services. In addition, as McWhirter argues, empowerment requires that clients "gain some degree of critical awareness of systemic power dynamics" (1991:225). One way counsellors can achieve this end is to provide clients with information on groups and organizations whose efforts are directed toward changing problematic elements of the system.

But the counselling process itself offers empowerment to clients. The beginning phase offers many clients a unique opportunity to explore their situation and their feelings. Active listening skills help clients bring long-forgotten or misunderstood feelings to the surface. Ventilation of feelings can energize clients, and it can lead to spontaneous insight into new ways of handling problems that seemed insurmountable. For some clients, the work of counselling is finished at this phase.

Empowerment Strategy Choices

Some clients need additional assistance as they work to change established patterns. This may involve counsellors in one or more of five empowering activities:

1. *Motivating*. Clients may have made conscious decisions to change, and their motivation may be high; but they may also have mixed feelings about replacing established behaviour with new ways of behaving. Sometimes change involves a "selling" job. Clients need to convince themselves that the benefits of change outweigh the risks, and they need to develop attitudes and beliefs about their capacity for change. Counsellors can help motivate clients to take the risk of developing and executing action plans based on measurable and achievable goals. But ultimately, the principle of self-determination requires that clients themselves make the decision to change. Yet adherence to this principle does not preclude counsellors from involving clients in critical thinking about their behaviour and the wisdom of change. Counsellors with a strengths perspective believe in the capacity of their clients to change, and this belief in them can be a powerful motivating factor.

2. *Confronting*. Confronting, one of the challenging skills introduced in Chapter 1, is a tool for providing new information to clients so that they critically evaluate their behaviour and ideas. Confrontation can be provocative because it challenges client perceptions and assumptions. It also brings to the foreground issues that clients might ignore, deny, or rationalize. In addition, confrontation may push clients to take responsibility for their actions, or it may cause them to face the painful reality of the effects of the behaviour on themselves and others.

3. *Helping clients think differently*. Sometimes clients remain stuck because they cling to established but ineffective ways of thinking. Counsellors can use a range of techniques for helping clients think differently. Reframing, for example, helps clients become unstuck from the limitations of their current thinking by providing alternative explanations for events. Counsellors can also help clients understand and make use of potential sources of power to help change their situation (e.g., politicians, government officials, advocacy groups, self-help/support organizations, community and government resources). However, in these situations, Sheafor and Horejsi (2006) note that some oppressed people who discover that they have power act impulsively or become overly aggressive. They

need to be counselled on how to exercise their power in an appropriate way so that they avoid alienating potential sources of help.

4. *Goal setting*. Goals provide specific targets for clients to work toward. Having clear goals is essential for developing action plans or strategies to reach these targets. Goal setting is used as a first step in helping clients to plan a systematic change in their lives. Setting small, achievable goals sets up a climate of success that energizes clients for further action and change.

5. *Action planning*. Action planning involves setting up strategies for achieving goals. Typically, this involves helping clients identify, evaluate, and select alternatives, then helping them execute systematic action plans. As a result, clients expand their repertoire of coping skills. For example, they develop new or expanded capacities to manage feelings and to make intelligent decisions, or they learn to be assertive and able to utilize community and societal resources.

The balance of this chapter discusses the skills of motivating, confronting, and helping clients to think differently, set goals, and plan their actions.

MOTIVATING CLIENTS

In counselling, **motivation** refers to the extent to which clients are willing to involve themselves in the change process. Johnson, McClelland and Austin identify three factors important for motivation: "the push of discomfort, the pull of hope that something can be done to relieve the problem or accomplish a task, and internal pressures and drives toward reaching a goal" (2000:133). Thus, not only must clients want to change, but they must also believe in their capacity for change. However, change is stressful, because it requires risk and energy to give up established patterns of behaviour and thinking, and clients differ in the extent to which they have the skill or energy to take the associated risks. The following are the essential elements of high motivation:

1. willingness to engage in the work of counselling
2. commitment to devote energy and resources to the change process
3. capacity to sustain effort over time and in the face of obstacles
4. sufficient self-esteem to sustain the courage to change (Shebib, 1997:252)

Counsellors can assess clients based on these four elements, then design appropriate strategies to meet each client's particular need. These four elements suggest two major motivational tasks for counsellors: engaging clients to commit to change and supporting and energizing clients as they deal with the stresses of obstacles to change.

The concept of secondary gain is a useful way of understanding why some people resist change despite the obvious pain or losses involved in maintaining their current situation. Secondary gain refers to the benefits that people derive from their problems. These benefits may include "increased personal attention, disability compensation, and decreased responsibility, as well as more subtle gratifications, such as satisfying the need for self-punishment or the vengeful punishment of others who are forced to take responsibility" (Nicoli, 1988:13).

CONVERSATION 7.1

WORKING WITH "LAZY" CLIENTS

STUDENT: The clients I have the most trouble with are the lazy ones—like the ones who won't even get out of bed in the morning to go looking for a job or the clients who never follow through on commitments.

TEACHER: Sure, these clients can be exceptionally difficult and frustrating to work with. Sometimes it's hard to do, but we should discipline ourselves to be nonjudgmental regarding motivation. Although it might be tempting to label some clients as lazy, we should remember that they may have given up for good reason. Perhaps society has not provided the resources or support they need for change. Clients may have given up in order to protect themselves from the further damage to their self-esteem that would come from repeated failure. In this way, their behaviour may be seen as adaptive. It's normal for counsellors to lose patience with them and give up, but it's important to remember that that's precisely what they did to themselves—give up. That's one of the reasons they need counselling.

Stages of Change

The **stages of change model**, also known as the transtheoretical model (Prochaska & Norcross, 2001), has received a great deal of attention in the literature since its inception in the 1980s. In this model, five changes of stage are recognized: precontemplation, contemplation, preparation, action, and maintenance. As well, in this model, change is viewed as progressive and developmental, with success at any phases dependent on the success of previous phases.

Individual clients may have characteristics from more than one stage. An essential assumption is that counselling interventions need to be selected to meet the needs and motivation of the particular stage. For example, discussing action with a client who is at the precontemplative stage is likely to meet with failure. But at this stage, the client may respond positively to attempts to understand his or her perspective and feelings.

Precontemplative Stage

Clients at this stage have no intention of changing. These clients do not perceive themselves as having a problem, despite the fact that their behaviour is problematic for themselves or others in their lives. These clients are not thinking about change.

For these clients, listening empathically and sensitively encouraging them to examine their situation and its consequences can be very helpful. Counsellors can provide information, offer feedback, or encourage reflection with questions such as "Is what you're doing now working to meet your needs?" But counsellors should proceed slowly when confronting denial, and they should remember that denial may be a defence mechanism that enables people to cope, perhaps by shielding them from feelings of hopelessness (George, in McNeece & DiNitto, 1998). DiClemente and Velasquez (2002) observe that "Sometimes the reluctant client will progress rapidly once he or she verbalizes the reluctance, feels listened to, and begins to feel the tension between the reluctance to change and the possibility of a different future" (p. 205). DiClemente and

Valasquez offer a counter-argument—that the natural tendency is to do more when the risk is higher:

> Clinicians often believe that more education, more intense treatment, or more confrontation will necessarily produce more change. Nowhere is this less true than with precontemplators. More intensity will often produce fewer results with this group. (2002:208)

Contemplative Stage

At the contemplative stage, clients know they have a problem, and they are thinking about change; but they have not developed a plan or made a commitment to take action. Contemplative clients may be ambivalent and may vacillate between wanting to alter their lives and resisting any shifts in their behaviour or lifestyle.

> Example: *Agnes has been in an abusive relationship for years. She wishes that she could leave and start over. In fact, she has left her husband twice in the past, but each time she returned within a few weeks.*

Contemplative-stage clients like Agnes are "burnt-out" from previous unsuccessful attempts at change. They are often in a state of crisis with considerable associated stress. Although they desire change, they doubt it will happen; and they believe that if change is to occur, it will be beyond their control. They also lack self-esteem and believe that they do not have the skill, capacity, or energy to change.

> Example: *Peter (55) has been unemployed for almost two years, but he has not looked for a job for months. He says, "There's no work out there. Besides, who is going to hire a man of my age?"*

Seligman's (1975) concept of learned helplessness is a useful perspective for understanding these clients. People with learned helplessness come to believe that their actions do not matter; as a result, they are unlikely to expend any effort to change. Moreover, they believe that they have no control over their lives and that what happens to them is a result of chance. They believe in a "luck ethic" rather than a "work ethic." Their beliefs are reflected in statements such as the following:

- "You have to be at the right place at the right time to succeed."
- "If I'm successful, it's because the task was easy."
- "It doesn't matter if I work hard."
- "There's nothing I can do about it."

The key to working with people with learned helplessness—indeed, most clients at the contemplation stage—is to assist them "in thinking through the risks of the behaviour and potential benefits of change and to instill hope that change is possible" (DiClemente & Velasquez, 2002:209). Many people with low self-esteem and learned helplessness are in fact quite capable; it is the way they think and feel about themselves that is problematic. Consequently, it is important that counsellors look for ways to counter client self-depreciating remarks (e.g., encourage clients to see their past failures as deficits "in the plan," not deficits in them). As well, counsellors can encourage clients to see elements of success in previous efforts (e.g., partial goal achievement, lessening of problem severity, short-term achievement).

Preparation Stage

When clients reach this third phase, they have made a decision to change, and motivating them is no longer the principal task. However, counsellors need to sustain the energy for change through support, encouragement and empathic caring. The principal task for the counsellor is to assist the client to develop concrete goals and action plan strategies. Without concrete, systematic plans, change efforts can be quickly frustrated and abandoned like New Years Resolutions. The essence of good planning consists of setting concrete goals, identifying and evaluating alternative ways of reaching goals, selecting an action plan, and anticipating potential obstacles. For clients with learned helplessness, setting small, achievable goals is crucial for establishing and maintaining a climate of success and hope.

> Example: *Iris, a young single parent, is excited about the possibility of returning to school. She sees a school counsellor for assistance with enrolment in the high school's special program for teen moms. But she has not yet considered issues like daycare.*

Using a strengths approach, counsellors can assist preparation-stage clients to draw from their past experiences (proven success strategies and lessons learned). As well, clients can learn about strategies that have worked for others. Finally, it is very important to coach these clients to anticipate potential obstacles and to plan strategies for addressing them, including the emotional stress of the change process.

Action Stage

At this stage, clients are actively involved in the change process. They are working on the goals and implementing the plans developed in the preparation stage. DiClemente and Velasquez offer this perspective on counsellor strategies for this stage:

> Clients in action may still have some conflicting feelings about the change. They may miss their old lifestyle in some ways and be struggling to fit into this new behaviour. Careful listening and affirming clients that they are doing the right thing are important in this stage. It is also important to check with the client to see if he or she has discovered parts of the change plan that need revision (2002:212).

When clients encounter anticipated obstacles, counsellors can remind them of previously developed contingency plans; or, if there are unanticipated obstacles, counsellors can assist with interventions to support clients as they deal with these potential setbacks.

Maintenance Stage

In the final stage, the challenge for the client is to maintain the changes that have been made and to deal with relapses, which may occur for a number of reasons (e.g., unexpected temptation, personal stress, letting down one's guard). Moreover, sometimes people are "actively sabotaged by others in their lives who were threatened by the changes" (Kottler, 2000:81). Achievement of goals does not guarantee that there will be no relapse. "This is particularly true if the environment is filled with cues that can trigger the problem behaviour. We all know [of situations] where an individual who has stopped drinking relapses just when everyone thinks the problem is finally resolved" (DiClement & Velasquez, 2002:213). But counsellors can help clients accept that relapses, while undesired, are part of the change process and do not signify complete regression or failure. In fact, counsellors can help clients to reframe the relapse as an opportunity for better success next time. "Frequently, people who do relapse have a better chance of success during the next cycle. They have often learned new ways to deal with old behaviours, and they now have a history of partial successes to build on" (DiClement & Velasquez, 2002:213).

CONVERSATION 7.2

WORKING WITH "INVOLUNTARY" CLIENTS

YOUTH COUNSELLOR: What are some strategies for working with involuntary clients?

COUNSELLOR: You work with street-involved youth. So why don't you tell me what you have learned about involuntary clients?

YOUTH COUNSELLOR: I have learned early what doesn't work. There's no point in lecturing, moralizing, or preaching about the dangers of drugs. What seems to work best is to focus on the relationship.

COUNSELLOR: How do you do that?

YOUTH COUNSELLOR: Sometimes, it's just little things, like bringing a cup of coffee to a sex-trade worker, or checking to see if they are all right or need anything. I try to be ready for the "teachable moment." That can happen anytime, such as after a "bad date" or when they're feeling down. Then empathy and listening skills are best.

COUNSELLOR: That's right. As you know, involuntary clients can be rebellious, and being forced into counselling arouses their defences. For example, I recently met with one who was referred by his employer because he could not get along with his co-workers. He claimed that others in his work team simply had difficulty dealing with his assertive manner and his high standards. He came in to see me, but it was evident that his main motivation was to preserve his job. With him, I found that it worked best to encourage him to express his anger about being told what to do. This diffused his resistance to the point where he no longer saw me as the enemy.

YOUTH COUNSELLOR: It's like that with our clients as well. With youth on probation, I like to look for ways to give them power and involve them in decision making. Here again, empathic listening can help them arrive at a plan that suits them, one that doesn't feel imposed.

COUNSELLOR: So involuntary clients are not necessarily precontemplative. Many are well aware of their problems and the need to change. They just don't like being told what to do, and that's the key to working successfully with them. When I worked in corrections, I found that many of my clients were initially resistant and overtly hostile towards authority. Clients with such antiauthoritarian values are not going to respond to directive, rigid attempts to control them. Such strategies will only serve to increase resistance. As always, paying attention to the relationship is crucial. For example, with clients coming out of prison, relationship credibility can be developed by helping them with basic needs, such as housing, clothes, food, and a job.

CONFRONTING CLIENTS

For many people, confrontation suggests conflict and hostility. But in counselling, effective confrontation is not considered a hostile act. Confrontation is simply a way of directing clients' attention to aspects of their personality or behaviour that they might otherwise overlook. It is a tool to move clients to a higher level of understanding of themselves and others. Moreover, caring confrontation can deepen the level of trust in the counselling relationship. It is also a major skill for helping clients develop fresh perspectives on themselves and their behaviour. Gilliland and James (1998) contend that caring confrontation is

TABLE 7.1	Stages of Change	
Stage of Change	**Counselling Goal**	**Strategy Choices**
Precontemplative: clients with no desire or intention to change	Increase awareness of need for change	• Listen empathically. • Provide information and feedback (if contracted). • Encourage clients to seek information and feedback from others. • Help clients become aware of attractive alternatives. • Use thought-provoking questions. • Avoid directive and confrontational techniques. • Use films, brochures, books, self-assessment questionnaires as tools to increase client insight. • Involuntary clients: explore feelings and concerns openly, self-disclose your own feelings about being forced, give clients choices, involve them in decision making, encourage client initiated goals.
Contemplative: clients who are thinking about change	Resolve ambivalence to engage in the change process	• Discuss risks and benefits of change, but avoid arguing in favour of change, which tends to make clients argue against change. • Help clients understand and manage self-depreciating remarks (e.g., reframe past failures as learning experience). • Identify elements of success in previous change efforts. • Explore deficits in previous change plans (emphasize failure of plans, not failure of clients). • Use support groups. • Convey hope.
Preparation: clients who are committed to change	Develop concrete strategies for action	• Set goals. • Plan systematic action. • Assemble/mobilize resources to support change. • Make contingency plans (anticipate obstacles).
Action	Implement change and sustain momentum	• Reward (praise, support, acknowledge) change efforts. • Assist clients to manage anticipated and unanticipated obstacles.
Maintenance	Sustain change	• Assist client to deal with periodic obstacles and/or relapses.

a way of valuing or respecting the client. They conclude that "confronting client excuses, explanations, or rationalizations is necessary to facilitate client movement toward responsible behaviour" (283). Egan (1998) describes confrontation as a way to encourage clients toward more effective living.

In general, confrontation may be useful for addressing incongruities between what clients believe and the way they act; self-defeating ways of thinking and behaving; behaviour that is harmful to self or others; blind spots; blaming behaviours; and communication problems. As well, confrontation can also target unrecognized or discounted strengths.

Types of Confrontation

The two main types of confrontation are feedback confrontation and confrontation of incongruities. **Feedback confrontation** provides new information to clients about who they are, including how they are perceived by others and the effects of their behaviour on others. Feedback confrontation can be used to help clients become aware of the consequences of their decisions and actions. But it is not reserved for negative or critical feedback—it can also be used to identify strengths.

In some cases, clients have blind spots about the harmful effects of their behaviour on themselves and others. They continue to behave in ways that are hurtful, yet they lack insight into how they are affecting others. Because they are unaware and fail to see their behaviour as problematic, they have no motivation to change. Feedback confrontation can help these clients examine the consequences of their actions. The following are examples of client blind spots:

• Jerry thinks of himself as humorous, but he is unaware that his jokes are offensive and sexist.
• Nathan has bad breath and body odour.
• Parvinder is unaware of how his aggressive behaviour pushes others away.
• Estelle has been in a series of relationships in which she has been battered. She does not understand how this has affected her children.

But despite its potential power as a helping tool, feedback confrontation is often misused. Some counsellors avoid it, perhaps because they fear that they might alienate their clients or arouse their anger. Other counsellors feel the need to keep the helping relationship pleasant, so they distort or lie to clients to sustain their approval. However, effective counsellors need to be willing and able to confront clients when necessary. Thus, counsellors must remain aware of their beliefs, fears, and expectations regarding confrontation to use this skill appropriately.

Sometimes, beginning counsellors (and some experienced ones too) are reluctant to confront. Here are some of their candid thoughts:

• "I was brought up to believe that if you don't have something good to say, then don't say anything at all."
• "If I confront, I might damage the relationship. I don't want to upset my clients."
• "I don't want to hurt my clients."
• "My clients might retaliate."

Yet most of the above beliefs arise from an erroneous understanding of confrontation as a "no holds barred" assault on clients. Assault-type confrontation strategies should, of course, be avoided. At the other extreme, refraining from confronting clients under any circumstance is an evasion of responsibility that cuts clients off from the potential benefits of new information and feedback. Competent counsellors should not withhold potentially useful feedback.

The second type of confrontation, **confrontation of incongruities**, is directed at inconsistencies and mixed messages:

- discrepancy between a client's verbal and nonverbal messages

    Client: *(crying) It's really nothing. I'm not bothered.*

- discrepancy between a client's values or beliefs and behaviour

    Client: *There's nothing more important to me than my kids. I know I haven't spent much time with them. It's just so hard to say no to my buddies when they ask me to help.*

- discrepancy between what a client says and what he or she does

    Client: *I'm committed to looking for work. But just like yesterday, something came up before I could get to the employment office.*

In confronting such discrepancies, counsellors need to remain calm and nonjudgmental while presenting clients with specific facts. Ivey offers these confrontation leads as suggestions: "The model sentence, 'On the one hand..., and on the other hand...,' provides a standard and useful format for actual confrontation. Variations include 'You say... but you do...,' 'I see... at one time, and at another time, I see...,' and 'Your words say..., but your actions say...'" (1982:196).

Confrontation Cautions and Risks

Although confrontation has potential for motivating clients to change and can assist clients in developing insight, misuse of confrontation can be destructive. As a rule, counsellors should use it sparingly and should be prepared to offer support and caring to ensure that confrontation does not overwhelm or devastate their clients.

There are risks to confrontation, and some clients do react poorly. They may respond with hostility and attempt to question the integrity or credibility of the counsellor. But such a hostile reaction may be a type of denial, indicating that the client is simply not ready to acknowledge the validity of the confrontation. Hostile reactions are more likely to occur when feedback or confrontation is unsolicited; but they may occur even when clients appear to be seeking information or feedback. Counsellors also need to consider that harsh client reactions may arise for legitimate reasons. Sometimes feedback is confusing, or the manner and tone of the counsellor are abrupt. Secure counsellors have to be open to the possibility that they may have erred.

Moreover, confrontation should never be used as an outlet for a counsellor's anger or frustration. When counsellors are not in control of their own feelings, clients are more likely to view them as aggressive and to feel their confrontation is unsupportive. The counselling relationship is formed to meet the needs of clients, and responsible counsellors forgo their own needs to this end. In addition, counsellors should be self-aware enough to know their reasons for wanting to confront.

Moreover, overly confrontational styles have been found to result in a high client dropout rate and poor outcomes. "Counsel in a directive, confrontational manner, and client resistance goes up. Counsel in a reflective, supportive manner, and resistance goes down while change talk increases (Miller & Rollnick, 2002:9). Ultimately, "the manner in which we present confrontations affects the way they are heard and accepted or rejected by the client (Sperry, Carlson, & Kjos, 2003:120).

Principles for Effective Confrontation

Principle Number 1

Unsolicited confrontation tends to result in resistance, hostility and defensiveness; but solicited (invited) feedback is more likely to be understood and result in action. The skills of contracting can be used to engage clients in accepting feedback:

> Counsellor: *One of the ways I might be able to help is by sharing some of my impressions about what you're doing, or even about our relationship. What do you think?*
>
> Client: *Sure. I'd appreciate that.*
>
> Counsellor: *Well, let's look ahead. Suppose I wanted to give you some feedback about something I thought you were doing wrong that you were not aware of. What would be the best way for me to approach you?*
>
> Client: *I don't like to be overwhelmed. And I like the good mixed with the bad.*

This example shows how contracting can be used to help the counsellor to "customize" feedback to meet the needs and expectations of the client. Subsequently, when the counsellor offers feedback, it is much less likely to meet with resistance. Contracting is also a way of asking for the client's permission to confront or give feedback. But as with all skills of counselling, counsellors must develop versatility so that they can confront or give feedback in a variety of ways. Some clients like blunt feedback; others prefer it "sandwiched" between positive statements.

Principle Number 2

Confrontation should be used sparingly in combination with other skills, particularly sensitive and empathic listening.

Confrontation may involve feedback that is unsettling for clients, and empathy reminds counsellors to remain sensitive to the impact of confrontation. In addition, counsellors should not confront clients without offering them assistance to develop new alternatives. Confrontation should also be measured to avoid overwhelming clients with more information than they can handle. Ideally, confrontation should not undermine the self-esteem of clients. Egan offers this valuable suggestion: "Confront only if you want to grow closer to the person you're confronting" (1977: 220). Corey and Corey reflect similar sentiments: "Challenge clients only if you feel an investment in them and if you have the time and effort to continue building the relationship with them" (1989:54).

At first, clients may respond defensively to feedback; but after reflection, they may be more accepting. Alternatively, they may appear to be accepting but later become resentful. Thus, it is important to check with clients how they feel about the feedback or confrontation.

Counsellors should monitor immediate reactions. As well, checking back with the client during the next session is a useful tool for identifying delayed reactions and for picking up on any feelings that might impair the relationship. The example below illustrates the process:

> Counsellor: *I'm wondering how you felt about our last meeting. Remember, I shared with you some of my opinions about the things you are doing that seem to distance you from your family.*
>
> Client: *I almost didn't come today.*
>
> *(silence)*
>
> Counsellor: *Because?*
>
> Client: *I was embarrassed by what you thought of me.*
>
> Counsellor: *You thought that I might think less of you?*
>
> Client: *Yes.*
>
> Counsellor: *Would you like to find out for sure what I think?*
>
> Client: *Okay.*

This counsellor's strategy sets the stage to help the client correct any distortions, and it is crucial for dealing with the aftermath of confrontation. It also reinforces that any feelings about what happens in the counselling relationship can be dealt with openly.

Principle Number 3

Confrontation should serve the goals of counselling by leading the client to improved ways of behaving, thinking, and feeling.

Relevant confrontation always meets the needs of the client. Thus, it is inappropriate for a counsellor to use confrontation as a means to vent frustration or anger. In these situations, the counsellor may frame the confrontation as being "in the client's best interests"; but in reality, it is meeting the needs of the counsellor. In fact, counsellors sometimes confront clients in order to punish them (Egan, 1998).

A counsellor can best deal with feelings related to the relationship or the work by using I-statements, rather than by trying to mask their feelings as helpful feedback (Gordon, 1971; Martin, 1983). I-statements are assertions about personal feelings or reactions that do not blame or judge others. Instead of saying "You don't care," an I-message would be "I feel confused when you don't answer my questions." I-statements are much less likely to cause resistance.

Principle Number 4

Confrontation must be timed appropriately at a point when clients are ready and willing to take advantage of feedback and when there is a reasonable possibility that feedback can motivate them to change.

Counsellors need to pay attention to timing and ensure that there is a well-developed counselling relationship to support confrontation. As a general rule, it is preferable to avoid strong confrontation in the beginning phase of counselling. Clients are more receptive and likely to accept feedback as credible when there is a relationship and climate of trust, when they won't feel insulted and misunderstood. Otherwise, they may never return.

Moreover, confrontation should be given as close as possible to the relevant behaviour, events, or circumstances that are being addressed. For example, if a counsellor uses confrontation to challenge a client's defensive behaviour, this is most appropriate immediately after a client is defensive, rather than a week later.

Furthermore, a client's ability to handle confrontation is a crucial variable. If clients are already overwhelmed with feelings, confrontation may add to their stress but contribute little to their ability to cope. Moreover, clients who are highly defensive and guarded may respond poorly to confrontation. In such situations, counsellors may find it wise to delay or avoid confrontation entirely.

After confronting, counsellors must be willing to invest time to help their clients understand any feedback. As well, counsellors must be available to help clients deal with any feelings that may result from the confrontation. Consequently, the end of a counselling interview is generally a poor time to confront.

Principle Number 5

Effective confrontation needs to be specific without attacking the personality of the client.

> Counsellor (Choice 1—ineffective confrontation): *You don't seem at all interested in what's happening here. If you're too lazy to care about our work, why don't you just quit?*

> Counsellor (Choice 2—more effective confrontation): *When you don't show up for appointments, I wonder whether you're as committed to your goals as you say you are.*

> Counsellor (Choice 3—most effective confrontation): *I think your best work has happened on those days when you came on time and when you took the effort to focus. My sense is that if you could make every appointment, you'd get a lot more out of our time together.*

In Choice 1, the counsellor's words attack the client. The counsellor judges the client's behaviour but provides no concrete or useable feedback. In Choice 2, the counsellor is more effective because the confrontation is linked to specific client behaviour. But Choice 3 focuses on strengths. The principle here is that people are motivated more by positive feedback than by negative feedback (Hamachek, 1982). Moreover, by focusing on strengths, clients can be clearer about what they can do that will be more effective.

HELPING CLIENTS THINK DIFFERENTLY

The fact that a client firmly defends a life style that he knows is unworkable is proof that he is in need of great assistance and support.
—*Wicks & Parsons, 1984:171*

Thinking Errors

Sometimes clients have difficulty breaking out of established patterns because of the way they think about issues or problems (De Bono, 1984). The five major types of **thinking errors** are distortion, incomplete analysis, egocentricity, rigidity, and self-defeating thought, all of which may overlap. These five types of thinking errors result in faulty logic, as discussed below.

Distortion

Distortion refers to misinterpretations, faulty assumptions, or cultural biases. For example, if a client is from a culture in which direct eye contact is discouraged and ends up working with a counsellor who interprets direct eye contact as a sign of warmth, there is a risk that the client may conclude that the counsellor is intrusive or disrespectful.

Incomplete Analysis

Incomplete analysis means failure to look at all aspects of a problem or situation. For example, prison inmates may overestimate their ability to cope with life outside jail. Their thinking may become clouded by unrealistic optimism that they will be able to avoid getting caught again or beat any charges if they are caught. In addition, they may neglect to consider the long-term consequences of their criminal behaviour, a pattern of thinking that is characteristic of lifestyle or habitual criminals. Walters reached this conclusion: "Until high rate offenders realize the self-destructive nature of their superoptimism, they will continue to resist change because they are operating on the mistaken belief that they can get away with just about any crime" (1991:36). Walters sees lazy thinking as the root of the offenders' problems. Even those with the best of intentions may find themselves in trouble because they failed to think about long-term outcomes.

Egocentricity or Lack of Empathy

Egocentric thinking errors come from a failure or inability to consider other people's ideas or to look at how one's behaviour affects others. Clients may adopt an arrogant position of self-righteousness, being confident that their ideas and conclusions are sound. Egocentric thinkers are likely to be seen by others as aggressive and insensitive, interested in meeting only their own needs. Egocentric thinkers are not only poor thinkers but also poor listeners. Typically, they believe that the purpose of thinking, listening, and responding is to prove themselves right. De Bono contends that self-protection is a major impediment to their thinking: "The main restriction on thinking is ego defence, which is responsible for most of the practical faults of thinking" (1985:29).

Rigidity

This common thinking problem is characterized by "black-and-white" thinking and by failure to be open to new ideas. De Bono made this important observation: "Unfortunately, Western thinking, with its argument habits, prefers to give a conclusion first and then to bring in the facts to support that conclusion" (1985:35). Rigid thinkers act as if to say, "We'll keep talking until you agree with me."

Self-Defeating Thoughts

Self-defeating thoughts are irrational ideas about one's own weaknesses. Albert Ellis has written a great deal about irrational thinking and its impact on emotions and behaviour (2004, 1993a; 1993b; 1984; 1962). Ellis argues that people's belief systems influence how they respond to and understand problems and events. When their beliefs are irrational and characterized by an unrealistic "should," they are likely to experience emotional anxiety or disturbance. This thinking is often accompanied by self-depreciating internal dialogue: "I'm no good," "Everyone must think I'm an idiot," and "No one likes me." Ellis concludes that irrational beliefs fall into three general categories with associated rigid demands or "shoulds":

1. "I (ego) absolutely must perform well and win significant others' approval, or else I am an inadequate, worthless person."
2. "You (other people) must under all conditions and at all times be nice and fair to me, or else you are a rotten, horrible person!"
3. "Conditions under which I live absolutely must be comfortable, safe, and advantageous, or else the world is a rotten place, I can't stand it, and life is hardly worth living." (1993a:7)

Wicks and Parsons offer a similar perspective when they suggest that many clients are discouraged because they set unattainable goals: "These goals are often based on irrational, simplistic views: (1) if a person acts properly, everyone will like him; and (2) either a person is totally competent or he is completely inadequate" (1984:170).

To counteract self-defeating thoughts, people need to change their way of thinking and correct irrational beliefs. Table 7.2 presents strategies for dealing with common thinking errors.

TABLE 7.2	Helping Clients Change Thinking Patterns	
Problem	**Example**	**Counselling Choices**
Distortion	A client assumes that quiet members in her social circle are "aloof and stuck-up."	Provide alternative explanations (e.g., cultural norms). Encourage clients to check the validity of assumptions (e.g., by talking with others about the meaning of their behaviour).
Incomplete Analysis	A young man decides to quit school so he can get a job and buy a new car.	Ask questions targeted to the overlooked area. Provide or encourage clients to find new information. Confront gaps in reasoning. Encourage clients to consult others. Challenge clients to consider the long-term implications of their actions.
Egocentricity or lack of empathy	A juvenile offender has no remorse and does not consider how his crimes adversely affect people. A client does not realize that his humour is sexist and offensive to others.	Teach empathy skills. Role play (i.e., ask clients to assume others' roles). Self-disclose personal feelings. Offer feedback or encourage clients to seek feedback from others.
Rigidity	An aggressive male believes that the only alternative to his present style is to say nothing. A client is prejudiced.	Stimulate new ideas through education and information. Use brainstorming to generate alternative ideas. Identify a range of alternatives. Suggest another frame of reference (reframing). Confront blind spots. Ask clients to assume the role of devil's advocate in order to self-critique their ideas. Assist clients in identifying and critically evaluating assumptions.
Self-defeating thought	A client demands perfection. A client constantly tells herself that she is inadequate.	Encourage clients to become aware of self-defeating thoughts. Teach techniques such as "thought stopping" to overcome self-defeating inner dialogue.

Reframing

Reframing is a counselling skill that helps clients shift or modify their thinking by suggesting alternative interpretations or new meanings. It empowers clients by focusing on solutions and redefining negatives as opportunities or challenges. Client stubbornness might be reframed as independence, or greediness as ambitiousness. (See Table 7.3 for additional examples.)

But before presenting reframed ideas, counsellors should use active listening skills to fully understand the client's current perspective. As well, empathy is crucial; otherwise, clients may conclude that their feelings are being discounted or trivialized.

Moreover, reframing should not be confused with platitudes, such as "It's always darkest just before dawn," which are typically not very supportive or helpful. An example of a well-meaning but misguided reframe that people give in times of grief over the loss of a child is "You're young—you can have more children." "Because strong emotions of sadness and loss are present, most people cannot accept a reframing that does not take into account the most salient feature of their experience—the grief itself" (Young, 1998:282). Reframing should not trivialize complex problems with pat answers; rather, it should offer a reasonable and useable alternative frame of reference.

TABLE 7.3	Reframing
Client's Perspective or Statement	**Counsellor's Reframed Idea**
This counselling is a waste of time.	Sounds as if you've done some thinking about how our work could be more relevant to you.
I don't fit in. I come from a different culture, and my ideas and values must seem strange.	Of course. Some people have not had experience with your culture, and they may be frightened. Perhaps you could look at this in a different way. Your experiences might also be fascinating for people who have not lived outside the country. They might welcome your fresh ideas.
I'm very shy. When I first join a group, I usually don't say anything.	You like to be patient until you have a sense of what's happening. People who are impulsive are working to develop this skill. You also seem to want to develop alternatives, such as being more expressive in the beginning.
For the first time in 20 years, I'm without a job.	Obviously, this is devastating. At the same time, I wonder if this might also be an opportunity for you to try something different.
Whenever I'm late for curfew, my mother waits up for me and immediately starts screaming at me.	I'm curious about why she might do this. Perhaps she has trouble telling you how scared she is that something may have happened to you. It might seem strange, but her anger could be her way of saying how much she loves you.

Clark (1998) offers guidelines for using reframing in group counselling, but the principles apply equally well to individual counselling:

1. Use reframing to help clients break out of thinking that is self-defeating, constricted, or at an impasse.

2. Make sure that clients are not so emotionally distracted that they are unable to hear or process the reframed idea.

3. Offer a reframed idea in a tentative way that invites consideration.

4. Ensure that reframed ideas are plausible.

5. Allow clients sufficient time to consider a reframed idea. Clients with firmly entrenched perspectives may not immediately accept logical and sound reframes; but with gentle persuasion and patience, they may begin to accept new ideas.

Even though it may be obvious that a client's thinking is distorted, it may be wise to hold back on reframing until the client's problem is fully explored. Moreover, as suggested above, it is important that the client's feelings be acknowledged through empathy. Exploration and empathy ensure that the counsellor understands the client's feelings and situation, and they provide a basis for the client to consider reframed ideas as reasonable or worthy of consideration. If counsellors push clients too quickly, clients may feel devalued and misunderstood and, in response, they may resist new ideas. Empathy helps workers to establish and maintain credibility with their clients.

In addition, counsellors can use directives to invite clients to use different language to describe the distorted idea (Young, 1998). For example, when clients avoid responsibility for their actions with statements such as "I can't get organized," counsellors can challenge them by proposing that they rephrase with statements such as "I won't let myself get organized." A client might say, "She makes me feel hopeless." In response, the counsellor can propose that the client rephrase the statement by stating, "I have decided to feel hopeless." The latter response underscores the client's control over personal feelings. As part of this work, counsellors can empower their clients by explaining that clients have ownership over their feelings and that no one can make them feel a certain way. After offering a reframe, counsellors should check for the client's questions and reactions to it. Then, if the reframed idea is accepted, they can encourage further exploration and problem solving based on the new perspective.

Reframing can energize clients. When clients are locked into one way of thinking about their problems, their solutions are limited. But when they consider new perspectives, problems that seemed insurmountable can yield new solutions. Moreover, reframing can serve to redirect client anxiety away from self-blame and onto other rational explanations that are less self-punishing. In these ways, effective reframing empowers clients to action, problem resolution and management of debilitating feelings. When counsellors "consider the question, 'What's good about it?' they give clients new perspectives on positive things that are already happening" (Miley, O'Melia, & DuBois, 2004:327).

GOAL SETTING

Obstacles are those frightful things you see when you take your eyes off your goals.
—Anonymous

The Importance of Setting Goals

Goal setting is a counselling process that helps clients define in precise, measurable terms what they hope to achieve from the work of counselling. Two types of goals are outcome goals and process or task goals (Shebib, 1997; Jacobs, Masson, & Harvill, 1998). **Outcome goals** relate to what the client hopes to achieve from counselling. These goals have to do with changes in the client's life, such as getting a job, improving communication with a spouse, dealing with painful feelings, or managing self-defeating thoughts. **Process goals** concern the procedures of counselling, including such variables as the frequency of meetings and the nature of the counselling relationship. Process goals are strategies for reaching outcome goals. In practice, there may be some overlap between process and outcome goals. For example, a process goal might be to develop trust in the counselling relationship. Success in achieving this process goal might assist the client in achieving an outcome goal targeted at improving communication with family and friends.

There is wide support in the counselling literature for the importance of setting goals (Egan, 1998; Young, 1998). Goal setting serves many important purposes, including giving direction, defining roles, motivating, and measuring progress.

Giving Direction

Goals help to give direction and purpose to the work of counselling. Clearly defined goals serve as beacons that guide and structure the client's actions. Moreover, goals help counsellors and clients decide which topics and activities are relevant. In addition, when clients are clear about their goals, they can begin to structure their thinking and action toward their attainment. Finally, setting goals helps clients make reasoned choices about what they want to do with their lives. Goal setting helps clients prioritize these choices.

Defining Roles

Goals provide a basis for defining roles. When goals are clear, counsellors know which skills and techniques are appropriate, and clients know what is expected of them. Moreover, when counsellors know the goal of the work, they can make intelligent decisions regarding whether they have the skills, capacity, and time to work with the client. If not, they may make a referral.

Motivating

Goals motivate clients. Setting and reaching goals is also therapeutic. It energizes clients and helps them develop optimism about change. Moreover, simply having goals can build self-confidence. Goal achievement confirms personal capacity and further promotes action. Writing down goals may add an extra measure of motivation.

Measuring Progress

Goals help provide benchmarks of progress, including defining when the counselling relationship should end—i.e., when the goals have been reached or their pursuit is no longer viable.

INTERVIEW 7.1   REFRAMING TECHNIQUES

The following interview excerpt illustrates how reframing might be used in a counselling session. The counsellor has been working with a community college student to help her deal with some of her fears about public speaking. Note: Reframing is only one of the ways that the counsellor might help this client deal with the situation. For example, relaxation techniques may help decrease the client's anxiety.

DIALOGUE	ANALYSIS
Client: Next week I have to make my class presentation. I'm so nervous, and it's still a week away. What am I going to be like on the day of my talk?	In all phases of counselling, empathy is an important response. More than any other skill, it tells clients that they have been heard and that their feelings have been understood.
Counsellor: You're wondering, "What if I'm so rattled I can't handle it at all?"	
Client: Exactly.	
Counsellor: Let's try something different for a minute. What if it were possible to look at your fears differently?	The counsellor introduces the technique of reframing with a brief rationale. Later in the interview, the counsellor or the client may wish to discuss the rationale in more detail. The counsellor's short self-disclosure communicates understanding and a nonjudgmental attitude.
Client: What do you mean?	
Counsellor: I think it's natural when we have a problem to dwell on all its unpleasant aspects. I know that I tend to do that unless I discipline myself not to. For example, when you think of how nervous you are, you think of all the negatives, such as that you might make a fool of yourself, or your mind might go blank while you're talking.	
Client (laughs): Or that I might throw up in front of everyone.	
Counsellor: Okay, those are real fears. But by considering only your fears, you become fixated on the negatives, and you may be overlooking some important positives. If you can look at it differently, you might discover	

(continued)

a whole new way of dealing with your class presentation.

Counsellor: Want to try it? (the client nods) Okay, try to identify some positive aspects of your fear.

Client: Well, I guess I'm not the only one who is scared of public speaking.

Counsellor: So you know that there will be other people in the class who understand and will be cheering for you to succeed.

Client: I never thought of that before. Here's another idea: Because I'm so nervous, I'm going to make sure that I'm super prepared.

Counsellor: Great. Do you think it might be possible to look at your fears differently? Consider that it's normal to be nervous. Or go a step further. Look at it positively. Maybe there's a part of it that's exciting—kind of like going to a scary movie.

Client: I did come back to school because I hated my boring job. One thing for sure, I'm not bored.

Counsellor: So the more you scare yourself, the more you get your money's worth. (the counsellor and client laugh)

Counsellor: Try this over the next few days. Every time you start to think negatively about your presentation, I want you to deliberately interrupt your thinking to focus on some of the positives.

Client: Okay. Do you think that will help?

Counsellor: Absolutely. (explains the theory behind thought stopping) But it takes practice, and you have to discipline yourself not to give up.

As a rule, it's more empowering for clients to generate their own suggestions before counsellors introduce their ideas and suggestions. In this way, clients become self-confronting and are more likely to come up with ideas that they will accept as credible.

The counsellor offers the client a reframed way of looking at nervousness. The client's response suggests that this notion is plausible.

Spontaneous humour adds colour and vitality to the counselling relationship.

The counsellor introduces thought stopping—a technique to help clients control self-defeating thinking (Gilliland & James, 1998; Cormier & Cormier, 1985). The basic assumption is that if self-defeating thoughts are interrupted, they will eventually be replaced by more empowering, positive perspectives.

Developing Effective Goal Statements

Sometimes clients are able to clearly articulate what they hope to achieve as a result of counselling. Others have difficulty identifying their goals. But through systematic interviewing, counsellors can help these clients define and target their goals. In addition, workers can use their knowledge base to develop simple checklists of potential goals, customized to the common needs and problems of particular client groups. However, these goals should always be concrete, measurable, challenging but realistic, and "owned" by the client.

Effective Goals Are Concrete

One defining feature of a counselling relationship is its goal-directed nature. But some clients begin counselling with vague and undefined goals:

- "I want to feel better."
- "My husband and I need to get along better."
- "I need to make something of my life."

These goals are useful starting points, but they are useless until they are described as clear and concrete targets. Beginning phase work that explores problems and feelings should lead to the development of goals that define and structure subsequent work. Then, in the action phase, clients can develop these goals as specific and measurable targets. This step is a prerequisite for action planning—the development of strategies and programs to achieve goals. Vague goals result in vague and ill-defined action plans, whereas explicit goals lead to precise action plans.

In Chapter 5, concreteness was introduced as the remedy for vagueness. Concreteness can add precision to unclear and ambiguous goals. For example, when clients are describing their goals, counsellors can use simple encouragers, such as "Tell me more" and "Yes, go on," to get a general overview of what clients hope to achieve. This is the first step in shaping workable goals. The next step is to use questions to identify goals, define terms, probe for detail, and develop examples. This step helps to cast the emerging goals in precise language and move from good intentions and broad aims to specific goals (Egan, 1998). Listed below are some examples of probes and directives that might be used to start the process:

- What is your goal?
- When you say you'd like to feel better, what exactly do you mean?
- Describe how your life would be different if you were able to reach your goal. Try to be as detailed as possible.
- If your problem were to be solved, what would need to be different in your life?
- What do you think would be the best resolution to your problem?
- What are some examples of what you would like to achieve?
- As a result of counselling, what feelings do you want to increase or decrease?
- What do you want to be able to do that you can't do now?
- If I could watch you being successful, what would I see?

Some clients are reluctant or unable to identify goals, and they may respond with a dead-end statement such as "I don't know" when they are asked for their goals. Counsellors can use some of these responses to break this impasse: "Guess." "What might your best friend (mother, father, teacher, etc.) suggest as your goal?" "What would you like to achieve, but don't think is possible?" A good general technique is to encourage clients to visualize themselves reaching their goals.

Note also that when clients say, "I don't know," their responses may indicate friction in the counselling relationship, and this answer is a way of sabotaging the work. In such cases, goal setting might be premature, and the focus of the interview may need to shift to relationship problem-solving (immediacy). Moreover, when clients say, "I don't know," they also might be saying, "I can't do it" or "I'm afraid." In such situations, suggesting a very small goal may be a starting point (for example, "If you could make just one tiny change in your life, what would it be?").

The **miracle question** (de Shazer, 1985) is widely used in brief or single-session counselling as a way to help clients who have difficulty coming up with defined goals. A typical miracle question might be formulated as follows: "Suppose that tonight while you're sleeping a miracle happens and your problem is solved. When you wake up, what will be different about your life?" Variations of this question may need to be developed to accommodate different clients. For example, some clients may object to the religious overtones in the question, and a more neutral term, such as *something remarkable*, could be used.

Effective Goals Can Be Measured

Goals need to be measurable in order to be effective. When goals are measurable, clients are able to evaluate progress, and they know precisely when they have reached their goals. Moreover, clear goals sustain client enthusiasm and motivation. Vague and unmeasurable goals, on the other hand, can result in apathy and vague action plans. Thus, goals need to be defined in terms of changes (increases or decreases) in behaviours, thoughts, or feelings.

> Example (skill): *"My goal is to express my opinion or ask a question once per class."*
>
> Example (thoughts): *"My goal is to manage self-depreciating thought patterns by substituting positive affirmations."*
>
> Example (feelings): *"My goal is to reduce anxiety."*

Whenever possible, goals should be framed in quantifiable language with questions such as "How often?" "How many times?" and "How much?" For example, a goal may be to target a weight reduction of nine kilograms. Goals should also have a realistic schedule or target date. Counsellors should help clients determine when they are going to start working toward their goals and when they expect to reach them. For example, "Target weight reduction of nine kilograms in ten weeks." "Make five calls per day to potential employers."

Effective Goals Are Challenging but Realistic

A goal has to be something that clients can reasonably expect to achieve, even though it may require effort and commitment. So counsellors need to consider variables such as interest in achieving the goals, skills and abilities, and resources (including the counsellor) available to help in reaching the goals. In addition, the goals need to be significant enough to contribute toward managing or changing the core problem situation.

But some clients may be reluctant to set challenging goals or even to set goals at all. This situation can occur for a number of reasons:

- poor self-esteem
- fear of failure
- lack of awareness of capacity for change
- fear of change and reluctance to give up established patterns
- lack of resources to support pursuit of the goal (Shebib, 1997:210)

So addressing these reluctance issues is a prerequisite for goal setting. In addition, for complex problems and situations, in which the client's capacity or self-esteem is low, setting short-term goals or subgoals is particularly useful. Short-term goals represent small, attainable steps toward long-term goals. Achieving them helps build optimism and helps clients overcome a sense of inadequacy (Pincus & Minahan, 1973).

In addition, during the beginning phase of counselling, counsellors may develop ideas or views on what might be appropriate goals for their clients. But they should share these ideas only as starting points for negotiation regarding what needs to be done, not as prescriptions.

Evelyn was referred to the counsellor for help in coping with Trevor, her 18-year-old stepson, who was involved in petty crime. Evelyn's immediate goal was to encourage Trevor to move out of the house, and she hoped that the counsellor might help her do this. During the interview, it became apparent to the counsellor that Evelyn needed help developing parenting skills for dealing with Trevor and her two other teenage stepsons. Without dismissing Evelyn's objective, the counsellor suggested that this be part of their agenda.

Effective Goals Are "Owned" by Clients

Clients need to see goals as relevant to their needs and consistent with their values. Thus, when clients are involved in the process of deciding what their goals are, they are more likely to be motivated to work toward achieving them. But when clients are forced to come to counselling by a third party, they may not feel committed to any of the goals of counselling. Thus, the chances of success are diminished greatly unless some mutually acceptable working agreement can be reached.

Understanding a client's values is an important part of goal setting. Some clients are motivated by spiritual values, some by material gain, and others by family values. Other clients focus on immediate gratification, while still others have objectives that are long term.

Ming left his family in China to come to North America. He has seen his wife only once in the last five years when he returned to his country for a short visit. He maintains regular contact with her and their six-year-old son. He sends much of his monthly pay home to support his wife and extended family. Although he hopes that one day his family will be able to join him, he has accepted that his purpose is to position future generations of his family for a better life.

But clients sometimes set goals that require others to change, such as "I want my husband to stop treating me so badly." Counsellors need to encourage clients to form goals based on what is under their control, namely their own feelings, behaviour, and thoughts.

Client complaints and problem statements can usually be reframed as positively worded goal statements. Here are some examples:

Example 1

Client: *Everyone always takes advantage of me.*

Counsellor: *Sounds as though you'd like to learn to stand up for yourself.*

Example 2

Client: *I'm tired of not working.*

Counsellor: *Put simply, your goal is to get a job.*

Example 3

Client: *My life is a mess.*

Counsellor: *You would like to find a way to get your life in order.*

TABLE 7.4	Sample Goals	
Target Area	**Vague Goal**	**Specific Goal Statements**
Behaviour	To do better in my courses	To improve my grade-point average from C to B- by the end of the semester
Feelings	To feel better	To overcome depression so I am able to enjoy life. That would include mixing socially with people and having a sense that life is worth living. I'll be more able to accept my problems without withdrawing or drowning in self-pity.
Thoughts	To stop putting myself down	To regard mistakes as normal and as learning opportunities. When I'm successful, I'll take credit. Overall, I'll be able to say to myself that I'm capable.
Skills	To get organized	To develop skill at organizing my time and setting priorities. I need to set up a schedule so I can plan at least a month in advance.
Relationship	To be able to communicate better with my husband	To reduce the number of fights that we have by not being so explosive. Instead of yelling, I need to remain calm. Instead of not listening, I need to check with him to make sure I understand what he wants too.
Health and fitness	To get in shape	To lose 5 kg over the next two months. To increase my weekly running from 5 to 10 km
Spiritual	To be closer to God	To attend religious services regularly—at least once a week. To make prayer a daily part of my life. To read something spiritual at least once a day. To walk in the forest three times a week

The above responses change the focus of the interview from problems to goals. Of course, the counsellor and client will have to work together to shape these vague goals into more explicit terms.

The overall goal of any counselling relationship is change; but depending on the needs of individual clients, the targets for change might focus on behaviour, feelings, thoughts, skills, relationship enhancement, or other areas of the client's life. Table 7.4 provides examples of vague goals and specific goals.

ACTION PLANNING

Counselling is a developmental process. In the beginning phase, the focus is on the development of a strong working relationship based on a contract that describes the work to be done and the respective roles of both the counsellor and the client. The beginning phase is also concerned with problem identification and exploration. This work provides the foundation for clients and counsellors to define goals. So attention to detail in the beginning phase helps prevent problems from premature action. Problem exploration leads to goal setting, which, in turn, forms the foundation for action planning.

Problem Exploration ⟶ Goals ⟶ Action Planning

Moreover, goals represent the outcomes that clients are working toward. Having clear goals is a prerequisite to defining action programs for reaching these goals. Once clients have their goals in mind, some may not even need further counselling assistance. The overall process of developing goals, including the important work of exploring their problems in the beginning phase, may be sufficient to meet their needs. But other clients will need additional coaching and support to develop and implement systematic action plans in order to avoid the New Years Resolution syndrome discussed earlier in this chapter.

Action planning and implementation consists of a series of steps leading to the client's goal (or subgoal). Put simply, action planning involves developing strategies to help clients get where they want to go. This involves four steps: (1) identify alternatives for action, (2) choose an action strategy, (3) develop and implement plans, and (4) evaluate outcomes.

Step 1: Identify Alternatives

The first task in selecting a plan is to list alternative ideas for achieving the goals. This step serves two purposes. First, it holds clients back from impulsive action based on the first alternative available, which may simply be a repeat of previous unsuccessful attempts at change. Second, it helps ensure that clients have choices based on a full range of possibilities. When there is choice, clients can make more rational decisions.

Both counsellors and clients may contribute ideas about possible plans. As well, consultation with others and brainstorming can generate ideas. Some basic rules for effective brainstorming are listed below (Egan, 1998; Shebib, 1997; Cragan & Wright, 1991; Young, 1998).

1. Do not evaluate or criticize ideas. Adherence to this principle ensures that self-censorship does not result. Clients might hold back potentially valuable and useable suggestions if they fear that they will be criticized or embarrassed.

2. Generate as many ideas as possible. Encourage wild and creative suggestions. At this stage, any alternative, however bizarre, is acceptable. Counsellors can use leads such as these to encourage clients to generate ideas: "Let your imagination run wild and see how many different ideas you can come up with that will help you achieve your goals." "Don't worry for now about whether it's a good idea or a bad one." Sometimes counsellors can prompt clients to be creative by generating a few "wild" ideas of their own.

3. Emphasize quantity—more is better.

4. Look for ways to combine or "piggyback" ideas. Sometimes apparently ridiculous proposals can be modified to work. Or they can be combined with other ideas to come up with new alternatives. Some key questions for stimulating further alternatives include "How can we join suggestions?" "In what ways can we sort or rearrange these ideas?"

INTERVIEW 7.2 GOAL SETTING

The following interview excerpt illustrates goal-setting techniques. Prior to this dialogue, exploration and active listening enabled the counsellor to develop a solid base of understanding. With this work apparently finished, it seems timely to move on to goal setting.

DIALOGUE	ANALYSIS
Counsellor: You've talked about how you're determined to change—as you put it, "now or never." That suggests to me that you're ready to set a change goal.	The counsellor recognizes the client's positive motivation for change and uses it to make a transition to goal setting. Problem statements can often be reframed to make goal statements.
Client: Yeah, I can't go on living like this. Something has to happen, and soon!	The client makes a general statement confirming motivation for change. This undeveloped goal is a useful starting point, but it is not yet an operational goal.
Counsellor: I think it might be helpful at this point to figure out what you want to achieve, what you'd like to change. This would give you something to work toward. What do you think?	The counsellor seeks to contract with the client to work on goal setting. The counsellor uses the criteria for effective goals as a reference point. As the interview progresses, other questions will be asked that help frame the goal. There is no secret agenda to this, and the counsellor might decide to review the process with the client. The final open question reaches for client input and agreement.
Client: Sounds good. I think it's time to do something. For one thing, I really haven't invested too much in my marriage. I have to change my priorities.	The client begins to identify an area for change.
Counsellor: What do you mean by "change your priorities"?	The counsellor requests more definition (goal specificity). This ensures that no assumptions are made.
Client: If possible, I've got to stop spending so much time at work. By the time I get home, I'm so tired that I have no energy or motivation to be involved with my family.	Often, as here, client goals are stated in the negative—i.e., in terms of what the client would like to stop doing.
Counsellor: Okay, I think I get a sense that what you'd like is to be more committed to your family. In order to do that, you'd have to cut back on work.	The counsellor attempts to help the client put an emerging goal statement in behavioural terms by reframing the idea.

(continued)

Client: Exactly.

Counsellor: Just so we can be clear, can you try to be more specific? Suppose you're successful. What will be different from the way things are now?

This request for more specificity encourages the client to reframe the goals in positive terms by stating what will be done differently.

Client: I don't understand. What do you mean?

The client is confused, but the relationship is strong enough that the client is able to ask for help.

Counsellor: Well, maybe you can't plan it out exactly, but what do you see happening in terms of the amount of time you'd like to spend with your family? Try to be specific so you'll have something to aim for.

The counsellor clarifies the question. This helps to educate the client regarding some of the criteria for goal setting.

Client (laughs): Oh, I see. You want to nail me down and close the deal. You should be a salesperson. Well, I think it's important that I free up the weekends and at least two nights a week. Sunday should be strictly family, a time to do something with the kids.

A clear goal statement has emerged, but the work is not yet finished.

Counsellor: From your excited tone, I get the sense that you'd feel really good if you could do that.

Empathy lets the client know that the counsellor has recognized the client's feelings and their importance.

Client: In my heart, it's what I've always wanted.

The client confirms acceptance of the counsellor's empathy.

Counsellor: A while back, you used the words "if possible" when you talked about cutting back on work. What problems do you anticipate?

An important part of goal setting is to assist the client to look at potential problems, including the relative advantages and disadvantages of goal attainment.

Client: I'd like to try for a management position at the company. But everyone's so competitive. I've got to put in the hours if I'm going to keep my sales above the others. And high sales is the first thing they look for when it's time for promotion.

Having identified this potential barrier, the client can address it—for example, by considering ways to overcome it—or make a decision about whether the costs involved are too high.

Counsellor: You're torn. To compete, you've got to put in the hours. But if you do that, it takes away from your time and energy with the family. That's a lot of stress.

The counsellor recognizes the client's ambivalence.

(continued)

Client: Now that you point it out, it seems obvious. I've been under stress for so long, I don't even think about it any more. It's clear to me now that the price of success is just too much.

Solutions to problems, however obvious, are often not acted upon because of such ambivalence.

Counsellor: Meaning that if you have to sacrifice time with your family in order to get ahead, you're not interested. (client nods)

The counsellor's empathy provides a basis for insight.

Sounds as if you've made a decision. But let me play devil's advocate. Suppose you cut back on your job and lost a promotion. How would you feel about that?

Such responses ensure that the client will not gloss over or minimize difficulties. The counsellor also prevents the client from acting impulsively. By anticipating risks, the client is challenged to decide whether the costs are acceptable.

Client: It would be hard on me. But I think not nearly so hard as what's happening now. At heart, I'm really a family man. I'm certain of it. Family has to be Number One. My career is important to me, but it's my second priority.

The client confirms a decision. If the counsellor is satisfied that the client has taken a serious look at all reasonable risks, it's time to move on.

Counsellor: Let's go back to your goal. What other problems do you anticipate?

The counsellor challenges the client to look ahead to see if there are other risks. Similar responses are called for until all difficulties are explored.

(20 seconds of silence)

Client: Here's one. My family is so used to getting along without me, they've developed lives of their own. I guess I can't expect them to drop everything for me.

The counsellor must be patient and give the client enough time to complete the thought process.

Counsellor: So, how can you deal with that reality?

Client: That's easy. I guess I'll just have to negotiate with the family on how much time we'll spend together.

This type of response ensures that the client sets goals and embarks on action plans with a clear sense of direction and planning. Problems may be prevented or anticipated, and the client is far less likely to face a crisis that leads to abandonment of otherwise healthy objectives.

Counsellor: One thought occurs to me. How will your boss react if you suddenly start spending less time on the job? Do you think that's something to consider?

It is appropriate for the counsellor to tentatively introduce some of her own ideas, leaving a lot of room for the client to respond. But as a rule, counsellors should let the client have the first opportunity.

Adapted from Shebib, 1997.

Case Study (Lisa)

Lisa, age 33, and her counsellor come up with a list of possibilities for Lisa to deal with her shyness and her need to meet more people. Some of the ideas they generated are listed below:

- *join a singles club*
- *take an acting class*
- *learn to sing*
- *put an ad in the personals column*
- *become a volunteer*
- *use counselling to role play problem situations in order to develop assertiveness*
- *forget the goal and become a nun*
- *use counselling to deal with self-depreciating inner talk*
- *try hypnosis*
- *join a social group at a place of worship*
- *participate in an assertiveness training group*

Step 2: Choose an Action Strategy

Once a creative list of alternative action strategies is identified, the next task is to assist clients in evaluating alternatives and making choices. At this point, the counsellor's role is to ensure that clients are able to make informed choices. This involves helping clients intelligently consider each alternative against a number of criteria. An obvious first criterion is that the alternative is potentially effective for meeting the client's goal. It must be sufficient to make a difference and relevant to the problem being addressed. A second criterion is that the alternative is within the capacity of the client. Otherwise, failure is inevitable. A third criterion is that the alternative is consistent with the values and beliefs of the client. A fourth is that the alternative is reviewed in terms of their potential cost. Cost might be measured by time, money, and energy expended in finding resources to execute the alternative. As well, alternatives might result in other losses for the client. For example, suppose a client wishes to end a pattern of alcohol abuse, but the person's friends are drinking buddies. If quitting drinking involves developing new activities, the potential loss of friends and social structure must be considered as a negative consequence that will have an impact on the client. Understanding and exploring this loss is important, for unless clients are aware of and prepared for these contingencies, they may be unable to sustain any efforts at changing.

Step 3: Develop and Implement Plans

Developing and implementing plans involves four substeps: (1) sequencing plans, (2) developing **contingency plans**, (3) putting plans into action, and (4) evaluating plans.

Effective plans are maps that detail the sequence of events leading to the final goal. Counsellors should avoid tailor-made plans in favour of customized strategies that are designed in collaboration with individual clients. Some of the important questions that need to be answered include the following:

- What specific strategies will be used?
- In what order will the strategies be used?
- What resources or support will be needed at each step?
- What are the risks and potential gains?
- What are the risks and potential obstacles?

Effective plans anticipate the potential obstacles that clients might encounter along the route. Once clients know and accept the possible barriers that could interfere with their plans, they can develop contingency plans to deal with these barriers. This preventive work helps keep clients from giving up when things don't go smoothly.

CASE STUDY (LISA, CONTINUED)

Lisa decided that joining a singles group would be a great way for her to meet people, but she admitted that she would probably back out before going to the first meeting. With her counsellor's help, she came up with two ideas for managing this problem. She recruited a friend to go with her to the group, and she phoned the group leader to volunteer to bring refreshments. Lisa knew that she wouldn't back down if it meant that others would be affected by her actions.

Lisa said that what bothered her most was the idea of first meeting someone. She told her counsellor, "I already feel so awkward. I just won't know what to say." Her counsellor helped Lisa accept that feeling awkward is normal under such circumstances. The counsellor self-disclosed some of her own anxieties and suggested that they could role-play some ideas for handling these tough moments.

Later, during the implementation phase, counsellors need to support and encourage clients as they deal with the stress of change. One way they can help is to remind clients that anxiety, awkwardness, and periodic slumps are normal when change is occurring. Meanwhile, counsellors can look for ways to reframe failure or setbacks as learning opportunities. Wilson's comments might be offered to clients:

> Although you may fail to reach the goal, there are benefits of having worked toward it. One benefit is the practical education of making the effort. Another is the opportunity to practice specific skills. A third is the recognition that meeting some goals and failing to meet others is part of the ebb and flow of life. Recognize that you probably will not achieve significant goals without some failures. Failing provides unique learning opportunities that ultimately contribute to your personal growth. (1994:18)

Moreover, empathy is particularly important at this time to support clients dealing with feelings that accompany change. During implementation, counsellors should also encourage clients to use family, friends, and support groups to assist them.

Step 4: Evaluate Outcomes

Effective plans include continual evaluation during the implementation phase. Evaluation recognizes and confirms success and is a powerful motivator. However, evaluation may also uncover problems that need to be addressed. For example, it may become apparent that the goals are too unrealistic. If they are too challenging and unreachable, counsellors can help clients define smaller goals. Similarly, if goals prove to be too easy, they can be modified to provide more challenge. Thus, regular review of progress ensures that goals and action strategies remain relevant and realistic.

When evaluation reveals that the plan is unlikely to be successful, efforts can be redirected toward redesigning the plan or selecting a different strategy for action. In some cases, the client may need help that is beyond the capacity of the counsellor; in this case, referral to another counsellor or service is appropriate.

CONVERSATION 7.3

I'VE TRIED EVERYTHING

STUDENT: I get stuck when a client says, "I've tried everything and nothing seems to work."

TEACHER: You feel stuck, which is precisely how the client feels. Clients often bring out in counsellors the same feelings that they are experiencing. This reality can be a useful tool for empathy. When clients say they've tried everything, it's important not to get into a "yes, but" game, whereby counsellors generate ideas and clients dismiss them with a "yes, but" response.

STUDENT: So, what are my choices?

TEACHER: I'd be interested in exploring what the client did. Did he or she try long enough? At the right time? In the right way? Sometimes problems get worse before they get better, and clients may give up too soon. A mother might try ignoring her child when he has a tantrum. She tells you ignoring doesn't work, but she may have abandoned this tactic after a few minutes when it appeared that the intensity of her child's tantrum was increasing. In this situation, you could help her anticipate this obstacle so that she would not be demoralized when it occurred. Or maybe she was giving her child lots of nonverbal attention, not realizing how this was reinforcing the tantrum.

STUDENT: I can think of another example. One of the members of my work group was having trouble with her supervisor. She told us that there is no point in talking to him because he doesn't listen anyway. But from the way she described how she talked to him, I wouldn't listen either. She was vicious and cruel.

TEACHER: So, if she were your client, she would need some help developing awareness about how she affects others.

BRIEF COUNSELLING

Be kind whenever possible. It is always possible.
—*Dalai Lama*

Brief counselling is an approach to counselling characterized by a focus on resources and solutions rather than problems. The purpose of brief counselling is "to provide people with a pleasant experience that turns problems into challenges, fosters optimism, enhances collaboration, inspires creativity, and, above all, helps them to retain their dignity" (Furman & Ahola, 1994:65).

How Brief Counselling Helps

Often counselling relationships are brief, sometimes limited to a few sessions, a single session, or even a brief encounter. Michael Hoyt (1994) reviewed the literature and found that single-session therapy is often the norm and that a significant number of clients and counsellors found it desirable and useful. In three systematic studies of the effectiveness of single-session therapy (SST), more than 50 percent of clients showed improvement (1994:41). Moreover, many people solve psychological problems without professional consultation. For others, the "light touch" of a single visit may be enough, providing experience, skills, and encouragement to help them continue in their life journey (Hoyt, 1994:153).

Furthermore, a change in some part of a client's life can affect other aspects of his or her life, including relationships with significant others. Thus, brief counselling that helps a client achieve some success (e.g., insight, reduction of painful feelings, new skills), however small, can have a dramatic long-term impact if it switches the client from a point of despair to a position of optimism, and a ripple effect occurs. "When clients alter their behaviors ever so slightly, it causes a chain reaction in response to the initial change. Those affected by the change find themselves adjusting their responses, which in turn elicits further changes in clients" (Sklare, 1997:11).

When clients come voluntarily for counselling, they may have already established a certain momentum for change. In fact, some clients realize progress while waiting for their first scheduled appointment.

De Shazer (1985) argues that it is not necessary to spend time searching for the root causes of a problem, nor is it necessary to have elaborate knowledge about the problem. In brief counselling, the goal is to help clients do something different to improve their situation, rather than repeating the same ineffectual solutions.

Brief counselling may help in many ways. Because of its emphasis on action and change, brief counselling helps clients to become "unstuck" from ineffectual ways of thinking, feeling, and acting. Clients can be encouraged to reframe by focusing their attention on what's working, thus interrupting their preoccupation with problems and failure. This focus may generate or renew the clients' optimism that change is possible. In addition, brief counselling, even a single session, can be therapeutic for clients if they are able to unload pent-up feelings. A caring and empathic counsellor can encourage such ventilation and reassure clients that their reactions and feelings are normal. This can significantly reduce feelings of isolation by disputing the belief that many clients hold: "I'm the only one who feels this way."

Brief counselling can also provide important information to clients. For example, they can be referred to appropriate alternative services. Or they can be given information that might help them deal with their situation. Finally, brief counselling can be used to demystify the counselling process and to help clients understand what they might reasonably accomplish in counselling. In this way, brief counselling may be useful for motivating reluctant clients to engage with or to continue with counselling.

But brief or single-session therapy is not appropriate for all clients. It is less likely to be effective with these client groups: clients who need inpatient psychiatric care, including those who are suicidal; clients with schizophrenia, bipolar disorder, or drug addiction; clients who need help in dealing with the effects of childhood abuse; and clients with chronic eating disorders (Hoyt, 1994).

Selected Brief Counselling Techniques

Helping Clients Get on Track

Counsellors need to shift their own thinking away from believing that they have to stay with clients until the clients' problems are solved and their lives are in order. For example, counsellors might assist clients to organize their thinking about grieving; but the process of grieving is normal and might last a long time, and counsellors do not have to be present for the entire grieving process (Walter & Peller, 1994). Counselling ends with the client still grieving but with a much greater sense of control and of being on track. If clients have a plan in mind for dealing with their problems, they have the capacity to put that plan into action. Moreover, if they are already implementing that process, counsellors should consider getting out of their way.

Looking for Exceptions

Huber and Backlund (1991) propose working with the exceptions to the times when clients are having difficulty. They contend that regardless of the severity of their clients' problems, there are moments when clients are managing their troubles. Moments when anxious persons feel calm, acting-out children listen to their parents, and angry people are peaceful can all be studied to discover potentially successful answers to chronic problems. Huber and Backlund believe that clients become fixated on their problems and on what doesn't work. By doing so, they often fail to notice those times when their problems have abated. In fact, they often continue to repeat or exaggerate "solutions" that have already proved unworkable. Using this exceptions approach, counsellors ask clients to focus on those moments, however rare, when they are coping successfully.

So when clients are asked, "What is different about those occasions when your child obeys you or at least responds more receptively to your requests?" or "What is different about those times that you're not angry or only minimally upset?" the counsellor is requesting that clients report on experiences to which they have paid almost no attention. Consequently, they have given little or no credence to the more successful manner in which they were resolving what at other times they experienced as a persistent difficulty. (66)

Working with exceptions provides a dramatic and quick way to motivate and energize clients to think about solutions rather than problems. In the following brief excerpt, the counsellor uses the technique to assist a client who is having trouble dealing with her teenage son.

> Counsellor: *From what you've been saying, it's a rare moment when you and your son can sit together and talk calmly.*
>
> Client: *Maybe once or twice in the last year.*
>
> Counsellor: *Let's look at those two times. I'm really curious about what was different about them that enabled you to talk without fighting. Pick one time that worked best.*
>
> Client: *That's easy. My son was excited because he was going to a rock concert, and he was in a really good mood. I felt more relaxed too. He just seemed more approachable that day.*
>
> Counsellor: *Have you considered that part of your success might have to do with your mood? Perhaps your son was more approachable because you were more relaxed.*
>
> Client: *Interesting point.*

Counsellor: *Let's explore that a bit further. Because you were more relaxed, what else was different about the way you handled this encounter?*

Client: *I didn't feel stressed so I think I was more open to listen to him.*

Counsellor: *What were you doing differently?*

Client: *I let him talk without jumping in to argue.*

The counsellor's goal in the above interview is to find what works, then to encourage the client to apply successful solutions more frequently. The process is as follows:

1. Identify exceptions to those times when the client is having difficulty.
2. Explore what was different about those times, including what (specifically) the client was doing differently.
3. Identify elements (e.g., behaviour, setting, timing) that contributed to a successful solution.
4. Help the client increase the frequency of the success elements when dealing with the problem situation.

Clients are often more experienced using ineffectual strategies to deal with their problems. Despite the fact that these strategies do not work, clients may compulsively repeat them to the point where they give up and conclude that their problems are hopeless. Consequently, counsellors need to encourage clients to apply the elements of success. For example, a behavioural rehearsal (role-play) that focuses on systematic exploration of the elements of success can be used. Counsellors also need to encourage clients to pay attention to what they are doing when they are managing their problem, as in the following case:

> Rodney came to counselling asking for help to quit what he described as "compulsive marijuana use." He was concerned that he might slip into heavy drug use. The counsellor asked him to observe what he was doing when he was not using marijuana and what he did to overcome his urge to use. This technique empowered Rodney by helping him become aware of successful strategies he was already using. Subsequently, he was encouraged to increase the frequency of these successful behaviours.

Using Solution Talk

Furman and Ahola (1994) introduced the idea of "solution talk" as a way to evoke a solution-oriented focus to the counselling interview. The goal is to create a climate of discovery and action. For example, in order to get clients to notice their skills and capacities, counsellors can use statements and questions such as the following:

- You have dealt with this problem for a long time. Many people would not have survived. How did you manage to keep going? What strengths were you able to draw on?
- When you've successfully coped, how did you do it?

In addition, counsellors need to be alert for opportunities to reinforce clients' strengths. Personal qualities, actions that underscore their determination, attitudes, positive decisions, accomplishments, effort toward change, and courage in the face of adversity can all be used to bolster clients' sense of capacity and self-esteem.

But clients may already have a rich understanding of their problems and the ways in which they might be solved. So counsellors need to tap their clients' expertise about possible answers to their problems. The central assumption here is that clients have the capacity to resolve their distress.

- What solutions have you already tried?
- What would your best friend advise you to do?
- Suppose one day you received an invitation to give a lecture to professionals about the kind of problem you have had to live with. What would you tell them? (Furman & Ahola, 1994:51)
- In order to solve your problem, what will you have to do?

Creative solution finding can be stimulated with statements and questions such as these:

- Let's try to identify something different for you to do to solve your problem.
- Let's brainstorm ideas. Don't censor anything. The wilder the idea, the better.

Earlier in this chapter, reframing was introduced as a way to help clients modify their thinking. Reframing suggests another way of looking at problems, which, in turn, generates new ways of looking at solutions. The miracle question, (Sklare, 1997; Hoyt, 1994) can also be used to direct clients to thinking about solutions:

- If a miracle occurred and your problem were solved, what would be different in your life?
- How could you make the miracle happen? What would you have to do differently?

A variation is to use the miracle question to probe for examples of success and exceptions to clients' problems:

- Tell me about the times when part of this miracle has already happened, even just a little bit. (Sklare, 1997:68)

The Change Continuum

The basic idea behind this technique is to assist clients to become motivated in the direction of positive change. A central assumption is that it is not necessary for the counsellor to be present for the whole change process. The counsellor's role is to promote/assist with small changes in the direction of larger goals.

STEP 1: Draw a continuum such as the one illustrated below. The continuum will be used to assist clients to represent where they are, what direction they are heading, and where they would like to be.

As bad as it could be   **As good as it could be**
(negative)   **(positive)**

STEP 2: Ask clients to add indicators to represent each end of the continuum.

<-->

As bad as it could be
(negative)

– using hard narcotics
– prostitution
– HIV positive
– criminal activity

As good as it could be
(positive)

– job
– drug free
– place of my own
– friends who are "clean"

STEP 3: Use questions such as the following to promote discussion and exploration.

• At this time in your life, where are you on the continuum?
• Where would you like to be?
• What direction are you heading?
• What might cause or help you to change directions?
• What would be an indicator that you are moving in the right direction?

STEP 4: Suggest to clients that the direction they are heading is more important than where they are on the continuum. Your role may be limited to assisting them to change direction. Help clients identify incremental steps towards their final goal. Remember: "less frequent" and "less severe" can also signal progress.

SUMMARY

The foundation for empowerment in counselling is the belief that clients are capable and have a right to manage their own lives. In order to empower clients, counsellors need to forgo controlling them, demystify the counselling process, promote client self-determination, advocate for progressive changes in the system, and assist clients to change established patterns of thinking and acting that are interfering with their lives. Counsellors can help clients change established patterns through five major activities: motivating, confronting, helping clients think differently, goal setting, and action planning.

Motivating involves engaging clients in a change process, as well as supporting and energizing them as they deal with the rigours of change. Counsellors may face a range of motivational challenges, and they can employ different strategies to address each of them. Clients may be at precontemplative, involuntary, burnt-out, contemplative, or energized stages of readiness.

Effective confrontation is not a hostile act. It is a way to move clients to a different level of understanding, behaving, or feeling. Confrontation can address incongruities between what clients believe and the way they act; self-defeating ways of thinking and behaving; behaviour that is harmful to self or others; blind spots; blaming behaviours; communication problems; and strengths. Confrontation should be relevant to the goals of counselling and timed appropriately to minimize defensive reactions.

In addition, clients may have trouble breaking out of established patterns because of the way they think about problems. Thinking errors include distortion, incomplete analysis, egocentricity or lack of empathy, rigidity, and self-defeating thought. An important goal of counselling is to help clients discontinue faulty reasoning. Reframing is a tool for helping clients examine problems from another perspective. It empowers clients by focusing on solutions and redefining negatives as opportunities or challenges.

Goal setting serves many important purposes, including giving direction, defining roles, motivating, and measuring progress. Effective goals need to be concrete, measurable, challenging but realistic, and owned by clients. Effective goals can be developed from problem statements.

Action planning consists of a series of steps leading to the client's goal or subgoal. Selecting a plan involves systematic identification and evaluation of the possibilities for action, then choosing one or more alternative action plans. Developing and implementing plans involves four substeps: sequencing plans, developing contingency plans, putting plans into action, and evaluating.

Often counselling relationships are limited to a few sessions or even a single session. Nevertheless, these brief encounters have the potential to be helpful for clients. Brief counselling works on the assumption that a change in some part of a client's life will affect other aspects of his or her life, including relationships with significant others. One major technique of brief counselling is working with the exceptions to the times when clients are having difficulty. Counsellors can help clients study moments such as when anxious people feel calm to discover potentially successful answers to chronic problems. A second major technique is to focus the work of counselling on solutions to problems.

EXERCISES

1. What style do you prefer others to use when they give you feedback? Compare your preference with those of your colleagues and develop a list of different options (e.g., straight and to the point, "sandwiched," etc.)

2. Consider the various ways in which your colleagues prefer to receive feedback. Which ways would you have most trouble with?

3. Consider areas in your life where change is possible, is necessary, or has already occurred. Classify your stage of change with each issue, based on the stages of change model: precontemplative, contemplative, preparation, action, maintenance. What could potentially "move" you from one stage to another?

4. What are the essential differences between a counselling confrontation and an attack?

5. Identify the person(s) from whom you would be most receptive to receiving feedback and those from whom you would be least receptive. Give your reasons why.

6. Self-evaluate your personal comfort when confronting others.
   a. What people would you have difficulty confronting?
   b. Do you avoid confronting?
   c. Think of times when it was reasonable to confront, but you didn't. What prevented you from confronting?
   d. Finish the following sentence: When I confront, I feel...

7. Write a short concept paper that describes what you believe are the elements of effective confrontation.

8. Hamachek says, "Do not confront another person if you do not wish to increase your involvement with that individual" (1982:230). Develop a rationale that supports this statement.

9. Work with a colleague to role-play an appropriate counsellor confrontation for each of the following situations.

   a. a client who has hygiene problems
   b. a colleague who has, in your opinion, behaved in an unprofessional manner
   c. a client who consistently arrives late for appointments

10. Identify an area in your own life that you are willing to accept feedback about (e.g., the first impressions you leave with others, your style of communication, the way others see you). Spend about 20 minutes with a friend or colleague exploring their opinions about the identified area.

   a. What were your feelings during the encounter? Did they change?
   b. What did your colleague say or do that made it easier to accept the feedback? What made it more difficult?
   c. What did you learn about giving or receiving feedback that will be useful to you in your work as a counsellor?

11. Evaluate the effectiveness of each of the confrontations below. Suggest improvements.

   a. Try to do better next time.
   b. You're an idiot.
   c. You're saying that you're okay, yet you're crying.
   d. Grow up and act your age.
   e. As long as you continue to act like a doormat, you're going to get abused. If you're serious about protecting yourself, leave him.

12. Suggest reframed responses for each of the following client statements.

   a. I can't do it.
   b. (a student counsellor) I feel so unnatural and phony expressing empathy all the time.
   c. I really want my kids to avoid making the same mistakes I did. I don't know why they don't listen to me.
   d. If he really loved me, he'd send me flowers.
   e. My life is a mess.
   f. I'm tired of being depressed all the time.

13. Name at least 10 different ways to motivate clients.

14. Evaluate how effectively the following statements meet the criteria for effective goals.

   a. to be a better person
   b. to get my boss to stop hassling me
   c. to drink less
   d. to be able to disagree with someone without dismissing them or their ideas
   e. to improve my fitness by next year to the point where I can run 1 km in 15 minutes

15. Practise brainstorming techniques. Identify 30 different action strategies for a client who wishes to quit drinking.

16. Use the concepts from this chapter to practise goal setting and action planning. Pick one or more target areas (behaviour, feelings, thoughts, skills, or relationship).

17. Work with a partner. Use selected brief counselling techniques from this chapter to help him or her deal with a problem area.

WEBLINKS

Links and resources on the topic of motivational interviewing:
www.motivationalinterview.org/

Links to articles and resources on goal setting:
www.selfgrowth.com/goal.html

Methods for changing thoughts, attitudes, self-concept, motivation, values and expectations:
www.southlakecenter.com/psyhelp/chap14/

chapter eight

Difficult Situations

PREVIEW

After reading this chapter you should be able to:

- Understand the different forms of client resistance.

- Explain reasons for resistance.

- Describe techniques for dealing with resistance.

- Explain the importance of counsellor self-awareness when dealing with clients who are resistant.

- Define intimidating and violent behaviour.

- Identify key variables for predicting which clients might become violent.

- Understand violence in relation to mental illness.

- List key questions for assessing the potential for violence.

- Describe techniques for preventing violence.

- Identify and describe the four phases of violence.

- Describe strategies for intervening at each phase of violence.

- Explain the importance of debriefing critical incidents.

- Identify debriefing techniques.

RESISTANCE

A term first introduced by Freud, **resistance** refers to a normal defensive reaction that comes from the natural drive to preserve the status quo. Change challenges people to alter existing and familiar patterns of communicating or coping. But these patterns, however painful, are at least familiar and the prospect of change represents some risk as well as potential gain. Thus, resistance protects clients from the stress and threat of change. Sheafor and Horejsi (2006) note that it is common for clients to be somewhat defensive, particularly in the beginning phase: "Clients usually begin a helping relationship feeling some conflict over whether the perceived need for change outweighs the disruption it may cause. Even a small amount of change can create a discomfort or fear for clients, especially if they hold rigid beliefs, are inflexible in their thought processes and behaviors, or are fearful about risking change in their relationships with others" (p. 205)

Most clients are ambivalent about the change process and may simultaneously desire and resist efforts and opportunities for change. The messages from clients seem to say, "I want to change, but I don't want to change." This ambivalence can freeze clients in a state of indecision; thus, "resolving ambivalence can be a key to change" (Miller & Rollnick, 2002:19). So counsellors should expect ambivalence and gear their activity toward helping clients understand and make decisions based on the relative risks and rewards of changing. For example, counsellors can use flip charts to help clients identify and visually evaluate the costs and benefits of any potential decision.

But sometimes clients are resistant because they have been forced to come for counselling. They do not see the need for change, and they resent being coerced. Other clients come voluntarily for counselling and appear motivated to change, but they resist it because of prior bad experiences with counsellors or because they fear the unknown risks and pain of changing. As Young observes, "When the helper begins to disrupt long-held and cherished beliefs about the world, the client tries to protect his or her core beliefs from sweeping changes that may bring chaos" (1998:251).

Harris and Watkins echo Young's sentiments, arguing that resistance to change indicates a degree of stability that would be upset if people changed randomly. They conclude that "resistance has positive value, and a counselor should expect to find some good reasons why clients don't change—at least from their point of view" (1987:17).

Yet sometimes clients become increasingly resistant as counselling progresses. This may signal that the process is moving too quickly or that there is unresolved conflict in the counsellor–client relationship. Resistance may also arise at critical moments in counselling, such as when counsellors challenge long-established behaviour or attempt to encourage discussion or goal setting in areas that clients would like to avoid. Miller and Rollnick (2002) developed the theory of **psychological reactance** to describe how painful consequences (e.g., personal suffering from drug addiction, nagging from concerned family members) may actually increase the undesired behaviour. This theory "predicts "an increase in the rate and attractiveness of a "problem" behaviour if a person perceives that his or her personal freedom is being infringed or changed (p. 18)."

Signs of Resistance

Resistance may reveal itself in a variety of ways, ranging from overt hostility to passivity that impedes the work. Here are some client behaviours and signs that may suggest resistance

(Gladding, 1996; Young, 1998; Miller & Rollnick, 2002; Hackney & Cormier, 2005; Shulman, 1999):

1. failure to comply with the basic procedures of counselling, including keeping appointments, being on time, and paying fees

2. hostile or argumentative statements (e.g., "This is a waste of time," "You can't make me cooperate," "That's none of your business," and "I don't want to be here.")

3. passivity (e.g., silence, withholding information, persistent short responses such as "I don't know," extreme self-censorship of ideas and feelings). Such passivity may indicate that the client does not want to be there, or it may mean that the feelings, content, and challenges of the interview are more than the client is willing or able to face.

4. diversion as a way of avoiding difficult, threatening, or incriminating content. (e.g., changing subject, using excessive humour, making small talk, introducing irrelevant material, being overly talkative, intellectualizing, restricting the conversation to particular topics).

5. uncooperative behaviour (e.g., failure to follow through with plans or homework, false promises)

6. subtle undermining (e.g., acting seductively, attempting to redefine the counselling relationship as a friendship, excessive praising, being sarcastic)

7. creating the illusion of work, described by Shulman (1999) as engaging in conversations that appear important but that in reality are empty and have no real meaning. Interviews may be filled with apparent cooperation and verbosity, but the work does not empower clients or enable them to change.

8. nonverbal cues suggesting a passive/aggressive response, such as not making eye contact, folding arms, sitting on the edge of the seat, using an angry tone of voice, clenching fists, raising eyebrows, frowning, and sighing

9. blaming, making excuses, expressing unwillingness to change

Otani (1989) cautions against using a single incident as evidence of resistance. For example, a client may become silent when a new topic is introduced. This silence may or may not be resistance. But if the client becomes silent again when the same topic is reintroduced, then resistance is likely.

Sometimes clients expect the worst from counsellors. These expectations may be based on past experience with helping professionals or other persons in authority; thus, it is understandable for clients to be cautious or suspicious when they fear the same outcome. Consequently, these clients will be quick to pick up on anything that might confirm their fears. Indeed, they view caring as manipulative and empathy as intrusive. As Irving Layton, a Canadian poet, commented, "The virtues of those we dislike irritate us more than their vices." Counsellors who understand the importance of such prior expectations are less likely to be taken aback by clients who reject or who are suspicious of their caring actions. It is crucial that counsellors monitor and manage their own emotional reactions to resistance. Common counsellor reactions include fear, anxiety, a sense of rejection, avoidance, defensiveness, anger, and pessimism.

Counsellor Self-Awareness and Management of Self

Client resistance can be unsettling and demoralizing for counsellors. Counsellors who have a high need to be liked by their clients may interpret resistance as personal rejection. Resistant clients can test almost every counsellor's ability to be nonjudgmental. Frequently, counsellors respond with their own insecurities and defences. In turn, clients may view their counsellors' annoyance as proof that the situation is hopeless. In worst-case scenarios, counsellors turn against their clients and blame them for their problems. Ultimately, they look for ways to refer them in order to get rid of them. Such referrals are a way of "dumping" the client, rather than an attempt to help them meet their real needs through connection with alternative resources. Thus, it is important that counsellors find ways to depersonalize the situation. Otherwise, they run the risk of further worsening the situation by rejecting the client or retaliating in subtle ways.

Counsellors also need to be able to objectively evaluate their own conduct and take their fair share of responsibility for resistance. When counsellors have high self-awareness of their actions, they are able to monitor themselves and change their behaviour to be more effective. Weisinger underscores the importance of counsellor self-awareness when dealing with difficult clients: "By being aware, for example, that your voice is getting louder and you are becoming increasingly angry at a client who is making yet another unreasonable demand—and recognizing, of course, how important your client is to your ongoing employment—you might lower your voice, defuse your anger, and respond to your client respectfully" (1998:xx). Hill (2004) echoes sentiments from many sources with the simple, yet profound advice to counsellors "to respond to client anger as they would to any other emotion" (p. 417).

Moreover, counsellors should use colleagues and supervisors for support when dealing with highly resistant clients, who can tax the patience of even the most dedicated counsellor. Collegial support can help counsellors unwind from tough sessions. Colleagues can also help counsellors process their reactions and regain or test objectivity, and they can be a source of fresh ideas for reaching difficult clients.

Dealing with Resistance

Some resistance is normal and perhaps desirable, so counsellors do not always have to treat resistance as problematic. Skilled counsellors recognize resistance, but they are not threatened by it; instead, they consider it a clue that their clients' defences are engaged. By understanding the nature of the resistance, counsellors can open a pathway to greater understanding of their clients. In the beginning phase of counselling, before trust and a working contract are negotiated, many clients tend to hold back. At this stage, their counsellors are strangers, and it would be unwise for clients to open up too quickly without knowing how precious personal information might be treated.

However, clients who are open and candid about their resistance may present less of a challenge than those who mask their resistance with silence or feigned cooperation. When resistance is clearly labelled by clients, frank discussion seems to follow; but when clients mask their uncooperativeness, they deny being resistant when counsellors introduce the subject. So before counsellors assume that their clients are resistant, they should eliminate other factors. For example, clients who appear resistant may not understand the expectations or the process of counselling; thus, they remain cautious and guarded. Counsellors should remember that whereas they have considerable training in how to be a counsellor, their clients have not had training in how to be a client. Unless the process is clarified, clients may remain frightened or confused. Counsellors also need to be explicit regarding their expectations. They should not assume that what is obvious to them will also be obvious to their clients.

Resistance may arise for a number of reasons: (1) relationship, (2) motivational, (3) attitudinal, (4) fearful, and (5) involuntary reasons. Client resistance may be unconscious and unintended, or it may be a deliberate act of sabotage or avoidance.

Relationship Resistance

This type of resistance is linked to variables in the counselling relationship. Clients may be resistant because of transference reactions or simply because they don't feel a good connection with their counsellors. Sometimes clients are influenced by past experiences with counsellors. For example, if they experienced other counsellors as rude or untrustworthy, they may be guarded and defensive with any new worker. This is a way to protect themselves from further rudeness, inconsistency, or breach of trust. Therefore, it is useful for counsellors to inquire about any past experiences that clients have had with other counsellors. This helps to bring feelings and issues into the open, including any preconceptions or fears about the current relationship. When counsellors do this, they should provide a brief explanation to let their clients know they are not prying for gossip:

> Counsellor: *Have you had any other experiences with counselling in the past?*
>
> Client: *Yes, my husband and I went for marital counselling about two years ago.*
>
> Counsellor: *What did you like and dislike about that experience? I'm asking because I think it will help me to understand a bit about your expectations. I'd like to learn what worked for you and what didn't.*

Resistance may also develop as a result of conflict in the current relationship. Counselling relationships, like all relationships, are subject to periodic stress and conflict. Counsellors can make mistakes and say the wrong thing, and they can offend their clients. Clients who are vulnerable may be overly sensitive, or they might misinterpret messages and feel angered. This is an inevitable reality of the chemistry of human encounters. But what sets effective counsellors apart is their ability to be sensitive to clues that all is not well in their relationships. Counsellors are alert for verbal and nonverbal shifts in the tone of the interview that might signal that there is friction. Effective counsellors are further distinguished by their willingness and capacity to address these issues in a caring and nondefensive manner. By doing so, they not only prevent further resistance, but they also build trust and understanding with their clients.

Motivational Resistance

This type of resistance results from some of the motivational problems discussed in Chapter 7. Clients who are in denial do not accept that they have a problem, even though there might be considerable evidence that their behaviour is problematic for them and others. If this is the source of resistance, one option is to provide accurate information to clients about the effects or consequences of their behaviour. With clients who deny they have an addiction problem, providing information (questionnaires, handouts, date and time of an open AA meeting, etc.) may persuade them to reassess their situation.

But some clients hold to their current mode of thinking, feeling, and acting because they lack the energy necessary for change or they are pessimistic that change is possible. Whatever the reason, these clients resist counselling because it is easier and safer than embracing change. Counsellors might deal with this resistance by communicating optimism and by helping clients set small but achievable goals. By supporting and reinforcing small successes, counsellors contribute to the empowerment of their clients. But in the process, counsellors should express empathy regarding the challenges and fears associated with any change. Clients need to understand that they will not be humiliated or overwhelmed by the demands of counselling or change and that counselling will be a way for them to find the resources, support, and motivation for change.

Attitudinal Resistance

Some clients are resistant because they believe that taking help is a sign of weakness. They may believe, as well, that counselling will undermine their personal autonomy. But one way for counsellors to address this resistance is to look for appropriate opportunities to reframe counselling as a sign of strength, rather than feebleness. Counsellors can also deal with fears about loss of independence by making sure that clients are active and informed partners in the work of counselling.

Sometimes counsellors can modify hostile intentions through goal setting. The following interview excerpt provides a brief illustration:

Counsellor: *What do you hope to achieve?*

Client: *Nothing.*

Counsellor: *What's behind that answer?*

Client: *I just think that counselling is a waste of time. What good does it do to talk about problems anyway?*

Counsellor: *You also seem to be saying that if counselling could in some way help you with your problems, you'd be more satisfied.*

Client: *I guess so.*

Another technique is to avoid any direct challenges to resistance which might precipitate a power struggle. This strategy identifies but accepts the resistance. To the uninformed observer, it seems to encourage further resistance, but often the response is a reduction in resistance. This approach is illustrated below.

Client: *I just think that counselling is a waste of time. What good does it do to talk about problems anyway?*

Counsellor: *Given your pessimism, it seems to me that you're wise to be cautious about what we might accomplish here.*

By responding in this way, the counsellor relieves the client of the burden of trying to convince the counsellor of the validity of his position. The client may begin to see the counsellor more as an ally. The wisdom of not attacking clients' beliefs and values directly is nicely illustrated by the following story:

A holy man and an atheist met one day. The atheist challenged the holy man to debate, exclaiming, "I don't believe in God!" The holy man replied, "Tell me about the God you don't believe in." The atheist talked at length about the absurd wars that had been fought in the name of God. He attacked the "hypocrites" who espoused their religious values and beliefs but behaved quite the opposite. The holy man listened patiently until the atheist had said his piece. Only then did he respond: "You and I have a lot in common. I don't believe in that God either."

At the same time, counsellors need to accept some truth in criticisms, such as "Counselling isn't going to put food on my table." They need to understand that for many clients, systemic change is what is needed. Harris and Watkins offer this perspective:

> Counselling cannot solve problems like discrimination and the economic punishment that goes with it. Counselling can help people choose how they want to respond to discrimination and how to take advantage of what economic resources may be available. But people who feel victimized by society see their problems as caused by circumstances outside themselves. Thus counselling, which seeks personal change, is viewed as valueless because it is society that needs changing. (1987:46)

Fearful Resistance

For most people, it is difficult to change from established routines and ways of coping. They communicate fears regarding the imagined consequences of change through resistance. Some clients have trouble with intimacy, and counselling may be seen as an unwanted intrusion that threatens their need to maintain personal distance and privacy. Depending on the situation, a variety of counselling initiatives might prove useful, including candid discussion with clients about their fears and the real risks of change. Here again, working on small but achievable goals is less threatening (see Chapter 7). As well, it is crucial that counsellors support and empathize with their clients' fears. Clients need to hear that they will not be pushed beyond their capacity. In addition, sometimes limited counsellor self-disclosure can be a useful way of normalizing fears about change.

Johnson and Yanka suggest that "resistance is the opposite of motivation and is sometimes a sign that other influences on a person are stronger than the need for change" (2004:281). For example, cultural and familial values or responsibilities may prevent clients from seeking or taking help. It is important that workers understand how clients may perceive them. For example:

> Clients and others typically do not understand the limits of the social worker's span of control and ascribe more authority to the worker than is legally allowed. Clients may believe that the worker can withhold an income maintenance cheque if they do not do what they think the worker wants them to do. Such situations can become complex when the client acts according to what she believes the worker wants rather than what the worker has said. (Johnson & Yanka, 2004:281)

When clients assume workers have more power than they actually have, they might withhold information, avoid meetings, or otherwise resist counselling. Therefore, frank discussion of roles, responsibilities, and the limits of power may assist in clients' fears. In addition, in cross-cultural situations, workers can try to modify their approach to be more congruent with their clients' culture, or they can use or partner with same-culture workers.

Involuntary Resistance

This type of resistance stems from client resentment at being forced to come for counselling and an inability to see a need for change. These clients may see themselves as fighting the "system," and they view the counsellor as a representative of the system (Harris & Watkins, 1987). Involuntary clients typically receive services from large bureaucratic organizations, but the structure and procedures of these agencies can make it difficult for workers to support their clients. Systems designed to help clients may overwhelm clients with rules and regulations, and the workers often have to make troubling decisions on how to use their scarce resources and time.

With involuntary clients, it is important to restore their sense of control and right to self-determination. These clients need to be able to answer the question "What can counselling do for me?" They need to see goals and outcomes that they desire as opposed to those imposed on them. Counsellors need to be patient with unwilling clients by remaining nonjudgmental and caring. Moreover, they can decrease resistance by demonstrating their ability to talk calmly with their clients about their reasons for not wanting to be there. Counsellors should be especially diligent about informing unwilling clients about their rights, including the limits of confidentiality. Clear, succinct statements about these issues will help to reduce their suspicions.

Table 8.1 provides some strategies for dealing with each type of resistance. Two points need to be emphasized. First, clients may show more than one type of resistance; and second, techniques always have to be adapted and modified to meet the needs, culture, and language of each client and situation. Creativity and flexibility are essential for handling resistance. Sometimes this can mean dealing with resistance directly by inviting clients to talk about their feelings. At other times, counsellors may prefer to avoid direct challenges to resistance. For example, a counsellor who observes that a client becomes hostile when a certain topic comes up can shift the focus to a less threatening topic until more trust is developed.

Immediacy and Resistance

Immediacy was introduced in Chapter 3 as the process of exploring, deepening, and evaluating counselling relationships. When resistance blocks the work of counselling, immediacy provides a way to deal directly with client concerns regarding the counselling process or the relationship itself. As a general rule, if resistance is increasing, it is wise to deal directly with it; otherwise, the client may never return. The following questions and statements illustrate the potential variety of responses that can be used to move the interview toward a discussion of resistance:

- How do you feel about being here?
- If I felt forced to come, I think I'd feel quite angry.
- I'm wondering what's happening between us. Are you feeling angry toward me?
- Let's see if we can agree on what we want to accomplish.
- If I'm not mistaken, every time I mention your father, you change the subject. Is that a topic you would rather avoid?

TABLE 8.1	Strategies for Dealing with Resistance	
Type of Resistance	**Description**	**Strategy Choices**
Relationship	There is unresolved conflict in the helping relationship, or clients are defensive because of prior bad experiences with counselling.	Solve relationship difficulties and problems. Discuss prior experiences with counselling, then negotiate contracts that clients can support (but do this in a way that does not undermine the integrity of other counsellors). Refer to other counsellors. Respond nondefensively and do not personalize.
Motivational	Clients lack motivation to change either because they see no problem or because they do not believe that change is possible.	Use confrontation to help clients become aware of problems. Use authority (personal or organization power). Deal with learned helplessness (see Chapter 7). Communicate optimism about client skills and abilities. Acknowledge and reinforce all efforts and progress. Set small achievable goals
Attitudinal	Personal or cultural values define taking help as a sign of weakness.	Encourage clients to voice concerns regarding counselling. Adjust counselling methods to be culturally sensitive. Persuade clients that taking help is a sign of strength. Use strategies that fully empower and involve clients in making decisions.
Fearful	Clients are afraid of the risks and potential pain of changing.	Encourage clients to share fears, then respond with empathy. Candidly discuss the risks of change. Support and encourage the client. Gear pacing toward small, achievable goals. Help clients identify and deal with self-defeating inner dialogue. Target the work in less threatening areas until confidence increases.
Involuntary	Clients do not want to be in counselling but have been forced by a third party (e.g., courts, school counsellor).	Encourage clients to share feelings, then empathize. Negotiate a contract to add voluntary objectives to those that are involuntary. Generate opportunities that give clients control, choices, and power. Help clients answer the question: "What's in it for me?" Redirect the work to less threatening areas.

- How committed are you to making changes?
- Do you believe it's possible for you to change?
- What does it mean to you to be seeing a counsellor?
- Are you worried that I will try to force you to do something you don't want to do?

Culture and Resistance

Sue and Sue (cited in Diller, 1999) present a case study that portrays how cross-cultural miscommunication can easily be misinterpreted as client resistance. The client was a 13-year-old girl who was referred to a school counsellor for allegedly selling drugs. The school counsellor consulted for help in dealing with the parents, whom she described as "uncaring, uncooperative and attempting to avoid responsibility for their daughter's delinquency." Describing the case, the counsellor said that she called the parents, a Hispanic family living in San José, California, and talked with Mrs. Martinez. She said she asked Mrs. Martinez to come in as soon as possible to see what could be done to resolve the situation. The counsellor said Mrs. Martinez hesitated and excused herself from the phone when pressed. The counsellor said she overheard whispering, then Mr. Martinez came on the line. He also avoided and made excuses, saying he had to work and could not come in for the meeting. The counsellor emphasized the importance of the meeting for his daughter's welfare and suggested that missing work for a few hours was not important, given the gravity of the situation. The father proposed an evening meeting, but the counsellor rejected this because school policy prohibited evening meetings. Finally, the father agreed, and a meeting was set up for the next day. Mr. and Mrs. Martinez and a brother-in-law (the girl's godfather) showed up. The counsellor reported that she was upset that the brother-in-law was present, and she explained that this would unduly complicate the session. She stressed that she wanted to see only the family. The counsellor said the meeting went badly, and the parents were evasive and not forthcoming with their answers.

Analyzing the counsellor's conclusions, Diller describes this encounter as a clear case of misunderstanding cultural differences. He cites a number of erroneous assumptions. For example, "The counsellor appears unaware that in a traditional Mexican family, the wife would not make a decision without first consulting her husband" (57). The counsellor also assumes that Mr. Martinez is unwilling to take off work because he is apathetic about his daughter. "Like any middle-class professional, she assumes he can make himself available during the day and even presumes to moralize at him, something he is probably not used to from a woman, about several hours of work being more important than his daughter" (57). As well, the counsellor hides behind school policy to excuse herself from accommodating an evening meeting. Finally, the counsellor has a narrow definition of family and has no appreciation of the appropriateness of the brother-in-law's presence. In Hispanic culture, godfathers are responsible for the spiritual welfare of their godchildren. In the eyes of this family, the girl was experiencing a serious spiritual crisis.

This case serves as a reminder to counsellors to be mindful of imposing their cultural values and expectations on clients. The Martinez family was clearly victimized by a culture-bound system that was unresponsive to their needs and wants. The very system that was designed to help them became oppressive. Its representative, the school counsellor, reached inaccurate and insulting conclusions because she was unable to view the Martinez family from their own frame of reference.

INTERVIEW 8.1	**DEALING WITH RESISTANCE**

The following interview excerpt shows some ways for dealing with client resistance. The client is a young male, age 19, who has been referred to an addiction counsellor as a condition of his probation. This excerpt is from the first interview, and it begins about 15 minutes into the interview. It is clear from the client's nonverbal behaviour that he doesn't want to be there (e.g., he has not removed his coat, he gives single-word or short answers to questions, and his voice tone is hostile).

DIALOGUE	ANALYSIS
Client: How long is this going to take? I'm really not in the mood to be cross-examined.	The counsellor decides to address the client's resistance directly. This is the first interview, and some softening of the client's hostility might be expected over time; but this degree of resistance seems pronounced enough that it should be dealt with directly. In her response, the counsellor also attempts to remind the client that he does have a choice about whether to stay or go. However, this is a bit risky, since the client may decide to walk out.
Counsellor: Of course, you're free to leave at any point. But before you do, why don't we take a moment to talk straight. I know that you were forced to come here by your probation officer. I'm wondering how you feel about that.	
Client (sarcastically): It's no big deal. I can handle it.	Frequently, clients deny that they are resistant. This can be exceptionally hard to deal with, since such clients evade taking responsibility for their behaviour.
Counsellor: We do agree on one thing. You don't want to be cross-examined, and I don't intend to try. You don't have to tell me about anything you don't want to talk about.	The counsellor tries to find a point of agreement, but her response is greeted by more anger. At this point, it is important that the counsellor not give up. Even though the client's response is less than ideal, he has heard what the counsellor said.
Client: Let's get one thing clear. I don't need your permission to do anything.	
Counsellor: Agreed. But since you've decided to stay, let's talk. If you're feeling angry because your probation officer thinks you need counselling, I can understand. I sure don't like it when I'm forced to do something against my will.	The counsellor tries to ally herself with the client by using self-disclosure to encourage him to talk about his resistance. She emphasizes that the client has made choices. Sometimes it is less threatening for clients when counsellors avoid questions (see Chapter 5). The client's earlier statement that he "doesn't want to be cross-examined" is a good indication that questions would be inappropriate in this interview.
Client: It's not you. I just don't see the point. There's nothing wrong with me. I don't understand why I have to come here.	The counsellor's persistence works, as the client begins to open up. At this point, it is important for the counsellor to avoid becoming defensive.

(continued)

If she starts to "sell" her client on the merits of counselling, she may lose him.

Cautiously, the client begins to share his feelings, including his reservations about what will happen in the relationship.

Counsellor: Sounds as if you really want to stand up and say, "This is my life. Butt out."

Client: Yeah. What gives them the right to say I'm crazy?

Counsellor: And now that you're here, you might be worried that I'll do the same thing. That I'll try to get into your head, tell you what to do.

Client: Of course. Isn't that how it works? I've been to counselling before. (laughs) You guys aren't happy unless you're mucking someone up.

Counsellor (laughs): Well, we have to shrink our quota of heads.

Client (laughs): My head is staying just where it is.

A little humour from the counsellor helps build rapport, while showing empathy with the client's feelings. The counsellor's humour affirms her ability to talk about the issues without becoming defensive. But when using humour, timing is critical. What works very well in one situation might result in disaster in another.

Counsellor: I'm impressed that you're able to say what you want.

The counsellor does not attempt to break down her client's defences, which are an important part of the way this client has coped.

Client: I don't believe in playing games.

Counsellor: Me neither. So, let's talk about what's going to happen here. Let's try to work out something that works for both of us.

There is much work to be done to establish a solid working relationship with this client. Resistance may be a reality throughout the life of the counselling relationship. However, an important beginning has been established.

CONVERSATION 8.1

SAYING NO

STUDENT: What are some ways to say "no" to clients? I really hate it when I have to deny them what they want or need.

TEACHER: That's my reaction too. None of us in the helping professions wants to be seen as harsh or uncaring. Saying "no" may evoke feelings of guilt in us, as well as strong negative reactions from our clients. We really need to be able address our own emotions as well as those of the client.

STUDENT: I suppose it's a reality of the business. Sometimes we have to make tough decisions, such as who gets the training money and who qualifies for assistance. In the residential part of the program where I work, we often have to say "no" when the kids want exceptions to the rules. No problem when you're able to give clients what they want. But what about when you have to turn down requests?

TEACHER: Even when you are saying "no," it's important that clients know you care. You need to listen and be available to respond with empathy and compassion. Find a way to show you understand, even if you are not able to give your clients what they want. Or, see if there is a way to compromise to help your client save face. What do you think?

STUDENT: I've learned a couple of things: Be direct, clear, and brief. Don't waffle, hint, or avoid the "bottom line." With kids, I've found that even when they test the limits, they may need limits and even welcome them when imposed. It increases their sense of safety and control when they learn the boundaries of acceptable behaviour.

TEACHER: I agree. I think it's important that you don't make a hasty retreat. Expect that anger, defensiveness, and counterattack are the ways that some clients respond to frustration. In extreme situations, you need to protect yourself. Anticipate potentially violent situations and take defensive action. Also, be sure to debrief with a colleague or supervisor after difficult encounters. And if necessary, take a break to ensure that your reactions do not contaminate your ability to deal with your next client objectively. Finally, remind yourself that no matter how your client reacts, you must stay in a professional role.

STUDENT: When someone says "no" to me, I find it a lot easier to accept if I know why. So I try to explain my rationale or the policy. Then I invite questions.

TEACHER: If you can, help your client identify other ways to meet their needs.

POTENTIALLY DANGEROUS CLIENTS

The deadliest form of violence is poverty.
—Gandhi

Many counsellors are employed by agencies in which their work may include some elements of social control (e.g., probation, involuntary clients, establishing eligibility). The nature of this work may leave counsellors increasingly vulnerable to violence (Newhill, 1995). For example, a counsellor's denial of a client's request for financial assistance may evoke retaliation.

Hospital emergency rooms are particularly dangerous places for social workers, counsellors, and other health-care professionals (Lanza et al., 1996). In one case, a 27-year-old social worker was shot, without provocation, while interviewing a client in a psychiatric emergency room; and in another case a social worker was stabbed to death by her client in her office (Newhill, 1995).

Although some statistical studies suggest that societal violence may be decreasing at a modest rate, anecdotal and some empirical evidence suggests that most of those who work in the counselling field admit that issues of personal safety are an increasing concern (Newhill, 1995). A study at one private psychiatric hospital found that the frequency of violence by male patients was 50 percent higher than a decade ago, and that violence by female patients was 150 percent higher than a decade ago (Tardiff et al., 1997). Newhill's review of the literature supported the conclusion that violence against social workers is increasing. In part, this is because "social workers handle frontline situations that previous generations of workers did not encounter (for example, increased violence attributed to female, elderly, and deinstitutionalized clients and new intervention roles in domestic violence situations, police–social worker teams, custody and divorce mediation, and emergency room work)" (1995:632).

Sometimes clients cause fear because their behaviour is threatening or they have a history of violent behaviour. At other times, counsellors' fears are based on intuition or hunches, the internal response to subtle signals that all is not well. In fact, some clients provide abundant reasons for fear, either because of intimidating behaviour or overtly violent acts.

Intimidating behaviour includes name calling, obscene or sexually harassing language and gestures, shouting, threatening displays of power such as fist shaking, invasion of personal space, stalking, and verbal threats. Clients also behave in an intimidating manner when they won't take *no* for an answer or when they refuse to leave the office. As well, clients may attack workers with personal insults, or they may intimidate them with threats to call the newspaper or civil rights groups. In general, intimidating behaviour should be controlled or managed in order to prevent escalation to violence. The following case examples of threatening behaviour are all based on real incidents:

- A new client to a welfare office says, "If I don't get some help, you'll be sorry."
- A man in his late 20s stares obstinately at an intake worker.
- An angry parent tells a child protection worker that if his child is not returned, the worker will know what it's like to lose someone you love.
- A teenager in a group home refuses to comply with house rules. He tells his childcare counsellor, "I've had enough. Things are going to change around here."
- A parole officer meets a new parolee for the first time. He is pleasant and cooperative, but the parole officer can't ignore the fact that this man has a long history of assault charges and is known to have a short fuse.
- A mental health counsellor deals with her client, a young male with a history of self-destructive behaviour. It is obvious that he is not taking his medication, and he seems unusually agitated.
- A 10-year-old child who witnessed abuse at home grabs a pair of scissors and lunges toward the counsellor.

Violent behaviour means hitting, pushing, biting, slapping, kicking, throwing objects, and using weapons such as guns, knives, or syringes. It also refers to kidnapping and stalking.

- A social worker in a hospital emergency ward is threatened with a syringe by an angry HIV-positive patient.
- An angry client picks up a chair and hurls it at the counsellor.
- A client, disgruntled with the counsellor's refusal to provide him with money, spits in the counsellor's face.

Nonetheless, it is important that counsellors do not become hypervigilant and conduct their work in constant fear. Such a stance makes it difficult for them to separate actual hazards from situations that present no real risk. Moreover, unwarranted fear of clients leads to uninformed responses. Though very real dangers exist in the workplace, by and large, it is a place of safety. The challenge is to be able to answer some basic questions:

- Which clients are likely to become violent? What are the indicators of potential violence?
- Under what conditions should a client's anger be cause for concern?
- What are the skills and behaviours that can be used to de-escalate dangerous situations?

Predicting Violence

Violence arises from a complex array of psychological, social, biological, and physiological factors. Although certain variables are more likely risk factors than others, risk assessment is difficult, and violence cannot be predicted with precision (Miller, 2000). There is simply no foolproof way to predict with certainty who is likely to become violent.

Violence may be perceived as a desperate act by an angry client to regain control and power. Multiple stressors, such as poverty, the loss or absence of supportive relationships, and substance abuse, may magnify a client's vulnerability and stress to the breaking point. Moreover, counsellors may be in positions of authority with the right to deny clients access to goods or services. Clients may perceive such denials as further threats to their fragile power and self-esteem, and the risk of violence may escalate. Attacking others works as a psychological defence against feelings of shame and humiliation.

Based on his review of the academic literature, Ross (1995) identifies five primary causes of violent crime in Canada: "interpersonal conflict situation (over status, resources, power, control, and reputation), presence of weapons, influence of drugs and/or alcohol, media facilitation, and cultural or subcultural reinforcement" (p. 348). The key variables that have been found to have some validity for predicting violence include (1) past and current behaviour, (2) substance abuse, (3) age and gender, and (4) personality. The more risk factors present, the greater the risk. But the presence of a risk factor does not mean that a given person will become violent in a given situation.

Past and Current Behaviour

The best predictor of future violence is a history of violence (Miller, 2000); and the more recent and severe the violent behaviour, the greater the risk. Kelleher's conclusion that a history of violent behaviour should always be given serious consideration is echoed consistently in the research on violence: "Although the argument can be made that historical evidence of violence is not a guaranty of future violent behavior, an understanding of any form of violent criminal activity clearly supports the contention that a history of violence is often a predictor of future violence" (1997:13).

Counsellors should be particularly interested in noting how a client has handled difficulties and frustrations in the past. Some clients who were victims of abuse as children grow up without a capacity for warmth and empathy for others, which can make them particularly oblivious to the suffering of others (Roth, 1987; Weaver, 1982, Miller, 2000). In extreme cases, violence may even bring these clients pleasure or sexual gratification. Counsellors should also be interested in the level of remorse that clients show for past acts of violence. Clearly, counsellors should be most concerned about clients who show no regret. On the other hand, clients who have learned other ways of managing their anger now have more choices and are less likely to act out physically. In this respect, it might be revealing for counsellors to explore how their clients are managing stress outside the counselling relationship.

For example, do they show evidence of a lack of concern for the safety of others? Are there indicators of inappropriate or uncontrolled anger? Are they typically extremely defensive, irritable, or self-centred? To what extent are they prone to impulsive behaviour? Impulsive clients might assure counsellors that they have no intent to harm anyone and then attack another client in the waiting room 10 minutes later.

Furthermore, clients who have a specific plan of violent action and the means to carry it out represent an immediate risk of violent behaviour. Counsellors need to consider their professional obligations and legal requirements to warn any intended victim by examining their codes of ethics, as well as relevant legislation or legal precedent.

Substance Abuse

Common sense and empirical research suggest that intoxicated and agitated clients should be approached cautiously. Substance abuse, particularly in combination with other risk factors, compounds the risk of violence (Miller, 2000) Reviewing the role of drugs in violence, Roth (1987:13–14) concludes:

- Hallucinogens such as LSD and PCP, glue sniffing, amphetamines, and barbiturates have been associated with aggressive and homicidal behaviour.
- Narcotics tend to suppress violence, but individuals might become violent in order to get these drugs.
- Alcohol has a disinhibiting effect on behaviour and is implicated as the most frequent drug linked to violence.

Furthermore, many studies link substance abuse to violent behaviour (Swanson et al., 1997; Tardiff et al., 1997). Newhill reviewed the available research and recorded that certain drugs subdue aggression, whereas others escalate it. "Anticholinergics, antipsychotics, antidepressants, sedative hypnotics, and analgesics tend to suppress aggression. Amphetamines and withdrawal from drugs such as morphine or alcohol induce aggression" (1992:70). Moreover, people who abuse drugs are at an increased risk of victimization (Conway, 1996). The link between drug abuse and violent behaviour may arise, at least in part, from the fact that alcohol and other drugs are more likely to be abused in a dangerous place.

Age and Gender

The vast majority of people who are violent and who have been arrested for violent behaviour are male. The highest risk for violence is found in people from 15 to 39 years of age. The rate of violent acts for this age group is three times that of the general population (Roth, 1987; Weaver, 1992).

Personality

Some clients deal with their sense of personal fragility by lashing out at others, and they are hypervigilant about protecting themselves from perceived threats from others. Miller (2000) notes:

> Tendencies toward low frustration tolerance, impulsive behavior, vulnerability to criticism, feeling humiliated and powerless, superficial relationships, lack of empathy, a pattern of externalizing problems, and failing to accept responsibility for one's own actions are all associated with more-violent behavior. (p. 300)

De Becker cautions that some people assume the worst possible motives and character and that they write their own scripts: "The Scriptwriter is the type of person who asks you a question, answers it himself, then walks away angry at what you said... The things that go wrong are the work of others who will try to blame him. People are out to get him, period" (1997:148–49). These clients believe that you are uncaring and out to get them. Whatever counsellors do and however caring their actions, these clients will react based on their expectations. They may try to control the relationship through manipulation and intimidation. But this behaviour should be interpreted as a warning signal only. These clients may not escalate to violence.

Violence and Mental Illness

The question whether people with mental illnesses are more dangerous than the general public continues to be the subject of research, debate, and controversy. Not surprisingly, many people believe that there is a strong link between mental illness and violence; but advocate groups argue that the media, through selective and exaggerated reporting, have stimulated the development of false assumptions about the dangers of people with mental illnesses. Sensationalized headlines such as, "Schizophrenic Man Kills Wife, Then Turns Gun on Himself" and "Voices Told Me to Kill My Child" create the impression that mental illness is associated with violence. However, objective research evidence supports different conclusions.

One comprehensive Canadian study of the literature on the link between mental illness and violence concluded that there is no scientific evidence that mental illness causes violence (Arboleda-Florez, Holley, & Crisanti, 1996). Echoing many other research findings, they also implicated substance abuse as the most significant risk factor, noting that studies suggest that "individuals are at greater risk of being assaulted by someone who abuses substances rather than someone who is suffering from major mental illness such as affective disorder, anxiety disorder, or schizophrenia." Another study (Swanson et al., 1997) confirms the links between violent behaviour and substance abuse, particularly when there has been absence of recent contact with mental health service providers. A recent study concluded that predictions of violence based on a history of violence were more accurate than clinical predictions based on diagnosis (Gardner et al., 1996). Overall, persons with mental illness are more than 2.5 times likely to be victims of violence than perpetrators, particularly when other factors such as poverty and substance abuse are present (Canadian Mental Health Association, 2005).

Although "major mental disorder and psychiatric disturbance are poor predictors of violence" (Harris and Rice, 1997), Miller (2000) found that certain mental disorders, such as schizophrenia with paranoia and command hallucinations, mania, substance use disorders, antisocial personality disorders, and borderline personality disorders, are more likely to be associated with violence. Moreover, in recent decades, deinstitutionalization of psychiatric patients has resulted in unprecedented numbers of people with mental illnesses in the community. Clients with a history of severe mental illness and violence who stop taking their medications can be very dangerous, particularly if they have command hallucinations (voices and images directing them to be violent).

A comprehensive followup study of patients discharged from psychiatric hospitals concluded that former patients who do not abuse drugs are no more violent than a random population sample (Bower, 1998). Pastor concluded that unrealistic and delusional thinking tends to increase the likelihood that violence will result. He also noted: "Manic symptoms, such as irritability, increased energy or activity, psychomotor agitation and grandiosity, also increases the risk of violent behavior. A belief that 'others' are responsible for the person's misfortune increases the likelihood of striking out against those persons" (1995:1173).

In addition, organic brain disease and head trauma may reduce a client's impulse control and cause him or her to act in ways that are dangerous to him or her self and others. Organic disease or injury should be suspected when clients show disturbance in attention, orientation, and short-term memory (Dubovsky & Weissberg, 1986:258).

Assessing Potential for Violence

Although long-term prediction of violence is difficult, counsellors should be able to make reasonable short-term forecasts based on consideration and assessment of the following questions and issues:

1. Does the client have a history of violent behaviour and/or an arrest record for violent crime? The counsellor should review agency file records and other anecdotal evidence for information.

2. To what extent does the client appear dangerous, as evidenced by marked or escalating agitation or threatening behaviour? The counsellor should consider verbal threats as well as nonverbal expressions of aggression.

3. If the client is threatening violence, are the threats concrete and specific? Does the client have a plan? Does the client have the means to carry out the stated plan? Does the client have a weapon or access to one, especially a gun?

4. Is the client under duress from one or more stressors, such as poverty, unemployment, or loss of social support? Has there been a recent precipitating event that represents the last straw for the client?

5. What agency factors might be exacerbating the situation (e.g., missed or delayed appointments, denial of benefits)?

6. What counsellor variables might be heightening the client's anger? Is the counsellor acting in ways that the client might see as provocative? For example, is the counsellor defensive or judgmental toward the client?

7. What high-risk symptoms are present? For example, is the client experiencing command hallucinations? Is the client prone to impulsivity? Is the client near panic? Is the client narcissistic or self-centred and prone to blame others for his or her misfortune? Is the client hypersensitive to any criticism or hint of rejection?

8. Is there evidence of substance abuse?

9. Has the client failed to take psychiatric medication? Has the client cut off or failed to keep scheduled contact with a psychiatric caregiver?

10. Does the client believe that he or she is able to control his or her behaviour? Is the client socially isolated?

These questions are references for the purpose of assessment only. The presence of any of the factors does not mean that the client will necessarily become violent. However, when there are numerous strong clues that suggest violence, counsellors should proceed cautiously and look for ways to reduce risk factors to establish safety.

Preventing Violence

Many clients come to counselling in a state of crisis, with low tolerance for added stress. Consequently, it is important that agency policies and routines do not compound the risk. Congested and noisy waiting rooms, unexplained delays for appointments, insensitive receptionists, and indifference to the clients' right to privacy can exacerbate frustration. Nevertheless, even when these factors are controlled, counsellors may have to deny assistance, and clients may believe that they are denying them access to goods or services. These clients may perceive themselves as "losers" and look for ways to save face, including resistance, with statements such as "I don't have to put up with this treatment."

Agency Safety Precautions

In settings where there is significant risk for violence, procedures should be developed for dealing with potentially violent clients. In fact, employers usually have a legal responsibility to provide a safe working environment. Minimum safety precautions might include the following:

POLICY Agencies should develop and regularly review policies and procedures for dealing with potentially violent situations. Policies should address issues such as the procedures for visiting homes, giving clients home phone numbers, using last names, and interviewing after hours. Generally, counsellors should not make home visits alone if there is a possibility for violence. Many counsellors who work with potentially dangerous clients use unlisted phone numbers as a way to ensure privacy and safety. In extreme situations, such as dangerous child abuse investigations, counsellors may need to be protected by police. Generally, counsellors should avoid making unescorted visits to high-crime areas; and only those counsellors with legal authority should investigate allegations of child abuse or neglect.

STAFF TRAINING Training should address tactics for dealing with difficult clients, including those who are involuntary, angry, or acting out. Front office and reception staff should also be trained so that they can relate to clients in ways that do not escalate the clients' frustration or anger. Periodic team simulations will ensure that everyone is familiar with their roles and responsibilities. This prevents members of the team from becoming confused during a critical incident. Simulations also help staff to build confidence in themselves and trust in their colleagues as backups.

INTERVIEWING PROCEDURES AND OFFICE DESIGN Counsellors who are interviewing difficult or dangerous clients should work in offices where access to immediate help can be provided. A silent system for alerting others that a dangerous situation is developing should be implemented (e.g., panic button, encrypted phone message). Leaving the door open during the interview can allow other staff to monitor any increasing danger, but this practice may violate the client's confidentiality. Ideally, both counsellors and clients should have a clear, unobstructed path to the doorway so they can leave abruptly if they choose.

Files on clients with a history of violence should clearly document details of any past violent behaviour or threats. For clients with a high propensity toward violence, a team approach may be desirable, with two or more persons being present during the interview. In such cases, it is usually preferable if only one person does the interviewing. This can lessen any feelings the client might have of being ganged up on. Too many people may heighten the client's anxiety. Backup help can be stationed out of sight, but on quick standby for dangerous situations.

Office furnishings should be carefully chosen to minimize risk. For example, shatter-proof glass can be used, and items that are potential weapons, such as scissors, should be removed. Also, soft lighting and calming colours may have some modest effect on mood. In addition, the agency itself should have good external lighting. Finally, during high-risk hours, such as late at night or early in the morning, access doors should be locked, and workers should not have to walk alone to dark parking lots.

CRISIS INTERVENTION A written script for staff who call police or emergency backup intervention ensures that relevant information is presented quickly and clearly. In a panic situation, people may forget basic information, such as emergency phone numbers. More-over, an organization needs to have in place a mechanism for debriefing after a violent or hostile act. This enables the counsellor to restore a sense of equilibrium. It is important to remember that a critical or violent incident may also affect and traumatize staff who were not directly involved, including clerical, janitorial, and kitchen personnel. Therefore, they should be involved in the debriefing.

The Phases of Violence

The National Crisis Prevention Institute (1993) has identified four **phases of violence** that describe how crises escalate to violence (see Table 8.2). Each phase is characterized by particular indicators and demands specific responses. But in applying this or any other model, remember that individual incidents may not conform to the model. The four phases are (1) anxiety, (2) defensiveness, (3) acting out, and (4) tension reduction.

Phase 1: Anxiety

In the anxiety phase there are often early-warning, marked changes in the client's behav-iour. The client's agitation and anxiety may include verbal challenges, such as refusal to follow directions or questioning of authority. Statements such as "You can't tell me what to do," accompanied by finger pointing, may suggest escalating anger. Shea (1988) cautions that other signs of escalation, such as pacing, intense staring, and refusing to sit down, should be noted. At this point, the client may respond to gentle directives and invitations, such as "Let's talk and see if we can work things out" and "I'm willing to listen." This phase offers counsellors the best opportunity to intervene early to prevent anger from intensifying into acting-out behaviour.

Usually, clients enter the anxiety phase because of stress, which can come from multi-ple sources, including jobs, relationships, health, and finances. Clients define stressful events; thus, counsellors cannot measure stress just by knowing the facts about a situation. What one client might see as an opportunity another might experience as a threat. Kelleher describes the triggering event as an incident that pushes the potentially violent person toward violence: "It is the proverbial 'straw that broke the camel's back, and, like the straw, may often be perceived by others with far less significance than it's perceived by the per-petrator" (1997:11). Before clients see counsellors, they may already be feeling helpless and abandoned. Any counsellor/agency behaviour that the client views as provocative or rejecting may further propel the client toward violence.

TABLE 8.2	Preventing and Managing Violent Behaviour
Phase	**Strategy Choice**
Preventive	Recognize risk factors. Structure the agency to reduce client stress and danger to personnel. Set up emergency response protocols. Practise crisis responses with simulations. Take steps to protect identified intended victims.
Phase 1: Anxiety	Promote client involvement in decision making to give them a sense of empowerment and control. Attend to changes in the client behaviour. Take "gut instincts" and threats seriously. Use empathy and reassurance to acknowledge and attend to client needs.
Phase 2: Defensiveness	Set clear, reasonable, and enforceable limits. Respect client need for increased space. Remain calm and avoid sudden movement. Avoid using an authoritarian tone. Respond assertively. Use basic counselling skills. Search for compromises and "win-win" solutions.
Phase 3: Acting Out	Call the police (do not try to disarm clients who have weapons and do not risk personal safety unless unavoidable). Try to ensure the safety of everyone, including bystanders, other staff, and the client. Use a team approach, including, if necessary and appropriate, physical restraint. Refer clients to hospital for assessment and/or medication. Try to reestablish verbal communication.
Phase 4: Tension Reduction	Support the client's return to a state of calm. Reestablish communication. Elicit available family support.
Followup	Involve clients in long-term counselling. Help clients learn nonviolent solutions to problems. Implement consequences, if any. Conduct individual and team debriefing. When clients have plans to harm a specific victim, warn the victim and/or notify the police. Review procedures for handling disruptive clients.

Individuals who are predisposed to violence respond to stress with increasing anger and anxiety. A person's emotional reaction can also influence whether he or she might become violent. Labig observes:

Emotional reactions that make it more likely that a person will become violent in reaction to a stressful situation are anger, hatred, blame, and terror. People who typically react emotionally in these ways are at higher risk of escalating into violence. Emotional reactions can also intervene to inhibit an individual's behavior. Empathy and guilt make it less likely that a person will strike out. (1995:24–25)

DEALING WITH THREATS Gavin de Becker, an expert on predicting violent behaviour, offers this strategy for dealing with threats:

> When any type of threat includes indirect or veiled references to things they might do, such as "You'll be sorry," or "Don't mess with me," it is best to ask directly, "What do you mean by that?" Ask exactly what the person is threatening to do. His elaboration will almost always be weaker than his implied threat. If, on the other hand, his explanation of the comment is actually an explicit threat, better to learn it now than to be uncertain later. (1997:117)

Counsellors need to take action when clients exhibit changes in their normal behaviour. This action could include referral for psychiatric assessment and reevaluation of medication. Immediate crisis intervention might result in moving the client out of the environment where others might be injured, for example, a crowded waiting room. As well, long-term counselling might focus on anger management or relaxation training. The immediate goal is crisis management, but the long-term goal is crisis prevention. This interesting conclusion reached by Quinsey et al. (1998) challenges one common misbelief: "encouraging angry individuals to relieve anger through catharsis (e.g., boxing, using a punching bag) is contraindicated because it may lead to increased hostility and aggression" (p. 204).

In addition, counsellors should be attuned to their own fears and anxieties. Appropriate anxiety is a clue that the situation is escalating and that remedial action is necessary. De Becker (1997) argues that people have a basic intuition that tells them when all is not well, but that they often disregard the red flags of danger. It is only in the aftermath that they reflect and realize that they had sufficient information to make better choices but that they ignored it.

Phase 2: Defensiveness

This is a late warning phase with clear indicators that the person is about to lose control. The client may become more challenging and belligerent by making direct threats and provocations. The client has become irrational, and clear warning indicators may be present, including clenching or raising of fists, grasping objects to use as weapons, and showing signs of movement toward attack (e.g., grasping the arms of the chair, denoting that they are about to rise and advance) (Shea, 1988:172).

At this point, it is crucial that counsellors refrain from reciprocating with the same aggressive behaviour that the client is using. This requires some discipline, as the counsellor's natural reaction might be to respond in kind, which only serves to escalate or precipitate violence. Decreased eye contact might be appropriate with some clients. As well, counsellors are wise to increase the physical distance between them and their clients, since potentially violent persons may have an increased need for space. Note that physical contact, however well intentioned, should be avoided. Sometimes counsellors try to calm clients by touching their shoulders; but this is ill advised, as clients may interpret it as aggression.

At this phase, counsellors need to be self-disciplined and to model calmness. When counsellors stay calm, clients are more likely to emulate their composure. This calmness should be reflected in their voice and manner with slow, nonjargonistic language. Counsellors who speak calmly and avoid any loud or authoritarian tone have a greater chance of calming their anxious clients. On the other hand, counsellors who match their clients' defensiveness and anger exacerbate the situation and increase the possibility of violent retaliation. Rigid and authoritarian counsellor reactions may leave clients feeling pressured or trapped.

It is essential that counsellors maintain their own equilibrium and remain in control. They need to develop their capacity to monitor their own feelings and behaviour, including their ability to ask for help or to withdraw when they are not in control. Counsellors also need to resist any tendency to be baited by clients into angry confrontation or retaliation, which only escalates the crisis. Moreover, if clients perceive that their counsellors are not in control, they may become more irrational. Clients, particularly those in institutional settings, may have an increased potential for violence if they perceive the staff to be overly anxious (Roth, 1987).

Labig (1995) says that some people can react with intense emotion because of the emotional tone with which they are addressed.

> A loud, intense, and menacing voice can create an instantaneous emotional response in certain people. This is all it takes to push some people into retaliatory action... Generally, the more emotionally calm and safe an individual feels, the less likely he is to become violent. The more frightening and threatening he finds his environment, the more likely he is to respond with violence. (p. 25)

Basic communication and counselling skills are excellent tools for both preventing violence and for dealing with clients who are on the verge of losing control. In particular, active listening skills communicate that counsellors are willing to listen to and learn about clients' wants and needs. Counsellors should try to speak calmly and avoid any mannerisms that clients might interpret as threatening (e.g., touching a client, making sudden movements, or invading a client's personal space). "Encourage the client to sit and to be comfortable. Listen, empathize, paraphrase, and summarize while avoiding defensiveness. As a general rule, respond to clients in the anxiety and defensive phases with supportive and empathic statements.

However, some clients may misinterpret empathy as an unwanted intrusion on personal privacy and react defensively. Counsellors should be alert to clients' reactions to certain topics or questions. This will help counsellors make intelligent decisions about when it is appropriate to challenge or confront and when they should back off because the subject is clearly agitating their clients to a dangerous level. Counsellors should be careful that they don't overreact and should avoid interview topics that could be controversial.

THE POWER OF COMPROMISE Violent clients often feel disempowered and disadvantaged. But when counsellors promote compromise, they restore some balance of power in the relationship and show their willingness to reach a solution. Conversely, when counsellors argue with, threaten, or ignore the needs of their clients, the clients may become increasingly belligerent. As Dubovsky and Weissberg conclude, the client "protects himself from feeling powerless, inadequate and frightened by attempting to demonstrate how powerful and frightening he can be" (1986:262).

Compromise helps clients find a way to save face and retain their dignity. While counsellors have the responsibility to set appropriate limits, they must not argue with, ridicule, challenge, threaten, or unfairly criticize clients. The language used by the counsellor can help to establish an atmosphere of compromise and mutual problem solving—for example, "Let's work together to find a solution we can both live with" and "I really do want to find a solution."

> Client: *(yelling loudly) I'm sick and tired of getting the runaround.*
>
> Counsellor: *(calmly) Your anger makes it clear to me how strongly you feel about this. I can see that this is an important issue for you. But we will work better if you stay calm and don't threaten. Let's see if there's another way to approach it.*
>
> Client: *(pacing and yelling) Are you going to help me or not?*
>
> Counsellor: *(calmly) I'm willing to work at this problem to solve it.*
>
> *(client sits, stares intently)*

Counsellor: *I understand that you think that this is the best solution. I also appreciate your reasoning. But there are two of us here. We need to find a solution that both of us can live with.*

Client: *(loud, but not yelling) I'm trying to be reasonable.*

Counsellor: *Okay, I'm listening. I'd like to hear your ideas on how to...*

Hocker and Wilmot (1995) identify five principles for establishing effective collaboration: (1) join with the other, (2) control the process, not the people, (3) use productive communication, (4) be firm in your goals, flexible in your means, and (5) remain optimistic about finding solutions to your conflict (p. 212). They suggest a variety of means for operationalizing the principles, such as using "we" language to affirm common interests; actively listening even when you disagree; and persuading rather than coercing. As well, they emphasize the importance of separating the issues from the relationship and dealing with the important items one at a time. Such a collaborative approach requires that counsellors remain positive, creative, and constructive. The general goal must be: "We, working together, can solve this problem that is confronting us" (Hocker & Wilmot, 1995:205). Dubovsky and Weissberg (1986) underscore the importance of promoting collaboration. They contend that the client "protects himself from feeling powerless, inadequate and frightened by attempting to demonstrate how powerful and frightening he can be. His threatening behavior increases if he feels he is not being taken seriously" (262).

Setting Limits Setting and enforcing reasonable limits makes it possible for counsellors and clients to continue working together. Failure to set limits reinforces acting-out behaviour which if unchecked could lead to more violent and destructive consequence. In the defensive phase, clients may still respond to appropriate limits. Limits let clients know what will and what will not be tolerated, but counsellors need to apply certain principles in setting limits. Counsellors should be specific and tell clients which behaviour is inappropriate since they may not be aware what is acceptable. Moreover, they may not know how their behaviour is affecting others. Limits should include enforceable consequences, and counsellors should state the consequences of noncompliance. However, it's usually better to state the limit with a positive tone, as in the following example: "If you stop yelling at me, then I will sit with you to see if we can find a solution. If not, then I will have no choice but to end our meeting and ask you to leave."

Phase 3: Acting Out

At this stage, the client has lost control and has become assaultive. Protection of self and others is the primary goal. Ideally, agency procedures are operative, and counsellors who are dealing with such situations will receive immediate assistance from the staff team. Police intervention and restraint of the acting-out client may also be required. When dealing with acting-out clients, a team approach with a well-organized and trained staff is the preferred way to address the crisis. A team approach provides increased safety for everyone, including the client. A well-trained team may subdue violent clients before they injure themselves or others, but staff should be trained in techniques for physical restraint and control (for a brief description of physical control techniques, see Roth, 1987:254). The team members provide support and can act as witnesses if litigation should arise as a result of the incident.

Police Intervention Counsellors should not hesitate to call the police if a client becomes too threatening or aggressive. No counsellor is expected to risk his or her life or endure physical assault as part of the job. Moreover, sometimes clients are unwilling or unable to constrain their hostility, and police or psychiatric restraint is essential for managing the crisis. Police intervention is particularly crucial when dealing with clients who have weapons. In addition, counsellors should not try to prevent a client who is determined to leave by blocking the exit. In general, counsellors who are assaulted by clients should consider laying criminal charges. This establishes the importance of clients' taking responsibility for their actions.

Phase 4: Tension Reduction

The tension reduction phase is characterized by a gradual reduction in aggressive behaviour and a return to more rational behaviour. The client may still be driven by adrenalin for up to 90 minutes (Kaplan & Wheeler, 1983), so it is important that counsellors proceed cautiously to avoid reactivating aggressive acting out.

FOLLOWUP COUNSELLING INTERVENTIONS Clients can be counselled to become alert to their own warning signs, such as "tenseness, sweating palms, a tightening of the stomach, pressure in the chest and a surge to the head" (Morrissey, 1998:6). Once clients are aware of their own triggers, they can be counselled on appropriate diversionary tactics, such as employing relaxation techniques, taking time out, and using **assertiveness** and other behavioural response alternatives. Morrissey describes a technique that a counsellor used with a client who was on the verge of violence. The counsellor reassured the client "that he was there to help him and commended the client for coming to see him rather than acting on his feelings of rage. He also asked the client what was keeping him in control thus far and used that as proof to reinforce the fact that he could indeed control himself" (1998:6).

At the end of the tension reduction phase and after the client has returned to normal, the client may be mentally and physically exhausted and show signs of remorse and shame. Consequently, counselling can be directed toward helping the client use the experience as a learning opportunity: for example, to develop alternative responses for future similar stresses. Interview 8.2 provides an example.

Counsellors are well prepared to teach their clients techniques for resolving conflict and crises nonviolently. The skills of counselling are also, to some extent, the skills of effective everyday communication. Communication skill training equips clients with more choices for asserting their rights and respecting others. Assertiveness training can help clients express feelings in a nonaggressive manner. When clients are able to respond assertively, they establish an atmosphere of cooperation and conflict can be peacefully resolved. Often conflict is difficult for clients to settle because they are unable to see the perspectives or feelings of others in the conflict. Clients who learn empathy and other active listening skills are better able to compromise because they are less likely to judge their own behaviour as absolutely right and that of others as absolutely wrong.

But sometimes, long before violence erupts, counsellors intuitively feel that the situation is worsening. This feeling may be based on unconscious reactions to subtle cues and indicators. Counsellors and clients might find it useful to try to concretely identify these clues. Doing so will assist clients in becoming sensitive to those initial psychological responses that signal the imminent onset of the anxiety phase. Clients who become adept at recognizing early warning indicators are in a much better position to take early warning action, such as withdrawing from an explosive situation or switching to healthier problem-solving strategies.

Critical Incident Debriefing

Counsellors who have been assaulted or threatened with assault may be traumatized and may experience symptoms such as recurrent images or thoughts of the event, distressing dreams, flashbacks, and intense stress when returning to the scene of the incident. There may be a marked decline in their ability to handle routine work tasks, and they may feel detached and isolated from colleagues. They may develop sleep difficulties and have difficulty concentrating. Frequently, they return to work in a state of hypervigilance, constantly expecting further trauma. Often they describe themselves as "numb" and unable to enjoy activities that usually gave them pleasure. When symptoms such as these are present, counsellors should consider obtaining medical assessment and/or professional counselling.

Even when counsellors are not injured, the threat of violence can be just as traumatic. Typical responses may include helplessness and thoughts of leaving the profession. These feelings may develop immediately or emerge after a delay of months or even years. Consequently, it is important to debrief critical incidents in order to lessen shock, reduce isolation, and restore personal control. Team debriefing should take place as soon as possible after the incident. Debriefing should be conducted by an objective third party in a safe setting. It should be held as soon as possible after the critical incident, usually within 24 to 72 hours in order to minimize the effects of any trauma that victims or witnesses may be experiencing. This is important in order to promote a return to the normal routine of the agency. A typical debriefing session is like a counselling interview. The debriefing should reinforce team interdependence. Sometimes counsellors are reluctant to ask colleagues for assistance, believing that asking for help is a sign of incompetence. One goal of a debriefing is to develop a staff culture in which asking for help is a sign of strength, rather than weakness. A critical incident debriefing generally has the following elements:

1. All team members are invited to share feelings and reactions about the current or prior incidents. Active listening can be used to promote this process. This helps individuals who were threatened or assaulted to "normalize" their own reactions. Counsellors should require little persuasion of the benefits of talking about their feelings. They might be reminded that sharing feelings is something they routinely ask of their clients. Helping team members manage feelings is the major objective of the debriefing. At this time, it is important to identify the potential physical and emotional reactions that staff may experience. As well, information regarding services, such as employee assistance programs (EAPs) that are available to staff who need additional help to manage their emotions, should be detailed.

2. The team conducts a postmortem on the violent event. A thorough analysis of what transpired is used to review and reinforce procedures for dealing with violent clients. An important question for the team to consider is: "What, if anything, could we have done to prevent this incident?" For example, the team can explore whether any early warning indicators of pending violence were overlooked. They can investigate whether there were things that individuals or the agency did or did not do that contributed to the client's behaviour.

INTERVIEW 8.2   FOLLOWUP TO A VIOLENT INCIDENT

In the following example, the counsellor, a group-home worker, is reviewing an incident with her client. The incident occurred two hours ago and was precipitated when the counsellor denied the client, a 16-year-old male, permission to meet with some of his friends later that night. The client smashed an ashtray on the floor and stormed out of the office while screaming obscenities.

DIALOGUE	ANALYSIS
Counsellor: Let's talk about what happened. Client: I guess I got a bit carried away. Counsellor: I was scared. Client: I'm sorry. I won't let it happen again.	Whenever possible, it's important that clients be invited to review prior incidents. By telling the client how she felt, the counsellor may be giving the client new information that will increase the client's capacity for empathy. Often, violent or acting-out clients are so preoccupied with their own needs and fears that they don't realize the impact they have on others.
Counsellor: I accept your apology.	This helps the client to retain some dignity. Notice that the counsellor's acceptance of her client's apology does not condone his behaviour, as would a statement such as "It's okay. Don't worry about it. No real harm was done."
Counsellor: It might be helpful for both of us to go over what happened to see how it might have been prevented. Client: I was still upset from seeing my mother. When you said *no*, it was just too much.	One goal of counselling is to help clients recognize their own early warning indicators that they are in danger of losing control.
Counsellor: It's never been easy for you to talk to your mom. You always seem to come back really wound up.	Empathy confirms that feelings have been heard and understood.
Client: Yeah, those are the days that people should stay out of my face.	The client rationalizes his behaviour, putting the responsibility on others.
Counsellor: Good point. Sounds like you know that you need some time alone when you're stressed. Client: You got it.	Without directly challenging the rationalization, the counsellor shifts the focus back on the client and a client strength.
Counsellor: As we talk, I'm wondering what prevented you from taking that time. If you'd	Feedback confrontation challenges the client to consider some new alternatives.

(continued)

taken the time to cool off before approaching me, things would have been a lot different.

Client: Sure, I know I have to learn to control my temper, but once I get going I just can't seem to stop myself.

Counsellor: Put another way, your hope is to find a way to deal with your feelings so that you don't get angry and hurt someone.	The counsellor takes advantage of an opportunity to reframe the client's problem statement into a goal.
Client: I don't know if that's possible.	
Counsellor: You've already shown me that you have some skill at doing this. You threw the ashtray and you said some awful things, but afterward you left the room without doing any more damage. This tells me that you have the ability to bring things under control. You need to find a way to do this a little earlier.	Acknowledgment of the client's restraint, however late, provides a base for further development. By doing so, the counsellor reinforces nonaggressive behavioural alternatives.

3. The team debriefing is an important "teachable moment," when staff are highly motivated toward skill development. It is a chance to explore alternative responses that might have been used at all stages of the critical incident. Role play and simulations can be used to practise alternative responses. This step helps empower individuals and the team by moving them away from any tendency to feel helpless.

SUMMARY

Resistance is a client's defensive reaction that interferes with or delays the process of counselling. Client resistance to counselling is common. It may be evident in a variety of ways, such as failure to cooperate with the basic routine of counselling, subtle or direct attacks, passivity, and nonverbal cues. Resistance arises for a number of reasons that may be categorized under five major groupings: (1) relationship, (2) motivational, (3) attitudinal, (4) fearful, and (5) involuntary resistance. Counsellors can use a range of techniques for dealing with each of the five types. Client resistance may be unconscious, or it may be a deliberate act of sabotage or avoidance. Since client resistance can be unsettling for counsellors, it is important that they objectively evaluate their own feelings and behaviour when dealing with it. Counsellors need to be sensitive to the possibility that cross-cultural miscommunication can be mistaken for resistance.

Intimidating behaviour includes name calling, using obscene language, shouting, threatening through displays of power such as fist shaking, invading personal space, stalking, and issuing verbal threats. Violent behaviour means hitting, pushing, biting, slapping, kicking, throwing objects, and using weapons such as guns, knives, or syringes.

Clients may become violent for a number of reasons. Although it is difficult to predict with certainty which clients will become violent, some risk factors may be isolated. The best predictor of violent behaviour is a history of violence. Substance abuse is also a common variable. Other factors that counsellors should consider when assessing risk are age, gender, and personality characteristics.

To prevent or minimize violent incidents, counselling agencies should develop policies and routines that address this issue. Simulations can be used to practise responses to potentially dangerous situations.

The four phases of violence are anxiety, defensiveness, acting-out, and tension reduction. In the anxiety phase, there is a marked change in the client's usual behaviour, with signs of increasing agitation. To prevent anxiety from escalating, counsellors should attempt to establish a climate of cooperation and mutual problem-solving. In the defensiveness phase, anxiety has increased to the point that the client is in danger of losing control. At this point, clients may still respond to appropriate limits. But in the acting-out phase, the client becomes assaultive, and emergency intervention is crucial. Since the client has lost control, protection of one's self and others is the primary goal. During the tension reduction phase, the client's aggressive energy gradual recedes, and the client returns to more rational behaviour.

It is important to debrief critical incidents in order to lessen shock, reduce isolation, and restore personal control. Team debriefing should take place as soon as possible after the incident. It should provide an opportunity for people to talk about their feelings. As well, the debriefing can be used to review what went wrong. Role plays and simulations can be used to practise alternative responses. Overall, debriefing is designed to empower individuals and the team and to move them away from any tendency to feel helpless.

EXERCISES

1. Review your experiences dealing with persons who are angry, resistant, or potentially violent. What is your natural reaction when someone's anger starts to escalate? Do you tend to fight back, or do you withdraw? What aspects of your experience will help you deal effectively with difficult situations? What aspects will impede your ability?

2. Interview counsellors from different settings regarding their experiences with violent or potentially violent clients. Discuss strategies that they have found effective.

3. Work in a small group. Assume that you are members of an inner-city needle exchange centre. Develop detailed policies and procedures for dealing with violent and potentially violent clients.

4. Suppose you review the file on your next client and discover that he was loud and abusive with his previous worker. What are some possible explanations for this client's behaviour? Suggest some strategies for working with this client.

5. Work in a small group to explore the potential benefits and risks of each of the following actions:
   a. having an unlisted phone number
   b. making home visits alone
   c. making home visits only when accompanied by a colleague
   d. conducting joint interviews for potentially hostile clients
   e. using only your first name with clients
   f. knowing that a client has a history of violence
   g. interviewing a client with a police officer present
   h. refusing to see a client with a history of violence

     i. striking a client in order to defend yourself

     j. calling the police

     k. warning an intended victim

     l. seeing a client who has been drinking

6. Research legal and ethical codes in order to explore your responsibility to notify intended victims of violence. Talk to counsellors and agencies for their opinions.

WEBLINKS

The Crisis Prevention Institute provides information about training programs and resources for nonviolent crisis information:
www.crisisprevention.com/program/nci.html

Information and links to sites on violence and violence prevention:
www.workplace-violence-hq.com/#abouthead

This website provides access and links to a wide range of health and emotional issues. Use the search feature to research topics:
www.mayoclinic.com/index.cfm

Comprehensive Canadian study on mental illness and violence:
www.phac-aspc.gc.ca/mh-sm/mentalhealth/pubs/mental_illness/index.htm

chapter nine

Variations with Selected Target Groups

PREVIEW

After reading this chapter you should be able to:

- Demonstrate knowledge of the impact of job loss.
- Identify and describe the four major activity target areas for employment counselling.
- Explain the structure and use of DSM-IV-TR.
- Describe the characteristics of and treatment for major mental disorders, including schizophrenia, mood disorders, anxiety disorders, and eating disorders.
- Identify suicide warning signs.
- Identify strategies for dealing with clients who are suicidal.
- Identify issues and strategies for counselling clients who are HIV positive and clients who have AIDS.

EMPLOYMENT COUNSELLING

The devastating impact of unemployment is well documented in the literature (Bolles, 2005; Borgen, Amundson, & McVicar, 2002; Soper & Von Bergen, 2001). Aside from the obvious loss of income from not having a job, there may be significant consequences to job loss (see Bolles, 2005; Steinweg, 1990; Sunley & Sheek, 1986; Kirsh, 1983). One Canadian study showed how unemployment can lead to increased stress; health and mental health problems, including depression; increased suicide rate; premature death; and increased hospitalization (Kirsh, 1983). Moreover, Holmes and Werbel (1992) reviewed the research on the physical and mental health effects of job loss. They found that job loss leads to higher incidence of coronary disease, hypertension, ulcers, headaches, depression, anxiety, and hostility, as well as increased family conflict and higher illness rates among children whose parents are unemployed.

For many people, a job or career is a pivotal part of their identity. A protracted period of unemployment can result in a loss of self-esteem and personality. Moreover, persons who are unemployed lose the routine of their daily lives, the structure of the workday, their sense of purpose, and the social contact with friends and colleagues at the workplace.

In addition, the financial impact of job loss can be devastating. Day-to-day survival can be tenuous at best as individuals and families struggle to survive on savings or meagre social assistance benefits. Financial problems become a crisis when unanticipated expenses such as car repairs, school fees, or medical bills appear. Job loss can easily result in the loss of one's savings, one's home, and the ability to maintain one's lifestyle, including one's social and recreational life. As Burman describes it, "It means not being able to reciprocate a dinner invitation, not seeing one's way clear to join a friend for lunch or a movie, and not being able to afford the price of a favourite recreation. As the weeks and months of unemployment pass, one's social orbit shrinks, placing a heavy emotional load on family relationships" (1988:xii).

Target Areas for Employment Counselling

In general, employment counsellors are concerned with four major activity target areas: (1) job loss counselling, (2) career counselling, (3) job search skills, and (4) life skills counselling (see Table 9.1). No assumptions should be made regarding client needs until an assessment interview is conducted to help counsellors determine if a client needs assistance with one or more of the four areas.

Job Loss Counselling

Job loss counselling aims to help clients regain equilibrium after being laid off and deal with the psychological stress that typically accompanies job loss and unemployment. As well, counsellors can help clients adjust to living on reduced or low incomes. They can help them access services that might help alleviate financial stress (e.g., welfare, employment insurance, loan negotiation, use of community resources such as subsidized daycare).

Self-esteem counselling is essential because it affects how job seekers market themselves. Sometimes clients develop learned helplessness as a result of repeated failure in

TABLE 9.1	Employment Counselling	
Activity Area	**Counselling Targets**	
Job loss counselling	Improving or restoring self-esteem Managing stress and the negative feelings associated with unemployment Assisting clients to deal with the financial impact of their unemployment	
Career counseling	Researching careers and educational opportunities Assisting clients to identify and explore their interests, aptitudes and values Researching employers Identifying career goals	
Job search skills	Overcoming barriers (e.g., age, a criminal record, racism, sexism) Writing résumés Identifying leads Networking Conducting informational interviews Getting interviews Preparing for interviews Using interview followup techniques Using electronic resources	
Life skills counselling	Teaching work and life skills Helping with job survival	

their job search. A number of strategies can be used to help unemployed clients overcome learned helplessness:

1. Short-circuit self-deprecation by ignoring such remarks, challenging the basis for the remarks, and inviting clients to rationally consider changing the basis for their beliefs. Counsellors might use reframing and other techniques for changing thinking (see Chapter 7).

2. Reassure clients that "perfection is neither attainable nor expected" (Arnhold & Razak,1991:103).

3. Reinforce current or past successes. "Positive comments on a neat desk, a new outfit, reliable punctuality, and other small past and present triumphs can be to the helpless-ness-oriented individual what a meal is to a starving person" (Arnhold & Razak, 1991:103). Assist clients to understand what they can control. This helps them to see the link between their efforts and success.

4. Encourage action. Setting small but achievable goals results in success, which helps clients break out of pessimism.

When dealing with clients who feel and act helpless it is important for counsellors to remember Arnhold and Razak's observation that "helplessness is a perception and not an accurate description of an individual. Many who are afflicted with crippling low self-esteem are in fact quite capable in some respects—the problem is that they think and feel otherwise about themselves" (102).

Amundson (1996) suggests a series of strategies that employment counsellors can use to help clients change their perspectives. These strategies include helping clients make positive affirmations, normalizing the experience of unemployment (i.e., assuring them that their feelings and reactions are normal), and encouraging them to avoid blaming themselves for unemployment. As well, counsellors can encourage clients to identify and use transferable skills (skills from other jobs, activities, hobbies, and experiences) in the job search. Amundson proposes challenging negative thinking patterns by having clients change "I can't" statements to "I won't" declarations. By changing the wording, clients can consider the power that they have to change any thinking or behaviour that might be acting as a barrier to action. Clients are often unemployed for reasons beyond their control, such as high unemployment rates, organizational downsizing, and economic downturns. They can help clients change their thinking about job loss by encouraging them not to blame themselves.

Amundson also suggests giving clients specific activities that interrupt established but ineffective patterns of activity. For example, counsellors could ask clients to research employers, develop contact lists, and make phone calls. "By actively engaging in meaningful activity, with support, clients will gain confidence and will have a greater likelihood of persisting with career exploration and job search" (Amundson, 1996:160).

Since sustained unemployment can be damaging to clients' self-worth and esteem, it is important for counsellors to encourage clients to maintain as much as possible their daily routine. In addition, whenever possible, clients should continue activities and commitments, such as parenting, volunteering, social contact, and exercise, all of which enhance self-esteem. In addition, counsellors can help clients "by providing general information on potential physical, psychological, financial, and social effects that they may experience" (Borgen et al, 2002:124).

Soper and von Bergen, 2001 suggest that employment counsellors can encourage clients to use expressive writing to express and explore their feelings. "Both historically and recently, researchers and practitioners have cited the expression of negative emotions as vital for good mental and physical health, whereas the inhibition of such emotion is often considered detrimental (p. 150).

Career Counselling

Career counselling helps clients to enhance their understanding about their aptitudes, values and interests. Job satisfaction is enhanced when there is a match between client aptitudes, values, and interests and their chosen career. Aptitudes are measures of a client's ability to learn different skills, for example verbal, numerical, and manual dexterity. Aptitudes are not based on current ability. Career values represent a client's preferred outcomes, for example, financial, creative, altruistic, and control. For clients who do not have a clear perspective on these variables, vocational testing can be used, but the results of such testing should never be used as prescriptions for dictating what clients must or should do. With clear career possibilities identified, clients can then use a variety of resources to find out about the occupations that match their unique interests, values, and personal styles. This process should result in the establishment of a career goal.

Job Search Skills

Counselling in job search skills includes tasks such as researching employers and careers, preparing for job interviews, handling difficult interview questions, and following up

TABLE 9.2	Traditional versus Modern Job Search Methods
Traditional Search Method	**Modern Strategies**
Mail the same résumé widely to employers.	Tailor multiple résumés to individual employers.
Be ready to take any job.	Link job and career objective to targeted employer or industry.
Learn about the job after you are hired.	Conduct prior research to learn about the organization. Prepare for the job interview by anticipating and rehearsing questions.
Emphasize specific skills and experiences.	Emphasize transferable skills. Use work skills derived from other areas (e.g., volunteer work, hobbies).
Gear job search to available vacancies.	Gear job search to aptitude and interests and not to one type of job.
Respond to job ads—"door to door" contact (dropping in on all employers in a defined geographic area to ask about job openings).	Use multiple approaches to job search, including: • networking • phone contact • use of Internet • direct contact with targeted employers • use of the hidden job market • follow-up of contacts • call back.
Effort is part time and sporadic.	Effort is full time.

phone calls or employment interviews. For example, counsellors can help clients anticipate interview questions, then role play answers. Video recordings can be used to help clients review their manner and the quality of their answers.

Job search skills training focuses on nontraditional job search methods, such as **networking** and using the **hidden job market** (see Table 9.2). Small groups for support and role playing may support this process.

Most uninformed job seekers rely on newspaper and other advertisements or employment agencies to find job vacancies. However, most jobs are never advertised. Only 15 to 20 percent of all jobs are filled through job ads (Angel and Harney, 1997; Farr, 1996). The remaining 80 to 85 percent of vacancies are part of what is known as the hidden job market.

Networking is the primary tool used to access the hidden job market. It involves using contacts such as friends, family, neighbours, and others who might provide information or access to others with information about job opportunities. An important part of networking is asking contacts for the names of other people who might have jobs or information about potential openings. In this way, the network contact list grows dramatically, and clients gain access to people that they would not otherwise have known about.

Life Skills Counselling

Life skills counselling may be appropriate for clients who lack basic abilities in such areas as managing finances, maintaining proper hygiene, getting to work on time, and getting along with supervisors and co-workers. For clients in this category, this work is essential in order for them to become job ready. Some clients will need continued support and assistance in the workplace.

Job Clubs

Steinweg's (1990) work confirms the importance of group support as a way to reduce isolation and to buffer the adverse impact of unemployment. One of the most popular forms of group support is the **job club method** developed by Azrin and Besalel (1980). The job club method is based on the notion that looking for work is in itself a full-time job that is best done with a group of people. The job club leader provides support, job search skills training, and materials and supplies for completing a successful job hunt. Job clubs provide participants with access to phones, computers, photocopying, stationery, daily newspapers, and other sources of job leads. Secretarial assistance for producing effective résumés is provided, as well. Internet access is now an essential tool for tapping the hidden job market and for researching careers and employers. An important part of the job club is the buddy system. Every job club participant has another member in the group who provides support and assistance.

    The job club has a single goal: to help members obtain a job. Job club leaders remain unwavering in their optimism that everyone is employable and that there are job opportunities even during times of recession or depression. Job clubs typically have 8 to 12 members who meet for a period of two to three weeks. Job club counsellors use behavioural methods and standardized routines to teach participants job-finding methods. The "brief talk" rule requires counsellors to speak very briefly about a technique or procedure, usually for a maximum of one or two minutes. Participants then immediately practise the skill. Every session has specific learning objectives. By taking part in a job club, participants have an opportunity to acquire the skills of an effective job search, including how to network with family, friends, acquaintances, and others for job leads; how to develop an effective résumé; how to make phone calls to secure interviews; and how to handle interview questions. Azrin and Besalel offer this summary of the job club method:

> The general counseling style in the Job Club method is one of continuous encouragement and praise while still being very structured and task oriented. The counselor is constantly complimenting and encouraging the job seekers, speaking to each of them very frequently and yet briefly... The counselor promotes mutual assistance among group members. He has a single overriding objective of helping each job seeker to obtain a good job and he devotes every moment of the meeting to instructing and encouraging the members in the specific activities that will help them obtain that objective. (1980:12)

Electronic Resources

In recent years, electronic technology has necessitated that clients become familiar with new strategies for managing their job and career searches. Fax machines, electronic databanks, software that guides users through résumé construction, and the Internet will likely continue to dramatically change the nature of the job search. The Internet, for example, offers unprecedented opportunities for clients to communicate with employers and other job seekers. As well, clients can visit company home pages for background information on the business, or they can search the Internet for detailed data on industry trends. The Internet has many resources for career information, self-assessment, job search tips, job bulletin boards, and government grants. The vast majority of colleges and universities now have websites where clients can get information on training programs and educational opportunities. The Internet can also help clients who may be considering moving by giving them geographic, economic, and demographic data. Chat rooms and other discussion groups can provide support, information, and sometimes network contacts. However, Bratina and Bratina caution, "Information found on the Internet is not necessarily accurate. Counsellors should encourage job seekers to give Internet sources the same critical review they would give to other sources" (1998:21).

Many companies are now inviting applicants to submit electronic résumés via the Internet. Electronic résumés are somewhat different from traditional paper résumés. Action verbs such as planned, directed, and organized are best for paper résumés, but nouns such as bachelor's degree, teller, top 10 percent of class, and WordPerfect are best for electronic versions because computers sort and screen electronic résumés based on nouns such as these (Bratina and Bratina, 1998).

There is a wide range of websites of significance to Canadian employment counsellors. For example, Job Futures (**www.hrdc-drhc.gc.ca/JobFutures/english/index.htm**) offers general information on the National Occupations Classification occupational groups, including projections for future growth in these groups. The Canada WorkInfoNet (**www.workinfonet.ca/cwn/english/main.html**) highlights hot jobs and provides a variety of labour market information.

Employment Counselling and Immigrant Clients

Westwood and Ishiyama called attention to the unique employment counselling needs of culturally diverse clients. They noted that clients from immigrant minority groups often face unique problems related to "language, racial prejudice, lack of knowledge of the world of work, limited contacts or networks, lack of cultural knowledge of job finding and interviewing techniques, plus the additional stress due to the cultural adjustment to a new society" (1991:130). In dealing with these clients, counsellors need to be particularly sensitive to the cultural attitudes and norms. For example, Asian immigrant clients consider their career search in "light of the financial burden that may fall to them by virtue of their place in the family" (140). Thus, counsellors need to take family into account more than they might when dealing with clients from other cultures. Westwood and Ishiyama offer this caution for employment counsellors working with immigrants:

> Client resistance and distrust in the counseling process may be set in motion by cross-cultural insensitivities, such as the counselor's disregarding the client's age and social status and calling him or her by the first name, using excessive informality and friendliness, probing into private feelings, demanding high levels of self-disclosure and expressiveness, and advice giving. (1991:137)

COUNSELLING PEOPLE WITH MENTAL DISORDERS

Historically, treatment of people with mental disorders was barbaric and included such practices as exorcizing, burning "witches," blood letting, whipping, starving, imprisoning, or housing in overcrowded "snake-pits," or insane asylums. During the 20th century, especially in the last 50 years, mental disorders have gradually been recognized as a health problem, and more humanitarian practices have been developed to replace procedures based on superstition, fear, and ignorance.

Over the past 40 years there has been a major and continuous shift in the delivery of mental health services from long-term treatment in hospitals to treatment of patients in the community, a process known as deinstitutionalization. Today, the population of mental hospitals in Canada is only about one-fifth of what it was 40 years ago (Sealy and Whitehead, 2004). The development and refinement of a range of psychotropic drugs has been the driving force behind deinstitutionalization because these drugs enable patients to control hallucinations and behaviour that might otherwise preclude them from living in the community. However, this move toward community treatment has often been poorly funded, and new problems for those with mental disorders have resulted, particularly homelessness and its associated problems.

Psychiatric assessment and diagnosis typically involve an in-depth interview, including a thorough history of the person's situation. As well, physical examinations, including brain scans, electroencephalograms (EEGs), and lab tests, may be used to rule out organic illness (brain tumours, AIDS, drug reactions, etc.). Psychological tests may be used to assess thinking, personality, and other variables. The purpose of psychiatric diagnosis is not to label clients, but to match diagnosis to treatment decisions based on the best scientific evidence regarding which treatments are likely to be most effective with each disorder (Reid, 1989).

It is beyond the scope of this book to fully explore mental disorders. However, it is important to note that the concept is influenced by cultural and societal values. For example, at various times in history, homosexuality has been considered both an aberration and a gift. It is no longer considered a mental disorder.

It is important to remember that there may be vast differences between individuals with the same mental disorder. Psychological, social, and biological variables influence how illness manifests in each person. In addition, people with mental disorders may have concurrent problems, such as poverty, substance abuse, and social/relationship difficulties. Dual diagnosis or concurrent disorder is a term used to describe a person who has both a substance abuse addiction and a psychiatric disorder.

DSM-IV-TR

DSM-IV-TR is the **Diagnostic and Statistical Manual of Mental Disorders**–Text Revised, published by the American Psychiatric Association. Psychologists, psychiatrists, and other psychotherapists throughout the United States, Canada and many other countries use use it to classify and diagnose mental disorders. In Europe and some other countries the International Classification of Diseases–10 (ICD–10) is used.

Counsellors should follow the lead of the DSM-IV–TR text, which "avoids the use of such expressions as 'a schizophrenic' or 'an alcoholic' and instead uses the more accurate,

TABLE 9.3	Mental Health: Canadian Facts

- 1 in 5 Canadians will experience a mental illness during their lifetime.
- Most mental illnesses begin in adolescence and young adulthood.
- Mental illness arises for a complex interaction of biological, genetic, personality and environmental factors.
- Social and workplace pressures, poverty, substance abuse, and learned behavioural and thinking patterns can influence the onset and outcome of mental illness.
- During any one year period:
  - over 8% of the Canadian population will experience a mood disorder
  - .3% will experience schizophrenia
  - 12% an anxiety disorder
  - almost 2.5% an eating disorder
  - 1 in 10 people experience some disability from a diagnosable mental disorder.
- In Canada during 2001–2002, there were almost 200,000 psychiatric hospital admissions with an average stay of 43 days—over 8 million patient days.
- More hospital beds in Canada (8%) are filled with persons with schizophrenia than with any other condition.
- Schizophrenia costs Canadians over $4.3 billion annually in direct and indirect costs.
- As many as one-third of the homeless have a mental disorder.
- Approximately 1% of Canadians will experience bipolar disorder.
- At least 2% of all deaths are from suicide.
- Personality disorders affect between 6% and 9% (estimated) of the Canadian population.
- Suicide accounts for 24% of all deaths among those 15 to 24 years old and 16% of those age 25 to 44 years old.
- Psychiatric problems are the second leading cause of hospital admissions among those 20 to 44 years old.
- The estimated annual impact of mental health problems in Canada is over 14 billion dollars per year.
- Most mental illness can be treated.
- Best practice intervention favours treatment in the community using a variety of counselling interventions, occupational therapy, and medication.

Sources: Statistics Canada, 2005, Public Health Agency of Canada, 2002; BC Schizophrenia Society, 2001; NIMH, 1998; Skidmore, Thackeray, and Farley,1991; Cleghorn and Lee (1991)

but admittedly more cumbersome, 'an individual with Schizophrenia' or 'an individual with Alcohol Dependence'" (American Psychiatric Association, 1994:xxii).

DSM-IV-TR strives to look at patients as more than just diagnostic labels. The manual recognizes that individuals are complex and that medical conditions, social circumstances, and other factors affect how people function. To facilitate a more comprehensive assessment, DSM-IV-TR uses a five-level multiaxial system, described below.

AXIS I: CLINICAL DISORDERS This axis is used to report the specific mental disorder that is being diagnosed. Two exceptions are personality disorders and mental retardation, which are reported on Axis II.

AXIS II: PERSONALITY DISORDERS, MENTAL RETARDATION Personality disorders and mental retardation are reported on this axis.

AXIS III: GENERAL MEDICAL CONDITIONS This axis is used for reporting relevant medical conditions that affect a current or past mental disorder (Axis I or Axis II). For example, hypothyroidism can cause depression; thus, the individual would be coded on Axis I with a mood disorder due to hypothyroidism and also on Axis III as hypothyroidism (American Psychiatric Association, (2000:29).

AXIS IV: PSYCHOSOCIAL AND ENVIRONMENTAL PROBLEMS This important axis is used for reporting significant stressors that might be contributing to the mental disorders. DSM-IV groups stressors into nine categories: (1) problems with primary support groups, (2) problems related to the social environment, (3) educational problems, (4) occupational problems, (5) housing problems, (6) economic problems, (7) problems with access to health-care services, (8) problems related to interaction with the legal system/crime, and (9) other psychosocial and environmental problems.

AXIS V: GLOBAL ASSESSMENT OF FUNCTIONING SCALE (GAF) This axis is used to report an individual's highest level of functioning on three major areas: social functioning, occupational functioning, and psychological functioning. This scale is based on a continuum from 0 to 100, in which 100 represents a superior level of adaptation (American Psychiatric Association, 1994:32). Predictably, people who have a higher level of functioning before their illness generally do better than those with a lower level (Saddock & Saddock, 2004).

APPROPRIATE USES OF DSM-IV-TR The overview in this chapter is a brief introduction to the basic structure of the manual. Counsellors should use the DSM-IV–TR classification system as a diagnostic tool only if they have appropriate specialized clinical training. Typically, individuals who use DSM-IV–TR in their counselling practice are licensed psychiatrists or those with graduate degrees in counselling or psychology. Untrained practitioners should not attempt to make psychiatric diagnoses.

However, all counsellors can use DSM-IV–TR as a tool for understanding the essential definitions and features of mental disorders. DSM-IV–TR contains valuable information regarding variations in culture, age, and gender with respect to particular mental disorders. The manual also provides counsellors with reference material on the prevalence of mental disorders, including lifetime risk, the typical patterns of disorders, and data on the frequency of specified disorders among biological family members.

There can be wide individual difference between individuals with the same diagnosis. One person with schizophrenia may suffer debilitating effects and their behaviour may present as bizarre, but another may respond to medication to the point where they function "normally" with no one suspecting that this person has a mental disorder.

Counsellors and DSM-IV-TR

Counselling is primarily concerned with individuals in a social context with an emphasis on helping them to deal with relationship problems, crisis events, difficulties related to inadequate resources, and problems dealing with organizations such as schools or government welfare offices. DSM-IV–TR, however useful as a tool for intellectually understanding mental disorders, is a model based on pathology and deficits. It does not address or prioritize human empowerment, which is a central objective of counselling. Contemporay counsellors adopt a strengths approach to problem solving that assumes the power of individuals to overcome adversity. Using a strengths approach they endeavour to find and respect the successes, assets, and resources of people, including those resources available within their culture such as sweat lodges and other healing rituals. As Compton and Gallaway see it:

> The emphasis is on knowing them in a more holistic way: acknowledging their hopes and dreams, their needs, their resources and the resources around them, their capacities, and their gifts. The strengths perspective invites a more affirming interaction with individuals and families; as a profession, you engage them conversationally as collaborators and peers, recognizing that they and you are both experts and have a mutual interest in improving their quality of life. (1999:17)

Structure of DSM-IV-TR

DSM-IV–TR organizes mental disorders into 16 major groups or classes. Each diagnostic class is further subdivided into specific disorders. A cursory overview of the 16 groups follows.

1. Disorders usually first diagnosed in infancy, childhood, or adolescence (e.g., mental retardation, learning disorders, autism, conduct disorders, Tourette's syndrome). Disorders in this category have their onset during childhood or adolescence, but they may not be diagnosed until adulthood.

2. Delirium, dementia, and amnestic and other cognitive disorders (e.g., dementia owing to HIV, Huntington's, Alzheimer's, or Parkinson's disease). The significant feature of disorders in this section is a disturbance in memory or thinking.

3. Mental disorders resulting from a general medical condition. Here, the distinguishing feature is the judgment that the mental disorder is the direct result of a medical condition.

4. Substance-related disorders (e.g., alcoholism and other addictions)

5. Schizophrenia and other psychotic disorders. Disorders in this section are typically accompanied by psychotic symptoms such as hallucinations and delusions.

6. Mood disorders (e.g., depression, bipolar disorder). The predominant feature is a disturbance in mood or feeling.

7. Anxiety disorders (e.g., panic attacks, agoraphobia, post-traumatic stress disorder, phobias, obsessive-compulsive disorder). The predominant feature of anxiety disorders is much greater than usual anxiety or tension.

8. Somatoform disorders (e.g., hypochondria or the fear that one has a serious disease). Here, the common feature is the presence of physical symptoms that suggest a medical problem, but there is no medical condition that is diagnosable.

9. Factitious disorders (e.g., Munchausen syndrome). These disorders are characterized by the fact that the patient intentionally fakes symptoms in order to assume the role of patient.

10. Dissociative disorders (e.g., amnesia, depersonalization disorder). Disorders in this category are characterized by significant changes in the consciousness, memory, or identity of the person.

11. Sexual and gender identity disorders (e.g., pedophilia, sexual sadism). These disorders concern disturbances in sexual desire and functioning.

12. Eating disorders (e.g., anorexia nervosa, bulimia nervosa). These disorders are noted by severe disturbance in eating behaviour.

13. Sleep disorders (e.g., insomnia, narcolepsy). Sleep disorders are characterized by abnormalities in the amount, quality, or timing of sleep.

14. Impulse control disorders not elsewhere classified (e.g., pathological gambling, pyromania, kleptomania). The essential feature of impulse control disorders is the inability to resist impulses or temptations.

15. Adjustment disorders. These disorders arise from stressful events, such as the end of a relationship or loss of a job.

16. Personality disorders (e.g., paranoid personality disorder, obsessive-compulsive personality disorder). A personality disorder "is an enduring pattern of inner experience and behavior that deviates markedly from the expectations of the individual's culture, is pervasive and inflexible, has an onset in adolescence or early adulthood, is stable over time, and leads to distress or impairment" (American Psychiatric Association, 2000:685).

Selected Major Mental Disorders

This section provides only a very brief synopsis of some of the most common mental disorders that counsellors are likely to encounter, including schizophrenia, mood disorders, anxiety disorders, and eating disorders.

Schizophrenia

According to the Schizophrenia Society of Canada (2005), schizophrenia is a chronic (continuing) mental disorder affecting about 1 percent of the population. In rare cases children can develop schizophrenia, but it usually starts in the late teens or early 20s for men, and in the 20s and early 30s for women. Although the exact cause remains unknown, it is believed that the disease is a biochemical brain disorder involving suspect neurotransmitters such as dopamine and serotonin. The children of a parent who has schizophrenia are ten times more likely to develop it than children of a parent who does not have it (NIMH, 1998). Most people with schizophrenia suffer from it throughout their lives, and an estimated one of every ten people with the illness dies by suicide (NIMH, 1998; Cleghorn & Lee, 1991; Dubovsky & Weissberg, 1986).

Contrary to popular opinion, people with schizophrenia do not have split personalities, like Dr. Jekyll and Mr. Hyde. Furthermore, although some once accepted it as truth, parents do not cause schizophrenia. The current perspective on the disorder is that it is caused by an imbalance of the complex, interrelated chemical systems of the brain (NIMH, 1998), but there may be no single cause. The symptoms of schizophrenia vary between individuals, sometimes dramatically. The symptoms are commonly classified as positive or negative. **Positive symptoms** may include hallucinations, delusions, bizarre behaviour, agitation, thought disorder, disorganized speech and behaviour, and catatonic behaviour. **Negative symptoms** include blunted or flattened affect, poverty of speech, emotional and social withdrawal, lack of pleasure (anhedonia), passivity, difficulty in abstract thinking, lack of goal directed behaviour (Ralph, 2003). Antipsychotic medications (neuroleptics) are the most effective way of treating the positive symptoms of schizophrenia.

There are a wide variety of early warning signs of schizophrenia including noticeable social withdrawal, deteriorating personal hygiene, irrational behaviour, sleep disturbances, extreme reactions, inappropriate laughter, cutting or strange use of words, and many others (for a more complete list, see BC Schizophrenia Society, 2001:6).

HALLUCINATIONS There may be wide variation in the symptoms of persons with schizophrenia. Most sufferers, however, experience hallucinations, usually auditory but sometimes visual or olfactory (related to smell). These hallucinations may be voices that tell clients what to do (command hallucinations), or they may be visions of things that do not exist. Persons with command hallucinations telling them to harm themselves or others are dangerous risks for suicide, homicide or other violent behaviour (Saddock & Saddock, 2004)

Hallucinations can affect any of a person's senses, causing them to hear, see, taste, touch, or smell what others do not. Auditory hallucinations are the most frequent type of hallucination and are most common for people with schizophrenia (Fauman, 2002). Visual hallucinations are much less common, and they are more likely to occur as a result of acute infectious disease. Olfactory hallucinations may occur because of schizophrenia and organic lesions of the brain. Tactile hallucinations (touch) may occur as a reaction to drugs. Kinesthetic hallucinations may occur after the loss of a limb ("phantom limb") and owing to schizophrenia. Withdrawal from drugs may cause vivid hallucinations, such as the sensation that insects are crawling under the skin (delirium tremens common with alcohol withdrawal) (Saddock & Saddock, 2004). In fact, the symptoms of alcohol withdrawal may be clinically indistinguishable from schizophrenia (Reid, 1989). With auditory hallucinations, clients may hear voices that command or compliment them, but with disorders such as schizophrenia, the voices are usually hostile (Shea, 1988). These voices may be so real that clients believe that they have had broadcasting devices planted in their bodies. For example, one client was convinced that her dentist had secretly implanted receivers in her fillings. It was so real to her that she could not dismiss it as imagination.

It is important to know that a wide range of factors can cause hallucinations, including psychosis, high fever, mind-altering drugs (marijuana, psilocybin, LSD, and opium), medications, withdrawal from depressant drugs such as alcohol, brain disease and injury, epilepsy, sensory deprivation or sensory overload, oxygen deprivation, hyperventilation, hypoglycemia, extreme pain, extended fasting, dehydration, and social isolation (Saddock & Saddock, 2004, Nicoli, 1988; Beyerstein, 1998). Hallucinations can also occur in persons who have impaired vision but no mental disorder.

DELUSIONS **Delusions** are false beliefs which "cannot be influenced or corrected by reason or contradictory evidence (Fauman, 2002:149). Persons with schizophrenia may experience delusions, or distorted beliefs involving bizarre thought patterns. Delusions of persecution, typical in paranoid schizophrenia, may lead people to believe they are being cheated, controlled, or poisoned. Other common delusions include religious delusions (belief that one is a manifestation of God), delusions of grandeur (bizarre beliefs about one's abilities), delusions of being controlled (e.g., belief that one is being directed by radio messages), thought broadcasting (belief that one's thinking can be heard by others) and thought insertion (belief that thoughts are being inserted into one's brain by others) (Nicoli, 1988).

Not all delusions are bizarre. Examples of nonbizarre delusions are the belief that one is being watched or that a famous person loves them (erotomania) (Saddock & Saddock, 2004; Fauman, 2002).

DISORDERED THINKING Another common feature of schizophrenia is disordered thinking. Individuals may be unable to think logically, or they may jump from one idea to another without any apparent logical connection. Thinking may be so disorganized and fragmented that it is totally confusing to others.

SOCIAL ISOLATION Persons with schizophrenia are often socially isolated and withdrawn. They may be emotionally numb, have poor communication skills, and show decreased motivation and ability to care for themselves.

TREATMENT OF SCHIZOPHRENIA Hospitalization may be a necessary first step in the effective treatment of acute psychotic symptoms, particularly if there is a risk of violence (Ralph, 2003). Antipsychotic medications such as clozapine, and risperidone are used to decrease the positive symptoms of the disorder—hallucinations, agitation, confusion, distortions, and delusions. There is no cure for schizophrenia, but long-term drug maintenance now enables most people with the disease to live outside a psychiatric institution.

Counselling is an important adjunct to antipsychotic medication. Counsellors typically target their activities toward helping clients deal with the social aspects of the disease. As well, counsellors can be instrumental in encouraging clients to seek psychiatric attention when necessary, and they can support psychiatric initiatives by encouraging clients to continue with any prescribed medication. This is crucial, since about 50 percent of people with schizophrenia are noncompliant in taking their medication (Dubovsky & Weissberg, 1986). Long acting (one to six weeks) antipsychotic medication is an option for those who have difficulty (Ralph, 2003).

One client, a young university student, gives us a sense of what the world of a person with schizophrenia is like:

> I want to sue my dentist. Over the past year he has been installing radio transmitters in my fillings. Now he uses them to control me. At first he was nice, then he raped me while he worked on my teeth. Sometimes he makes me sleep with complete strangers. If I don't get them removed soon, I might be forced to do something awful... There are others. I talked to a woman on the phone the other day. Her dentist did the same thing. We need to go underground where we can be safe from the enemy.

CONVERSATION 9.1

WHEN CLIENTS ARE HALLUCINATING

STUDENT: What should I do when clients begin hallucinating?

TEACHER: Let's talk about what not to do. First, counsellors need to resist the temptation to argue with clients about the reality of their hallucinations. Although some clients are aware of when they are hallucinating and have learned to live with it, others are convinced of their authenticity and dismiss arguments to the contrary. Their experience is very real and has to be accepted as such.

Second, counsellors should avoid patronizing or humouring clients about their hallucinations, as this behaviour may promote further hallucinating.

STUDENT: Okay, but what can counsellors do?

TEACHER: Hallucinations are generally treated with antipsychotic medications. Consequently, referral to a physician or psychiatrist is essential to make sure that clients have been assessed for an appropriate medication to control their hallucinations. Subsequently, it is important to ensure that clients are taking their medication and that their dosage is appropriate.

One way that counsellors can respond without arguing is to simply state that they do not sense what their clients are sensing. They can combine this statement with empathic statements that acknowledge the feelings that clients may be experiencing as a result of their hallucinations.

Counsellors also can help clients deal with any stressors that may be increasing the frequency of hallucinations. For example, if being in large crowds or missing sleep brings on hallucinations, clients can take steps to minimize these precursors. It may be helpful to work with clients to help them learn skills for controlling their hallucinations. For example, they can discipline themselves to direct their thoughts and activities elsewhere. One researcher found that silence, isolation, and attention to oneself tend to promote hallucinations, but distraction, exploratory activity, movement, and external stimulation tend to impede hallucinations (Silva & Lopez de Silva, 1976). So simply diverting client attention can be a useful strategy.

STUDENT: I learned something from one of my clients that I found helpful and profound. I remember him saying to me, "I have a mental disorder, but don't forget, I have the same needs and fears as everyone else." I was reminded that he and I were more alike than unlike each other.

Mood Disorders

The two most severe mood disorders (also known as affective disorders) are major **depression** and **bipolar disorder**, or manic-depressive illness.

DEPRESSION About one in four women and one in ten men in North America will experience major depression during their lifetimes, but almost 90 percent of people who develop depression can be treated (Cleghorn & Lee, 1991:55). Although everyone has bad days, the depressed feelings that accompany them usually pass quickly. A clinical diagnosis of depression is made when a person's depressed mood becomes pervasive over time and interferes with the person's ability to cope with or enjoy life. In this way, depression is differentiated from the normal mood swings that everyone experiences. Depression is almost certainly more widespread than statistics suggest since it often goes untreated. In fact, it is sometimes referred to as the "common cold of mental illness." The signs of depression, sometimes described as clinical depression or major depression to separate it from ordinary sadness, can be organized into four major categories with specific symptoms:

1. Mood disturbances
   - constant sad, anxious, or empty mood
   - feelings of hopelessness or pessimism
   - feelings of guilt, worthlessness, or helplessness

2. Changes in behaviour
   - diminished interest or pleasure in daily activities, including sex
   - decreased energy and fatigue
   - withdrawal from others
3. Alterations in thinking
   - difficulty thinking, concentrating, remembering
   - inability to make decisions
   - recurrent thoughts of death or suicide
4. Physical complaints
   - restlessness or irritability
   - fatigue or loss of energy
   - sleep disturbances, including insomnia
   - loss or gain of appetite and weight
   - chronic pain or other persistent bodily symptoms that are not caused by physical disease
   - suicide attempts (NIMH, 1998; American Medical Association, 1998, American Psychiatric Association, 1994; Cleghorn & Lee, 1991)

Scott Simmie, a Canadian journalist, describes how his depression included obsession with thoughts of suicide:

> I spent weeks in bed, unable to find a reason to get up. Sleep was my drug—the only, albeit temporary, way to escape what had befallen me. When awake I brooded, almost obsessively, on death. Pictured myself rigging pulleys so I could hang myself in the condo... Most mornings, the first thought that entered my head was to put a gun to it. Bang. Problem solved. (Simmie & Nunes, 2001:27)

In a report on diagnosis trends by Intercontinental Medical Statistics Inc. (IMS, 2001), which compiles statistical information for the Canadian health care community, researchers noted that visits to a doctor for depression have shown the largest increase among Canada's leading diagnoses. During the period 1995–2000, IMS statistics revealed that visits to doctors in Canada for depression increased 36 percent with 7.8 million consultations with doctors for depressive disorders. Put another way, almost three percent of all physician visits were for depression. Women represented 66 percent of those diagnosed with depression. About 47 percent of individuals (male and female) diagnosed with depression were in the age group 40–59, and 31 percent were from the next largest group made up of 20–39 year-olds. Significantly, depression now ranks second behind essential hypertension as the leading reason for visiting a physician. Moreover, the report suggested that almost three million Canadians have serious depression but less than one-third seeks help.

Depression is believed to be caused by a complex combination of three primary variables—biological, genetic (inherited), and emotional and/or environmental (American Medical Association, 1998). Biological origins are associated with brain chemistry and hormonal activity. Research has demonstrated that some families are more likely to have members who suffer depression. Although no specific gene has been linked to depression, there appears to be ample evidence that heredity leads to an increased vulnerability to depression. Emotional and environmental causes might include stressors such as death of a loved one, job loss, or the break up of a relationship. As well, depression might be the result of sleep disturbances, illness, or drug reaction. Depression that originates from physical illness usually abates once the physical illness is treated. Depression is symptomatic of a medical condition in about 10 percent to 15 percent of all cases. Known physical causes of depression include thyroid disease, adrenal gland disorders, hyperparathyroidism, diabetes, infectious diseases such as viral hepatitis, cancer, autoimmune disorders, vitamin and mineral deficiencies, and cancer (American Medical Association, 1998; O'Conner, 1997). Thus, clients who are dealing with depression should be referred for a medical checkup as an adjunct to counselling.

Current thinking suggests that it is the combination of factors that results in depression. For example, if people with a predisposition to depression experience stressful life crises, they may develop depression. Subsequently, their first depressive episode may stimulate changes in brain chemistry that leave them more vulnerable to further episodes, when even small stressful events can trigger depression (American Medical Association, 1998).

Counsellors can assist people who are depressed in a number of ways, including:

- helping them recognize and identify the symptoms of depression
- referring them for appropriate medical examination and treatment which might include medication or hospitalization
- helping them to develop coping strategies for dealing with stress
- counselling them for loss or grief
- assessing and managing suicide risk
- helping them develop cognitive/behavioural strategies for overcoming low self-esteem and other self-defeating thought patterns that often accompany depression
- supporting and understanding emotions
- providing family counselling to interrupt communication patterns that contribute to or escalate depression.

BIPOLAR DISORDER With bipolar illness, depression alternates with manic episodes. During manic periods people typically experience heightened energy, a euphoric mood, and a greatly increased sense of confidence, sometimes to the point of grandiosity. They may have sharpened and unusually creative thinking, along with a much decreased need for sleep. Or they may experience a flight of ideas (thoughts without logical connection). Although they may engage in increased goal-directed activities at work or school, they often engage in them without regard to the consequences, thus leading to irrational behaviour, such as uncontrolled buying sprees, sexual indiscretion, and foolish business investments (American Psychiatric Association, 1994; NIMH, 1998; Nicoli, 1988). Scott Simmie's recollection of his mindset when he was in the midst of the manic phase illustrates the irrationality of this state:

> Despite everything I'd been through, I was still convinced that I was in perfect health, that the real problem was the failure of others to recognize that something extraordinary and wonderful had happened to me. That I had been spiritually reborn. That my limitless potential had finally been free. (Simmie & Nunes, 2001:25)

Thus, it is very difficult, but not impossible, to persuade people to accept treatment, including hospitalization, during the manic phase of the illness. Supportive counsellors, family and friends may convince them to seek treatment; but in some cases, particularly where behaviour has become self-destructive or dangerous, involuntary hospitalization may be necessary.

Bipolar disorder usually begins in adolescence or early adulthood and continues throughout life. It is often not recognized as an illness, and people who have it may suffer needlessly for years or even decades. There is evidence that bipolar disorder is inherited (NIMH, 1998). Persons with untreated bipolar illness may experience devastating complications, including marital breakup, job loss, financial ruin, substance abuse, and suicide. However, almost everyone with bipolar illness can be helped through the use of medications such as lithium, which has demonstrated effectiveness in controlling both depression and mania. Bipolar disorder cannot be cured, but for most people treatment can keep the disease under control.

Anxiety Disorders

Anxiety disorders are characterized by higher than normal levels of fear, worry, tension, or anxiety about daily events. High anxiety may be present without apparent reason. Four serious anxiety disorders are obsessive-compulsive disorder (OCD), phobias, panic disorder, and post-traumatic stress disorder (PTSD).

OBSESSIVE-COMPULSIVE DISORDER (OCD) An obsessive-compulsive disorder involves recurrent, unwanted thoughts and conscious, ritualized, seemingly purposeless acts, such as counting the number of tiles on the ceiling or needing to wash one's hands repetitively. Behavioural techniques and medication have proved effective in treating this disorder.

PHOBIA A phobia is an irrational fear about particular events or objects. Phobias result in overwhelming anxiety in response to situations of little or no danger. Most people have phobias of one sort or another, such as fear of flying, heights, public speaking, or snakes. For the most part, people deal with their phobias through avoidance, which decreases the anxiety associated with the fear. Unfortunately, avoidance increases the fear of the particular object or situation. Treatment of phobias is necessary when they interfere with a person's capacity to lead a normal life. For example, agoraphobia (fear of open or public spaces) prevents people from leaving the safety of their homes. Treatment in such cases is essential to help clients overcome what would otherwise be severely restricted lives.

With systematic desensitization, persons with a phobia are first taught how to manage anxiety through relaxation. With the help of the counsellor, they construct a hierarchy of anxiety-provoking events associated with the phobia. Finally, they learn how to control their anxiety with progressively more difficult exposures to the anxiety-producing object or event. In addition, other specialized behavioural techniques, such as flooding, relaxation training, and pharmacologic (drug) treatment, may be necessary to relieve anxiety disorders.

PANIC DISORDER A panic disorder involves sudden attacks of terror and irrational fear, accompanied by an overwhelming sense of impending doom. During a panic attack, a person may experience symptoms such as an accelerated heart rate, sweating, shaking, shortness of breath, chest pain, and nausea, as well as a fear of dying or losing control (American

Psychiatric Association, 1994). Medication and psychotherapy have proved effective in treating this disorder.

POST-TRAUMATIC STRESS DISORDER (PTSD) PTSD symptoms develop following traumatic events, such as rape, assault, natural disasters (earthquakes, floods, etc.), war, torture, or automobile accident. Symptoms may occur immediately after the event, or they may be delayed by months or years (Nicoli, 1988). Recollections of the event result in disabling symptoms, such as emotional numbness; sleep disturbance (nightmares, difficulty sleeping); reliving the event; intense anxiety at exposure to cues that remind the person of the trauma; avoidance of activities, people, or conversations that arouse recall of the trauma; hypervigilance; and outbursts of anger (American Psychiatric Association, 1994; Nicoli, 1988). PTSD symptoms often dissipate within six months; but for some people, the symptoms may last years. Relaxation training and counselling are effective tools for treating this disorder.

EATING DISORDERS The two most common eating disorders, anorexia nervosa and bulimia, are most likely to affect adolescent and young adult women, with about 90 percent of all those afflicted coming from this group (NIMH, 1998; Nicoli, 1988; Cleghorn and Lee, 1991). Approximately 1 percent of adolescent girls develop anorexia nervosa (NIMH, 1998), and as many as 10 percent develop bulimic disorder (Nicoli, 1988). Eventually, half of those with anorexia will develop bulimia (NIMH, 1998). Eating disorders are difficult to treat because many people refuse to admit that they have a problem and resist treatment. Counsellors and family need to persuade those affected to seek treatment; but this can be hard, because people with these disorders may argue that their only problem is the "nagging" people in their lives. Because of the life-threatening nature of eating disorders, involuntary treatment or forced hospitalization may be necessary, particularly when there has been excessive and rapid weight loss, serious metabolic disturbances, and serious depression with a risk of suicide.

The National Eating Disorder Information Centre (NEDIC), a Toronto-based, non-profit organization offers this explanation on the cause of eating disorders:

> Eating disorders are caused by a combination of societal, individual, and family factors. They are a manifestation of complex underlying struggles with identity and self-concept, and of problems that often stem from traumatic experiences and patterns of socialization. Eating disorders are coping behaviours which provide the individual with an outlet for displacement of feelings or with a (false) sense of being in control. Common to all eating disorders is a pervasive underlying sense of powerlessness. (2005)

SOCIAL AND CULTURAL VARIABLES For most of recorded history, plumpness in women was deemed desirable and fashionable. During the last 50 years, particularly in Western cultures, women have been bombarded with media messages that promote slimness as the route to a successful and happy life. Societal emphasis on dieting, combined with the unrealistic body image of supermodels, has contributed to an obsessive preoccupation with body image and dieting (Abraham & Llewellyn-Jones, 1997). One study found that the top wish of a group of girls aged 11 to 17 was "to be thinner," while another survey discovered that girls were more afraid of becoming fat than they were of cancer, nuclear war, or losing their parents (Berg, 1997:13). Mothers and fathers who are overly concerned or critical about their daughters' weight and physical attractiveness may put the daughters at increased risk of developing an eating disorder. People pursuing professions or activities that emphasize thinness, such as modelling, dancing, or gymnastics, are more susceptible to the problem (Nicoli, 1988; NIMH, 1998).

ANOREXIA NERVOSA Anorexia nervosa occurs when people reject maintaining minimally healthy body weight. Driven by low self-esteem and an intense fear of gaining weight, people with anorexia use techniques such as purging (e.g., fasting, vomiting, taking laxatives) and excessive exercise to reduce body weight. Even though they may diet to the point of starvation and they look emaciated, they will still insist that they are too fat. Anorexia nervosa can be life threatening, and as many as 10 to 15 percent of sufferers die of the effects of prolonged starvation (Cleghorn & Lee, 1991; NIMH, 1998).

The symptoms of anorexia include excessive weight loss, belief that the body is fat, and continuation of dieting despite a lower than normal body weight, cessation of menstruation, obsession with food, eating in secret, obsessive exercise, and depression. People with anorexia are often perfectionists with superior athletic ability. There is some evidence to suggest that people with anorexia starve themselves in order to gain a sense of control in some area of their lives (NIMH, 1998).

Treating eating disorders requires a team approach consisting of physicians, counsellors, nutritionists, and family therapists. Group therapy may be a helpful adjunct to individual counselling to reduce isolation. Reframing and other methods for helping clients change their distorted and rigid thinking patterns may be extremely helpful (see Chapter 7). As well, antidepressant medications such as fluoxetine (Prozac) and imipramine may be used.

BULIMIA Bulimia occurs when people adopt a pattern of excessive overeating followed by vomiting or other purging behaviours to control their weight. Individuals with bulimia usually binge and purge in secret. Typically, persons with bulimia feel isolated, and they deal with their problems through overeating; then, feeling guilty and disgusted, they purge. Because they may have normal or even above normal body weight, they often hide their problem from others for years. By the time they finally seek treatment (sometimes not until in their 30s or 40s), their eating disorder is firmly entrenched and difficult to treat.

The symptoms of bulimia may include cessation of menstruation; obsession with food; eating in secret; obsessive exercise; serious depression; binging, vomiting, and other purging activities (often with the use of drugs); and disappearances in the bathroom for long periods of time. In addition, as a result of excessive vomiting, the outer layer of the teeth can be worn down, scarring may be present on the backs of hands (from pushing fingers down the throat to induce vomiting), the esophagus may become inflamed, and glands near the cheeks can become swollen (NIMH, 1998). Persons with bulimia are at increased risk for substance abuse and suicidal behaviour.

Treating Mental Disorders

Ideally, persons with mental disorders should be dealt with through a team approach that includes psychiatrists, psychiatric social workers, social service workers, counsellors, occupational counsellors, nurses, and volunteers. As a team, they share common objectives:

1. motivating clients to seek and remain in treatment and, in severe cases, arranging for involuntary treatment

2. supporting clients to return or remain in the community (helping with housing, life skills training, employment, and career counselling, assistance with the negative symptoms of the illness)

3. assisting clients in dealing with the challenges of medication (e.g., compliance, side effects)

4. educating clients and their families about the nature of their disorder

5. assisting clients in dealing with the consequences of mental disorders including stigma

6. helping clients and their families develop and use support systems, including self-help groups and professionals

Psychiatric Medications

The 1950s witnessed the introduction of powerful chemicals that have resulted in dramatic advances in the treatment of mental disorders. Medications have enabled the vast majority of persons with mental disorders to be treated and managed in the community and not locked up in psychiatric facilities. Medications may be able to control the symptoms of mental disorders, such as hallucinations, but they do not cure the illness. They can increase the effectiveness of counselling by increasing the capacity of the clients to hear and respond. Many people need to take medication to control their illness for the rest of their lives.

There may be wide variations in people's reaction to medication (e.g., some respond better to one than another, some need bigger doses, some experience side effects and others do not). Medications may result in unwanted side effects, such as tardive dyskinesia (characterized by uncontrollable movement), drowsiness, weakness, tremors, slurred speech, sleep disturbances, sexual dysfunction, increased heart rate, dry mouth, and headaches (Walsh & Bentley, 2002). Some clients may stop taking medication in order to avoid these side effects.

Psychotropic medications alter the neurotransmission processes, the chemical/electrical system of the brain. There are roughly five categories of psychotropic medication (Walsh & Bentley, 2002) as outlined below.

Antipsychotic (or neuroleptic) medications, such as loxapine, haloperidol, clozapine, and risperidone, are used to treat illnesses such as schizophrenia. Antipsychotic medications may be taken daily, but some medications are available through injection (once or twice a month). Injections are particularly useful for ensuring that clients take the medication. Newer antipsychotic medications (e.g., clozapine, risperidone, olanzapine, quetiapine), also known as novel or atypical antipsychotics, do not have the same level of adverse side effects as some of the older (conventional) drugs (e.g., chlorpromazine, thorazine, haldol). Antipsychotic medications have enabled most persons with schizophrenia to be treated in the community rather than in institutions, the primary method used for the first half of the 20th century.

Antidepressant medications, such as Prozac, Paxil, and Zoloft, are used to help people deal with serious depression. As well, some are used to treat certain anxiety disorders (Walsh & Bentley, 2002).

Mood-Stabilizing medications, such as lithium carbonate, are used to control the manic symptoms of bipolar disorder.

Antianxiety medications, such as valium and librium, are used to control serious and persistent anxiety, phobias, and panic attacks.

Psychostimulants such as ritalin and cylert are used to treat attention-deficit hyperactivity disorder (ADHD).

CONVERSATION 9.2

WHEN CLIENTS DON'T TAKE THEIR MEDICATION

STUDENT: My practicum is at an inner-city drop-in centre for persons with mental disorders. One of the big problems we face is clients who don't take their drugs. They end up relapsing or going to the emergency room on a regular basis.

TEACHER: I know when you say "drugs" you're referring to their prescribed medication. Since many clients use street drugs, it's better to use the term medication to keep the distinction separate. As you suggest, failure to take prescribed medication is an enormous problem. I read recently that approximately 50 percent of persons with schizophrenia are noncompliant, and there is a high correlation between medication non-compliance, violence, and suicide, particularly when there is a co-occurring substance abuse problem. (Leo, Jassal, & Bakhai, 2005). Non-compliance can mean not taking medication at all, not using it correctly, or mixing it with street drugs.

STUDENT: So, what can we do about it?

TEACHER: First, I think it is important to understand factors that contribute to clients not taking their medications, such as adverse side effects, medication costs, or the complex nature of their medication regimen. Their illness may also cause a lack of will or motivation to take their medication. Some may simply be unable to understand or follow the routines. Moreover, clients who are paranoid might fear they are being poisoned or controlled by medication and thus be unwilling to comply. And clients who are manic may prefer to stay that way.

STUDENT: I think a big problem is homelessness and isolation.

TEACHER: Yes, clients will tend to do better if they live in supportive environment. And for some, this means a structured and supervised setting, such as a mental health boarding home, where professional help and encouragement are available. When clients resist medication because of adverse side effects, it is crucial that this be discussed with their doctors, since side effects can often be addressed with alternative medications, particularly if the client is taking some of the older medications. Long-acting injections are another useful alternative.

STUDENT: What can counsellors do?

TEACHER: They can make sure that clients have access to adequate information about their illness and its treatment. They can also assist clients in developing and using routines to manage their medication. Moreover, counselling can help clients resolve ambivalence about using medication (for example, by providing information about the potential consequences of prolonged noncompliance and the benefits of compliance). As well, counsellors may be able to help family members with information and ideas on how they can support medication compliance. And, as you said, it is important to assist clients to find supportive housing.

SUICIDE COUNSELLING

The American Association of Suicidology (1998) describes suicide as a permanent solution to a temporary, treatable problem. Suicide intervention is crisis counselling that requires counsellors to assess the immediate risk and intervene to prevent their clients from completing the suicide. This challenges counsellors to rapidly establish a supportive relationship. Active listening skills are crucial; for unless suicidal clients can be convinced that the counsellor is genuinely interested in their welfare, they may cut off communication. In Canada, it is not illegal to attempt suicide, but aiding or abetting suicide is an illegal act.

Warning Signs and Risk Assessment

While there is no absolute way of predicting that a person will attempt suicide, there are some important warning signs: threats of suicide, history of attempts, methodology, stressors, personality factors, alcoholism, social supports, and gender and demographic variables (Center for Suicide Prevention, 2005; Saddock & Saddock, 2004; American Association of Suicidology, 1998; Harvard Medical School, 1996; San Francisco Suicide Prevention Institute, 1998).

Threats of Suicide

Clients who talk about suicide or who appear preoccupied with death and dying should be considered at risk. Research has shown that 8 out of 10 suicidal persons give some sign of

TABLE 9.4	Suicide: Canadian Facts

- In Canada, the known annual death rate from suicide is 21 per 100,000 for males and 6.8 per 100,000 for females.
- For males 20–24 years old, the suicide rate is 33 per 100,000.
- For males over 65 years old, the suicide rate is 30 per 100,000.
- In 1999, suicide was the leading cause of death for Aboriginals up to age 44.
- Suicide accounts for 38% of the deaths among Aboriginal youth.
- Men commit suicide at a rate of four times that of women, whereas women attempt suicide at a rate of four times that of men.
- Men are more likely than women to use lethal methods (e.g., guns, hanging).
- Physical illness is estimated to be a contributing factor in up to 50 percent of suicides.
- Approximately 40 percent of people who commit suicide have made a previous attempt.
- Some drugs can produce depression that leads to suicide.
- The death rate from suicide is higher that the death rate from motor vehicle accidents.
- The suicide rate for persons married with children is about half of that of never-married, single people.
- The suicide rate for persons under psychiatric care is 3 to 12 times that of nonpatients. Key risk factors are substance abuse, depression, and schizophrenia.
- Suicide is higher among persons who are unemployed, and it increases with economic recessions and depressions.
- High risk groups are male physicians (2–3 times that of the general male populations), dentists, musicians, law enforcement officers, lawyers, and insurance agents.

Sources: (Statistics Canada, 2005c; Center for Suicide Prevention, 2005; Saddock and Saddock, 2004;; Health Canada, 2003; American Association of Suicidology, 1998; Cleghorn & Lee, 1991)

their intentions. Sometimes the clues are clear, such as clients directly threatening to take their lives. At other times, there are only hints of suicidal objectives, such as giving away their possessions, making final arrangements (e.g., expressing wishes for their funeral, writing a will), or involving themselves in increased risk-taking behaviour. Threats of suicide and other warning signs are a cry for help, and counsellors should take them seriously.

History of Suicide Attempts

About 30 to 40 percent of people who commit suicide have made a previous attempt, and about 10 percent of those who attempt suicide succeed within ten years. But eight to ten times as many people make suicide attempts as those who complete suicide (Cleghorn & Lee, 1991, (Harvard Medical School, 1998). However, it is likely that the number of completed suicides is underreported, since in some cases, what appear to be accidental deaths are, in fact, suicides.

Methodology

As a rule, clients who have a specific plan and a lethal method for taking their lives are at greater risk than those who do not have such a plan and method. Moreover, the more developed the plan and the greater the potential lethality of the proposed method, the greater the risk. For example, "hanging, shooting and jumping from high places are serious, mostly successful suicide methods" (Othmer & Othmer, 1989:267).

Certain, drugs, such as antipsychotic medication, sleeping pills, antidepressants, and analgesics (aspirin), are all potential overdose drugs, especially when taken in combination with other drugs. Roberts reports that, as a rule, a lethal dose is ten times the normal dose; but in combination with alcohol, as little as half the normal dose can result in death (1991:58).

Stress

Clients who are currently coping with significant stress, such as death, divorce, loss of job, money, status, self-confidence, self-esteem, or spiritual crisis, are at greater risk. As well, recent medical illness may be a factor. About two-thirds of the clients who commit suicide have seen a doctor shortly before their death (Hirschfeld & Russell, 1997).

Personality Changes

Counsellors should explore whether there have been recent and drastic changes in their clients' usual manner. Changes such as social withdrawal, sudden changes in their moods, loss of interest in activities that previously gave them pleasure (sex, work, friends, family, job, hobbies), increased substance abuse, changes in sleep patterns, and loss of interest in personal appearance ought to be closely assessed. As well, counsellors should look for signs of depression, apathy, anxiety, and general pessimism about the future. Not all suicidal people are depressed, nor are all depressed people suicidal. Some people contemplating suicide may seem at peace, even euphoric. However, depression is a signal to counsellors to assess suicide risk.

Alcohol Addiction

Research has shown that persons who are addicted to alcohol have an increased risk of suicide compared with the general population. As many as 15 percent of people addicted to alcohol commit suicide; and the suicide rate for people who are heroin dependent is 20 times that of the general population (Saddock & Saddock, 2004:391-392).

Gender and Demographic Differences

Women attempt suicide three or four times as often as men, but men tend to use more lethal methods and account for 80 percent of all completed suicides. One study (cited in Cleghorn & Lee, 1991:204) identified high-risk groups as those with a mental disorder, young people, seniors, Aboriginal people, and those in prison. They highlighted the risk for males aged 15 to 24 who often choose violent means to end their lives.

A study by Devons (1996) revealed that the suicide rate for elderly people was the highest of all age groups, perhaps as high as double the rate in the general population. She suggests that the profound losses associated with aging leave elderly persons vulnerable, but early identification of depression can lead to appropriate treatment intervention.

Counselling Intervention

Suicide prevention and crisis intervention require that counsellors be aware of the dangerous myths about suicide:

Myth 1: Suicide occurs without warning signs.

Myth 2: People who talk about suicide aren't serious about killing themselves.

Myth 3: Bringing up the topic promotes suicide as an option.

Myth 4: People who attempt suicide are just trying to get attention.

Myth 5: The best response to a threat is to say, "Go ahead." (Devons, 1996)

Assess the Risk

Although no counsellor can determine with certainty whether a client will try to commit suicide, knowing about and exploring risk factors is essential for intelligent intervention. As described earlier in this section, some of the key risk factors that counsellors should consider include past attempts, current mental and physical status, the presence of a viable plan, the means to kill oneself, talk about suicide, personal losses, efforts to put one's affairs in order, and substance abuse. Counsellors need to explore these variables in a calm, nonjudgmental manner, without moralizing, and offer support and empathy throughout the process.

To assess the potential lethality of a plan, counsellors should investigate factors such as the lethal potential of the suicide method (e.g., time between attempt and likely death), the extent to which the person has access to the means (e.g., presence of a gun or sleeping pills), and possibility of discovery and access to rescue.

Ask about Suicide Intent

Counsellors need to overcome any reluctance to ask clients if they have considered suicide as a solution to their problems. Roberts (1991) reports that there is clinical and empirical evidence to strongly support the value of direct inquiry. Asking about suicide will not plant the idea in the client's mind. In fact, bringing the issue into the open can relieve clients of the stress of trying to hide their intent, whereas avoiding the topic increases feelings of isolation and hopelessness in the suicidal person. As Roberts concludes, "Critically, direct inquiry gives the potentially suicidal individual permission to discuss feelings that may have seemed virtually undiscussable. Direct inquiry can bring great relief to the client—at last the inner battle of life or death can be openly discussed and explored in a safe, supportive, and accepting climate" (59).

Moreover, a counsellor should always take seriously any veiled or vague comment about suicide. When clients make statements such as "Sometimes life doesn't seem worth it," a follow-up question such as "Have you thought about killing yourself?" should be used to put the issue on the discussion table.

Crisis Intervention

Counsellors have a responsibility to prevent suicide once the client makes this intent known. Crisis intervention strategies may include the following.

1. Removing the means of suicide from the client (e.g., flushing pills down the toilet, confiscating guns). This prevents clients from acting impulsively.

2. Negotiating a "no-suicide" contract. This involves an agreement that the client will not hurt him- or herself until the next contact with the counsellor, when a new contract may be negotiated. This plan should be very concrete and detailed, outlining exactly what the client will be doing, hour by hour, until the next contact with the counsellor.

3. Emergency hospitalization. All jurisdictions have mental health legislation that defines when clients can be hospitalized. Typically, imminent risk for suicide is a compelling reason for involuntary hospitalization.

4. Future linkage. This involves setting up short- and long-term goals that give the client something to anticipate. Through this process the client is diverted from the present crisis to thinking about an improved future.

5. Decreasing isolation and withdrawal. For many clients, talking about their problems with a counsellor is sufficient to reverse the drive to suicide. In addition, counsellors should make every effort to recruit capable family members or friends to be with the client through the crisis phase. For their support to be helpful, the client must perceive these people as credible and supportive. They may need to be available on a 24-hour-a-day basis during the crisis period.

6. Treatment of coexisting problems, including addictions and mental disorders.

7. Management of problems such as poverty, unemployment, and uncontrolled pain.

8. Initiatives to increase self-esteem.

COUNSELLING HIV-POSITIVE CLIENTS AND CLIENTS WITH AIDS

HIV is the acronym for **Human Immunodeficiency Virus,** a virus that attacks the immune system, weakening its ability to fight off infections. People may have the virus and not be aware of it, and they may have no symptoms for as long as 5 to 15 years. HIV is spread when HIV-infected blood, semen, or vaginal fluids enter the body of another person. Sharing dirty needles (through drug taking, tattooing, body piercing, etc.) and unprotected sex (anal, vaginal, and oral) are considered high-risk behaviours. But HIV cannot be transmitted by hugging or kissing, nor can it be transmitted through the air by coughing or sneezing. It also cannot be transmitted through water, food, or insect bites.

AIDS is the acronym for **Acquired Immune Deficiency Syndrome**, the syndrome caused by HIV infection, which results in a number of different illnesses and opportunistic infections, such as karposi sarcoma (cancer) and thrush. AIDS is a fatal disease, and there is currently neither cure nor vaccination for it. HIV infection becomes AIDS when a person's immune system is seriously compromised and the immune system's T-cell count drops below 200.

Since the discovery of AIDS in 1981 and the first reported case in Canada in 1982, remarkable progress in its treatment has been realized in the Western world. Aggressive treatment routines using antiretroviral therapies (HIV is a retrovirus) have resulted in a decline in the number of AIDS-related deaths in the industrialized nations; but a cure and a vaccine for the disease are not expected in the immediate future. Meanwhile, in poorer nations, particularly those in Africa, where communities are ill equipped to handle the massive costs of treatment, the ravage of AIDS continues unabated. According to Health Canada (2005), there have been an estimated 20 000 cases of AIDS reported and 56 000 people living with HIV.

TABLE 9.5	Global AIDS Facts and Statistics for 2004

- 40–45 million people were living with HIV/AIDS, including over 2 million children.
- 5–6 million people were newly infected with HIV in 2004.
- Over 3 million people died from AIDS in 2004.
- More than 8000 people per day die from AIDS.
- AIDS has left more than 15 million orphans.
- Sub-Saharan Africa is the worst affected area, but the epidemic in Asia (particularly China) is growing quickly.
- Social norms and ignorance about protection have put the women of many countries at risk; for them, choosing to abstain or have safer sex is not an option.

Source: United Nations, 2004

Prevention and Testing

Prevention of HIV infection is the best way of controlling the AIDS epidemic. Counsellors can play a significant role in educating target populations to prevent new HIV infections.

Testing is an important first step. But some clients are reluctant to be tested. In part, this may arise from their mistaken belief that there is nothing they can do about positive results. They may fear (often justifiably) that an HIV-positive diagnosis may lead others to devalue and oppress them. In addition, fears about homophobia may lead individuals to isolate themselves from services that could provide information. But educating clients and the public about new treatments and the importance of early intervention may help to overcome their aversion to being tested.

In some jurisdictions HIV-positive test results must be reported. As a result, people may resist testing because they fear systematic discrimination. But when anonymous testing is available, the anonymity can be used to encourage people to take the test. Rapid testing with results in as little as 15 minutes is useful for testing people who are highly anxious. These tests have high reliability, but they are always confirmed later with more standard tests, such as a Western Blot test.

The primary preventive goal for counsellors is to educate clients to abandon high-risk behaviours, such as unprotected sex and needle sharing. This goal may involve initiatives to help clients deal with barriers to making changes (e.g., reluctance of partners to use condoms, fatalistic attitudes). A second counselling goal is to help clients resolve reluctance or ambivalence about taking an HIV test by exploring the advantages of testing. For example, counsellors might reframe the test as an opportunity to achieve peace of mind if it shows the client has no HIV infection. Counsellors can also inform clients that an HIV-positive diagnosis puts them in a better position to take advantage of new treatments and allows them to direct their focus to nutrition and wellness in order to keep their immune systems strong. They need to know that current AIDS therapies enable clients to prolong their lives.

Counselling Interventions

Awaiting test results is an anxious time for most clients. Counsellors may effectively use this period to help clients explore the meaning they attribute to the results. In the process, they need to support client feelings and fears.

In addition, client reactions to testing positive may vary. Predictably, most clients who test negative experience relief. At this time, counsellors may take advantage of the opportunity to educate these clients about appropriate preventive routines. But when the results are positive, some clients are completely shocked, whereas others see the results as confirmation of what they already knew. Some see the diagnosis as a death sentence, while others experience denial and act as though the results mean nothing (Kain, 1996). Clients who receive the results as death sentences need immediate help to deal with the psychological shock of receiving the diagnosis. At this point, counsellors should encourage clients to explore and cope with complex feelings, which might include guilt, anger, fear, despair, and thoughts of suicide. As well, they need to be educated regarding contemporary therapies which have successfully kept AIDS at bay for many people. Support and education about the realities of the disease can help them reach a more rational understanding about their future. In the 1980s, counselling focused on assisting clients in dealing with the shock of their diagnosis and their impending death. Now that an HIV-positive diagnosis no longer means imminent death in the industrialized world, counselling goals have shifted to helping people live with the disease.

But a particularly difficult situation arises when counselling HIV-positive men who have engaged in high-risk homosexual activity while remaining in heterosexual relationships. They need considerable support and counselling to deal with both the trauma of their diagnosis and the unique challenge of telling their partners.

But in all AIDS situations, an important counselling goal is to help clients sustain health. For example, counsellors can work with clients to ensure that they have access to the latest information regarding the disease and its treatment. This may mean referral to appropriate physicians who specialize in the area. Or it may mean helping clients use databases of information so that they make intelligent choices about their physical and psychological health and wellness, as well as that of others in their lives. Counsellors can support clients while they adopt new healthy practices, including aggressive treatment that bolsters their immune systems. They should also promote lifestyle practices that prevent the spread of infection.

Spirituality

Frequently, clients living with HIV-positive diagnosis and AIDS raise spiritual questions regarding the meaning of life and life after death. Client spiritual values and beliefs are legitimate considerations in the counselling process (Kelly, 1995), and effective counsellors must be open and nonjudgmental when dealing with spirituality issues. It requires that they understand the different ways that individual clients might define and approach religion and spirituality. Kain underscores the importance of spirituality in counselling persons with HIV:

> We need to remember that many people living with HIV disease may feel alienated from all sources of spiritual guidance; the counseling session may be the only place where they feel comfortable enough to risk elaborating on issues of faith. At times we may be surprised to find that when we provide clients with the room to pursue spiritual matters accelerated psychological growth often occurs. (1996:117).

But keep in mind that counselling is not an opportunity for counsellors to convert clients to their religious beliefs. Instead, counsellors must be open to the wide range of spiritual paths that individuals choose. This may be an appropriate time to refer them to an appropriate spiritual leader or teacher.

Counselling Goals

Specific counselling activities and goals for working with clients who are HIV positive or have AIDS include the following:

- providing empathy and support to help clients deal with their fears and anxieties while awaiting test results
- helping clients deal with the feelings associated with a positive test and living with the disease
- helping clients deal with the complex challenges of disclosure (to family, friends, sexual partners)
- assisting clients in dealing with issues of discrimination
- supporting clients to make lifestyle adjustments and to prevent spread of the infection, including adopting safe sex practices
- helping clients deal with the challenges of dating and maintaining relationships
- educating clients about preventive treatment, personal health, nutrition, and wellness issues
- working with families to help them understand how to create a safe and supportive environment for people who are HIV positive
- helping caregivers (i.e., partners, family, friends) deal with their emotional and physical stress
- helping clients meet basic needs (living arrangements, finances, medical, transportation)
- helping clients with sexual identify confusion issues
- supporting couples where one partner is HIV-positive and one is negative
- linking clients to appropriate support groups and community services
- assisting clients in dealing with the feelings associated with this disease, such as fear of death, depression, and fear of being abandoned
- grief counselling to help clients cope with the decline and loss of significant others who have AIDS
- helping clients find meaning and purpose to their lives
- supporting clients who are dying (e.g., helping with funeral arrangements, saying goodbye to significant others, exploring the process and meaning of death, hospice care, wills, pain control)
- referring clients to appropriate religious organizations for spiritual support

In addition, counsellors working with people with AIDS need to make sure that they don't neglect their own needs for emotional support and wellness. For example, those who work in hospice settings may have to deal with multiple deaths each week. These counsellors need to be able to recognize and deal with their own grief when their clients die. Thus, support and consultation with colleagues is essential for dealing with the feelings and stress of counselling people with AIDS.

SUMMARY

Job loss or unemployment can have a significant impact on a person's well-being. Issues of self-esteem and identity and financial consequences can lead to increased stress and mental health problems. Employment counsellors deliver service in four major areas: (1) job loss counselling, (2) career counselling, (3) job search skills, and (4) life skills counselling.

Modern job search methods differ significantly from traditional strategies. Modern strategies focus on a targeted approach to particular careers and employers with customized résumés and use of the hidden job market through networking. Electronic technology has necessitated that clients become increasingly familiar with new strategies for managing their job and career search.

The job club method is a group approach that provides support, job search skills training, and materials and supplies necessary to complete a successful job hunt. Job clubs provide participants with phones, computers, photocopying, stationery, and daily newspapers and other sources of job leads.

The last 40 years have witnessed dramatic shifts in the delivery of services to people with mental disorders. Deinstitutionalization, propelled by the introduction of new medications, has enabled the majority of people with mental disorders to live in the community.

DSM-IV is the Diagnostic and Statistical Manual of Mental Disorders published by the American Psychiatric Association. Psychologists, psychiatrists, and other psychotherapists use it to classify and diagnose mental disorders. It uses a multiaxial system—a comprehensive evaluation system that includes not only mental disorders, but also medical conditions, psychosocial and environmental problems, and an assessment of a client's overall level of functioning.

Schizophrenia is a serious mental illness that results in a range of symptoms, including hallucinations, delusions, disordered thinking, and social isolation. There may be wide variations in the symptoms people experience.

The two most severe mood or affective disorders are major depression and bipolar illness. Major depression affects as many as one in four women and one in ten men in North America. The defining symptoms of depression include feelings of hopelessness and difficulty sleeping, thinking, or concentrating, as well as thoughts of suicide.

Anxiety disorders are characterized by greater than normal levels of fear, worry, tension, or anxiety about daily events, or anxiety without apparent reason. Four serious anxiety disorders are obsessive-compulsive disorder (OCD), phobias, panic disorder, and post-traumatic stress disorder (PTSD).

The two most common eating disorders, anorexia nervosa and bulimia, are most likely to affect adolescent and young adult women. Eating disorders can be life threatening, and involuntary hospitalization is necessary in some cases.

There is no certain way to predict that a person may attempt or complete suicide, but certain warning signs and risk factors can be considered. The principal risk factors include past attempts, current mental and physical status, the presence of a viable plan and the means to kill oneself, talk about suicide, personal losses, efforts to put one's affairs in order, and substance abuse.

Counsellors have important educational roles to play in preventing the spread of HIV infection. Counsellors can help by promoting practices such as safer sex, particularly the use of condoms, and the use of clean needles for injection drug users. The focus of counselling people with HIV and AIDS is to support them in adopting healthy practices, including aggressive medical treatment that bolsters their immune systems. As well, counsellors need to insure that they pay attention to their own wellness when working with HIV/AIDS populations.

EXERCISES

1. If you were responsible for defining mental illness, how would you define it?
2. Explore how you and your family/friends might react to the following events:
   a. you or someone else has a mental illness
   b. learning that you or a member of your family is HIV positive or has AIDS
   c. losing a job
   d. you or someone in your family has an eating disorder
   e. someone you know commits suicide
3. For what reasons might a person stop taking psychiatric medication?
4. Scan magazines to identify feature stories highlighting dieting. Discuss how these might impact self-image and behaviour.
5. Examine your own attitudes and beliefs about mental illness. How have your values been shaped by personal experience? By the media?
6. Do you believe that it is ethically acceptable for counsellors to openly explore with their clients without judgment their clients' desire to kill themselves? Should counsellors be required to prevent clients in advanced stages of AIDS or other fatal illnesses from killing themselves?
7. Review your personal experiences with death and dying. How might these experiences help or hinder your work if you were counselling clients with AIDS?
8. How might you respond to a client who says, "I'm not going to get AIDS because I'm not gay."
9. Your client is HIV positive but continues to engage in unsafe practices. Explore your ethical, moral, and legal responsibilities—for example, the dilemma of whether to reveal the client's HIV status to a known sexual partner. What if this client is a prostitute?

WEBLINKS

The Ontario Centre for Addiction and Mental Health has resources on addiction and mental health issues (formerly the Clark Institute of Psychiatry and Addictions Research Foundation):
www.camh.net/mental_health/index.html

Canadian based website providing information, training, and research on suicide:
http://suicideinfo.ca/

Canada WorkInfoNet provides career, education, and labour market information:
www.workinfonet.ca/cwn/english/main.html

Comprehensive reports and information on mental illness in Canada:
www.phac-aspc.gc.ca/publicat/miic-mmac/chap_1_e.html

Canadian Mental Health Association website with fact and information sheets on a wide range of mental health issues:
www.cmha.pe.ca/bins/index.asp?lang=1

chapter ten

Cultural Diversity: The Future of Counselling

PREVIEW

After reading this chapter you should be able to:

- Describe the diverse nature of Canadian society.
- Define worldview and its importance to counselling.
- Explain why realities such as oppression and racism impact counselling.
- Explain the key elements and issues of cross-cultural understanding and multicultural counselling.
- Demonstrate knowledge of skills and attitudes necessary for working with First Nations people.
- Explain the importance of traditional healing practices.
- Describe the importance of spirituality in counselling.

THE CANADIAN CONTEXT

No matter how similar we are, there will be differences. No matter how different we are,
there will be similarities.
—Pedersen, 2001:18

Canada's arts and community celebrations mirror the rich diversity of its citizens. Throughout the year, festivals, religious ceremonies, and various cultural events provide people with opportunities to honour their own heritage and take part in the ceremonies of others. But this has not always been the case. Until 1968, immigrants to Canada were largely of European ancestry. The Immigration Act of 1968 replaced criteria for entry that were perceived as racist. As a result, the ratio of visible minorities among immigrants changed from less than one percent (pre-1960) to more than 75 per cent today. These changing demographics have challenged all institutions, including social service providers, to reexamine their structures, philosophies, and service delivery methodologies. Even the theoretical basis of counselling practice is under pressure to become more culturally sensitive to the diverse worldviews of the client population.

Immigration policies in the latter part of the twentieth century increased the need for counsellors to develop skills to relate to increasingly heterogeneous caseloads. In fact, typical counselling caseloads in Canada are characterized by diversity in terms of culture, age, race, gender, and sexual orientation. It is a certainty that counsellors will work with clients who have different cultural backgrounds than their own. The 2001 Canadian Census reveals the rich ethnic mix of the Canadian population. Table 10.1 shows that among Canada's 30 million people, more than 5 million speak a mother tongue other than English or French. While culture is defined by many variables, including religion, dress, customs, and food, language is a major defining variable. Table 10.2 shows that almost 20 percent of Canada's people were born in another country and immigrated to Canada. However, there are significant regional differences. For example, in British Columbia, 33 percent of the population is immigrant, and 37 percent of the Vancouver area is immigrant.

The Immigration and Refugee Protection Act recognizes six categories of immigrants: skilled workers, business class, provincially nominated, family class, international adoption, and refugees. Skilled workers qualify based on education, skills, and work experience. The business class includes entrepreneurs and investors. Provincially nominated immigrants fill regional labour shortages. Family class immigrants are those sponsored by close relatives. International adoption allows Canadians to adopt foreign children. And a refugee claimant is one who is seeking protection as defined by the United Nations' Geneva Convention Relating to the Status of Refugees.

Canada and the United States

Comparisons of Canadian internal approaches to ethnic relations with the United States often suggest that the American "melting pot" contrasts with the Canadian "cultural mosaic." The assumption is that the United States promotes integration of cultures whereas Canadians encourage preservation of ethnic culture. However, studies have shown that the differences between the two countries are not as distinct as the two models suggest (Isajiw, 1999). In fact, the US more closely resembles the Canadian mosaic metaphor than the melting pot. In both countries, the tendency is for ethnic groups to retain their distinct individual identity. Of course, each culture contributes to the national identity and is in turn

TABLE 10.1	Population by Mother Tongue, 2001 Census, Canada
Total Population	29 639 035
English	17 352 315
French	6 703 325
Non-official languages	5 202 245
Chinese	853 745
Italian	469 485
German	438 080
Polish	208 375
Spanish	245 495
Portuguese	213 815
Punjabi	271 220
Ukrainian	148 085
Arabic	199 940
Dutch	128 670
Philipino	174 060
Greek	120 360
Vietnamese	122 055
Cree	72 885
Inuktitut (Eskimo)	29 010
Other non-official languages	1 506 965

Source: Statistics Canada, 2001a. Adapted from the Statistics Canada website <www.statcan.ca/>.

subject to its influence. One clear example is the extent to which the non-Asian population in North America celebrates the Chinese New Year.

Nevertheless, Isajiw (1999) highlights one important difference in race relations between Canada and the US:

> In the US the largest groups setting priorities for ethnic relations are Blacks, now called Afro-Americans, and the Hispanics, mainly immigrants from Latin America, particularly Mexico. In Canada, the two main groups that set priorities are, above all, the French of Quebec, and the Native Peoples. (58)

In Canada, First Nations claims for self-government and territorial rights have reached a much higher profile than in the US. In addition, French Canadian struggles for cultural equality and preservation of their language parallel those of Hispanics in the US. For French Canadians, language has become the principal battleground for preserving their cultural heritage; however, the issue of Quebec separation from Canada continues to remain important. Increases in Asian immigration to Canada have also greatly impacted the cultural mix

TABLE 10.2	Immigrant Population by Place of Birth and Period of Immigration, 2001 Census, Canada
Place of Birth	**Total—Immigrant Population**
All countries	5 448 480
Southern Europe	715 370
United Kingdom	606 000
Eastern Asia	730 600
Northern and Western Europe	494 825
Eastern Europe	471 365
South-east Asia	469 105
Southern Asia	503 895
Caribbean and Bermuda	294 050
Central and South America	304 650
United States	237 920
Africa	282 600
West-central Asia and the Middle East	285 585
Oceania and Other	52 525

Source: Statistics Canada, 2001b. Adapted from the Statistics Canada website <www.statcan.ca/>.

of many areas, particularly large urban centres such as Vancouver, Toronto, and Montreal. Isajiw (1999) suggests that substantial increases in immigration has resulted in tension:

> Yet, the mood in the country appears to be an uneasy balance between an understanding and acceptance of the immigrants and feelings of suspicion and even moderate hostility towards them and towards minority ethnic groups in general. A factor in this mood is a degree of racist feeling against the predominately non-white immigrants. (93)

As well, economic stressors, including company downsizing and consequent unemployment, can result in the scapegoating of immigrants and minorities for societal problems.

Ethnic Minorities and Counselling

Capuzzi and Gross (2001) report that research has demonstrated that ethnic minority clients do not seek help from mainstream counselling agencies except in emergency situations. In addition, they are typically not satisfied with the outcomes of counselling and "may distrust the counseling experience which may be viewed as intrusive, objectifying, and dehumanizing" (417). "Overlooking client strengths, misreading nonverbal communication, and misunderstanding family dynamics are among the most common errors made in cross-cultural helping. Behaviours motivated by religion and spirituality, family obligation, and sex roles are often misunderstood" (Sheafor & Horejsi 2006:177).

Reviewing some of the literature, Ruskin and Beiser (1998) conclude that Asians are more likely to avoid seeking mental health services because of the fear of the possible stigma. They are also less likely to accept referrals for assistance and typically terminate service more prematurely than Caucasians. This is not surprising, given Ivey's (1995) observation that "traditional counseling and therapy theory are White, male, Eurocentric, and middle-class in origin and practice" (p. 55).

A Canadian study reached this conclusion:

> Ethnic groups in Canada avoid the mental health system because they feel that barriers impeding access to appropriate services are often insurmountable. They also feel that, even if they sometimes succeed in overcoming barriers, the treatment they receive is inappropriate or ineffective... Large cultural groups who have been in Canada for generations also feel disenfranchised from care. (Canadian Task Force, 1988:37)

In addition, ethnic groups may differ in their expectations of counselling. While Western-trained counsellors may favour more passive approaches that empower clients to develop solutions to problems, other cultures may expect that the helper will be more active and give them direct answers.

Barriers

A review of the literature (Turner & Turner, 2000; Sue & Sue, 1999) suggests a number of barriers and recurrent themes that prevent culturally sensitive practice from being the norm:

1. Ignorance regarding the "underlying philosophy, structural, and technological alterations" that are necessary.
2. Inability or reluctance to develop agency services from a "one-size fits all" approach to one founded on respect for multicultural diversity.
3. Failure of professionals to recognize, accept, and honour cultural diversity.
4. Lack of counsellor self-awareness regarding how their cultural values and socialization impact their practice.
5. Evidence that counsellors do not invest equal time and energy to their work with minority group clients.
6. Failure of training programs to adequately address ethnic issues.

CROSS-CULTURAL UNDERSTANDING

Worldview

Worldview is the looking glass through which clients see the world. Dodd (1995) describes worldview as:

> ...a belief system about the nature of the universe, its perceived effect on human behaviour, and one's place in the universe. Worldview is a fundamental core set of assumptions explaining cultural forces, the nature of humankind, the nature of good and evil, luck, fate, spirits, the power of significant others, the role of time, and the nature of our physical and natural resources. (105)

Because the worldviews of counsellors and their clients may involve different belief systems based on different assumptions and explanations, communication misunderstandings can easily occur. Counsellors may, for example, encounter clients whose essential worldview is fatalistic (i.e., they believe that they have little control over what happens to them and that luck is the primary factor governing their fate). This fatalism has profound implications for counselling and may serve to explain (at least partially) why some clients persist with passivity and pessimism.

Moreover, culture is not an adjunct to counselling. It is not "something to be gotten over or gotten around in order to get on with the real business" (Ruskin & Beiser, 1998:438). Instead, it provides the essential context for understanding and responding to clients. Counsellors need to understand how cultural origin influences client behaviour and worldview. Similarly, they need to be aware of how their own cultural past influences their assumptions and responses. Moreover, counsellors need to remember that they are members of a professional community that adheres to a specific social/political ideology, and they hold to a belief system that may be at odds with that of their clients. This awareness is a prerequisite for developing consciousness to ensure that they don't impose their world-view on their clients. By developing such consciousness, they can avoid some of the problems described by Evans et al. (1979) who reported that:

> Workshops on listening skills conducted in Alaska and the Canadian Northwest Territories have floundered on the critical issue of cultural differences. Eye contact among some Eskimos and Inuit is considered inappropriate and distracting. In the US, patterns of eye contact among Blacks sometimes differ from those of Whites. Individuals in the Middle East stand closer together when they talk than people in the United States and Canada; therefore, interviewing at what is considered normal distance in America would be uncomfortable for individuals from Egypt or Lebanon. The direct approach of staying on one topic and focusing on problems may be inappropriate for some Asian populations who may prefer more indirect, subtle approaches. (12)

Ross (1992) suggests we should expect differences that lead to different interpretations of our words and actions. He proposes:

> Whenever we find ourselves beginning to draw negative conclusions from what the other has said or done, we must take the time to step back and ask whether those words and acts might be open to different interpretations, whether that other person's actions may have a different meaning from within his cultural conventions. (5)

Problems Faced by Immigrants and Refugees

Immigrants to Canada face a wide range of practical problems that may result in their coming for or being referred for counselling. Here are some examples of the issues that counsellors might expect to emerge when working with immigrants:

1. Language. Clearly, one of the most challenging problems for any immigrant is to acquire sufficient knowledge of the country's language so that he or she can participate in the society.
2. Unemployment. For many immigrants, coming to Canada results in loss of status, as credentials acquired in their home country may not be accepted in Canada. For some, the problems are insurmountable, and they never return to their former occupations.
3. Poverty. Immigrants who have escaped oppressive conditions may have been forced to leave their possessions and wealth behind. Others may be required to take entry level or minimum wage jobs in Canada and, as a result, subsist on marginal income.
4. Discrimination. Discrimination can frustrate an immigrant's ability to find employment and housing. Moreover, the experience of discrimination can evoke feelings of bitterness or hostility and affect their psychological well-being.

5. Culture shock. This phenomenon, which may be experienced in varying degrees, can include bewilderment, increased self-consciousness, embarrassment, shame, and loss of self-esteem.

6. Parent-child relationship problems. As a rule, children learn the host language more quickly than their parents and they adapt more quickly to Canadian life. Thus, parents may adapt by overreliance on their children for translation or interacting with their new country. Fears for their children may lead them to become overprotective, which can lead to parental child conflicts or acting-out behaviour.

7. Male-female role adjustment issues. Clients may come from cultures where male dominance is accepted and embedded in the routines and beliefs of their society.

Recent Immigrants and Refugees

There are unique challenges for counsellors who work with recent immigrants, particularly those who do not speak English or French. These challenges are magnified when clients are refugees, who may be poorly prepared for life in Canada:

> Not only is their arrival usually preceded by an arduous, often dangerous journey, their flight was usually precipitated by social, ethno-racial, religious, or political strife—even war. Many refugees have been the victims of, or witnessed, torture and other atrocities. (Turner & Turner, 2001:171)

Counsellors who cannot draw on their own experiences for understanding need to be willing to actively learn from these clients about the enormous trauma and suffering they have experienced. Such empathic interest will help them avoid duplicating the experience of many survivors of concentration camps, who were prevented from getting treatment and assistance "because the examining psychiatrists were unable to comprehend the enormity of their suffering" (Ruskin & Beiser, 1998:428).

> Example: *Parivash fled from her home in the Middle East after a long period of religious prosecution. Her father and her brother were both executed for refusing to deny their faith, although she claims the official explanation cited various fictitious crimes against the state. As a teenager, she was imprisoned and was subjected to torture, but then, without explanation, she was released from jail. Her eldest brother still remains imprisoned with his fate unknown. Newly arrived in Canada, Parivash has only marginal English, but strong determination to make a new life. Her spiritual commitment remains central to her worldview.*

Socio-Political Realities

With ethnic minority clients, there are typically historical and sociopolitical realities of oppressive racism that cannot be ignored. In Canada, this is particularly relevant when working with First Nations clients, whose cultures, including their languages, spirituality, customs, leadership, and social structure, have been eroded through colonization and systematic undermining by Canadian government policies and legislation (Poonwasie & Charter, 2001; Backhouse, 1999). Residential schools were established to force children to assimilate and accept Christian values. These schools, which operated until 1972, have a well-documented legacy of physical and sexual abuse.

Counsellors should not be surprised to find that their culturally different clients present with suspicion and caution, expecting that counselling will be yet another experience where overt or subtle evidence of bias will come to the foreground. Sue and Sue (1999) argue that counsellors need to remember that "many problems encountered by minority clients reside externally to them (bias, discrimination, prejudice, etc.) and they should not be faulted for the obstacles they encounter. To do so is to engage in victim blaming" (29). They suggest that in counselling sessions with culturally different clients, "[s]uspicion, apprehension, verbal constriction, unnatural reactions, open resentment and hostility, and passive or cool behaviour may all be expressed" (39). They conclude that culturally effective counselling requires professionals to understand these behaviours nonjudgmentally, to avoid personalizing them, and to resolve questions about their credibility.

Counsellors should acknowledge racial differences early in the relationship. Davis and Proctor (1989) argue that "[a]cknowledgment by the worker of a worker-client dissimilarity will convey to the client the worker's sensitivity and awareness of the potential significance of race to the helping relationship. It will also convey to the client that the worker probably has the ability to handle the client's feelings regarding race" (120). They suggest using direct questions, such as "How do you think my being white and your being nonwhite might affect our working together?" along with statements that voice openness to discuss issues related to culture. When counsellors and clients are from different cultures, frank discussion of their differences is an opportunity to "put on the table" variables related to dissimilar values and perspectives that might otherwise adversely impact the work. Although this is an important process with all clients, it should be a priority whenever there are sharp differences between counsellors and clients. This will assist counsellors in understanding their clients' worldviews, including their priorities for decision making.

> Counsellor: *Clearly, you and I are very different. I wonder if it might help me to spend a bit of time talking to you about your culture and your take on things.*

> Client: *Lots of people here in Canada think it's rather odd that my wife's mother and father live with us. But, they just don't understand.*

> Counsellor: *What don't they understand?*

> Client: *In Canada, kids grow up and once they reach 19 or 20, they can't wait to get away from home to establish their independence. In our culture, we want to be with our families as much as possible. Living with our parents is natural and expected. We don't see it as a burden. It's a great blessing that we can be together.*

Counsellors also need to consider the notion that not all groups in Canada have the same status or power, despite the fact that all groups have the same legal rights. Power differentials that lead to oppression and discrimination can exist by virtue of race ("white privilege"), sexism, heterosexism and classism (Miley, O'Melia, & Dubois, 2004).

KEY ELEMENTS OF CROSS-CULTURAL UNDERSTANDING

A multicultural orientation to counselling begins with a quest to understand our own worldview, then continues with curiosity and willingness to discover the unique and personal worldview of the client. Although different priorities may emerge for each client, the following broad areas should be considered:

1. Individual identity and role within family and community
2. Verbal and emotional expressiveness
3. Relationship expectations

4. Style of communication
5. Language
6. Personal priorities, values, and beliefs
7. Time orientation

Individuality and Family

When working with clients of different cultures, it is important to determine where the client's identity emphasis lies: within the individual or within the family/community (Hackney & Cormier, 2005). North Americans place high value on individuals becoming independent from their family; but in many cultures, separation from family is neither sought nor desired. In North America, rugged individualism tends to be prized; but among many Asian and Hispanic groups, greater priority is given to family and community (Sue & Sue, 1990). In general, counsellors should remember that for many African, Asian, Middle Eastern, and First Nations clients, "individual identity is always subsumed under the mantle of family" (Ruskin & Beiser, 1998:427). Consequently, counsellors need to consider whether clients would expect that extended family or even members of their community should be included in counselling. For example, many African, Asian, Middle Eastern, and First Nations people expect that their families will be involved (Ruskin & Beiser, 1998).

Culturally sensitive counsellors need to be aware of the influence of extended family in decision making. Consider, for example, the potential dilemmas regarding confidentiality with the client who comes from a family where the family leader, not the client, is responsible for decisions regarding counselling. There may be sharply different role and relationship expectations between cultures. In addition, culture-bound counsellors, who define a healthy male-female relationship as one based on equal division of household responsibilities, will find themselves in difficulty if they try to impose their assumptions on a family who hold a more traditional gender division of roles and power.

Although all cultures tend to have at least some respect for their elders, some cultures place very high value on the elders of the community. Many Africans, especially younger ones, defer decision making until they consult with older family members; and in Asian cultures, elders may be valued more than one's children (Dodd, 1995). The North American tendency to stress individuality and personal decision making might be regarded as disrespectful to parents in many African, Middle Eastern, and Asian cultures. In these cultures, "to honour one's parents throughout life is considered one of the highest virtues" (Dodd, 1995:117). Obligation to one's family or even to the community may take precedence over self, and failure to fulfill one's obligation may bring shame and embarrassment to the family.

Counsellors should consider family and community helping networks that exist within their clients' cultural community. Such natural helping opportunities should be used as adjuncts or alternatives to professional counselling. However, involving others should be with the permission of the client, except under unusual circumstances such as when the client is incapacitated or incapable of making an informed choice. For example, First Nations and Middle Eastern people may include the deceased as part of their natural helping network. Many Iranians believe that deceased relatives can appear in their dreams to offer guidance and support. Morrisseau (1998) from the Ontario Couchiching First Nation eloquently describes his belief:

> Since all life is based on a circle, and a circle has no beginning and no end, life cannot end in death but rather takes on a different form and meaning. When we understand "all our relations," we will know our ancestors are just as much a part of us today as when they were physically walking Mother Earth. In this sense, we are never alone. Our relations are still present to help us. (90)

The 1978 Iranian revolution resulted in large numbers of Iranians, mostly Muslims and Baha'is, coming to Canada. Shahmirzadi (1983) noted that Iranians are highly family-oriented, and counsellors can expect that elder relatives may accompany them to counselling. As well, Iranians will tend to be formal, particularly when dealing with people in authority, so last names should be used until familiarity is established.

Verbal and Emotional Expressiveness

Another important consideration is the client's beliefs regarding emotional expression and disclosure of personal information. The Western approach to counselling "involves heavy dependence on verbal expressiveness, emotional disclosure, and examination of behavior patterns" (Hackney & Cormier, 2005:125). This may be in stark contrast to other cultures, notably Asian and Hispanic, where emotional control is favoured. Also, what is acceptable in one culture may be offensive in another. For example, what is considered assertive behaviour in North America might be seen as arrogance in other parts of the world, and what North Americans interpret as shyness might be defined as respectful behaviour elsewhere.

Many counsellors place heavy emphasis on exploration of problems and feelings as a means to assist clients to develop insight and understanding. But this course of action may conflict with the approach favoured by some cultures, namely to ignore feelings by concentrating on activity. Sue and Sue (1999) highlight this issue:

> The Rogerian process of paraphrasing, reflecting feelings, and summarizing can be incompatible with cultural patterns. African Americans, for example, may find the patient, waiting and reflective type of a nondirective technique to be antagonistic to their values... Directive, confrontive, and persuasive approaches are more compatible. (223)

Similarly, Sue and Sue (1999) observe that since many Asians have difficulty expressing their feelings openly to strangers, counsellor attempts to empathize and interpret feelings may result in shaming the client. Consequently, they propose more indirect or subtle responses: "In many traditional Asian groups, subtlety is a highly prized art, and the traditional Asian client may feel much more comfortable when dealing with feelings in an indirect manner" (45). Whereas Western counselling methods tend to emphasize open expression and exploration of feelings as a method to develop insight and manage pain, many cultural groups do not favour this approach. First Nations people, for example, may feel threatened by demands for personal disclosure, particularly from non-native counsellors (Diller, 1999). Sue and Sue observe that many Asians believe that "the reason why one experiences anger or depression is precisely that one is thinking about it too much!... 'Think about the family and not about yourself' is advice given to many Asians as a way of dealing with negative affective elements" (1999: 65). Consequently, counsellors should consider that keeping one's emotions private is for some cultures an indicator of maturity. This will assist counsellors to avoid negatively labelling such clients as resistant, uncooperative, or depressed. However, this does not rule out open discussion between counsellors and clients about the merits of dealing with repressed or painful feelings.

Versatile counsellors are able to shift away from introspective approaches that emphasize insight and exploration of feelings when this shift meets the needs of culturally different clients. For example, action-based strategies that focus on developing skills or accessing resources is sometimes more culturally appropriate. This shift has equal validity when working with clients with limited economic means whose primary need may relate to getting a job, finding housing, or feeding their families.

Alexander and Sussman (1995) suggest creative approaches to multicultural counselling that draw on the minority client's everyday life experiences. Culturally relevant music, for example, might be used in waiting rooms as a way of welcoming clients. Similarly, agency and office architecture and art should be culturally inviting.

Relationship Expectations

Clients from some cultural groups may have expectations that test the North American guidelines for counsellors. Ruskin and Beiser (1998) provide examples related to the field of psychiatry that parallel the challenges faced by counsellors:

> In many cultures, people expect to express positive feelings by giving a gift. Should a therapist accept patients' gifts? Is this an aspect of transference that must always be interpreted? Is a gift a bribe? Giving a gift to a therapist may be a culturally appropriate expression of gratitude and respect. Depriving the patient of this culturally sanctioned process may invoke feelings of hurt pride, shame, or anger that interfere with the therapy. Inviting the psychiatrist to family ceremonies and special occasions may at first seem inappropriate, but is not at all unusual. In such instances, the therapist may be well advised to consult with other therapists or culturally literate colleagues before making a decision. (437)

> Example: *Joyce, a young social worker, recalled how she became anxious when her client, a Jamaican single parent, told her that she wished to give her a gift to thank her for her help. Joyce did not want to insult the woman by refusing the gift, but she was acutely aware that her client was poor and could barely afford to feed her family. Moreover, she was concerned that she not violate professional ethics. Fortunately, her client resolved the dilemma when she presented Joyce with a grapefruit tied with a red ribbon. For Joyce's client, the grapefruit had great symbolic value.*

Another area where counsellors need to carefully navigate concerns physical contact and culture. Cultural groups differ on the extent that touch is expected or tolerated, with further issues related to gender a complicating factor. Both the Canadian Counselling Association and the Canadian Association of Social Workers codes of ethics are silent on the issue except to prohibit contact of a sexual nature. The National Association of Social Workers (1996) code outlines the responsibility of social workers to set "culturally sensitive boundaries" (Standard 1.10) regarding physical contact, but no specific guidance beyond this directive is offered.

Moreover, there are cross-cultural variations on how people greet each other and the spatial distance that is maintained during conversation or greeting. Whereas a handshake is common in North America, people from other cultures bow, hug, nod, or kiss on introduction, and this may vary depending on setting, degree of intimacy, or nature of the relationship. Vietnamese men do not shake hands with women or their elders, nor do two Vietnamese women shake hands (Dodd, 1995). Another variation concerns how people greet each other. Some clients are comfortable with first names only, but others are more formal and prefer to use titles. Some cultures expect one to greet the head of a family or elders first (Dodd, 1995). Iranians, who favour formality, may stand up when counsellors enter or leave the room (Shahmirzadi, 1983). Iranian same-sex members stand closer than in North America, but opposite sex members are likely to be further away (Shahmirzadi, 1983). Middle-Easterners may expect that offers of refreshments be given several times with encouragement to accept.

Relationships between various cultures may have historic roots of friction and oppression. Counsellors may expect that the feelings minority group clients have towards the dominant culture will influence the counselling relationship, particularly when counsellors are perceived to be representatives of the controlling culture. In some cases, feelings such as anger and suspicion will be overtly expressed; but they may also be unexpressed and revealed only through subtle or indirect ways. Clients who are overly compliant or ingratiating may, in fact, be masking their anger or hiding the fact that they feel inadequate in a relationship of unequal power. In any case, clients will carefully observe how counsellors process and deal with their feelings, with the future of the relationship and/or decisions about returning for a second session hinging on their counsellors' capacity to address such feelings non defensively.

Many clients, such as Iranians, have limited experience with counselling (Shahmirzadi, 1983). Consequently, it is important that roles and procedures be defined clearly, a step that is, of course, important for all counselling relationships regardless of experience with the process.

Style of Communication

Some clients are expressive and keen to talk about their experiences and feelings, whereas others are more reserved and carefully guard their privacy. Some clients like to get to the point and task quickly, but others prefer to informally build up to it. Clients may also differ sharply in their nonverbal communication style, including how comfortable they are with eye contact, their need for physical space and distance, their comfort with touch, their concept of time, and the way they use silence. Some clients find that a conversational distance of 1 to 1.5 metres is comfortable, whereas others find the same distance intrusive. For example, many people from the Middle East stand close enough to breathe on others. "In fact, the breath is like one's spirit and life itself, so sharing your breath in close conversation is like sharing your spirit" (Dodd, 1995:166).

Generally, First Nations people tend to speak more softly, use less eye contact (indirect gaze), and delay their responses (using silence) (Sue & Sue, 1999). A similar style is evident among Asians who also maintain a low-key approach and are more likely to defer to persons in authority. McDonald (1993) offers this simple, but impressive suggestion: "Interviewers must also be careful to remember that a response is not necessarily over when the speaker pauses. There may be more. Give time for full expression" (19).

Eye contact is another area of difference. In the dominant Caucasian Canadian community, eye contact is experienced as a sign of listening and showing respect, and lack of eye contact is evasive and inattentive. But in other cultures, casting one's eyes downward is the sign of respect. For Navaho Indians and many other First Nations people, direct eye contact communicates harsh disapproval (Dodd, 1995). Ross (1992) relates some important principles he learned from a Native mentor and elder from Northern Ontario, Charlie

Fisher, who commented on communication errors Ross made in speaking to an elder of the local First Nations community:

> Verbal expressions of praise and gratitude are embarrassing and impolite, especially in the presence of others. The proper course is to quietly ask the person to continue making his contribution next time around. Looking someone in the eye, at least among older people in the community, was a rude thing to do. It sends a signal that you consider that person in some fashion inferior. The proper way to send a signal of respect was to look down or to the side, with only occasional glances up to indicate attention. (3)

Ross also notes that Fisher reassured him that his errors probably did not offend the elder who "knew, after all, that a great many white men simply hadn't learned how to behave in a civilized manner" (4).

Sue and Sue (2003), emphasizing how communication styles are strongly linked to culture, make this observation:

> Whether our conversation proceeds with fits or starts, whether we interrupt one another continually or proceed smoothly, the topics we prefer to discuss or avoid, the depth of our involvement, the forms of interaction (ritual, repartee, argumentative, persuasive, etc.) and the channel we use to communicate (verbal-nonverbal vs. nonverbal-verbal) are all aspects of communication style. (p.126)

Language

Counsellors need to listen carefully to the vocabulary and idioms that their clients use to express ideas and feelings while keeping in mind that minority clients who are not fluent will have trouble expressing their thoughts. The more that counsellors can match their clients' style, the greater their rapport with them will be. When counsellors use jargon or unfamiliar words, clients may feign understanding, or the experience may leave them feeling vulnerable and disempowered. Of course, counsellors also need to avoid talking down to clients. Sometimes interpreters will be necessary; but family and friends of the client should not be used because of the risk of breaking confidentiality and the fact that their inclusion may introduce bias.

In addition, words may have different meanings or connotations for different cultures. For example, the word "school" may evoke terror from some First Nations people who associate the term with the abuses of residential schools. Counsellors should also consider the degree of formality that may be expected by clients. Addressing clients as *Mr.* or *Mrs.* may be much more appropriate than using first names. Some clients may see indiscriminate use of first names as overly familiar and insulting.

Culturally different clients are often particularly attuned to nonverbal communication (Sue & Sue, 1999), and they will respond very quickly to subtle indicators of counsellor bias. In counselling, they may test counsellors with questions about their racial views and attitudes to measure how much they can be trusted. Counsellors' nonverbal responses to such inquires will often reveal more about their real views than their words.

Racial Labels

It is important for counsellors to use appropriate terms when referring to their clients. African Americans have historically been called Coloured, Negro, black and more recently African American. Reviewing the literature, Paniagua (1998) concluded that the term *African American* is more acceptable since it does not emphasize skin colour, but includes reference to cultural heritage and the African connection. Since some clients may have different preferences—preferring to be called black, for example—it is prudent for workers to ask clients what they favour. In Canada, the term *First Nations* is preferred; but in the US, *American Indian* is more commonly favoured.

Personal Priorities, Values, and Beliefs

Everyone is differently motivated. Some people are career oriented, and others are driven by spiritual beliefs. Counsellors may find themselves working with clients whose views and attitudes on such major issues as gender equality, spirituality, and sexuality differ sharply from their own. But when counsellors understand their clients' priorities, they are in a much better position to support decision making and problem solving that is consistent with their clients' beliefs. Counsellors need to be self-aware and to have self-discipline in keeping their personal views and values from becoming a burden to their clients. If counsellors cannot work with reasonable objectivity, referral may be necessary.

For some clients, ideas and values that define personal and familial responsibilities and priorities are deeply rooted and defined in the traditions of their culture. There may be little room for individual initiative and independent decision making that is separate from considerations of family and one's position in the hierarchy of the family. For these clients, family and community are their sources of help and this reality has enormous implications for counsellors. To proceed without understanding, involving, or considering central family figures predestines counselling initiatives to failure.

European and North American notions of healthy adaptation include a focus on "self-reliance, autonomy, self-actualization, self-assertion, insight, and resistance to stress" (Diller, 1999:61). In contrast, Asians have different value priorities that include "interdependence, inner enlightenment, negation of self, transcendence of conflict, and passive acceptance of reality" (Diller, 1999:61). Thus, individualism and personal assertion are not as important for Asians as they tend to be for the dominant cultures of Canada. In order to process information correctly and make accurate assessments, "counsellors need to determine what is relevant behaviour within the client's current cultural context that may be quite different from that of the dominant group" (Arthur & Stewart, 2001:8). For example, they need to know when the value of family or tribal responsibility supersedes personal need. Moreover, with some Asian groups, for example, humility and modesty are preferred over confrontation, and conflict or disagreement may be expressed through silence or withdrawal. Thus, all behaviour must be interpreted based on its learned and cultural origins.

Pedersen (2001) offers an amusing, but profound, comment on the natural tendency to assume that others see the world the same as ourselves: "We have been taught to 'do unto others as you would have them do unto you' whether they want it done unto them or not!" (21)

A client's personal values can be identified through interviewing or simple tests and questionnaires. Lock (1996), for example, uses an inventory that assists people to rank-order 21 different values (e.g., need for achievement, creativity, power, wealth, etc.) based on their relative priority.

Beliefs about How People Should Act

This includes clients' beliefs about receiving help from counsellors. Do they believe that taking help is a sign of weakness? Do they think that families should be able to solve their own problems without outside intervention? Who do they believe should initiate conversations? What are their expectations of the role of the counsellor? What expectations do they have of people in authority? How do they feel men and women should relate to each other?

Clients from some cultures will tend to defer to authority and wait for their counsellors to take the lead in the interview, rarely volunteering information or taking the initiative. They may be reluctant to challenge the authority of their counsellors or even to admit that they do not understand.

Time Orientation

There are interesting and important differences between cultures regarding how they view time. The dominant Canadian society tends toward preoccupation with time, with people's lives divided and regulated by appointments and time constraints. The common saying "Time is money," describes the drive towards getting ahead and making progress. But other societies may be less future oriented and more focused on the present or past. Consider, for example, the importance that Asians and First Nation peoples place on one's ancestors and elders in defining one's life. First Nations peoples are more grounded in the present and "artificial division of time, as in making schedules, is disruptive to the natural pattern" (Sue & Sue, 1999:110).

COUNSELLING IMMIGRANTS AND MULTICULTURAL CLIENTS

Multiculturalism has been described as a "fourth force" in counselling, supplementing psychodynamic (emphasis on thoughts and feelings), behavioural, and humanist counselling ideologies (Pedersen & Locke, 1996). Diversification of society has made it imperative that counsellors develop new attitudes and skills in order to deliver effective service to their multicultural clientele, particularly since research has shown that "many traditional counselling approaches are not effective (and in some cases are even harmful) when used among culturally and racially diverse client populations" (D'Andrea, 1996:56).

Controlling the Tendency to Stereotype

Counsellors are expected by their codes of ethics to appreciate and respect the uniqueness and individuality of each client and to avoid being blinded by stereotyping groups and cultures. Stereotyping may be defined as holding firm judgments about people based on preconceptions. This is illustrated by such statements as "Jews are miserly," and "Indians can't hold their liquor." Abundant evidence of stereotypes can be found in ethnic jokes that typecast and smear various ethnic groups.

It is critical that counsellors realize and accept that people from different cultures have different standards of behaviour, and that they often respond to or interpret actions in widely divergent ways. Counsellors can study particular cultures and may reach conclusions that support certain broad generalizations about that culture; but this is no guarantee that any one member of that culture will adhere to the defining norms of their subgroup. Consequently, counsellors should make no assumptions. In fact, clients are simultaneously under the influence of many cultural groups, each of which may exert powerful, but contradictory leverage.

Example: *Baljit, a twenty-year-old East Indian woman, is a first-generation Canadian. Her parents emigrated from India shortly before her birth. They retain many of the values of their traditional culture, including the expectation that Baljit will have an arranged marriage. Baljit respects her parents, but this conflicts with her growing desire to choose her own marriage partner. She also wants to honour her spiritual traditions. Baljit is active in the Indian community, but she also has many Caucasian friends.*

Thus, a client like Baljit belongs "to multiple groups, all of which influence the client's perceptions, beliefs, feelings, thoughts, and behavior. The counsellor must be aware of these influences and of their unique blending or fusion in the client if counselling is to be successful" (Patterson, 1996:230). In general, one's personal culture is influenced by many factors, including family of origin, social circle, community, and education. As well, it may change over time and be influenced by catastrophic events, such as illness and war, or by economic realities, such as poverty.

Although individuals within cultural or other groups tend to share certain values and customs, individual differences may prevail, and any one person within the group may or may not conform to the cultural norms. There may also be wide diversity within the same group. In Canada, for example, there are many First Nations, including (to name only a few) Algonquin, Blackfoot, Cree, Haida, and Ojibway. Two key questions need to be considered:

1. To what extent does the client hold cultural values and traditions consistent with his or her own culture of origin?

2. What cultural values and traditions are unique to this individual (i.e., different from their own culture of origin)?

Exploring and understanding the culture, language, and history of the populations counsellors work with is an important step in preventing stereotyping. To some extent, books and films can provide this knowledge base, but direct contact and experience with different cultures is a better way to learn. Counsellors can gain this experience in a number of ways, such as by visiting ethnic districts, attending cultural festivals, and cultivating friendships with a diversity of people. However, it is important to remember that a member of a particular culture does not necessarily hold the cultural values that characterize that culture. Within any culture there can be a wide range of individual differences. Even members of an individual family may exhibit wide variations in their cultural identity.

Diversity and Individual Differences

As noted earlier in this chapter, there have been dramatic shifts in the demographics of Canada with a significant increase in non-White populations. In some cities and provincial areas, non-White populations have, or soon will become, the majority. The implications of these changes have meant that counsellors are increasingly called on to serve clients from diverse cultures. But Speight et al. (1991) caution counsellors against seeing multicultural counselling as something different from "regular" counselling. They warn against using a "multicultural 'cookbook' with each group receiving a 'recipe' that includes a checklist of the group's characteristics and some instructions regarding how the counselling should proceed" (30). Such an approach may result in stereotypes and in a failure to recognize individual differences. Since within-group cultural differences may actually exceed between-group differences, "all counselling, and, in fact, all communications are inherently and unavoidably multicultural" (Pedersen, 2001:18).

Respect for diversity challenges counsellors to modify their approaches to fit the needs and expectations of their clients. Counsellors need to become alert to any conflicts between how they see and do things and the different worldviews that drive their clients' perceptions and actions. To achieve this, counsellors need to develop self-awareness of their own cultural worldview, including their values, assumptions, biases and assumptions about others. They need to remember that everyone is somewhat culture-bound and that their heritage and socialization limits their capacity to be fully objective about the worldview of others.

Learning from Clients

Given the range of diverse clients that counsellors work with, it is not realistic to expect that counsellors can know about the cultural values and customs of all groups. Fortunately, counsellors can use clients as sources of information by asking clients to teach them about their beliefs. Smith and Morrisette (2001) stress that counsellors should avoid the "expert role" when working with First Nations people by becoming students of the client's culture. Simple questions such as, "What do you think I need to know about your culture and values in order for me to understand your situation?" can start the process. Additionally, the process of inquiry serves to deepen the development of the basic foundation of counselling—namely, the counsellor/client relationship. In fact, this approach empowers clients, and it should be followed with all clients, not just those who are culturally different.

Every client represents diversity with his/her own cultural mix. In this respect, Kadushin's (1983) comments on cultural attitudes are particularly relevant:

> What may ultimately be more important than knowledge is an attitude. The interviewer needs to feel with conviction that her culture, way of life, values, etc., are only one way of doing things; that there are equally valid ways, not better or worse, but different. Cultural differences are easily transmuted into cultural deficiencies. There needs to be an openness and receptivity toward such differences and a willingness to be taught by the client about such differences... Because the interviewer is less likely to have had the experience which permits empathic understanding of the racially different interviewee, she needs to be more ready to listen, less ready to come to conclusions, more open to guidance and corrections of her presuppositions by the interviewee. (304)

Table 10.3 summarizes major guidelines for working with multicultural clients.

FIRST NATIONS CLIENTS

Throughout the period of colonization and the evolution of Canada as a nation state, we maintained ourselves as a distinct social and political order. We retained our identity as a distinct society, as a nation. We continued to possess and exercise our right of self-government, a right recognized in both international and domestic law. We have never relinquished our right of self-determination.
—Chief Joe Mathias, 2001

One way for counsellors to deepen their knowledge about aboriginal issues is through film. Since 1996, the National Film Board of Canada has supported the Aboriginal Filmmaking Program. The Board has a rich variety of culturally informative and sensitive films that explore Aboriginal issues, such as (to name a few) cultural heritage, healing practices, arts, family, and sweat lodges. On line resource catalogues are available at **www.nfb.ca**.

TABLE 10.3	Guidelines for Multicultural Work

1. Openly acknowledge and discuss differences in race, gender, sexual orientation, and so forth.

2. Avoid stereotyping by exploring expecting individual differences. Encourage clients to teach you about their values, beliefs, and customs. Physical appearance does not necessarily mean that a person speaks the language or adheres to the values or customs of the culture they appear to represent.

3. Increase multicultural self-awareness through personal study, professional development, and personal involvement (e.g., cultivate multicultural friendships, attend multicultural events). Understand and appreciate how your culture, attitude, beliefs, customs, experience, and religion influence what you say and do in counselling.

4. Seek to understand how historical events, such as residential schools and internment of Japanese Canadians, influence current beliefs and behaviour.

5. Explore how problems like poverty, unemployment, agency policy/procedure, and systemic prejudice affect your client. Whenever possible, advocate for appropriate systemic change. For example, examine how agency structure, policy, staffing, and even architecture serve dominant groups while excluding minorities.

6. Remain non-defensive when dealing with clients who have experienced discrimination. Expect that they may be distrustful, sometimes hostile, towards professionals who represent what they perceive as the oppressive power of the dominant group.

7. Stay alert on how language, including nonverbal variables, has different meanings for people.

8. Adapt counselling strategies and goals to meet the needs of individual clients instead of expecting clients to fit into your style and expectations. Consider cultural context when working with all clients, especially ethnic minority clients.

9. Pay particular attention to family, community, or tribal expectations and roles. (Who makes important decisions? Who should be invited to counselling meetings?)

10. Seek and use natural helping networks, including family and community resources. For example, encourage First Nations clients to access and use traditional healing practices (as appropriate). Remember that spiritual and religious values are important components of multicultural understanding. Spiritual leaders from the client's community may, in some cases, be used in the counselling process.

11. Basic needs (food, shelter, employment) may need to be discussed first.

12. When dealing with clients for whom English is a second or subsequent language, speak slower (not louder). Sometimes single words or phrases are easier for them to understand than complete sentences.

13. If you are using a translator, look at your client, not the translator. When using translators, avoid using family and friends of the client.

First Nations Worldviews

First Nations people view mental and physical health in a unique way. "Illnesses, both mental and physical, are thought to result from disharmony of the individual, family, or tribe from the ways of nature and the natural order. Healing can only occur when harmony is restored" (Diller, 1999:61). Traditional healing practices are directed at restoring this harmony. Jack Lawson, a Native addictions counsellor, summarized his approach in an interview:

> We sit in a talking circle, but it is the issues we talk about that are important. The issues have to do with Native culture, identity, how they see themselves as Native People, the effects of stereotyping, justified anger, positive identity development, and ceremony. And we use ritual objects and ceremonies as part of the process: eagle feathers and pipes, smudging, sweat lodges, and so on, introducing our culture into the treatment process and acknowledging what they are going through ritually and with ceremonies. Such a process fits naturally with our cultural understanding of health and sickness. We also discuss the effects of oppression, while at the same time addressing the issues around denial, relapse prevention planning, and recovery maintenance. (Diller, 1999:171)

Poonwassie and Charter (2001) attempted to describe the clash of worldviews that occurred when European Christians encountered Aboriginal peoples:

> European Christian Canadians believed that they were meant to dominate the Earth and its creatures. The Aboriginal peoples believed that they were the least important creatures of the universe and that they were dependent upon the four elements (fire, water, earth and air) and all of creation for survival. (65)

Working with First Nations People

McDonald (1993) offers a number of pointers for working with First Nations people:

1. In contrast to mainstream Canadians, whose responses are quick, First Nations people may pause before offering a response.
2. First Nations people tend not to engage in "small talk." As a result, they may be misjudged as "shy, reticent, or uncooperative by an interviewer when, in fact, the behaviour may actually indicate they feel that there is nothing worthwhile to say, so there is no reason to comment" (19).
3. First Nations people may appear stoic or unconcerned because of a belief that it is improper to share personal feelings or information with a stranger.
4. Expect short and direct answers to questions. As well, there may be a cultural tendency not to "volunteer" information.
5. Lack of eye contact from First Nations people may mean respect for the person.

Poonwassie and Charter (2001), and others stress the importance of accepting First Nations practices as valid and preferred alternatives:

> In order to facilitate community empowerment, all those who collaborate with Aboriginal communities in healing initiatives must understand and accept that Aboriginal peoples have practiced viable healing methods based on their worldview throughout their history, and these methods must be recognized and accepted as equal to Euroamerican therapeutic approaches. (70)

Smith and Morrissette (2001) conducted a study of the experiences of white counsellors who work with First Nations clients. Some of their key observations and conclusions are summarized below:

- Honouring difference, maintaining flexibility, and using creative approaches, is critical to effective counselling. A central part of this is willingness of counsellors to understand First Nations experiences and culture in terms of their traumatic historical context.
- Counselling relationships may need to include extended families, elders, and traditional healers. Counsellors need to believe in the community's capacity to solve its own problems.
- Willingness to learn from clients, elders, and Native co-workers is important to relationship development and success in counselling. Counsellors must be willing to relinquish the expert role and adopt "a willingness to have one's knowledge challenge, to work with uncertainty, and seek guidance from the Native community." (80)
- Counsellors need to respect and be open to the power of Native spirituality. They need to be willing to become involved in community events, which may test and redefine contemporary professional boundaries.

These conclusions are echoed by Choney, Berryhill-Paapke and Robbins (1995), who also remind counsellors to consider such variables as "differences in communication styles, gender role definitions, medicine, and social support networks, including family relationships" (87).

CONVERSATION 10.1

WHO ARE THE ABORIGINALS?

STUDENT: I have trouble sorting out all the terms. Who are the Aboriginals? What is the correct term to use—Aboriginal, Indian, First Nations?

ABORIGINAL ELDER: In Canada, there are almost one million Aboriginal people. Aboriginals refer to the descendants of the original inhabitants of North America. In Canada, the Constitution defines three groups of Aboriginal people—Indian, Métis, and Inuit—each of which has unique culture, language, custom, religious practices, and so forth. Métis have mixed First Nation and European ancestry. They may have cultures influenced by their ancestral roots, such as French, Scottish, Ojibway, and Cree. The 2001 census reported that there are almost 300 000 Métis in Canada. Inuit are the descendants of the original people of the North, formerly known as Eskimos. The country's 45 000 Inuit live in northern regions of Canada, but you should know that Inuit also live in Alaska, Greenland, and Siberia. Indians are all Aboriginals who are not Inuit or Métis. More than 600 000 Canadians are of North American Indian descent.

The terminology is still very problematic. Many terms are accepted by some Aboriginals and rejected by others for various political and philosophical reasons. It is important to acknowledge the diversity of opinions that exist among First Nations people. In general, most seem to prefer the terms First Nations or Aboriginal, but some people prefer to acknowledge their nation, for example, the Oweekeno or the Klahoose. Some have a strong negative reaction to the term "Indian" but others still use it affectionately as an "insider" term of endearment.

In Canada, 60 percent of Aboriginals live on more than 600 reserves, land reserved for the exclusive use of the First Nation. Each band or First Nation has its own governing system. As you might expect, the members of each First Nation are uniquely bonded by common values, traditions, and practices from their ancestral heritage. But remember, there is wide diversity between Nations.

STUDENT: What is meant by the term Status Indian?

ABORIGINAL ELDER: In fact, three legal terms apply to Indians in Canada: Status Indians, Non-Status Indians, and Treaty Indians. Status Indians are registered under the Indian Act and have access to certain rights and programs. Treaty Indians have Status and are members of a First Nations community that has signed a treaty with the government that gives them certain land, hunting, fishing, and monetary rights. Precise treaty rights will vary between various First Nations. Nonstatus Indians have Indian ancestry and retain their Indian identity, but have lost their legal status under the Act.

STUDENT: What is the Indian Act?

ABORIGINAL ELDER: This is an 1876 Canadian law that outlines the federal government's role in regulating and managing Indian reserve lands. You should know that it is controversial. Aboriginal self-government refers to governments designed, established, and administered by Aboriginal peoples. As well, you should also know that our history includes much pain as we were robbed of our land and our children were removed to abusive residential schools where they were forbidden to practise their culture or speak their language. In the boarding schools, the goal was to make the children forget their Indian culture and adopt White and Christian values. Government policies were based on the assumption that we were primitive and that we needed to adopt the culture of the European settlers. Canadian governments systematically attacked the tribal systems, and this has resulted in marginalization and a loss of identity for First Nations peoples.

Traditional Healing Practices

For First Nations People, various practices and ceremonies are used where the "underlying goal of these ceremonies is almost always to offer thanks for, create, and maintain a strong sense of connection through harmony and balance of mind, body, and spirit with the natural environment" (Garrett, Garrett, & Brotherton, 2001:18). Examples of the various ceremonies include the sweat lodge, vision quest, and powwow. They are used in a number of ways such as "honouring or healing a connection with oneself, between oneself and others (relationships; i.e., family, friends, and community), between oneself and the natural environment, or between oneself and the spirit world" (19). In the tradition of First Nations people, life is embraced through the senses, which includes the awareness of medicine, which might include physical remedies (herbs and spices) but also extends beyond:

> Medicine is in every tree, plant, rock, animal, and person. It is in the light, the soil, the water, and the wind. Medicine is something that happened 10 years ago that still makes you smile when you think about it. Medicine is that old friend who calls you up out of the blue because he or she was thinking about you. There is medicine in watching a small child play. Medicine is the reassuring smile of an elder. There is medicine in every event, memory, place, person and movement. There is even medicine in empty space if you know how to use it. And there can be powerful medicine in painful or hurtful experiences as well. (Garrett et al, 2001:22)

Elders are being reaffirmed as central figures, and many First Nations people are once again adopting traditional holistic healing approaches. Poonwassie and Charter (2001) include the following examples:

- Medicine wheels
- Story telling
- Teaching and sharing circles
- Ceremonies (e.g., sundances, medicine lodges, fasts, sweats, pipe ceremonies, moon ceremonies, give-aways, and potlatches)
- Traditional role models, such as elders, healers, medicine people, traditional teachers, or healthy community members

SPIRITUALITY AND COUNSELLING

The 2001 census highlights a shift in the religious affiliation of Canadians. The majority of Canadians (70 percent) are still Christian, but this is a significant drop from over 80 percent a decade earlier (Statistics Canada, 2005) The changing nature of the nation's religious makeup is due to the shifts in immigration described earlier in this chapter.

Counsellors may hesitate or be uncomfortable about making spirituality a component of counselling. Fear of imposing one's values and beliefs, general discomfort with discussing religious issues, and lack of knowledge or skill in addressing religious issues—all may lead counsellors to unnecessarily avoid making spiritual beliefs a target for counselling discussion. Many counselling texts fail to address or even mention this important dimension. One major counselling textbook with more than 600 pages is completely silent on the issue. When spirituality is addressed, typically the discussion is confined to ethical issues, usually confined to discussion of the professional requirement that practitioners respect and accept diversity. However, spiritual and/or religious dimensions, often intimately entwined with culture, are beginning to receive increased attention in the literature and professional organizations. For example, The Association for Spiritual, Ethical, and Religious Values in Counseling has been formed under the auspices of The American Counseling Association.

The majority of people are likely to report some religious affiliation or conviction. Moreover, for some individuals and many cultural sub groups, religious organization plays a central role in their social lives and may be seen as a major source of support. Indeed, all cultures have important religious perspectives that must be understood as part of the process of understanding clients and their worldviews. Consequently, counsellors should not refrain from work in this important area, particularly when it meets the needs and expectations of their clients.

Counsellors may work in a religious setting where their work is clearly framed and guided by the values of their particular faith. Others may work in secular settings without any religious connection. In such settings, spiritual counselling is geared to the client's spiritual values and beliefs, not the counsellor's. This requires that counsellors become comfortable with religious diversity. They do not impose their religious or personal views on their clients. Examples of spiritual issues that might be discussed in counselling include:

- emotional struggles to reconcile emerging personal beliefs that are in conflict with one's religious background (e.g., a client "losing his/her faith")

- feelings such as guilt that emerge from lifestyle choices that are in conflict with one's religious values (e.g., a client contemplating an abortion)
- exploring client feelings such as anger towards God (e.g., client whose child has died)
- familial conflict (e.g., common law unions in violation of religious laws)
- family discord related to one's level of involvement (e.g., children who lose interest in attending religious services)
- meaning of life (e.g., exploring experiences that clients describe as spiritual or religious in order to discern the meaning of these experiences for them)
- death and dying (e.g., position regarding an afterlife, meaning of life's difficulties)
- establishing life plan or problem solving that is consistent with spiritual values (e.g., dealing with a divorce)

Frequently, cultural identity is meshed with religious identity. To understand culture, counsellors must understand religion and spirituality. Religion influences the way that people think; it shapes their values and sways their behaviour. Ethnic customs, calendar observances, music, and art may all be rooted in religious beliefs and practices. For people in many cultural minorities (and some from the dominant culture), their lives centre around their religious institution.

Moreover, ethnic minority clients may be more inclined to seek help from elders and religious leaders from within their own community. Clients with a strong religious connection respond best to counselling initiatives that take into account their spiritual community, values, and practices. This might include helping them to access and consider relevant sacred writings as well as helping them to use the resources and practices of their faith, including prayer and meditation. But counsellors who are not informed or do not consider spiritual issues when they are important for their clients have difficulty establishing credibility in this kind of counselling relationship. Not surprisingly, research has demonstrated that highly religious clients do better in counselling and are less likely to drop out prematurely when they are matched with counsellors who have similar religious values (Kelly 1995). For example, members of the Baha'i faith, who tend to come from a variety of ethnic origins, generally strive to obtain counselling services from professionals who are versed in their faith. Cultural understanding requires appreciation of spiritual values.

Counsellors who are versed in the spiritual teachings of their clients' belief system should discuss with them the extent that they wish counselling to be framed within tenets of their faith. Counsellors who are not versed in the spiritual teachings of their clients can establish credibility by demonstrating that they are open to spiritual elements as their clients experience them. Subsequently, they can best assist clients by helping them to articulate and/or sort out spiritual/religious issues. As well, counsellors can refer clients to religious leaders from their faith or enlist their assistance. Kelly (1995) offers this perspective:

> A counselor who understands and respects the client's religious dimension is prepared to enter that part of the client's world. At this point, the counsellor does not need an expert knowledge of the client's particular spiritual or religious belief but rather an alert sensitivity to this dimension of the client's life. By responding with respectful understanding to the spiritual/religious aspect of the client's problem, the counsellor in effect is journeying with the client, ready to learn from the client and to help the client clarify how his or her spirituality or religiousness may be understood and folded into fresh perspectives and new decisions for positive growth and change. (117)

Empathic responses are powerful ways to respect clients and communicate understanding of clients' feelings. An illustrative counsellor response to a client struggling with spiritual issues might be "Seems like you're feeling a bit lost or disconnected. This frightens you, and you're looking for a way to find spiritual peace."

But in the same way that there are wide variations within cultures, it is important to remember that there may be variations within religions. For some, religion and spirituality are central to their lives and all of their decisions and choices in life are considered in the context of their spiritual commitment. Others may identify with a particular religious belief, but their involvement and the extent that religion influences their actions may be marginal. Moreover, complexity is increased because individuals may give a different interpretation to religious teachings. Clients may self-identify as spiritually oriented without being affiliated with any organized religion; or they may be members of a particular faith but report that spirituality is not central to their lives.

Counsellors need to acquire a broad knowledge of the world's major religions. This is a formidable task considering the wide array of beliefs and traditions that exist. In Canada, counsellors will certainly encounter clients from the following groups: Christianity, Judaism, Islam, Hinduism, Sikhism, Buddhism, and Baha'i. Although basic knowledge can be obtained from books, this should be supplemented with appropriate field exploration. Many faiths permit visitors at religious ceremonies and sponsor public information events.

CONVERSATION 10.2

PRAYING WITH CLIENTS

STUDENT: What should you do if a client asks you to pray with him/her?

COUNSELLOR: It's unlikely that you'd ever get such a request in a secular or nonreligious setting. However, in religious settings, or when clients seek help from counsellors affiliated with an organized religion, prayers might be used at the beginning and the end of a session. For clients, this helps to establish the spiritual nature of this particular counselling work. Certainly, clients who come for religious counselling expect that prayer may be part of the work. But in a secular setting, most counsellors and agencies would agree that it is usually inappropriate to pray with clients. They might witness a client who wishes to pray, but not participate actively.

STUDENT: In fact, it did happen to me. I have a field placement at a hospital where I was assisting a Catholic woman. Her husband was terminally ill, and she asked if I would join the family as they celebrated last rites with their priest. I accepted, but I wonder if perhaps I've broken any ethical or professional rules.

COUNSELLOR: From the circumstances you describe, I don't believe that anyone could reasonably accuse you of unprofessional conduct. In a situation such as this, I think you need to ask two important questions. First, did you interfere with your client's right to self-determination? The request was initiated by your client, and given the context, your response seems supportive and appropriate. What's important is that you did not impose your religious views on her. Second, did you violate the legitimate boundaries of your role? It doesn't appear that you compromised your role with her by entering into a dual relationship. This would occur if you started to meet her outside of your professional mandate: for instance, if you agreed to accompany her to church on a regular basis or invited her to attend one of your religious ceremonies. In fact, you may have enhanced your capacity to work with her in that you gained further insight into her spiritual values and beliefs. Kelly (1995) argues that when a counsellor and a client have the same religious values, the counsellor may accept an invitation to participate in a prayer, but he advises extreme caution.

STUDENT: Suppose clients ask me about my religion. What should I do?

COUNSELLOR: Our role is to help clients make informed choices based on independent investigations. You might answer the question about your religion directly, then ask what prompted the question. You could assist them to explore spiritual questions, but this must be done from a position of neutrality without any attempt to convert them to your religion, which would clearly interfere with their rights to self-determination. As for teaching them your religion, I wouldn't go there. Instead, refer clients to religious specialists to help them meet their spiritual needs.

STUDENT: When prayer and spirituality are important for clients, I think it's okay to assist to set goals and action plans that will help them fulfil this need.

COUNSELLOR: Sure, and this might include encouraging them to use prayer—if they believe that this is an important part of their life.

STUDENT: I also think that it's okay to pray for your clients. A significant part of the population believes that others will benefit from our prayers. So, why should we deny our clients this benefit?

ACHIEVING CROSS-CULTURAL COMPETENCY

In recent years, there has been a shift toward a broader definition of culture and multicultural competence to include factors such as sexual orientation, physical disability, and socioeconomic status (Fuertes, Bartolomeo & Nichols, 2001). Johnson, McClelland and Austin offer this perspective on diversity for the Canadian context with its wide cultural mix:

> The human diversity approach considers human behaviour from the stance of cultural relativity. It sees normal behaviour as an irrelevant concept and behaviour as functional or dysfunctional relative to the social situation in which a person is functioning. What may be functional in one situation may be dysfunctional in another. Deviations of developmental patterns found in different cultures should not be considered as necessarily abnormal. (2000:10)

Respect and acceptance of diversity compels counsellors to be sensitive and aware of their own cultures as well as those of their clients. Competent counsellors don't just tolerate diversity; rather, they welcome and value individual and cultural differences. Thus, cross-cultural counselling competence requires counsellors to adjust their approaches to understand and respond effectively to clients with a different worldview. In order to achieve knowledge about the factors that shape their client's worldviews:

> Counsellors need to possess knowledge about the history, values, and socialization practices of cultural groups within Canadian society, and how their heritages, including the socio-political issues facing these groups may have influenced their personal and social development... Cultural knowledge includes information about the client's cultural roots, values, perceived problems and preferred interventions, as well as any significant within group diversity, including differing levels of socioeconomic status, acculturation and racial-identity commitment. (Arthur & Stewart, 2001:7)

Sue, Arredondo, and McDavis (1992) have proposed a series of multicultural counselling competencies (Table 10.4), which have been adopted by The American Counseling

TABLE 10.4	Cross-Cultural Competencies

I. Counsellor Awareness of Own Cultural Values and Biases

A. Beliefs and Attitudes

1. Culturally skilled counsellors have moved from being culturally unaware to being aware and sensitive to their own cultural heritage and to valuing and respecting differences.

2. Culturally skilled counsellors are aware of how their own cultural background and experiences, attitudes, and values and biases influence psychological processes.

3. Culturally skilled counsellors are able to recognize the limits of their competencies and expertise.

4. Culturally skilled counsellors are comfortable with differences that exist between themselves and clients in terms of race, ethnicity, culture, and beliefs.

B. Knowledge

1. Culturally skilled counsellors have specific knowledge about their own racial and cultural heritage and the way it personally and professionally affects their definitions and biases of normality-abnormality and the process of counselling.

2. Culturally skilled counsellors possess knowledge and understanding about how oppression, racism, discrimination, and stereotyping affect their work. This allows them to acknowledge their own racist attitudes, beliefs, and feelings. Although this standard applies to all groups, White counsellors may need to understand how they may have directly or indirectly benefited from individual, institutional, and cultural racism (White identity development models).

3. Culturally skilled counsellors possess knowledge about their social impact upon others. They know how communication styles differ, how styles may clash with or facilitate the counselling process with minority clients, and how to anticipate the impact communication style may have on clients.

C. Skills

1. Culturally skilled counsellors seek out educational, consultative, and training experiences to enrich their understanding and effectiveness in working with culturally different populations. Being able to recognize the limits of their competencies, they (a) seek consultation, (b) seek further training or education, (c) refer out to more qualified individuals or resources, or (d) engage in a combination of these.

2. Culturally skilled counsellors are constantly seeking to understand themselves as racial and cultural beings and are actively seeking a nonracist identity.

II. Counsellor Awareness of Client's Worldview

A. Attitudes and Beliefs

1. Culturally skilled counsellors are aware of their negative emotional reactions toward other racial and ethnic groups that may prove detrimental to their clients in counselling. They are willing to contrast their own beliefs and attitudes with those of their culturally different clients in a nonjudgmental fashion.

2. Culturally skilled counsellors are aware of their stereotypes and preconceived notions that they may hold toward other racial and ethnic minority groups.

B. Knowledge

1. Culturally skilled counsellors possess specific knowledge and information about the particular group that they are working with. They are aware of the life

| TABLE 10.4 | Cross-Cultural Competencies (Continued) |

experiences, cultural heritage, and historical background of their culturally different clients. This particular competency is strongly linked to the "minority identity development models" available in the literature.

2. Culturally skilled counsellors understand how race, culture, and ethnicity may affect personality formation, vocational choices, manifestation of psychological disorders, help-seeking behaviour, and the appropriateness or inappropriateness of counselling approaches.

3. Culturally skilled counsellors understand and have knowledge about sociopolitical influences that impinge upon the life of racial and ethnic minorities. Immigration issues, poverty, racism, stereotyping, and powerlessness all leave major scars that may influence the counselling process.

C. **Skills**

1. Culturally skilled counsellors should familiarize themselves with relevant research and the latest findings regarding mental health and mental disorders of various ethnic and racial groups. They should actively seek out educational experiences that foster their knowledge, understanding, and cross-cultural skills.

2. Culturally skilled counsellors become actively involved with minority individuals outside the counselling setting (community events, social and political functions, celebrations, friendships, neighbourhood groups) so that their perspective of minorities is more than an academic or helping exercise.

III. **Culturally Appropriate Intervention Strategies**

A. **Attitudes and Beliefs**

1. Culturally skilled counsellors respect client religious and/or spiritual beliefs and values, including attributions and taboos, because they affect worldview, psychosocial functioning, and expressions of distress.

2. Culturally skilled counsellors respect indigenous helping practices and respect the intrinsic help-giving networks of minority communities.

3. Culturally skilled counsellors value bilingualism and do not view another language as an impediment to counselling. They recognize that monolingualism may be the real impediment.

B. **Knowledge**

1. Culturally skilled counsellors have a clear and explicit knowledge and understanding of the generic characteristics of counselling and therapy (culture bound, class bound, and monolingual) and the ways these characteristics may clash with the cultural values of various minority groups.

2. Culturally skilled counsellors are aware of institutional barriers that prevent minorities from using mental health services.

3. Culturally skilled counsellors have knowledge of the potential bias in assessment instruments. For this reason, they keep in mind the cultural and linguistic characteristics of the clients when they use procedures or interpret findings.

4. Culturally skilled counsellors have knowledge of minority family structures, hierarchies, values, and beliefs. They are knowledgeable about the community characteristics and the resources in the community as well as the family.

5. Culturally skilled counsellors should be aware of relevant discriminatory practices at the social and community level that may affect the psychological welfare of the population being served.

TABLE 10.4	Cross-Cultural Competencies (Continued)

C. Skills

1. Culturally skilled counsellors are able to engage in a variety of verbal and nonverbal helping responses. They are able to send and receive both verbal and nonverbal messages accurately and appropriately. They are not tied down to only one method or approach to helping but recognize that helping styles and approaches may be culture bound. When they sense that their helping style is limited and potentially inappropriate, they can anticipate and ameliorate its negative impact.

2. Culturally skilled counsellors are able to exercise institutional intervention skills on behalf of their clients. They can help clients determine whether a "problem" stems from racism or bias in others (the concept of healthy paranoia) so that clients do not inappropriately blame themselves.

3. Culturally skilled counsellors are not averse to seeking consultation with traditional healers and religious and spiritual leaders and practitioners in the treatment of culturally different clients when appropriate.

4. Culturally skilled counsellors take responsibility for interacting in the language requested by the client; otherwise, they make appropriate referral. A serious problem arises when the linguistic skills of the counsellor do not match the language of the client. In these cases, counsellors should (a) seek a translator with cultural knowledge and appropriate professional background or (b) refer to knowledgeable and competent bilingual counsellor.

5. Culturally skilled counsellors have training and expertise in the use of traditional assessment and testing instruments. They not only understand the technical aspects of the instruments but are also aware of the cultural limitations. This allows them to use test instruments for the welfare of the diverse clients.

6. Culturally skilled counsellors should attend to as well as work to eliminate biases, prejudices, and discriminatory practices. They should be cognizant of sociopolitical contexts in conducting evaluations and providing interventions and should develop sensitivity to issues of oppression, sexism, and racism.

7. Culturally skilled counsellors take responsibility in educating their clients to the processes of psychological intervention, such as goals, expectations, legal rights, and the counsellor's orientation.

Source: Sue, Arredondo, and McDavis, 1992:484–86. Adapted and reprinted with permission of the American Counselling Association.

Association. They are organized into three clusters: counsellor awareness of own values and biases, counsellor awareness of clients' worldviews, and culturally appropriate intervention strategies, which in turn are detailed in terms of the counsellor's attitudes and beliefs, knowledge, and skills.

Awareness of Self

Counselors who presume that they are free of racism seriously underestimate the impact of their own socialization.
—*Pedersen, 1994:58*

Culturally competent counsellors are committed to understanding their own ethnic and value base. They consider how factors such as their own race, culture, sexual orientation, and religion shape their worldview and impact their work with clients who are different from them. They strive to develop and demonstrate understanding and comfort with diversity.

Counsellors must constantly question the relevance of their behaviour, values, and assumptions for particular clients and cultures. **Ethnocentrism** is the inclination to judge others negatively in relation to one's own cultural values and norms. Counsellors who work from an ethnocentric perspective may be predisposed to discount the importance of cultural traditions and beliefs. Worse still, they may see cultural traits as something to be treated or changed because they use their traditions, standards, and majority norms as a measure of normal behaviour. But respect for individual and cultural diversity implies more than just tolerance. It requires counsellors to accept that other cultures and lifestyles are equally valid, albeit different. This is an ethical responsibility for professional counsellors. For example, Standard A.9 of the Canadian Counselling Association's Code of Ethics directs counsellors to pursue knowledge and experiences that help them understand diversity:

> Counsellors strive to understand and respect the diversity of their clients, including differences related to age, ethnicity, culture, gender, disability, religion, sexual orientation, and social-economic status.

Typically, counsellors are well-meaning individuals who see themselves as moral and accepting. Thus, as Sue and Sue (1999) suggest, it may be very difficult for them to understand how their actions may be hurtful to their minority clients through the following:

- Stereotyping (for example, accepting the commonly held, but erroneous belief that First Nations people can't hold their liquor).
- Adhering to counselling strategies that are culture bound (for example, many people of colour prefer that "the helper [should be] more active, self-disclosing and not adverse to giving advice and suggestions where appropriate") (Sue & Sue, 1999:29).
- Believing that one's own cultural heritage and way of doing things is superior. Unchecked, this can lead to oppression.

The Importance of Personal Involvement

Books, films, courses, and seminars can be invaluable sources of information for counsellors in their quest for cultural deepening and understanding. These tools can greatly deepen intellectual knowledge and awareness about cultural customs and variations. They are also important for stimulating thought and broadening knowledge about diversity. However, counsellors also need to embrace experiential learning. Multicultural events, travel, visits to various churches, synagogues, and other places of worship, will expose counsellors to the subtleties of culture, including the wide variations in style and practice that exist within various groups. Multifaith calendars can be used as a starting point to learn about the religious holidays and festivals that different people celebrate. Cultivating multicultural friendships and involvement in multicultural organizations help counsellors broaden their worldview, increase their tolerance, and learn about the many different ways to make sense of the world.

Moreover, cross-cultural experiential learning exposes counsellors to the reality that there may be many different ways to view and solve the same problem. But achieving cross-cultural competence is difficult, perhaps impossible, if counsellors remain personally isolated within their own cultural community of friends and family.

In addition, contact with different cultures provides opportunities to rehearse adaptive functioning skills that help us survive in the diversified global village of the future. By learning to work with those different from ourselves, we learn that we can develop the facility for working with future cultures that we do not yet know (Pedersen, 2001:20).

Reminder

The importance of avoiding stereotypes needs to be emphasized. Individuals of any culture may or may not hold to the values and customs of their group. Some adhere completely, while others may be assimilated into the mainstream society. As well, physical appearance does not mean that the person speaks the language or adheres to the culture that they appear to represent.

SUMMARY

The increasing diversity of the Canadian population means that counsellors must develop their understanding and capacity for working with different cultures.

Stereotyping means holding firm judgments about people based on preconceptions. Individuals may adhere strongly to the values and customs of the culture to which they belong, or their worldview may differ sharply. Counsellors must avoid assumptions while accepting that people from different cultures have different standards of behaviour. However, since it is not realistic to expect to know about all cultures, counsellors need to use clients as sources of information.

Worldview is the looking glass through which clients see the world, including their core beliefs and assumptions. Counsellors need to understand how cultural origin influences their clients' worldviews. Similarly, they need to be aware of how their own cultural past influences their assumptions and responses.

Research has shown that ethnic minority clients avoid seeking counselling, and when they do, they are typically not satisfied with the outcomes. Moreover, they may have different expectations than Western clients.

Counsellors need to be sensitive to the needs and problems faced by refugees who may have faced considerable hardship in their move to Canada. Other clients need to be understood in the context of their history that might have included oppression and racism.

The elements of cross-cultural understanding include the following: individual identity and role within family and community, verbal and emotional expressiveness, relationship expectations, style of communication, use of language, personal priorities, values, and beliefs, and time orientation.

Cross-cultural counselling might address such issues as language, unemployment, poverty, discrimination, culture shock, parent-child relationship problems, and male-female role issues.

Successful work with First Nations people is more likely to occur when counsellors honour differences, include extended families and elders in the process, demonstrate their openness to learn from First Nations people, and respect Native spirituality. As well counsellors need to consider differences in communication styles and gender roles. Understanding and respect of the value of traditional healing practices is essential. Frequently, cultural identity is meshed with religious identity. To understand culture, counsellors must understand religion and spirituality.

Culturally competent counsellors try to understand their own ethnic and value base, including how factors such as their own race, culture, sexual orientation, and religion shape their worldview. They need to deepen their understanding of different cultures. Although books, films, courses, and seminars can be sources of information about cultures, counsellors also need to embrace experiential learning.

EXERCISES

1. In what ways do diversity issues such as ethnicity, gender, and sexual orientation affect counsellor effectiveness?

2. Develop a personal plan for increasing your multicultural sensitivity. Include strategies for experiential learning (e.g., increasing your circle of multicultural friends, involvement in multicultural events, etc).

3. What is your emotional reaction when you meet or counsel someone from a different culture?

4. Research how mental illness may be interpreted by different cultures.

5. Describe how counsellors can be sensitive to cultural norms while honouring individual differences.

6. What are some of the barriers that clients from ethnic minorities face when seeking counselling services?

7. To what extent does your cultural membership give your privilege?

8. Explore the religions of the world (e.g., attend services and festivities, acquire a multi-faith calendar).

9. How can counsellors assist clients to explore spiritual and religious issues without imposing their own religious values?

10. Do you think it's appropriate for counsellors to privately pray for their clients?

11. Use library databases or the online database of Statistics Canada (**www.statcan.ca**) to research the demographic characteristics of your community. Identify the places of birth and mother tongues of the immigrant community. Explore statistics related to Aboriginal groups in your area. What are the implications of your data for counsellors who hope to work in your locality?

12. Invite an Aboriginal person to share with you some of his or her experiences in a residential school. Remember that this is a very sensitive topic, so be prepared to be empathic in response to powerful feelings that might be revealed.

13. What unique problems might arise when counsellors and clients are from the same culture?

14. Think about specific customs and beliefs that you might encounter when you work with different cultures. In what areas do you have difficulty working with objectivity? Examples: arranged marriages, male dominance in the family, and female genital mutilation.

15. Interview several people who are culturally different to learn about their worldviews.

16. Try to analyze the worldviews of selected TV characters and personalities such as Tony Soprano of *The Sopranos*, Donald Trump, and Oprah Winfrey.

17. In what ways is your worldview the same as or different from that of your parents? Your colleagues? Your teacher?

18. Pedersen (1994) says "Counsellors who presume that they are free of racism seriously underestimate the impact of their own socialization" (58). Do you agree or disagree with this statement?

19. Take a cultural inventory of your friends. To what extent do they come from different cultures?

 # WEBLINKS

Canadian Heritage promotes Canadian content and cultural understanding:
www.canadianheritage.gc.ca/index_e.cfm

The official website of Indian and Northern Affairs Canada provides extensive information on federal programs and services as well as readings on the culture and history of Aboriginal people:
www.ainc-inac.gc.ca/index_e.html

The main Statistics Canada website:
www.statcan.ca/start.html

Appendix A

CCA Code of Ethics

Contents

Reprinted with the permission of the Canadian Counselling Association. The CCA Code of Ethics was approved by the CCA Board of Directors in May 1999 and amended by the CCA Board of Directors in May 2002.

PREAMBLE

This Code of Ethics expresses the ethical principles and values of the Canadian Counselling Association and serves as a guide to the professional conduct of all its members. It also informs the public which they serve of the standards of ethical conduct for which members are to be responsible and accountable. The Code reflects such values as integrity, competence, responsibility and an understanding of and respect for the cultural diversity of society. It is part of a social contract, based on attitudes of mutual respect and trust by which society supports the autonomy of the profession in return for the commitment of its members to act ethically in the provision of professional services.

Members of CCA have a responsibility to ensure that they are familiar with this Code of Ethics, understand its application to their professional conduct, and strive to adhere to its principles and values. Counsellors should also be familiar with other sources of information which will assist them in making informed professional decisions. These include the laws, regulations, and policies which are professionally relevant to their working environment.

Members are accountable to both the public and their peers and are therefore subject to the complaints and disciplinary procedures of the Canadian Counselling Association. Violations of this Code, however, do not automatically imply legal liability. Such a determination can only be made by legal and judicial proceedings. This peer review process is intended to enable the Association to advise and discipline its members in response to complaints originating either with peers or the public.

Although a Code of Ethics is essential to the maintenance of ethical integrity and accountability, it cannot be a substitute for the active process of ethical decision-making. Members increasingly confront challenging ethical demands and dilemmas in a complex and dynamic society to which a simple and direct application of this code may not be possible. Also, reasonable differences of opinion can and do exist among members with respect to how ethical principles and values should be rank-ordered when they are in conflict. Therefore, members must develop the ability and the courage to exercise a high level of ethical judgment. For these reasons, the code includes a section on ethical decision making.

This Code is not a static document but will need revisions over time because of the continuing development of ethical knowledge and the emergence of consensus on challenging ethical issues. Therefore, members and others, including members of the public, are invited to submit comments and suggestions at any time to CCA.

ETHICAL PRINCIPLES

The expectations for ethical conduct as expressed in this Code are based on the following fundamental principles:

a. respect for the dignity of persons
b. not wilfully harming others
c. integrity in relationships
d. responsible caring
e. responsibility to society
f. respect for self-determination

THE CCA PROCESS OF ETHICAL DECISION-MAKING

This brief overview of a process of ethical decision-making is provided here so that counsellors will have a sequence of steps to follow when making ethical decisions and resolving ethical dilemmas.

Step One—What are the key ethical issues in this situation?

This first step consists of the counsellor clearly identifying the ethical issues and/or behaviours which are of concern in the particular situation.

Step Two—What ethical guidelines are relevant to this situation?

The second important step consists of referring to the CCA Code of Ethics to see if the situation is dealt with under one or more of the articles in the Code. If there are appropriate articles (for example, on confidentiality or informed consent), following it may be sufficient to address the ethical issue. If the ethical problem is more complex, however, the following further steps will be needed.

Step Three—What ethical principles are of major importance in this situation?

The third step consists of examining the ethical principles that are important in the situation including those that may be in conflict. This would include a review of the six ethical principles as stated in this Code of Ethics.

Step Four—What are the most important principles, and what are the risks and benefits if these principles are acted upon?

The fourth step consists of choosing the most important principles and relevant ethical articles and beginning to implement some possible action by:

(a) generating alternatives and examining the risks and benefits of each,
(b) securing additional information, including possible discussion with the client
(c) consulting with knowledgeable colleagues, with provincial or CCA ethics committees, or with other appropriate sources, and
(d) examining the probable outcomes of various courses of action.

Step Five—Will I feel the same about this situation if I think about it a little longer?

Until this point, this decision-making process has concentrated on fairly cognitive, rational steps, so at the fifth step counsellors should acknowledge and include in their decision making process the feelings and intuitions evoked by the ethical challenge. In so doing, they could use such techniques as:

(a) Quest - a solitary walk in the woods or park where your emotions evoked by the ethical challenge are brought into full awareness,
(b) Incubation - "sleep on it",
(c) Time projection - projecting the ethical situation into the future and thinking about the various probable scenarios.

Step Six—What plan of action will be most helpful in this situation?

The sixth step consists of taking some action. Counsellors should follow a concrete action plan, evaluate the plan, and be prepared to correct any negative consequences that might occur from the action taken.

For a more comprehensive treatment of Ethical Decision-Making, members are directed to the CCA Counselling Ethics Casebook, available from the CCA National Office

A. PROFESSIONAL RESPONSIBILITY

A1. General Responsibility

Counsellors maintain high standards of professional competence and ethical behaviour, and recognize the need for continuing education and personal care in order to meet this responsibility.

A2. Respect for Rights

Counsellors participate in only those practices which are respectful of the legal, civic, and moral rights of others, and act to safeguard the dignity and rights of their clients, students, and research participants.

A3. Boundaries of Competence

Counsellors limit their counselling services and practices to those which are within their professional competence by virtue of their education and professional experience, and consistent with any requirements for provincial and national credentials. They refer to other professionals, when the counselling needs of clients exceed their level of competence.

A4. Supervision and Consultation

Counsellors take reasonable steps to obtain supervision and/or consultation with respect to their counselling practices and, particularly, with respect to doubts or uncertainties which may arise during their professional work.

A5. Representation of Professional Qualifications

Counsellors claim or imply only those professional qualifications which they possess, and are responsible for correcting any known misrepresentation of their qualifications by others.

A6. Responsibility to Counsellors and other Professionals

Counsellors understand that ethical behaviour among themselves and with other professionals is expected at all time.

A7. Unethical Behaviour by Other Counsellors

Counsellors have an obligation when they have serious doubts as to the ethical behaviour of another counsellor, to seek an informal resolution with the counsellor, when feasible and appropriate. When an informal resolution is not appropriate or feasible, or is unsuccessful, counsellors report their concerns to the CCA Ethics Committee. When the counsellors are members of a CCA Affiliate organization that has agreed to manage Complaints and Disciplinary Procedures for its members, counsellors will report their concerns to the appropriate committee of the CCA Affiliate.

A8. Sexual Harassment

Counsellors do not condone or engage in sexual harassment, which is defined as deliberate or repeated verbal or written comments, gestures, or physical contacts of a sexual nature.

A9. Sensitivity to Diversity

Counsellors strive to understand and respect the diversity of their clients, including differences related to age, ethnicity, culture, gender, disability, religion, sexual orientation and social-economic status.

A10. Extension of Ethical Responsibilities

Counselling services and products provided by counsellors through classroom instruction, public lectures, demonstrations, publications, radio and television programs, computer technology and other media must meet the appropriate ethical standards of this Code of Ethics.

B. COUNSELLING RELATIONSHIPS

B1. Primary Responsibility

Counsellors have a primary responsibility to respect the integrity and promote the welfare of their clients. They work collaboratively with clients to devise integrated, individual counselling plans that offer reasonable promise of success and are consistent with the abilities and circumstances of clients.

B2. Confidentiality

Counselling relationships and information resulting therefrom are kept confidential. However, there are the following exceptions to confidentiality:

  (i) when disclosure is required to prevent clear and imminent danger to the client or others;

 (ii) when legal requirements demand that confidential material be revealed;

(iii) when a child is in need of protection.

B3. Duty to Warn

When counsellors become aware of their clients intent or potential to place others in clear or imminent danger, they use reasonable care to give threatened persons such warnings as are essential to avert foreseeable dangers.

B4. Client's Rights and Informed Consent

When counselling is initiated, and throughout the counselling process as necessary, counsellors inform clients of the purposes, goals, techniques, procedures, limitations, potential risks and benefits of services to be performed, and other such pertinent information. Counsellors make sure that clients understand the implications of diagnosis, fees and fee collection arrangements, record keeping, and limits to confidentiality. Clients have the right to participate in the ongoing counselling plans, to refuse any recommended services, and to be advised of the consequences of such refusal.

B5. Children and Persons with Diminished Capacity

Counsellors conduct the informed consent process with those legally appropriate to give consent when counselling, assessing, and having as research subjects children and/or persons with diminished capacity. These clients also give consent to such services or involvement commensurate with their capacity to do so.

B6. Maintenance of Records

Counsellors maintain records in sufficient detail to track the sequence and nature of professional services rendered and consistent with any legal, regulatory, agency, or institutional requirement. They secure the safety of such records and, create, maintain, transfer, and dispose of them in a manner compliant with the requirements of confidentiality and the other articles of this Code of Ethics.

B7. Access to Records

Counsellors understand that clients have a right of access to their counselling records, and that disclosure to others of information from these records only occurs with the written consent of the client and/or when required by law.

B8. Dual Relationships

Counsellors make every effort to avoid dual relationships with clients that could impair professional judgment or increase the risk of harm to clients. Examples of dual relationships include, but are not limited to, familial, social, financial, business, or close personal relationships. When a dual relationship cannot be avoided, counsellors take appropriate professional precautions such as informed consent, consultation, supervision, and documentation to ensure that judgment is not impaired and no exploitation occurs.

B9. Respecting Diversity

Counsellors actively work to understand the diverse cultural background of the clients with whom they work, and do not condone or engage in discrimination based on age, colour, culture, ethnicity, disability, gender, religion, sexual orientation, marital, or socioeconomic status.

B10. Consulting with Other Professionals

Counsellors may consult with other professionally competent persons about the client. However, if the identity of the client is to be revealed, it is done with the written consent of the client. Counsellors choose professional consultants in a manner which will avoid placing the consultant in a conflict of interest situation.

B11. Relationships with Former Clients

Counsellors remain accountable for any relationships established with former clients. Those relationships could include, but are not limited to those of a friendship, social, financial, and business nature. Counsellors exercise caution about entering any such relationships and take into account whether or not the issues and relational dynamics present during the counselling have been fully resolved and properly terminated. In any case, counsellors seek consultation on such decisions.

B12. Sexual Intimacies

Counsellors avoid any type of sexual intimacies with clients and they do not counsel persons with whom they have had a sexual relationship. Counsellors do not engage in sexual intimacies with former clients within a minimum of three years after terminating the counselling relationship. This prohibition is not limited to the three-year period but extends indefinitely if the client is clearly vulnerable, by reason of emotional or cognitive disorder, to exploitative influence by the counsellor. Counsellors, in all such circumstances, clearly bear the burden to ensure that no such exploitative influence has occurred, and to seek consultative assistance.

B13. Multiple Clients

When counsellors agree to provide counselling to two or more persons who have a relationship (such as husband and wife, or parents and children), counsellors clarify at the outset which person or persons are clients and the nature of the relationship they will have with each person. If conflicting roles emerge for counsellors, they must clarify, adjust, or withdraw from roles appropriately.

B14. Multiple Helpers

If, after entering a counselling relationship, a counsellor discovers the client is already in a counselling relationship then, the counsellor is responsible for discussing the issues related to continuing or terminating counselling with the client. It may be necessary, with client consent, to discuss these issues with the other helper.

B15. Group Work

Counsellors have the responsibility to screen prospective group members, especially when group goals focus on self-understanding and growth through self-disclosure. They take reasonable precautions to protect group members from physical and/or psychological harm resulting from interaction within the group, both during and following the group experience.

B16. Computer Use

When computer applications are used as a component of counselling services, counsellors ensure that: (a) client and counsellor identity is verified; (b) the client is capable of using the computer application; (c) the computer application is appropriate to the needs of the client; (d) the client understands the purpose and operation of client-assisted and/or self-help computer applications; and (e) a follow-up of client use of a computer application is provided to assist subsequent needs. In any case, computer applications do not diminish the counsellor's responsibility to act in accordance with the CCA Code of Ethics, and in particular, to ensure adherence to the principles of confidentiality, informed consent, and safeguarding against harmful effects.

B17. Referral

When counsellors determine their inability to be of professional assistance to clients, they avoid initiating a counselling relationship, or immediately terminate it. In either event, members suggest appropriate alternatives, including making a referral to resources about which they are knowledgeable. Should clients decline the suggested referral, counsellors are not obligated to continue the relationship.

B18. Termination of Counselling

Counsellors terminate counselling relationships, with client agreement whenever possible, when it is reasonably clear that: the goals of counselling have been met, the client is no longer benefitting from counselling, when clients do not pay fees charged, when previously disclosed agency or institutional limits do not allow for the provision of further counselling services.

However, counsellors make reasonable efforts to facilitate the continuation of counselling services when services are interrupted by such factors as counsellor illness, client or counsellor relocation, client financial difficulties, and so forth.

C. CONSULTING AND PRIVATE PRACTICE

C1. General Responsibility

Counsellors provide consultative services only in those areas in which they have demonstrated competency by virtue of their education and experience.

C2. Undiminished Responsibility and Liability

Counsellors who work in private practice, whether incorporated or not, must ensure that there is no diminishing of their individual professional responsibility to act in accordance with the CCA Code of Ethics, or in their liability for any failure to do so.

C3. Accurate Advertising

Counsellors, when advertising services as private practitioners, do so in a manner that accurately and clearly informs the public of their services and areas of expertise.

C4. Consultative Relationships

Counsellors ensure that consultation occurs within a voluntary relationship between a counsellor and a help-seeking individual, group, or organization, and that the goals are understood by all parties concerned.

C5. Informed Consent

Counsellors who provide services for the use of third parties, acknowledge and clarify for the informed consent of clients, all obligations of such multiple relationships, including purpose(s), entitlement to information, and any restrictions on confidentiality. Third parties include, courts, public and private institutions, funding agencies, employees, and so forth.

C6. Respect for Privacy

Counsellors limit any discussion of client information obtained from a consulting relationship to persons clearly involved with the case. Any written and oral reports restrict data to the purposes of the consultation and, every effort is made to protect client identity and to avoid undue invasion of privacy.

C7. Conflict of Interest

Counsellors who engage in consultation avoid circumstances where the duality of relationships, or the prior possession of information could lead to a conflict of interest.

C8. Sponsorship and Recruitment

Counsellors present any of their organizational affiliations or membership in such a way as to avoid misunderstanding regarding sponsorship or certification. They also avoid the use of any institutional affiliation to recruit private practice clients.

D. EVALUATION AND ASSESSMENT

D1. General Orientation

Counsellors adequately orient and inform clients so that evaluation and assessment results can be placed in proper perspective along with other relevant information.

D2. Purposes and Results of Evaluation and Assessment

Counsellors take responsibility to inform clients about the purpose of any evaluation and assessment instruments and procedures and the meaning of evaluation and assessment results.

D3. Evaluation and Assessment Competence

Counsellors recognize the limits of their competence and offer only those evaluation and assessment services for which they have appropriate preparation and which meet established professional standards.

D4. Administrative and Supervisory Conditions

Counsellors ensure that evaluation and assessment instruments and procedures are administered and supervised under established conditions consistent with professional standards.

They note any departures from standard conditions, and any unusual behavior or irregularities which may affect the interpretation of results.

D5. Use of Technology

Counsellors recognize that their ethical responsibilities are not altered, or in any way diminished, by the use of technology for the administration of evaluation and assessment instruments. Counsellors retain their responsibility for the maintenance of the ethical principles of privacy, confidentiality, and responsibility for decisions regardless of the technology used.

D6. Appropriateness of Evaluation and Assessment

Counsellors ensure that evaluation and assessment instruments and procedures are valid, reliable, and appropriate to both the client and the intended purposes.

D7. Reporting Evaluation and Assessment Results

Counsellors ensure that when reporting evaluation and assessment results to clients and other individuals care is taken to provide, in an appropriate manner, accurate and sufficient information for an understanding of any conclusions and recommendations made, and to identify the basis for any reservations which might exist.

D8. Release of Evaluation and Assessment Data

Counsellors ensure that evaluation and assessment data are released only to persons qualified to interpret and use them properly.

D9. Integrity of Evaluation and Assessment Instruments and Procedures

Counsellors who use psychological tests and other assessment instruments, the value of which depends on their novelty to the client, ensure that they are limited to and safeguarded by those with the professional interest and competence to do so.

D10. Sensitivity to Diversity when Assessing and Evaluating

Counsellors proceed with caution when judging and interpreting the performance of minority group members and any other persons not represented in the group on which the evaluation and assessment instruments and procedures were standardized. They recognize and take into account the potential effects of age, ethnicity, disability, culture, gender, religion, sexual orientation, and social-economic status on both the administration of, and the interpretation of date from, such instruments and procedures.

D11. Security Maintenance

Counsellors ensure the integrity and security of evaluation and assessment instruments and procedures consistent with any legal and contractual obligations. They refrain from appropriating, reproducing, or modifying established evaluation and assessment instruments without the expressed permission and adequate recognition of the original author, publisher, and copyright holder.

E. RESEARCH AND PUBLICATIONS

E1. Researcher Responsibility

Counsellors plan, conduct, and report on research in a manner consistent with relevant ethical principles, professional standards of practice, federal and provincial laws, institutional regulations, cultural norms, and standards governing research with human subjects.

E2. Subject Welfare

Counsellors are responsible for protecting the welfare of their research subjects during research, and avoid causing injurious psychological, physical or social effects to persons who participate in their research activities.

E3. Principal Researcher Responsibility

Counsellors when in the role of principal researcher are responsible for ensuring that appropriate ethical research practices are followed and, with respect to research involving human subjects, they obtain an independent and appropriate ethical review before proceeding with the research. Research associates involved in the research activities share ethical obligations and full responsibility for their own actions.

E4. Voluntary Participation

Counsellors ensure that participation in research is voluntary. However, involuntary participation may be appropriate when it can be shown that participation will have no harmful effects on subjects, is essential to the research, and meets ethical review requirements.

E5. Informed Consent of Research Subjects

Counsellors inform all research subjects of the purpose(s) of their research. In addition, subjects are made aware of any experimental procedures, possible risks, disclosures and limitations on confidentiality. Subjects are also told they are free to ask questions and to discontinue at any time.

E6. Research Confidentiality

Counsellors ensure that research information on subjects is confidential and the identity of participants is protected unless otherwise authorized by them, consistent with all informed consent procedures.

E7. Further Research

Counsellors have an obligation to collaborate with colleagues by making available original research data to qualified researchers who may wish to replicate or verify the research.

E8. Research Sponsors

Counsellors when conducting research obtain informed consent form sponsors and institutions and ensure that sponsors and institutions are given feedback information and proper acknowledgment.

E9. Review of Manuscripts

Counsellors who review material submitted for publication, research or other scholarly purposes respect the confidentiality and proprietary rights of those who submitted the research.

E10. Reporting Results

In reporting research results, counsellors mention any variables and conditions that might affect the outcome of the investigation or the interpretation of the results, and provide information sufficient for others who might wish to replicate the research.

E11. Research Contributions

Counsellors give due credit through joint authorship, acknowledgment, footnote statements, or other appropriate means to those who have contributed significantly to the research and/or publication, and to those who have done previous work on the topic. For an article that is based mainly on a student thesis or dissertation, the student is listed as principal author.

E12. Submission for Publication

Counsellors do not submit the same manuscript or one essentially similar in content for simultaneous publication consideration by two or more journals. In addition, manuscripts published in whole or in substantial part in another journal or published work should not be submitted for publication without acknowledgment and permission from the previous publication.

F. COUNSELLOR EDUCATION, TRAINING, AND SUPERVISION

F1. General Responsibility

Counsellors who are responsible for counsellor education, training, and supervision adhere to current CCA guidelines and standards with respect to such activities and conduct themselves in a manner consistent with the CCA Code of Ethics and Standards of Practice.

F2. Boundaries of Competence

Counsellors who conduct counsellor education, training, and supervision have the necessary knowledge and skills to do so, and limit their involvement to such competencies.

F3. Ethical Orientation

Counsellors who are responsible for counsellor education, training, and supervision have an obligation to make their students, trainees, and supervisees aware of their ethical responsibilities as expressed in the CCA Code of Ethics, and Standards of Practice.

F4. Clarification of Roles and Responsibilities

Counsellors who engage in counselling supervision of students or trainees take responsibility for clarifying their respective roles and obligations.

F5. Welfare of Clients

Counsellors who engage in counselling supervision of students or trainees take steps to ensure the welfare of clients during the supervised practice period, and intervene, when necessary, to ensure that this obligation is met.

F6. Program Orientation

Counsellors responsible for counsellor education programs and training activities take responsibility to orient perspective students and trainees to all core elements of such programs and activities, including to a clear policy with respect to all supervised practice components, both those simulated and real.

F7. Relational Boundaries

Counsellors who work as counsellor educators, trainers, and supervisors establish relationships with their students, trainees, and supervisees such that appropriate relational boundaries are clarified and maintained, and dual relationships avoided.

F8. Obligation to Inform

Counsellors who work as counsellor educators, trainers, and supervisors take steps to inform students, trainees, and supervisees, at the beginning of activities associated with these roles, of all reasonably foreseeable circumstances under which confidentiality maybe breached during such activities.

F9. Self-Development and Self-Awareness

Counsellors who work as counsellor educators, trainers, and supervisors, encourage and facilitate the self-development and self-awareness of students, trainees, and supervisees, so that they learn to integrate their professional practice and personal insight.

F10. Dealing with Personal Issues

Counsellors responsible for counsellor education, training, and supervision recognize when such activities evoke significant personal issues for students, trainees, and supervisees and refer to other sources when necessary to avoid counselling those for whom they hold administrative, or evaluative responsibility.

F11. Self-Growth Activities

Counsellors who work as counsellor educators, trainees, and supervisors ensure that any professional experiences which requires self-disclosure, and engagement in self-growth activities are managed in a manner consistent with the principles of informed consent, confidentiality, and safeguarding against any harmful effects.

Appendix B

Canadian Association of Social Workers Code of Ethics

Contents

ACKNOWLEDGEMENTS

The Canadian Association of Social Workers (CASW) acknowledges with thanks the National Association of Social Workers (NASW) for permission to use sections of the copyrighted NASW 1999 *Code of Ethics* in the development of the CASW 2005 *Code of Ethics* and CASW 2005 *Guidelines for Ethical Practice*.

The CASW also acknowledges that other codes of ethics and resources were used in the development of this *Code* and the *Guidelines for Ethical Practice*, in particular the *Code of Ethics* of the Australian Association of Social Workers (AASW). These resources can be found in the Reference section of each document.

PURPOSE OF THE CASW CODE OF ETHICS

Ethical behaviour lies at the core of every profession. The Canadian Association of Social Workers (CASW) *Code of Ethics* sets forth values and principles to guide social workers' professional conduct. A code of ethics cannot guarantee ethical behaviour. Ethical behaviour comes from a social worker's individual commitment to engage in ethical practice. Both the spirit and the letter of this *Code of Ethics* will guide social workers as they act in good faith and with a genuine desire to make sound judgements.

This *Code of Ethics* is consistent with the International Federation of Social Workers (IFSW) *International Declaration of Ethical Principles of Social Work* (1994, 2004), which requires members of the CASW to uphold the values and principles established by both the CASW and the IFSW. Other individuals, organizations and bodies (such as regulatory boards, professional liability insurance providers, courts of law, boards of directors of organizations employing social workers and government agencies) may also choose to adopt this *Code of Ethics* or use it as a basis for evaluating professional conduct. In Canada, each province and territory is responsible for regulating the professional conduct of social workers to ensure the protection of the public. Social workers are advised to contact the regulatory body in their province or territory to determine whether it has adopted this *Code of Ethics*.[1]

Recognition of Individual and Professional Diversity

The CASW *Code of Ethics* does not provide a set of rules that prescribe how social workers should act in all situations. Further, the *Code of Ethics* does not specify which values and principles are most important and which outweigh others in instances of conflict. Reasonable differences of opinion exist among social workers with respect to which values and principles should be given priority in a particular situation. Further, a social worker's personal values, culture, religious beliefs, practices and/or other important distinctions, such as age, ability, gender or sexual orientation can affect his/her ethical choices. Thus, social workers need to be aware of any conflicts between personal and professional values and deal with them responsibly.

---

[1]To find the IFSW declarations or information about your relevant regulatory body, visit the CASW web site: http://www.casw-acts.ca

Ethical Behaviour Requires Due Consideration of Issues and Judgement

Social work is a multifaceted profession. As professionals, social workers are educated to exercise judgement in the face of complex and competing interests and claims. Ethical decision-making in a given situation will involve the informed judgement of the individual social worker. Instances may arise when social workers' ethical obligations conflict with agency policies, or relevant laws or regulations. When such conflicts occur, social workers shall make a responsible effort to resolve the conflicts in a manner that is consistent with the values and principles expressed in this *Code of Ethics*. If a reasonable resolution of the conflict does not appear possible, social workers shall seek appropriate consultation before making a decision. This may involve consultation with an ethics committee, a regulatory body, a knowledgeable colleague, supervisor or legal counsel.

PREAMBLE

The social work profession is dedicated to the welfare and self-realization of all people; the development and disciplined use of scientific and professional knowledge; the development of resources and skills to meet individual, group, national and international changing needs and aspirations; and the achievement of social justice for all. The profession has a particular interest in the needs and empowerment of people who are vulnerable, oppressed, and/or living in poverty. Social workers are committed to human rights as enshrined in Canadian law, as well as in international conventions on human rights created or supported by the United Nations.

As professionals in a country that upholds respect for diversity, and in keeping with democratic rights and freedoms, social workers respect the distinct systems of beliefs and lifestyles of individuals, families, groups, communities and nations without prejudice (United Nations Centre for Human Rights, 1992). Specifically, social workers do not tolerate discrimination[2] based on age, abilities, ethnic background, gender, language, marital status, national ancestry, political affiliation, race, religion, sexual orientation or socio-economic status.

CORE SOCIAL WORK VALUES AND PRINCIPLES

Social workers uphold the following core social work values:

Value 1: Respect for Inherent Dignity and Worth of Persons

Value 2: Pursuit of Social Justice

Value 3: Service to Humanity

Value 4: Integrity of Professional Practice

Value 5: Confidentiality in Professional Practice

Value 6: Competence in Professional Practice

---

[2]Throughout this document the term "discrimination" refers to treating people unfavourably or holding negative or prejudicial attitudes based on discernable differences or stereotypes. It does **not refer** to the positive intent behind programs, such as affirmative action, where one group may be given preferential treatment to address inequities created by discrimination.

The following section describes each of these values and discusses their under-lying principles.

Value 1: Respect for the Inherent Dignity and Worth of Persons

Social work is founded on a long-standing commitment to respect the inherent dignity and individual worth of all persons. When required by law to override a client's wishes, social workers take care to use the minimum coercion required. Social workers recognize and respect the diversity of Canadian society, taking into account the breadth of differences that exist among individuals, families, groups and communities. Social workers uphold the human rights of individuals and groups as expressed in The *Canadian Charter of Rights and Freedoms* (1982) and the United Nations *Universal Declaration of Human Rights* (1948).

Principles:

- Social workers respect the unique worth and inherent dignity of all people and uphold human rights.
- Social workers uphold each person's right to self-determination, consistent with that person's capacity and with the rights of others.
- Social workers respect the diversity among individuals in Canadian society and the right of individuals to their unique beliefs consistent with the rights of others.
- Social workers respect the client's right to make choices based on voluntary, informed consent.
- Social workers who have children as clients determine the child's ability to consent and where appropriate, explain to the child and to the child's parents/guardians, the nature of the social worker's relationship to the child.
- Social workers uphold the right of society to impose limitations on the self-determination of individuals, when such limitations protect individuals from self-harm and from harming others.
- Social workers uphold the right of every person to be free from violence and threat of violence.

Value 2: Pursuit of Social Justice

Social workers believe in the obligation of people, individually and collectively, to provide resources, services and opportunities for the overall benefit of humanity and to afford them protection from harm. Social workers promote social fairness and the equitable distribution of resources, and act to reduce barriers and expand choice for all persons, with special regard for those who are marginalized, disadvantaged, vulnerable, and/or have exceptional needs. Social workers oppose prejudice and discrimination against any person or group of persons, on any grounds, and specifically challenge views and actions that stereotype particular persons or groups.

Principles:

- Social workers uphold the right of people to have access to resources to meet basic human needs.

- Social workers advocate for fair and equitable access to public services and benefits.
- Social workers advocate for equal treatment and protection under the law and challenge injustices, especially injustices that affect the vulnerable and disadvantaged.
- Social workers promote social development and environmental management in the interests of all people.

Value 3: Service to Humanity

The social work profession upholds service in the interests of others, consistent with social justice, as a core professional objective. In professional practice, social workers balance individual needs, and rights and freedoms with collective interests in the service of humanity. When acting in a professional capacity, social workers place professional service before personal goals or advantage, and use their power and authority in disciplined and responsible ways that serve society. The social work profession contributes to knowledge and skills that assist in the management of conflicts and the wide-ranging consequences of conflict.

Principles:

- Social workers place the needs of others above self-interest when acting in a professional capacity.
- Social workers strive to use the power and authority vested in them as professionals in responsible ways that serve the needs of clients and the promotion of social justice.
- Social workers promote individual development and pursuit of individual goals, as well as the development of a just society.
- Social workers use their knowledge and skills in bringing about fair resolutions to conflict and in assisting those affected by conflict.

Value 4: Integrity in Professional Practice

Social workers demonstrate respect for the profession's purpose, values and ethical principles relevant to their field of practice. Social workers maintain a high level of professional conduct by acting honestly and responsibly, and promoting the values of the profession. Social workers strive for impartiality in their professional practice, and refrain from imposing their personal values, views and preferences on clients. It is the responsibility of social workers to establish the tenor of their professional relationship with clients, and others to whom they have a professional duty, and to maintain professional boundaries. As individuals, social workers take care in their actions to not bring the reputation of the profession into disrepute. An essential element of integrity in professional practice is ethical accountability based on this *Code of Ethics*, the IFSW *International Declaration of Ethical Principles of Social Work*, and other relevant provincial/territorial standards and guidelines. Where conflicts exist with respect to these sources of ethical guidance, social workers are encouraged to seek advice, including consultation with their regulatory body.

Principles:

- Social workers demonstrate and promote the qualities of honesty, reliability, impartiality and diligence in their professional practice.

- Social workers demonstrate adherence to the values and ethical principles of the profession and promote respect for the profession's values and principles in organizations where they work or with which they have a professional affiliation.
- Social workers establish appropriate boundaries in relationships with clients and ensure that the relationship serves the needs of clients.
- Social workers value openness and transparency in professional practice and avoid relationships where their integrity or impartiality may be compromised, ensuring that should a conflict of interest be unavoidable, the nature of the conflict is fully disclosed.

Value 5: Confidentiality in Professional Practice

A cornerstone of professional social work relationships is confidentiality with respect to all matters associated with professional services to clients. Social workers demonstrate respect for the trust and confidence placed in them by clients, communities and other professionals by protecting the privacy of client information and respecting the client's right to control when or whether this information will be shared with third parties. Social workers only disclose confidential information to other parties (including family members) with the informed consent of clients, clients' legally authorized representatives or when required by law or court order. The general expectation that social workers will keep information confidential does not apply when disclosure is necessary to prevent serious, foreseeable and imminent harm to a client or others. In all instances, social workers disclose the least amount of confidential information necessary to achieve the desired purpose.

Principles:

- Social workers respect the importance of the trust and confidence placed in the professional relationship by clients and members of the public.
- Social workers respect the client's right to confidentiality of information shared in a professional context.
- Social workers only disclose confidential information with the informed consent of the client or permission of client's legal representative.
- Social workers may break confidentiality and communicate client information without permission when required or permitted by relevant laws, court order or this *Code*.
- Social workers demonstrate transparency with respect to limits to confidentiality that apply to their professional practice by clearly communicating these limitations to clients early in their relationship.

Value 6: Competence in Professional Practice

Social workers respect a client's right to competent social worker services. Social workers analyze the nature of social needs and problems, and encourage innovative, effective strategies and techniques to meet both new and existing needs and, where possible, contribute to the knowledge base of the profession. Social workers have a responsibility to maintain professional proficiency, to continually strive to increase their professional knowledge and skills, and to apply new knowledge in practice commensurate with their level of professional education, skill and competency, seeking consultation and supervision as appropriate.

Principles:

- Social workers uphold the right of clients to be offered the highest quality service possible.
- Social workers strive to maintain and increase their professional knowledge and skill.
- Social workers demonstrate due care for client's interests and safety by limiting professional practice to areas of demonstrated competence.
- Social workers contribute to the ongoing development of the profession and its ability to serve humanity, where possible, by participating in the development of current and future social workers and the development of new professional knowledge.
- Social workers who engage in research minimize risks to participants, ensure informed consent, maintain confidentiality and accurately report the results of their studies.

GLOSSARY

Capacity

The ability to understand information relevant to a decision and to appreciate the reasonably foreseeable consequences of choosing to act or not to act. Capacity is specific to each decision and thus a person may be capable of deciding about a place of residence, for example, but not capable with respect to deciding about a treatment. Capacity can change over time (Etchells, Sharpe, Elliot and Singer, 1996).

Recent references in law point to the concept of "a mature minor," which Rozovsky and Rozovsky (1990) define as " . . . one with capacity to understand the nature and consequences of medical treatment. Such a person has the power to consent to medical treatment and parental consent is not necessary" (p. 55). They quote the comments by The Honorable Justice Lambert in *Van Mol v. Ashmore*, which help clarify common law with respect to a minor's capacity to consent. He states:

> At common law, without reference to statute law, a young person, still a minor, may give, on his or her own behalf, a fully informed consent to medical treatment if he or she has sufficient maturity, intelligence and capacity of understanding what is involved in making informed choices about the proposed medical treatment . . . once the capacity to consent has been achieved by the young person reaching sufficient maturity, intelligence and capability of understanding, the discussions about the nature of the treatment, its gravity, the material risks and any special and unusual risks, and the decisions about undergoing treatment, and about the form of the treatment, must all take place with and be made by the young person whose bodily integrity is to be invaded and whose life and health will be affected by the outcome.

Child

The *Convention on the Rights of the Child* passed by the United Nations in 1959 and ratified by Canada in 1990, define a child as a person under the age of 18 years unless national law recognizes an earlier age of majority (Alberta Law Reform Institute, 1991). The age of majority differs in provinces and territories in Canada. Under the *Criminal Code of Canada*, the age of consent is held to be over the age of 14 years; age in the context of the criminal code frequently refers to capacity to consent to sexual relations. All jurisdictions in Canada have legislation regarding child protection, which defines the age of a child for the purposes of protection. In Canada, in the absence of provincial or territorial legislation, courts are governed by common law. Social workers are encouraged to maintain current knowledge with respect to legislation on the age of a child, as well as capacity and consent in their jurisdiction.

Client

A person, family, group of persons, incorporated body, association or community on whose behalf a social worker provides or agrees to provide a service or to whom the social worker is legally obligated to provide a service. Examples of legal obligation to provide service include a legislated responsibility (such as in child welfare) or a valid court order. In the case of a valid court order, the judge/court is the client and the person(s) who is ordered by the court to participate in assessment is recognized as an involuntary client.

Conduct Unbecoming

Behaviour or conduct that does not meet social work standard of care requirements and is, therefore, subject to discipline. In reaching a decision in Matthews and Board of Directors of Physiotherapy (1986) 54 O.R. (2d) 375, Saunders J. makes three important statements regarding standards of practice, and by implication, professional codes of ethics:

1. Standards of practice are inherent characteristics of any profession.
2. Standards of practice may be written or unwritten.
3. Some conduct is clearly regarded as misconduct and need not be written down, whereas other conduct may be the subject of dispute within a profession. (See "Standard of Practice.")

Confidentiality

A professional value that demands that professionally acquired information be kept private and not shared with third parties unless the client provides informed consent or a professional or legal obligation exists to share such information without client informed consent.

Discrimination

Treating people unfavourably or holding negative or prejudicial attitudes based on discernable differences or stereotypes (AASW, 1999).

Informed Consent

Voluntary agreement reached by a capable client based on information about foreseeable risks and benefits associated with the agreement (e.g., participation in counselling or agreement to disclose social work report to a third party).

Human Rights

The rights of an individual that are considered the basis for freedom and justice, and serve to protect people from discrimination and harassment. Social workers may refer to the *Canadian Charter of Rights and Freedoms* enacted as Schedule B to the *Canada Act* 1982 (U.K.) 1982, c. 11, which came into force on April 17, 1982, as well as the *Universal Declaration of Human Rights* (1948) proclaimed by the United Nations General Assembly December 10, 1948.

Malpractice and Negligence

Behaviour that is included in "conduct unbecoming" and relates to social work practice behaviour within the parameters of the professional relationship that falls below the standard of practice and results in, or aggravation of, injury to a client. It includes behaviour that results in assault, deceit, fraudulent misrepresentations, defamation of character, breach of contract, violation of human rights, malicious prosecution, false imprisonment or criminal conviction.

Self-Determination

A core social work value that refers to the right to self-direction and freedom of choice without interference from others. Self-determination is codified in practice through mechanisms of informed consent. Social workers may be obligated to limit self-determination when a client lacks capacity or in order to prevent harm (Regehr and Antle, 1997).

Social Worker

A person who is duly registered to practice social work in a province or territory; or where mandatory registration does not exist, a person with social work education from an institution recognized by the Canadian Association of Schools of Social Work (CASSW) or an institution from outside of Canada that has been approved by the CASW, who is practising social work and who voluntarily agrees to be subject to this *Code of Ethics*. **Note:** Social workers living in Quebec and British Columbia, whose social work education was obtained outside of Canada, follow a separate approval process within their respective provinces.

Standard of Practice

The standard of care ordinarily expected of a competent social worker. It means that the public is assured that a social worker has the training, the skill and the diligence to provide them with social work services. Social workers are urged to refer to standards of practice that have been set by their provincial or territorial regulatory body or relevant professional association (see "Conduct Unbecoming").

Voluntary

"In the context of consent, 'voluntariness' refers to a patient's right to make treatment decisions free of any undue influence, such as ability of others to exert control over a patient by force, coercion or manipulation. ... The requirement for voluntariness does not imply that clinicians should refrain from persuading patients to accept advice. Persuasion involves appealing to the patient's reason in an attempt to convince him or her of the merits of a recommendation. In attempting to persuade the patient to follow a particular course of action, the clinician still leaves the patient free to accept or reject this advice." (Etchells, Sharpe, Dykeman, Meslin and Singer, 1996, p. 1083).

REFERENCES

AASW. (1999). *AASW code of ethics*. Kingston: Australian Association of Social Workers (AASW).

Alberta Law Reform Institute. (1991). *Status of the child: Revised report* (Report No. 60). Edmonton, Alberta: Law Reform Institute.

BASW. (2002). *BASW: A code of ethics for social workers*. British Association of Social Workers (BASW).

Canadian Charter of Rights and Freedoms Enacted as Schedule B to the *Canada Act* 1982, c.11 (1982). [**http://laws.justice.gc.ca/en/charter/**]

CASW. (1994). *Social Work Code of Ethics*. Ottawa: Canadian Association of Social Workers (CASW).

Criminal Code, R.S., c. C-34, s.1. (1985). [http://laws.justice.gc.ca/en/C-46/40670.html]

Etchells, E.; G. Sharpe; C. Elliott and P. Singer. (1996). Bioethics for clinicians: 3: Capacity. *Canadian Medical Association Journal,* 155, 657-661.

Etchells, E.; G. Sharpe; M.J. Dykeman and P. Singer. (1996). Bioethics for clinicians: 4: Voluntariness. *Canadian Medical Association Journal,* 155, 1083-1086.

IFSW. (1994). *The ethics of social work: Principles and standards.* Geneva, Switzerland: International Federation of Social Workers (IFSW).

(2004). *Ethics in social work: Statement of principles*. Geneva, Switzerland: International Federation of Social Workers (IFSW).

Lens, V. (2000). Protecting the confidentiality of the therapeutic relationship: Jaffe v. Redmond. *Social Work,* 45(3), 273-276.

Matthews and Board of Directors of Physiotherapy (1986) 54 O.R. (2d) 375.

NASW. (1999). *Code of Ethics*. Washington: National Association of Social Workers (NASW).

Regehr, C. and B.J. Antle. (1997). Coercive influences: Informed consent and court-mandated social work practice. *Social Work,* 42(3), 300-306.

Rozovsky, L.E. and F.A. Rozovsky. (1990). *The Canadian law of consent to treatment.* Toronto: Butterworths.

United Nations. (1948). *Universal Declaration of Human Rights.* New York: United Nations. [http://www.unhchr.ch/udhr/]

United Nations Centre for Human Rights. (1992). Teaching and learning about human rights: A manual for schools of social work and the social work profession (Developed in co-operation with International Federation of Social Workers and International Association of Schools of Social Workers). New York: United Nations.

Glossary

Absolute Confidentiality: An assurance that client disclosures are not shared with anyone.

Action Planning: Helping clients make changes in their lives; involves setting goals, identifying strategies for change, and developing plans for reaching goals.

Active Listening: A term describing a cluster of skills that are used to increase the accuracy of understanding. Attending, using silence, paraphrasing, summarizing, questioning, and showing empathy are the basic skills of active listening.

Affect: A term that counsellors use to describe how people express emotions.

Affective Area: How clients feel.

Affective Disorders: Disturbances in mood, including depression and mania.

AIDS: An acronym for **Acquired Immune Deficiency Syndrome**. Caused by HIV infection, AIDS results in a number of different illnesses and opportunistic infections, such as tuberculosis, pneumonia, persistent diarrhea, fever, and skin cancer.

Ambivalence: Multiple and often contradictory feelings about the same problem or experience. Ambivalence, though normal, can complicate clients' decision making and add stress to their lives.

Anorexia Nervosa: An eating disorder that occurs when people reject maintaining a minimally healthy body weight. Driven by low self-esteem and an intense fear of gaining weight, people with anorexia use techniques such as purging (e.g., fasting, vomiting, taking laxatives) and excessive exercise to reduce body weight.

Antianxiety Medication: Medications such as valium and librium that are used to control

serious and persistent anxiety, phobia, and panic attacks.

Antidepressant Medication: Medications such as Prozac, Paxil, and Zolof that are used to help people deal with serious depression.

Antimanic Medication: Medications such as lithium that are used to control the manic symptoms of bipolar disorder.

Antipsychotic Medication: Medications such as chlorpromazine, haloperidol, clozapine, and pisperidone that are used to treat illnesses such as schizophrenia.

Anxiety Disorders: More than normal levels of fear, worry, tension, or anxiety about daily events.

Assertiveness: Behaving and expressing thoughts and feelings in an open and honest manner that respects the rights of others.

Assumptions: Distortions or false conclusions based on simplistic reasoning, incomplete information, or bias.

Attended Silence: Counsellor silence characterized by making eye contact, physically and psychologically focusing on the client, and being self-disciplined to minimize internal and external distraction.

Attending: A term used to describe the way that counsellors communicate to their clients that they are ready, willing, and able to listen. Verbal, nonverbal, and attitudinal cues are the essence of effective attending.

Basic Empathy: A counsellor's acknowledgment of a client's clearly communicated feelings.

Behavioural Area: What clients are doing.

Bipolar Disorder: A mood disorder characterized by alternating periods of depression and abnormally heightened mood, sometimes to the point of grandiosity. Persons with bipolar disorder may behave irrationally (e.g., going on uncontrolled buying sprees, committing sexual indiscretions, and taking part in foolish business investments).

Brief Counselling: An approach to counselling characterized by a focus on resources and solutions rather than problems.

Bulimia: An eating disorder that occurs when people adopt a pattern of excessive overeating followed by vomiting or other purging behaviours to control their weight.

Burnout: A state of emotional, mental, and physical exhaustion that reduces or prevents people from performing their job.

Catharsis: Verbalization of ideas, fears, past significant events, and associations, which results in a release of anxiety or tension.

Challenging Skills: Skills used to encourage clients to critically evaluate their behaviour and ideas.

Closed Question: Questions that can easily be answered with a simple *yes* or *no* (e.g., "Did you go by yourself?").

Cognitive Area: How clients think about their situations.

Command Hallucination: Distorted perception of voices and images directing one to perform some action (e.g., attack or kill someone).

Concreteness: A term used to describe the level of specificity. It is "a way to ensure that general and common experiences and feelings such as depression, anxiety, anger, and so on are defined idiosyncratically for each client" (Cormier & Cormier, 1985:48).

Confrontation: Counselling initiatives that challenge clients to critically examine their actions and/or consider other viewpoints.

Confrontation of Incongruities: Used to point out inconsistencies in a client's verbal and nonverbal messages, values or beliefs, and behaviour.

Congruence: The capacity to be real and consistent with clients; matching behaviour, feelings, and actions.

Contingency Plan: A preventive plan that anticipates possible barriers that clients might encounter as they carry out action plans.

Contract: A negotiated agreement between counsellors and clients regarding the purpose of the work, their respective roles, and the methods and routines that will be used to reach their agreed-on objectives. (*See also* sessional contract.)

Controlled Emotional Involvement: "The empathic sensitivity of the worker to the client's feelings, disciplined by self-awareness, such that the worker's feelings do not inappropriately affect his or her understanding and purposeful response" (Hancock, 1997:131).

Core Conditions: Warmth, empathy, and genuineness.

Counselling: A process of helping clients to learn skills, deal with feelings, and manage problems.

Counselling Relationship: A time-limited period of consultation between a counsellor and a client in order to achieve a defined goal.

Countertransference: Tendency of counsellors to inappropriately transfer feelings and behaviours to clients.

Critical Incident Debriefing: A team meeting held to defuse the impact of a violent or traumatic event such as an assault on a staff member. Debriefing assists workers to normalize and deal with the feelings that may be aroused as a result of the event. As well, debriefing is used to review and revise preventive and crisis intervention procedures.

Defence Mechanisms: Mental process or reaction that shields a person from undesirable or unacceptable thoughts, feelings, or conclusions that, if accepted, would create anxiety or challenges to one's sense of self. Common defence mechanisms include denial, displacement, rationalization, suppression, and regression.

Delusion: Distorted belief involving bizarre thought patterns that cannot be challenged by others using reason or evidence.

Dependent Relationship: A counselling relationship in which clients become overly reliant on their counsellors for decision making. Symptoms include excessive permission seeking, frequent phone calls or office visits for information, and inability to make simple decisions or take action without consulting.

Depression: Pervasive deflation in mood characterized by symptoms such as sadness, hopelessness, decreased energy, and difficulty concentrating, remembering, and making decisions.

Directives: Short statements that provide direction to clients on topics, information, and pace (e.g., "Tell me more.").

Diversity: Variations in terms of lifestyle, culture, behaviour, sexual orientation, age, ability, religion, and other factors.

Doorknob Communication: A phenomenon described by Shulman (1992) wherein clients bring up important issues at the end of the interview/relationship when there is little or no time to address them.

DSM-IV-TR: The **Diagnostic and Statistical Manual of Mental Disorders** published by the American Psychiatric Association. It is used by psychologists, psychiatrists, and other psychotherapists to classify and diagnose mental disorders.

Dual Diagnosis: A person who has both a substance abuse addiction and a psychiatric disorder.

Dual Relationship: A relationship in which there is both a counselling relationship and another type of relationship, such as friendship or sexual intimacy.

Duty to Warn: Professional responsibility that counsellors have to inform people whom they believe a client may harm.

Emotion: A state of mind usually accompanied by concurrent physiological and behavioural changes and based on the perception of some internal or external object.

Emotional Literacy: The ability to experience all of one's emotions with appropriate intensity and to understand what is causing these feelings (Parrott, 1997:260).

Empathy: The process of accurately understanding the emotional perspective of another person and the communication of this understanding without imposing one's own feelings or reactions.

Empowering Skills: Skills used to help clients develop confidence, self-esteem, and control over their lives.

Empowerment: The process of helping clients to discover personal strengths and capacities so that they are able to take control over their lives.

Ethical Dilemma: Situation involving competing or conflicting values or principles.

Ethics: Guidelines that define the limits of permissible behaviour.

Ethnocentrism: The inclination to judge others negatively in relation to one's own cultural values and norms.

Exploring/Probing Skills: Skills counsellors use to gather information, clarify definition, seek example, and obtain necessary detail.

Feedback Confrontation: Used to provide new information to clients about who they are, including how they are perceived by others and the effects of their behaviour on others.

Genuineness: A measure of how authentic or real one is in a relationship.

Goal Setting: A counselling process that helps clients define in precise, measurable terms what they hope to achieve from the work of counselling.

Hallucination: Hearing, seeing, tasting, touching, or smelling what others do not.

Hidden Job Market: Jobs that are not advertised or made public; 80 percent or more of all jobs are filled through the hidden job market.

HIV: An acronym for **Human Immunodeficiency Virus**. This virus attacks the immune system, weakening its ability to fight off infections. People may be unaware that they have the virus, as they may have no symptoms for as long as 5 to 15 years.

Illusion of Work: As defined by Shulman (1992:171), a process in which the worker and the client engage in a conversation that is empty and that has no real meaning.

Immediacy: A tool for exploring, evaluating, and deepening counselling relationships.

Indirect Question: Statements that imply questions (e.g., "I'm curious how you responded.").

Inferred Empathy: A counsellor's identification of a client's feelings based on nonverbal cues and indirect communication.

Interviewing: Acquiring and organizing relevant information using active listening skills, including attending, silence, paraphrasing, summarizing, questioning, and empathy.

Interview Transition: A shift in the topic of the interview.

Intimidating Behaviour: Behaviours such as name calling; using obscene or sexually harassing language and gestures; shouting; and threatening through displays of power such as fist shaking, invading personal space, stalking, and issuing verbal threats. These behaviours should be restrained in order to prevent escalation to violence.

Invitational Empathy: A tool a counsellor uses to encourage clients to explore emotions.

I-Statement: Clear assertions about personal feelings or reactions that do not blame or judge others.

Job Club Method: An intensive and structured approach to job finding based on group support and structured learning activities. The sole purpose of a job club is to help participants find work.

Leading Question: A question that suggests a preferred answer (e.g., "Don't you think our session went really well today?").

Learned Helplessness: A state of mind that occurs when individuals have learned through failure that their efforts will not result in change.

Listening: A process aimed at receiving and understanding messages without distortion.

LIVE: An acronym that describes the four essential steps in summarizing: listen, identify, verbalize, evaluate.

Miracle Question: Used in brief or single-session counselling as a way to help clients who have difficulty coming up with defined goals. The miracle question challenges clients to imagine how their lives would be different if a miracle solved their problems.

MOANS: An acronym for five words—must, ought, always, never, and should—that signals irrational or self-defeating thought.

Mood Disorders: See affective disorders.

Motivation: The extent to which clients are willing to involve themselves in the change process.

Negative Symptoms: Include blunted or flattened affect, poverty of speech, emotional and social withdrawal, lack of pleasure (anhedonia), passivity, difficulty in abstract thinking, and lack of goal directed behaviour.

Networking: An integral part of job searching used to access the hidden job market. It involves using contacts, such as friends, family, and neighbours, who might provide information or access to others with information about possible job opportunities.

Nonhelping Behaviours: Variables that can lead to poor outcomes in counselling.

Objectivity: Ability to understand feelings, thoughts, and behaviour without allowing personal values, beliefs, and biases to interfere.

Obsessive-Compulsive Disorder (OCD): Recurrent, unwanted thoughts and conscious, ritualized, seemingly purposeless acts, such as counting the number of tiles on the ceiling or needing to wash one's hands repetitively.

Open Questions: Questions that promote expansive answers. These types of questions cannot be answered with a simple *yes* or *no* (e.g., "How do you feel about her?").

Outcome Goal: A goal related to what the client hopes to achieve from counselling.

Panic Disorder: Sudden attacks of terror and irrational fear, accompanied by an overwhelming sense of impending doom. During a panic attack a person may experience symptoms such as an accelerated heart rate, sweating, shaking, shortness of breath, chest pain, nausea, and fear of dying or losing control.

Paraphrase: A nonjudgmental restatement of the client's words and ideas in the counsellor's own words.

Partialization: The process of breaking large problems into priorities.

Phases of Counselling: Sequential steps through which counselling tends to evolve. The four phases are preliminary, beginning, action, ending.

Phases of Violence: Four-phase model (anxiety, defensiveness, acting out, and tension reduction) that describes how crises escalate to violence.

Phobia: An irrational fear about particular events or objects that results in overwhelming anxiety in response to situations where there is little or no danger.

Positive Regard: The ability of counsellors to recognize the inherent worth of people.

Positive Symptoms: Symptoms of psychosis that include include hallucinations, delusions, bizarre behaviour, agitation, thought disorder, disorganized speech, and behaviour and catatonic behaviour. (*See also* negative symptoms).

Post-Traumatic Stress Disorder (PTSD): Disabling symptoms such as emotional numbness, sleep disturbance (nightmares, difficulty sleeping), or reliving the event following a traumatic event such as rape, assault, natural disaster (earthquakes, floods, etc.), war, torture, or automobile accident.

Preparatory Empathy: A counsellor's attempt to consider (in advance of the interview) the feelings and concerns that the client may communicate indirectly.

Principle of Positive Reinforcement: The idea that behaviour tends to increase or continue when it is rewarded.

Process Goal: The methods and procedures that will be used in counselling to assist clients to reach their goals.

Proxemics: A term used to describe how people use space and distance in social behaviour.

Pseudo-counselling: Counselling that lacks real meaning, evidenced by irrelevant exploration of issues, use of clichés and patronizing platitudes, intellectual exploration of issues, and avoidance of subjects or feelings that involve pain in favour of "safe" topics.

Psychological Reactance: Tendency for people to increase problem behaviour if they believe their freedom is threatened. This theory can help us understand why nagging by concerned friends and family may have a paradoxical effect.

Psychotherapy: Advanced counselling targeting severe emotional or behavioural difficulties or disorders.

Questioning: An active listening skill that involves probing for information to confirm understanding and seek clarification.

Reframing: Technique for helping clients to look at things differently by suggesting alternative interpretations or new meanings.

Relationship-Building Skills: Tools for engaging clients and developing trust.

Relative Confidentiality: The assumption that client disclosures may be shared within the agency with supervisors or colleagues, outside the agency with client permission, or with others because of legal requirements, such as those contained within child-abuse legislation.

Rescuing: Also called band-aiding, this involves a counsellor's actions that prevent or protect clients from dealing with issues or feelings. Rescuing arises from the counsellor's need to avoid tension and keep the session cheerful.

Resistance: Defensive reaction by clients that interferes with or delays the process of counselling.

Schizophrenia: A chronic mental disorder involving symptoms such as hallucinations, delusions, disordered thinking, and social isolation.

Selective Perception: A term used to describe the natural tendency to avoid being overwhelmed by information by screening out material that is irrelevant.

Self-Awareness: Process of becoming alert and knowledgeable about one's own way of thinking, acting, and feeling.

Self-Defeating Thought: Inner dialogue of critical messages.

Self-Determination: The principle that promotes the rights of clients to have autonomy and freedom of choice.

Self-Talk: Mental messages people give to themselves (e.g., "I'm no good.").

Sessional Contract: An agreement between counsellor and client regarding the topic and expected outcome of an interview or session. (*See also* contracting.)

Silence: A tool used in counselling when the client is thinking, the client is confused and unsure of what to say or do, or the client has encountered painful feelings. Because it is culturally defined, silence can also signal trust issues or closure.

Simple Encouragers: Short phrases and gestures, such as "Tell me more," "Go on," "Uh huh," and head nods that encourage clients to continue with their stories.

Skill Clusters: Categories of skills based on their intended purpose or helping activity.

Stages of Change Model (transtheoretical model): Theory of motivation that recognizes five changes of stage: precontemplation, contemplation, preparation, action, and maintenance

Strengths Approach: A counselling perspective that assumes the inherent capacity of people. Individuals and communities are seen to have assets and resources that can be mobilized for problem solving.

Structured Interview: An interview that follows a predetermined sequence of questions.

Summary: A way of condensing content. A simple summary focuses on content and is an unedited condensing of the client's words. Theme summaries edit out unnecessary detail and attempt to identify key patterns and areas of urgency.

Thinking Errors: Faulty reasoning caused by distortion, incomplete analysis, egocentricity, rigidity, and self-defeating thought.

Thought Broadcasting: The delusional belief that one's thinking can be heard by others.

Thought Insertion: The delusional belief that thoughts are being inserted into one's brain by others.

Transference: The tendency of clients to communicate with their counsellors in the same way that they communicated to significant people in the past.

Unstructured Interview: An interview that does not have a preset plan that restricts direction, pace, or content.

Values: What individuals and groups consider important or worthwhile.

Ventilation: *See* catharsis.

Versatility: The need for counsellors to develop a broad range of skills in order to adapt their approach to fit the distinctive complexities of each individual and context.

Violent Behaviour: Hitting, pushing, biting, slapping, kicking, throwing objects, and using weapons such as guns, knives, or syringes.

Worldview: Belief system about the nature of the universe, its perceived effect on human behaviour, and one's place in the universe. Worldview is a fundamental core set of assumptions explaining cultural forces, the nature of humankind, the nature of good and evil, luck, fate, spirits, the power of significant others, the role of time, and the nature of our physical and natural resources (Dodd: 1995:105).

An excellent general resource is http://socialpolicy.ca, which provides an online glossary of hundreds of social work terms.

References

Abraham, S., and D. Llewellyn-Jones. *Eating Disorders: The Facts.* 4th ed. New York: Oxford University Press, 1997.

Alexander, C.M., and L. Sussman. "Creative Approaches to Multicultural Counseling." In J.G. Ponterotto, J.M. Casas, L.A. Suzuki, and C.M. Alexander, *Handbook of Multicultural Counseling.* Thousand Oaks, CA: Sage Publications, 1995: 375–384.

American Association of Suicidology. [Online, accessed 10 August 1998]. Available: http://www.cyberpsych.org/aas/

American Counseling Association (ACA). *Code of Ethics and Standards of Practice.* Alexandria, VA: American Counseling Association, 1995.

American Medical Association. *Essential Guide to Depression.* New York: Pocket Books, 1998.

American Psychiatric Association. *Diagnostic and Statistical Manual of Mental Disorders.* 4th ed. Text Revision. Washington: American Psychiatric Association, 2000.

Amundson, N.E. "Supporting Clients Through a Change in Perspective." *Journal of Employment Counseling* 33, no. 4 (1996): 155–62.

Angel, D.L, and E.E. Harney. *No One Is Unemployable: Creative Solutions for Overcoming Barriers to Employment.* Hacienda Heights, CA: WorkNet Training Services, 1997.

Arboleda-Florez, J., H.L. Holley, and A. Cristianti. *Mental Illness and Violence: Proof or Stereotype.* Ottawa: Health Canada, 1996 [Online, accessed June 12, 2005]. Available: http://www.phac-aspc.gc.ca/mh-sm/mentalhealth/pubs/mental_illness/index.htm

Armitage, A., *Social Welfare in Canada Revisited: Facing Up to the Future.* 3rd ed. Don Mills, ON: Oxford University Press, 1996.

Arnhold, R.M., and W.N. Razak. "Overcoming Learned Helplessness: Managerial Strategies for the 1990s." *Journal of Employment Counseling* 28 (September 1991): 99–106.

Arthur, N., and J. Stewart. "Multicultural Counselling in the New Millennium: Introduction to the Special Theme Issue." *Canadian Journal of Counselling* 35, no. 1 (2001): 3–14.

Azrin, N.H., and V.A. Besalel. *Job Club Counselor's Manual: A Behavioral Approach to Vocational Counseling.* Austin: Pro-Ed., 1980.

Backhouse, C. *Colour-Coded: A Legal History of Racism in Canada, 1900–1950.* Toronto: University of Toronto Press, 1999.

Barker, R.L. *The Social Work Dictionary.* 3rd ed. Washington: NASW Press, 1995.

Beckman, C.S., S.G. Turner, M. Cooper, D. Polnerow, and M. Swartz. "Sexual Contact With Clients: Assessment of Social Workers' Attitudes and Educational Preparation." *Social Work* 45, no. 3 (2000): 224.

Benjamin, A. *The Helping Interview.* 3rd ed. Boston: Houghton Mifflin, 1981.

Berg, F.M. *Afraid to Eat: Children and Teens in Weight Crisis*. Hettinger, ND: Healthy Weight Journal, 1997.

Beyerstein, B.L. "Believing Is Seeing: Organic and Psychological Reasons for Hallucinations and Other Anomalous Psychiatric Symptoms." *Medscape*. [Online, accessed 7 August 1998]. Available: http://www.medscape.com/Medscape/MentalHealth

Black, K. *Short-Term Counseling: A Humanistic Approach for the Helping Professions*. Menlo Park, CA: Addison-Wesley, 1983.

Bolles, R.N. *The 2005 What Color Is Your Parachute: A Practical Manual for Job-Hunters and Career Changers*. Berkeley: Ten Speed Press, 2005.

Borgen, W.A., N.E. Amundson, J. McVicar. "The Experience of Unemployment for Fishery Workers in Newfoundland: What Helps and Hinders." *Journal of Employment Counseling* 39, no. 3 (2002):117–126.

Bower, B. "Study Tracks Violence Among Mentally Ill." *Science News* (May 1998): 309.

Brammer, L.M. *The Helping Relationship: Process and Skills*. 3rd ed. Englewood Cliffs, NJ: Prentice-Hall, 1985.

Brammer, L.M., and G. MacDonald. *The Helping Relationship: Process and Skills*. 7th ed. Needham Heights, MA: Allyn & Bacon, 1999.

Bratina, T.G., and T.A. Bratina. "Electronic Career Search." *Journal of Employment Counseling* 35 (March 1998): 17–25.

Brill, N.I., and J. Levine. *Working with People: The Helping Process*. 8th ed. Boston: Pearson Education, 2005.

British Columbia Schizophrenia Society. *Basic Facts About Schizophrenia*. Richmond, BC: BC Schizophrenia Society

Burman, P. *Killing Time, Losing Ground: Experiences of Unemployment*. Toronto: Thompson Educational Publishing Inc., 1988.

Canadian Association of Social Workers. *Guidelines for Ethical Practice*, 2005.

Canadian Mental Health Association. *Violence and Mental Illness*. [Online, accessed June 12, 2005]. Available: http:// www.cmha.pe.ca/bins/content_page.asp?cid=3-108.

Canadian Task Force on Mental Health Issues Affecting Immigrants and Refugees. *After The Door Has Been Opened: Mental Health Issues Affecting Refugees and Immigrants in Canada: Report of the Canadian Task Force on Mental Health Issues Affecting Immigrants and Refugees*. Ottawa: Multiculturalism and Citizenship Canada, 1988.

Capuzzi, D., and D.R. Gross. *Introduction to the Counseling Profession*. 3rd ed. Needham Heights, MA: Allyn & Bacon, 2001.

Carkhuff, R.R. *The Art of Helping*. Amherst, MA: Human Resource Development Press, 1981.

Carniol, B. *Case Critical: The Dilemma of Social Work in Canada*. 3rd ed. Toronto: Between the Lines, 1995.

Center for Suicide Prevention. [online] Available: http://suicideinfo.ca/csp/go.aspx

Chappell, R. *Social Welfare in Canadian Society*. 2nd ed. Scarborough, ON: Nelson Thomson Learning, 2001.

Choney, S.K., E. Berryhill-Paapke, and R. Robbins. "The Acculturation of American Indians: Developing Frameworks for Research and Practice." In Pedersen, P.B., and D.C. Locke, eds. *Cultural and Diversity Issues in Counseling*. Greensboro, NC: ERIC Counseling and Student Services Clearinghouse, 1996: 73–92.

Clark, A.J. "Reframing: A Therapeutic Technique in Group Counseling." *Journal for Specialists in Group Work* 23, no. 1 (1998): 66–73.

Cleghorn, J.M., and B.L. Lee. *Understanding and Treating Mental Illness: The Strengths and Limits of Modern Psychiatry*. Toronto: Hogrefe & Huber, 1991.

Compton, B., and B. Galaway. *Social Work Processes*. 3rd ed. Homewood, IL: Dorsey Press, 1984.

———. *Social Work Processes*. 6th ed. Pacific Grove, CA: Brooks/Cole, 1999.

Corey, M., and G. Corey. *Becoming a Helper*. Pacific Grove, CA: Brooks/Cole, 1989.

Cormier, W.H., and L.S. Cormier. *Interviewing Strategies for Helpers*. Monterey, CA: Brooks/Cole, 1985.

Cormier, S., and H. Hackney. *Counseling Strategies and Interventions*. Boston: Pearson, 2005.

Corsini, R.J. *Encyclopedia of Psychology*. New York, NY: John Wiley & Sons, 1984.

Cottone, R.R., and V.M. Tarvydas. *Ethical and Professional Issues in Counseling*. Englewood Cliffs, NJ: Prentice-Hall, 1998.

Cowger, C. "Assessing Client Strengths." *Social Work* 39, no. 3 (1994): 262–268.

Cragan, J.F., and D.W. Wright. *Communication in Small Group Discussions: An Integrated Approach*. 3rd ed. St. Paul, MN: West Publishing Company, 1991.

D'Andrea, M.J. "White Racism." In P.B. Pedersen and D.C. Locke, *Cultural and Diversity Issues in Counseling*, eds. Greensboro, NC: ERIC Counseling and Student Services Clearinghouse, 1996.

Daniluk, J.C., and B.E. Haverkamp. "Ethical Issues in Counseling Adult Survivors of Incest." *Journal of Counseling and Development* 72, no. 1 (1993): 16–22.

D'Augelli, A.R., J.F. D'Augelli, and S.J. Danish. *Helping Others*. Monterey, CA: Brooks/Cole, 1981.

Davis, L.E., and E.K. Proctor. *Race, Gender, and Class: Guidelines for Practice with Individuals, Families, and Groups*. Englewood Cliffs, NJ: Prentice-Hall, 1989.

De Becker, G. *The Gift of Fear: Survival Signals That Protect Us from Violence*. Boston: Little, Brown and Co., 1997.

De Bono, E. *Six Thinking Hats*. Toronto: Key Porter, 1985.

DiClemente, C.C., and M. Velasquez. "Motivational Interviewing and the Stages of Change" In W.R. Miller and S. Rollnick, eds. *Motivational Interviewing: Preparing People for Change*, 2nd ed. New York: The Guilford Press, 2002.

de Shazer, S. *Keys to Solution in Brief Therapy*. New York: Norton, 1985.

Devons, C. "Suicide in the Elderly: How to Identify and Treat Patients at Risk." *Geriatrics* 51, no. 3 (1996): 67–72.

Diller, J.V. *Cultural Diversity: A Primer for the Human Services*. Scarborough, ON: Brooks/Cole, 1999.

Dodd, C.H. *Dynamics of Intercultural Communication*. 4th ed. Duguque, IA: Brown & Benchmark, 1995.

DuBois, B., and K. Miley. *Social Work: An Empowering Profession*. 2nd ed. Needham Heights, MA: Allyn & Bacon, 1996.

Dubovsky, S.L., and M.P. Weissberg. *Clinical Psychiatry in Primary Care*. 3rd ed. Baltimore: Williams & Wilkins, 1986.

Dumont, M. *The Absurd Healer*. New York: Viking Press, 1968.

Egan, G. *You and Me: The Skills of Communicating and Relating to Others*. Belmont, CA: Brooks/Cole, 1977.

———. *The Skilled Helper*. 4th ed. Monterey, CA: Brooks/Cole, 1990.

———. *The Skilled Helper*. 6th ed. Monterey, CA: Brooks/Cole, 1998.

Elbourne, R. "Is Silence Suspicious?" [Online, accessed 30 September 1997]. Available: http://home.vicnet. net.au/~gnaust/vic2/25-10.html.

Ellis, A. *The Road to Tolerance: The Philosophy of Rational Emotive Behavior Therapy*. Amherst, NY: Prometheus, 2004

Ellis, A. *Reason and Emotion in Psychotherapy*. New York: Stuart, 1962.

———. "Fundamentals of Rational-Emotive Therapy for the 1990s." In W. Dryden and I. Hill, eds. *Innovations in Rational-Emotive Therapy*. Newbury Park, CA: Sage, 1993: 1–32.

———. "Reflections on Rational-Emotive Therapy." *Journal of Counseling and Clinical Psychology* 62, no. 2 (1993b): 199–201.

———. *Rational-Emotive Therapy and Cognitive Behavior Therapy*. New York: Springer, 1984.

Erdman, P., and P. Lampe. "Adapting Basic Skills to Counsel Children." *Journal of Counseling and Development* 74, no. 4 (1996): 374–77.

Evans, D.R., M.T. Hearn, M.R. Uhlemann, and A.E. Ivey. *Essential Interviewing: A Programmed Approach to Effective Communication*. Monterey, CA: Brooks/Cole, 1979.

Farr, J.M. *The Very Quick Job Search: Get a Better Job in Half the Time*. 2nd ed. Indianapolis: JIST Works, 1996.

Fauman, M.A. *Study Guide to DSM-IV–TR*. Washington: American Psychiatric Publishing, 2002.

Fortune, A.E. "Terminating with Clients" In A.R. Roberts and G.J. Green, eds. *Social Workers' Desk Reference*. New York: Oxford, 2002:458-463.

Fuertes, J.N., C. Nichols, and M. Bartolomeo. "Future Research Directions in the Study of Counselor Multicultural Competency." *Journal of Multicultural Counseling and Development*, vol. 29 (Jan. 2001): 3–13.

Furman, B., and T. Ahola. "Solution Talk: The Solution-Oriented Way of Talking about Problems." In M.F. Hoyt, ed. *Constructive Therapies*. New York: The Guilford Press, 1994: 41–66.

Gardner, W., C. Lidz, E. Mulvey, and E. Shaw. "Clinical versus Actuarial Predictions of Violence in Patients with Mental Illness." *Journal of Consulting and Clinical Psychology* 64, no. 3 (1996): 602–10.

Garrett, A. *Interviewing: Its Principles and Methods.* 3rd ed. Revised and enlarged by Margaret M. Mangold and Elinor P. Zaki. New York: Family Service Association of America, 1982.

Garrett, M.T., J.T. Garrett, and D. Brotherton. "Inner Circle/Outer Circle: A Group Technique Based on Native American Healing Circles." *Journal for Specialists in Group Work,* 26, no. 1, March 2001.

Garvin, C.D., and B.A. Seabury. *Interpersonal Practice in Social Work: Processes and Procedures.* Englewood Cliffs, NJ: Prentice-Hall, 1984.

George, R.L., and T.S. Cristiani. *Counseling Theory and Practice.* 2nd ed. Englewood Cliffs, NJ: Prentice-Hall, 1986.

Gilliland, B.E., and R.K. James. *Theories and Strategies in Counseling and Psychotherapy.* 4th ed. Needham Heights, MA: Allyn & Bacon, 1998.

Gladding, S.T. *Counseling: A Comprehensive Profession.* 3rd ed. Englewood Cliffs, NJ: Prentice-Hall, 1996.

Glicken, M.T. *Using the Strengths Perspective in Social Work Practice: A Positive Approach for the Helping Professions.* New York: Allyn & Bacon, 2004

Glosoff, H.L., B. Herlihy, and E.B. Spence. "Privileged Communication in the Counselor-Client Relationship." *Journal of Counseling and Development* 78, no. 4 (2000): 454–462.

Golden, B.J., and K. Lesh. *Building Self-Esteem: Strategies for Success in School and Beyond.* 2nd ed. Scottsdale, AZ: Gorsuch Scarisbick, 1997.

Goleman, D. *Emotional Intelligence.* New York: Bantam Books, 1995.

Gordon, T. *Parent Effectiveness Training: The "No-Lose" Program for Raising Responsible Children.* New York: Peter Wyden, Inc., 1971.

Government of Canada. "Chapter 27."*Immigration and Refugee Protection Act, Statutes of Canada 2001.* Assented November 2001.

Grinder, J., and R. Bandler. *The Structure of Magic II.* Palo Alto, CA: Science and Behavior Books, 1976.

Hackney, H.L., and L.S. Cormier. *The Professional Counselor: A Process Guide to Helping.* 5th ed. Needham Heights, MA: Pearson Education, 2005.

Hall, E.T. *The Silent Language.* Greenwich, CT: Fawcett Publications, 1959.

Hamachek, D.E. *Encounters with Others: Interpersonal Relationships and You.* New York: Holt, Rinehart and Winston, 1982.

Hammond, C., D. Hepworth, and V. Smith. *Improving Therapeutic Communication.* San Francisco: Jossey-Bass, 1977.

Hancock, M.R. *Principles of Social Work Practice: A Generic Approach.* Binghamton, NY: The Haworth Press, 1997.

Harris, G.A., and D. Watkins. *Counseling the Involuntary and Resistant Client.* College Park, MD: American Correctional Association, 1987.

Harris, G.T., and M.E. Rice. "Risk Appraisal and Management of Violent Behavior." *Psychiatric Services* 48, no. 9 (1997): 1168–76.

Harris, H.S., and D.C. Maloney. *Human Services: Contemporary Issues and Trends*. Needham Heights, MA: Allyn & Bacon, 1996.

Harvard Medical School. *Harvard Mental Health Letter* 13, no. 6 (December 1996).

Health Canada, HIV and AIDS, [online, accessed Aug 19, 2005] Available: http://www.hc-sc.gc.ca/dc-ma/aids-sida/index_e.html

Health Canada, First Nations and Inuit Health Branch. *A Statistical Profile on the Health of First Nations in Canada*. Ottawa: Queen's Press, 2003.

Hepworth, D.H., R.H. Rooney, and J. Larsen. *Direct Social Work Practice, Theory and Skills*. 5th ed. Pacific Grove, CA: Brooks/Cole, 1997.

Hess, H., and P. McCartt Hess. "Termination in Context." In *Social Work Processes*, 3rd ed., by B. Compton and B.Galaway. Homewood, IL: Dorsey Press, 1984, 559-70

Hill, C.E. B. Thompson, and N. Ladany. "Therapist Use of Silence in Therapy: A Survey." *Journal of Clinical Psychology* 59, no. 4, 2003, 513-525.

Hill, C.E. *Helping Skills: Facilitating Exploration, Insight, and Action*, 2nd ed. Washington: American Psychological Association, 2004.

Hirschfeld, R.M., and J.M. Russell. "Assessment and Treatment of Suicidal Patients." *The New England Journal of Medicine* 337, no. 13 (1997): 910–16.

Hocker, J.L., and W.W. Wilmot. *Interpersonal Conflict*. 4th ed. Dubuque, IA: Wm. C. Brown Communication, 1995.

Holmes, B.H., and J.D. Werbel. "Finding Work Following Job Loss: The Role of Coping Resources." *Journal of Employment Counseling* 29, no. 1 (1992): 22–29.

Hoyt, M.F., ed. *Constructive Therapies*. New York: The Guilford Press, 1994.

Huber, C.H., and B.A. Backlund. *The Twenty Minute Counselor: Transforming Brief Conversations into Effective Helping Experiences*. New York: The Continuum Publishing Company, 1991.

Intercontinental Medical Statistics Inc. [Online, accessed March 31, 2001] Available: http://www.imshealthcanada.com/htmen/4_2_1_35.htm.

Isajiw, W.W. *Understanding Diversity, Ethnicity and Race in the Canadian Context*. Toronto: Thompson Educational Publishing, 1999.

Ismael, J.S. (ed). *The Canadian Welfare State: Evolution and Transition*, Edmonton: The University of Alberta Press, 1987.

Ivey, A.E. *Intentional Interviewing and Counseling*. Monterey, CA: Brooks/Cole, 1982.

Ivey, A.E., M.B. Ivey, and L. Simek-Downing. *Counseling and Psychotherapy: Integrating Skills, Theory, and Practice*. 2nd ed. Englewood Cliffs, NJ: Prentice-Hall, 1987.

Ivey, A.E. "Psychotherapy as Liberation: Toward Specific Skills and Strategies in Multicultural Counseling and Therapy." In J.G. Ponterotto, J.M. Casas, L.A. Suzuki, and C.M. Alexander, eds. *Handbook of Multicultural Counseling*. Thousand Oaks, CA: Sage, 1995: 53–72.

Jacobs, E., R. Masson, and R. Harvill. *Group Counseling Strategies and Skills*. Pacific Grove, CA: Brooks/Cole, 1998.

Jobes, D.A., and A.L Berman. "Crisis Intervention and Brief Treatment for Suicidal Youth." In A.R. Roberts, ed. *Contemporary Perspectives on Crisis Intervention and Prevention*. Englewood Cliffs, NJ: Prentice-Hall, 1991, 53–69.

Johnson, L.C., Yanca, S. J., *Social Work Practice: A Generalist Approach*. 8th ed. Needham Heights, MA: Allyn & Bacon, 2004.

Johnson, D.W. *Reaching Out: Interpersonal Effectiveness and Self-Actualization*. 6th ed. Boston: Allyn & Bacon, 1997.

Johnson, L.C. *Social Work Practice: A Generalist Approach*. 4th ed. Needham Heights, MA: Allyn & Bacon, 1992.

Johnson, L.C., R.W. McClelland, and C.D. Austin. *Social Work Practice: A Generalist Approach*. Canadian Edition. Scarborough, ON: Prentice Hall Allyn & Bacon Canada, 2000.

Kadushin, K. *The Social Work Interview: A Guide for Human Service Professionals*. 3rd ed. New York: Columbia University Press, 1990.

Kadushin, A., and G. Kadushin. *The Social Work Interview: A Guide for Human Service Professionals*. 4th ed. New York: Columbia University Press, 1997.

Kain, C.D. *Positive HIV Affirmative Counseling*. Alexandria, VA: American Counseling Association, 1996.

Kaplan, S.G., and E.G. Wheeler. "Survival Skills for Working with Potentially Violent Clients." *Social Casework* (June 1983): 339–46.

Keith-Lucas, A. *The Giving and Taking of Help*. Chapel Hill, NC: University of North Carolina Press, 1972.

Kell, B.L., and W.L. Mueller. *Impact and Change*. New York: Appleton Century-Crofts, 1966.

Kelleher, M.D. *Profiling the Lethal Employee: Case Studies of Violence in the Workplace*. Westport, CT: Praeger, 1997.

Kelly, E.W. *Spirituality and Religion in Counseling and Psychotherapy: Diversity in Theory and Practice*. Alexandria, VA: American Counseling Association, 1995.

Kirsh, S. *Unemployment: Its Impact on Body and Soul*. Canadian Mental Health Association, 1983.

Kottler, J.A. "When Clients Don't Get Better: Facing Failure as a Counselor." *American Counselor* 2, no. 4 (1993): 14–19.

Labig, C.E. *Preventing Violence in the Workplace*. New York: AMACOM, 1995.

Lanza, M., H. Kayne, I. Pattison, C. Hicks, S. Islam, J. Bradshaw, and P. Robins. "The Relationship of Behavioral Cues to Assaultive Behavior." *Clinical Nursing Research* 5, no. 1 (1996): 6–28.

Lazarus, A.A., and L.E. Beutler. "On Technical Eclecticism." *Journal of Counseling & Development* 71, no. 4 (1993): 381–85.

Leeds, D. "The Art of Asking Questions." *Training and Development* 47, no. 1 (1993): 57–62.

Leo, R.J., K. Jassal, and Y. Bakhai. "NonAdherence with Psychopharmacologic Treatment Among Psychiatric Patients." *Primary Psychiatry*, June 2005: 33-39.

Lock, R.D. *Taking Charge of Your Career Direction*. 3rd ed. Pacific Grove, CA: Brooks/Cole, 1996.

Martin, D.G. *Counseling and Therapy Skills*. Belmont, CA: Brooks/Cole, 1983.

Martin, G., and J. Pear. *Behavior Modification: What It Is and How to Do It*. 4th ed. Englewood Cliffs, NJ: Prentice-Hall, 1992.

Maslow, A.H. *Motivation and Personality*. New York: Harper & Row, 1954.

Mathias, Chief Joe. Quotation taken from a permanent public display. Stanley Park, Vancouver, BC, 2001.

McDonald, N. *Interviewing Aboriginal Peoples: A Guide to Effective Cross-Cultural Interviews*. Winnipeg: Cross-Cultural Communications International, 1993.

McNeece, C.A., and D.M. DiNitto. *Chemical Dependency: A Systems Approach*. 2nd ed. Needham Heights, MA: Allyn & Bacon, 1998.

McWhirter, E.H. "Empowerment in Counseling." In *Journal of Counseling and Development* 69, no. 3 (1991): 222–27.

Meharabian, A. *Silent Messages: Implicit Communication of Emotions and Attitudes*. 2nd ed. Belmont, CA: Wadsworth, 1981.

Mehr, J.J. *Human Services: Concepts and Intervention Strategies*. 7th ed. Boston: Allyn & Bacon, 1998.

Middleman, R.R., and G.G. Wood. *Skills for Direct Practice in Social Work*. New York: Columbia University Press, 1990.

Miley, K.K., M. O'Melia, and B. Dubois. *Generalist Social Work Practice: An Empowering Approach*. Boston: Allyn & Bacon, 2004.

Miller, M.C. "A Model for the Assessment of Violence." *Harvard Review of Psychiatry* 7, (2000):299-304.

Miller, W.R., and S. Rollnick. Motivational Interviewing: Preparing People for Change, 2nd Ed., New York: The Guilford Press, 2002.

Minuchin, S., and H. Fishman. *Family Therapy Techniques*. Cambridge, MA: Harvard University Press, 1981.

Morrisseau, C. *Into the Daylight: A Wholistic Approach to Healing*. Toronto: University of Toronto Press, 1998.

Morrissey, M. "Safety Issues for Counselors Who Work with Violent Clients." *Counseling Today* (February 1998): 6.

National Association of Social Workers. *Revised Code of Ethics*. Washington: NASW Press, 1996.

National Crisis Prevention Institute. *Nonviolent Crisis Intervention: The Preventative Techniques*. Vol. 1. [videorecording] National Crisis Prevention Institute, 1993

National Eating Disorder Information Centre. *Questions and Answers*. [online, accessed 21 June, 2005]. Available: http://www.nedic.ca/qa.html#3.

National Institute of Mental Health (NIMH). [Online, accessed 5 August 1998]. Available: http://www. nimh.nih.gov/home.htm.

Newhill, C.E. "Assessing Danger to Others in Clinical Social Work Practice." *Social Service Review* (March 1992): 65–79.

———. "Client Violence Toward Social Workers: A Practice and Policy Concern for the 1990s." In *Social Work* 40, no. 5 (September 1995): 631–39.

Nicholi, A.M. (ed). *The New Harvard Guide to Psychiatry*. Cambridge, MA: Belknap Press, 1988.

Noesner, G.W., and M. Webster. "Crisis Intervention: Using Active Listening Skills in Negotiations." *The FBI Law Enforcement Bulletin* 66, no. 8 (1997): 13–20.

O'Connor, R. *Undoing Depression: What Therapy Doesn't Teach You and Medication Can't Give You*. Toronto: Little, Brown and Company, 1997.

Otani, A. "Client Resistance in Counseling: Its Theoretical Rationale and Taxonomic Classification." *Journal of Counseling and Development* (1989): 458–61.

Othmer, E., and S.C. Othmer. *The Clinical Interview Using DSM-III–R*. Washington: American Psychiatric Press, 1989.

Paniagua, F.A. *Assessing and Treating Culturally Diverse Clients: A Practical Guide*. 2nd ed. Thousand Oaks, CA: Sage, 1998.

Parrott, L. *Counseling and Psychotherapy*. New York: McGraw-Hill, 1997.

Pastor, L.H. "Initial Assessment and Intervention Strategies to Reduce Workplace Violence." In *American Family Physician* 52, no. 4 (1995): 1169–75.

Patterson, C.H. "Multicultural Counseling: From Diversity to Universality." *Journal of Counseling and Development* 74, no. 3 (1996): 227–31.

Pedersen, P.B. "Multiculturalism and the Paradigm Shift in Counselling: Controversies and Alternative Futures." *Canadian Journal of Counselling* 35, no. 1 (2001): 15–25.

Pedersen, P.B., D.C. Locke, eds. *Cultural and Diversity Issues in Counseling*. Greensboro, NC: ERIC Counseling and Student Services Clearinghouse, 1996.

Pedersen, P. *A Handbook for Developing Multicultural Awareness*. 2nd Ed. Alexandria, VA: American Counseling Association, 1994.

Pincus, A., and A. Minahan. *Social Work Practice: Model and Method*. Itasca, IL: F.E. Peacock, 1973.

Poonwassie, A., and A. Charter. "An Aboriginal Worldview of Helping: Empowering Approaches." *Canadian Journal of Counselling* 35, no. 1 (2001): 63–73.

Public Health Agency of Canada. *A Report on Mental Illness in Canada, 2002* [online, accessed 25 June, 2005]. Available: http://www.phac-aspc.gc.ca/publicat/miic-mmac/index.html.

Prochaska, J.O., and J. Norcross. "Stages of Change" *Psychotherapy:Theory, Research, Practice, Training* 38, Issue 4:443–448.

Quinsey, V.L., G.T. Harris, M.E., Rice, and C. Cormier. *Violent Offenders: Appraising and Managing Risk*. Washington: American Psychological Association, 1998.

Ralph, I. *Psychotropic Agents*, 13th Edition. Grand Forks, BC: IGR Publications, 2003.

Reamer, F.G. "Ethical Issues in Social Work." In A.Roberts and G. Greene, eds. *Social Workers Desk Reference*. New York: Oxford University Press, 2002.

Reamer, F.G. *Ethical Standards in Social Work: A Critical Review of the NASW Code of Ethics*. Washington: NASW Press, 1998.

Reid, W.H. *The Treatment of Psychiatric Disorders: Revised for the DSM-IIIR*. New York: Brunner/Mazel, 1989.

Roberts, A.R. *Contemporary Perspectives on Crisis Intervention and Prevention*. Englewood Cliffs, NJ: Prentice-Hall, 1991.

Roberts, A.R., and G. Greene, eds. *Social Workers Desk Reference*. New York: Oxford University Press, 2002.

Rogers, C.R. *Client-Centered Therapy: Its Current Practice, Implications, and Theory*. Boston, MA: Houghton Mifflin, 1951.

———. *On Becoming a Person*. Boston: Houghton Mifflin, 1961.

———. *A Way of Being*. Boston: Houghton Mifflin, 1980.

Ross, J.I., ed. *Violence in Canada: Sociopolitical Perspectives*. Don Mills, ON: Oxford, 1995.

Roth, L.H. *Clinical Treatment of the Violent Person*. New York: Guilford Press, 1987.

Ruskin, R., and M. Beiser. "Cultural Issues in Psychotherapy." In P. Cameron, J. Ennis, and J. Deadman, eds. *Standards and Guidelines for the Psychotherapies*. Toronto: University of Toronto Press, 1998: 422–445.

Saddock, B.J., and V. Saddock. *Concise Textbook of Clinical Psychiatry*. Philadephia: Lippincott Williams & Wilkins, 2004.

Saleeby, D. *The Strengths Perspective in Social Work Practice*. 3rd. New York: Allyn & Bacon, 2002.

San Francisco Suicide Prevention Institute. *Suicide Facts and Statistics*. [Online, accessed 10 August 1998]. Available: http://www.sfsuicide.org/html/facts.html.

Schram, B., and B.R. Mandell. *An Introduction to Human Services Policy and Procedure*. 3rd ed. Needham Heights, MA: Allyn & Bacon, 1997.

Sealy, P., and P. Whitehead. "Forty Years of Deinstitutionalization of Psychiatric Services in Canada: An Empirical Assessment." *Canadian Journal of Psychiatry* 49 (2004): 249-257.

Seligman, M.E. *Helplessness: On Depression, Development and Death*. San Francisco: W.H. Freeman, 1975.

Shahmirzadi, A. "Counseling Iranians." In *The Personnel and Guidance Journal* (April 1983): 487–489.

Shea, S.C. *Psychiatric Interviewing: The Art of Understanding*. Philadelphia: W.B. Sanders, 1988.

Sheafor, B.W., and C.R. Horejsi.. *Techniques and Guidelines for Social Work Practice*. 7th ed. Boston: Allyn & Bacon, 2006.

Shebib, B. *Counseling Skills*. Victoria, BC: Province of British Columbia, Ministry of Education, Skills and Training, 1997.

Shilling, L.E. *Perspectives on Counseling Theories*. Englewood Cliffs, NJ: Prentice-Hall, 1984.

Shulman, L. *Skills of Helping Individuals and Groups,* 4th ed. Itasca, IL: F.E. Peacock, 1999.

Shulz, W.E. *Counselling Ethics Casebook 2000*. Ottawa: Canadian Counselling Association, 2000.

Silva, F., and M. Lopez de Silva. "Hallucinations and Behavior Modification." *Analisis y Modificacion de Conducta* 2, no. 2 (1976).

Simmie, S., and J. Nunes. *The Last Taboo: A Survival Guide to Mental Health Care in Canada*. Toronto: McClelland & Stewart, 2001.

Sklare, G.B. *Brief Counseling That Works: A Solution-Focused Approach for School Counselors*. Thousand Oaks, CA: Corwin Press, 1997.

Soper, B., and C.W. Von Bergen. "Employment Counseling and Life Stressors: Coping Through Expressive Writing." *Journal of Employment Counseling* 38, no. 3 (2001): 150-150.

Smith, D.B., and P.J. Morrissette. "The Experiences of White Male Counsellors Who Work with First Nations Clients." *Canadian Journal of Counselling* 35, no. 1 (2001): 74–88.

Specht, H. "Social Work and the Popular Psychotherapies." *Social Service Review* 64, no. 3 (1990): 345–357.

Speight, S.L., L.J. Myers, C.I. Cox, and P.S. Highlen. "A Redefinition of Multicultural Counseling," *Journal of Counseling and Development* 70, no. 1 (1991): 29–36.

Sperry, L., J. Carlson, and D. Kjos. *Becoming and Effective Therapist.* Boston: Allyn & Bacon, 2003.

Statistics Canada. *GD Sourcing: Research and Retrieval[NMI].* [online] http://www.gdsourcing.com/works/HealthStatsCan.htm, June 2005.

Statistics Canada. *Overview: Canada still predominantly Roman Catholic and Protestant* [online] http://www12.statcan.ca/english/census01/Products/Analytic/companion/rel/canada.cfm#noreligion. February, 2005

Statistics Canada. [online] http://www.statcan.ca.

Statistics Canada. *Suicides, and suicide rate, by sex and by age group.* [online] http://www40.statcan.ca/l01/cst01/health01.htm?sdi=suicide. June, 2005c.

Steinweg, D.A. "Implications of Current Research for Counseling the Unemployed." *Journal of Employment Counseling* 27, no. 1 (March 1990): 37–41.

Sudman, S. and N.M. Bradburn. *Asking Questions: A Practical Guide to Questionnaire Design.* San Francisco: Jossey-Bass, 1983.

Sue, D.W., P. Arredondo, and R. McDavis. "Multicultural Counseling Competencies and Standards: A Call to the Profession." *Journal of Counseling and Development* 70, no. 4 (1992): 477–86.

Sue, D.W., and D. Sue. *Counseling the Culturally Different: Theory and Practice.* 3rd ed. New York: John Wiley and Sons, 1999.

Sue., D.W., & D. Sue. *Counseling the Culturally Diverse.* New York: Wiley, 2003.

Sunley, R., and G.W. Sheek. *Serving the Unemployed and Their Families.* Milwaukee, WI: Family Service America, 1986.

Swanson, J., S. Estroff, M. Swartz, R. Borum, W. Lachicotte, C. Zimmer, and R. Wagner. "Violence and Severe Mental Disorder in Clinical and Community Populations: The Effects of Psychotic Symptoms, Comorbidity, and Lack of Treatment." *Psychiatry: Interpersonal and Biological Processes* 60, no. 1 (1997): 1–22.

Tardiff, K., P. Marzuk, A. Leon, L. Portera, and C. Weiner. "Violence by Patients Admitted to a Private Psychiatric Hospital." *American Journal of Psychiatry* 154, no. 1 (1997): 88–94.

Thoreson, R.W., P. Shaughnessy, P.P. Heppner, and S.W. Cook. "Sexual Contact During and After the Professional Relationship: Attitudes and Practices of Male Counselors." *Journal of Counseling and Development* 71, no. 4 (1993): 429–34.

Truax, C., and R. Carkhuff. *Toward Effective Counseling and Psychotherapy: Training and Practice.* Chicago: Aldine, 1967.

Turner, J.C., and F.J. Turner, eds. *Canadian Social Welfare.* 2nd ed. Don Mills, ON: Collier Macmillan Canada, 1986.

————. *Canadian Social Welfare*. 4th ed. Toronto: Pearson Education Canada, 2001.

United Nations. *AIDS Epidemic Update*. [online, accessed June 30, 2005]. Available: http://www. unaids.org/wad2004/EPIupdate2004_html_en/epi04_00_en.htm.

Vaillant, G.E. "Defense Mechanisms." In A.M. Nicholi, ed. *The New Harvard Guide to Psychiatry*. Cambridge, MA: Belknap Press, 1988: 200–7.

Walrond-Skinner, A. *Dictionary of Psychotherapy*. London: Routledge & Kegan Paul, 1986.

Walsh, J., and K. Bentley. "Psychopharmacology Basics." In A.Roberts and G. Greene, eds. *Social Workers Desk Reference*. New York: Oxford University Press, 2002.

Walter, J.L., and J.E. Peller. "On Track' in Solution-Focused Brief Therapy." In M.F. Hoyt, ed. *Constructive Therapies*. New York: The Guilford Press, 1994: 111–25.

Walters, G.D. "Identifying and Confronting Resistance in Lifestyle Criminal Offenders." In G.A. Harris, ed.*Tough Customers: Counseling Unwilling Clients*. Laurel, MD: American Correctional Association, 1991: 25–42.

Weaver, A.J. "Working with Potentially Dangerous Persons: What Clergy Need to Know." *Pastoral Psychology* 40, no. 5 (1982): 313–23.

Weaver, C.H. *Human Listening: Processes and Behavior*. Indianapolis: Bobbs-Merrill Company, 1972.

Weisinger, H. *Emotional Intelligence at Work*. San Francisco: Jossey-Bass, 1998.

Wells, C.S., and M.K. Masch. *Social Work Ethics Day to Day: Guidelines for Professional Practice*. Prospect Heights, IL: Waveland, 1991.

Westwood, M.J., and F.I. Ishiyama. "Challenges in Counseling Immigrant Clients: Understanding Intercultural Barriers to Career Adjustment." *Journal of Employment Counseling* 28, no. 4 (1991):130–43.

Wicks, R.J., and R.D. Parsons. *Counseling Strategies and Intervention Techniques for the Human Services*. New York: Longman, 1984.

Wilson, S.B. *Goal Setting*. New York: AMACOM, 1994.

Wolvin, A., and C. Coakley. *Listening*. 5th ed. Dubuque, IA: Brown & Benchmark, 1996.

Woodside, M., and T. McClam. *An Introduction to Human Services*. Belmont, CA: Brooks/Cole, 1990.

Young, M.E. *Learning the Art of Helping*. Upper Saddle River, NJ: Merrill, 1998.

Zastrow, C. *Introduction to Social Welfare: Social Problems, Services, and Current Issues*. 4th ed. Belmont, CA: Wadsworth, 1990.

Index